History of Lebanon, N.H.,

1761-1887

Charles Algernon Downs

Alpha Editions

This edition published in 2020

ISBN : 9789354011856

Design and Setting By
Alpha Editions
email - alphaedis@gmail.com

As per information held with us this book is in Public Domain.
This book is a reproduction of an important historical work. Alpha Editions uses the best technology to reproduce historical work in the same manner it was first published to preserve its original nature. Any marks or number seen are left intentionally to preserve its true form.

HISTORY

OF

LEBANON, N. H.

1761-1887

BY

REV. CHARLES A. DOWNS

ILLUSTRATED

CONCORD, N. H.
RUMFORD PRINTING CO.
1908

REV. CHARLES ALGERNON DOWNS,

Historian.

BORN IN SOUTH NORWALK, CONN., MAY 21, 1823.
DIED IN LEBANON, N. H., SEPTEMBER 20, 1906.

Rev. Charles A. Downs prepared for college at Concord, N. H., under the tutelage of his maternal uncle, Rev. Nathaniel Bouton, D. D., the eminent historian, and entered the Concord Literary Institute in 1839, from whence he proceeded to Dartmouth College, where he remained something over one year, when he transferred himself to the University of the City of New York, where he graduated in 1845.

Mr. Downs came to Lebanon July 5, 1848, as a candidate for the pastorate of the Congregational Church, to succeed Rev. Phineas Cook, who had served the church for nineteen years; he was installed as pastor November 22, 1845, and continued in that office for twenty-five years, when, at his own request, the connection was dissolved. He continued to reside in Lebanon, but for a few years was the acting pastor of the church at Hanover Centre.

He served the state as superintendent of public instruction, and the town as selectman, representative, police judge, superintendent of schools, precinct clerk and treasurer, and town clerk, and spent much time and labor in the preparation of this volume. For fifty-eight years Mr. Downs was known to every citizen of Lebanon, and he left this earth without an enemy. He once said to the writer of these lines, " I have tried to live so my obituarist would have nothing to say."

F. C. C.

PREFATORY NOTE.

The warrant for the annual meeting of the town of Lebanon held March 9, 1880, contained the following:

"Article 12. To see what action the town will take in relation to a preparation of a history of the town and raise money therefor or act thereon." Whereupon the following resolution was adopted:

"*Resolved*, That the selectmen be authorized to secure a proper person or persons to prepare a history of the town and to use such sums of money as may be necessary therefor out of any monies not otherwise appropriated."

At the annual meeting March 11. 1884, the following resolution was adopted:

"*Resolved*, That the selectmen be authorized to take such action as they deem expedient in regard to the printing of the town history and that the expense of the same be paid from any monies in the treasury not otherwise appropriated."

Under the resolution passed March 9, 1880, Rev. Charles A. Downs was engaged to write a history of the town, but no definite action was taken regarding its publication until the annual town meeting, March 12, 1895, when the following resolutions were adopted:

"*Resolved*, That the selectmen be authorized to appoint three suitable persons whose duty it shall be to supervise the publication of the history of the town, as prepared by the historian, Rev. Charles A. Downs; that such sums of money as may be necessary for the completion, publication and illustration of said work be and is hereby appropriated therefor.

"*Resolved*, That said committee when appointed shall have authority and they are thereby empowered to make a contract for the publication of said history and to fix the number of copies to be published."

Under the resolutions the selectmen appointed Alpheus W. Baker, William H. Cotton and Frank C. Churchill said committee. This committee met on March 12, 1895, and organized by choosing Alpheus W. Baker, chairman; William H. Cotton, treasurer; and Frank C. Churchill, secretary; at which time it was voted to ask the historian to meet the committee for conference on March 16, 1895. The conference brought out the fact that the manuscript was not yet complete and the further fact that it was Mr. Downs' intention to finish his work at an early day. Mr. William H. Cotton died August 25, 1904, and Mr. Alpheus W. Baker died April 11, 1905, the manuscript not being in the hands of the committee at the time of the decease of my associates.

On January 4, 1906, I turned over to the selectmen the record book of the committee and all papers and pictures that had come into its hands.

At the annual town meeting held March, 1906, the following resolution, offered by Mr. Solon A. Peck, was passed:

"*Resolved*, That the selectmen be a committee to act with Frank C. Churchill, whose duty it shall be to supervise the publication of the history of the town, as prepared by Rev. C. A. Downs."

The manuscript was placed in the hands of the committee in August, 1906, and on September 20, 1906, Rev. Charles A. Downs died. September 3, 1906, the committee entered into an agreement with the Rumford Printing Co. of Concord, N. H., to print 1,500 copies.

FRANK C. CHURCHILL.

LEBANON, N. H., 1908.

TABLE OF CONTENTS.

	PAGE.
Introduction	1
Charter	2
Names of Grantees	4
Provisions of Charter	5
Persons	7
Records	8
Town	20, 21, 23, 24, 26, 28, 29, 31, 33, 39, 43
Proprietors'	20, 22, 23, 25, 27, 28, 30, 37, 41
Territory of Lebanon	45
Survey of the Town	47
Settling	51
First Meeting House	59
Boundaries	64
Controversy with Enfield	66
Condition of the Town, 1775	67
Revolution	71
Provision Bill	84
Revolutionary Papers	86
Soldiers in the Revolution	95
Major Whitcomb's Battalion	97
Committee of Safety	100
Vermont Controversy	108
Settlement of the Controversy	140
Development of the Town	144
Eight School Districts	153
New Meeting House	165
Town in 1900	190
Property in Town	190
Roads and Bridges	198
Lyman's Bridge	202, 203, 305
Fourth New Hampshire Turnpike	202, 204, 262
War of 1812	222
State and Town Officers	229

TABLE OF CONTENTS.

	PAGE.
The Toleration Act	243
Political Affairs 248, 256, 279, 289,	300
Meeting House 249,	265
Poor Farm	250
New Roads	251
Support of Primary Schools	253
Railings on Bridges	253
Railroad in Prospect	254
Public Money from United States Surplus Revenue	254
Town Clerk's Recording Deeds	255
Meeting House Uneasy	255
Dividing Grafton County	262
Surplus Revenue	262
Sale of Spirituous Liquors	266
Railroads	268
Opening of Northern Railroad to Lebanon	269
Capital Punishment	276
Extinguishment of Fires	276
Vote of Thanks to George H. Lathrop	277
Teachers' Institutes 277,	281
New Burying Ground	278
Tomb	279
Town House 281,	296
Horse Sheds	283
Common	284
Humphrey Wood Bridge	285
Firemen's pay	285
Railroad Tax	286
Cemetery at West Lebanon	286
School Districts	286
Fence Around Village Burying Ground	287
Instruction to Collector of Taxes	287
Groceries	288
Railroad Bridges and Crossing	288
Hearse for West Lebanon 289,	304
Police Officers	289
County Farm	291
Burying Grounds	292
Shade Trees	293

TABLE OF CONTENTS.

	PAGE.
Engine Company, No. 2	294
Hearse	294
To Provide Place for the Poor	294
Sextons for Cemeteries	295
Encouragement of Manufactures	293, 303
Park on Hanover Street	295
Roads Discontinued Across the Common	296
Purchase of Hose	299
Common—Regulations	299
Town Pound	300
Town Bonds	302
Hay Scales	302
Hanover Street Bridge	302
Survey of Streets	304
First Board of Health	304
Fire Precinct Extended	305
Bequests to the Town	311
Centennial Fourth of July	312
Town Pump	312
Sale of Cider and Sewage	313
Hog Reeves	313
Coasting	317
Soldiers' Monument	318
C. C. Benton's Bequest	318
Stocking Streams with Trout	319
Heating and Lighting Town Hall	319
Street Lights	320
Manufacturers' Exemption from Taxation	321
Spring at West Lebanon	321
Town Clocks	322
Balance of the Dog Tax	322
Colburn Park	324
Postmasters of Lebanon	324
Town in the Rebellion	325
Town Meetings	325
Selectmen During the War	329
Soldiers in the War	329
State Aid, Etc.	351
Reimbursement	351

TABLE OF CONTENTS.

	PAGE.
Centennial and Patriotic Celebration	352
Exercises on the Stand	353
Toasts and Speeches	353
Volunteer Toasts	363
Memorial Building	364
Village Fire Precinct and Great Fire of 1887	370
At Last	384
List of Losses	393
Insurance	395
Resurgam	399
Notes About the Fire	399
Relief Work	402
Who Will Rebuild	402
Churches of the Town	405
Congregational Church	405
Decade 1817 to 1827	410
West Congregational Church	417
Baptist Church	418
Methodist Episcopal Church	429
Universalist Society	432
Sacred Heart Church	436
Index	437
General Index	437
Index of Names	446

LIST OF ILLUSTRATIONS.

Rev. Charles A. Downes	Frontispiece
Old Lafayette Hotel	facing page 24
Old Lebanon Bank Building	40
Maj. Wm. Willis Bliss	52
Hon. Experience Estabrook	58
Prof. Ira Young	64
Capt. John Bliss	72
Maj. John Griswold	76
Richard Burleigh Kimball	80
Prof. Charles A. Young	88
Dr. Cyrus H. Fay	104
William P. Gallup	120
Hon. George S. Towle	128
Sally Truman	136
Diarca Allen	144
Lucinda Howe Storrs	148
Hiram A. Simonds	152
Orren Hubbard	156
James Hubbard	160
Abel Storrs	164
Col. Constant Storrs	168
Seth Blodgett	170
George Blodgett	172
The Old Meeting House on the Common—Present Town House	174
Old View of the Common	176
Clement Hough	180
Clark Hough	184
Rev. Story Hebard	188
Abram Pushee	192
Simeon S. Post	196

ILLUSTRATIONS.

	PAGE.
Halsey R. Stevens	204
Oliver Lathrop Stearns	204
Dr. Phineas Parkhurst	208
Timothy Kenrick	238
Ami B. Young	240
Dr. Benjamin Gallup	240
Dr. Caleb Plastridge	240
Robert Byron Kimball	254
Robert Kimball	254
J. W. Peck Homestead	264
John W. Peck	265
Harvey Murch	266
Elisha P. Liscomb	266
Hon. A. H. Cragin	278
William G. Perley	286
Daniel Richardson	286
Jesse C. Sturtevant	292
Col. Frank C. Churchill	296
William H. Cotton	296
Joseph W. Gerrish	296
Alpheus W. Baker	296
Edward J. Durant	298
Albert M. Shaw	298
Solon A. Peck	304
Postmasters of Lebanon	324
Col. James G. Benton	328
Harry H. Hosley, U. S. N.	332
Maj. N. H. Randlett	346
Call for Troops, Spanish War	350
Col. Henry L. Kendrick	362
Laying Corner Stone Memorial Building	364
Sergt. Jesse E. Dewey	364
After the Fire, 1887	384
After the Fire, 1887	392
Charles H. Dana	406
Rev. Phinehas Cooke	412
Baptist Church	418
Elias H. Cheney	420
Gilman C. Whipple	420

ILLUSTRATIONS. xiii

	PAGE.
First Baptist Church and Parsonage	422
Rev. John Moore	432
Colbee C. Benton	432
Rev. G. W. Bailey	434
Map of Proprietors' Lots, 1761–1803	436

HISTORY OF LEBANON.

INTRODUCTION.

The final conquest of Canada in 1760 gave peace to the frontiers of New Hampshire. The Indians, who had for so many years been a source of terror and distress, were no longer feared.

The various Indian and French wars, by the continual passage of soldiers, had made the lands in the valley of the Connecticut well known. They were eagerly sought by both adventurers and speculators. Benning Wentworth, the royal governor of New Hampshire, always alive to his own interest, "availed himself of this golden opportunity, and by advice of his council ordered a survey to be made of the Connecticut river for sixty miles, and three lines of townships on each side to be laid out." This survey was made by Joseph Blanchard. Townships of six miles square were laid out on both sides of the river and granted to various petitioners, and so numerous were the applicants that in the year 1761 not less than sixty townships were granted on the west side of the river and eighteen on the east side.

Nor was this movement wholly speculative. In the older settlements of Massachusetts and Connecticut there came upon the people one of those mysterious impulses which prompt men to leave their homes and seek new abodes in unoccupied territory. "There was a passion for occupying new lands." In the various expeditions to repel French and Indian aggressions, soldiers had passed through the Connecticut valley in going to and returning from Canada. They had noticed the fertile intervales and well timbered hills of the Cohos country. They pictured to themselves the farms and homes with which the hills and valleys might be beautified. Among those who had noted these lands were certain soldiers from the southeastern towns of Connecticut. They reported what they had seen to their neighbors, and as soon as peace was secured by the conquest of Canada, they took measures to give reality to the pictures which had so often filled their fancies upon the scout and march.

A number of persons in the towns of Norwich, Lebanon and Mansfield, Conn., associated themselves together to procure charters of townships in the new territory of the Connecticut valley. They formed two companies, though each was composed mainly of the same persons. One company sought a charter of a town to be called Lebanon, the other company proposed to call their town Enfield; both names of Connecticut towns. They appointed Jedediah Dana their agent to go to Portsmouth and obtain from Governor Wentworth charters for the towns. He was successful in his mission and on the same day, July 4, 1761, charters were issued for Lebanon and Enfield. The following is the charter of Lebanon:

CHARTER.

Province of New Hampshire—

George the Third By the Grace of God of Great Britain, France and Ireland, King, Defender of the Faith &c—To all Persons To whom these presents shall come

GREETING

KNOW Ye that we of our special grace, certain knowledge and mere motion, for The due encouragement of settling a new Plantation within our said Province, by and with the advice of our Trusty and well beloved BENNING WENTWORTH. E s q., our governor and commander in chief of said Province of Newhampshire, in New England & of our council of the said Province—Have upon the conditions and reservations hereinafter made given and Granted, and by these presents for us and our heirs & succefsor, do give and Grant in equal shares unto our loving Subjects, inhabitants of our said Province of Newhampshire and our other Governments & to their heirs and afsigns forever, whose names are Entered on this grant—To be divided to and among them into sixty-eight equal shares, all that tract or parcel of land situate lying and being within our said Province of Newhampshire, containing by admeasurement Twenty-three thousand acres, which tract is to contain six miles square, and no more, out of which an allowance is to be made for highways and unimprovable lands, by rocks, Ponds mountains and Rivers, one Thousand and forty acres free, according to a plan and survey hereof made by our said Governor's order and returned into the secretary's Office, & hereunto annexed, butted and bounded as follows (v i z): Beginning at a white Pine Tree marked with the figures three on one side and four on the other, which tree is about eighteen miles on a point from the upper end of Charleston, and stands on the bank of Connecticut river, from thence South, seventy-two degrees East six miles; from thence North, thirty-six degrees East five miles and one

INTRODUCTION. 3

half; from thence North sixty-four West seven miles to Connecticut River, To a hemlock tree marked four and five that stands just at the head of white river falls; from thence down the river to the first bound mentioned; and that the same be & hereby is incorporated into a Township by the name of Lebanon; and the inhabitants that do or shall hereafter inhabit the said Township are hereby declared to be enfranchized with and Entitled to all & every the privileges & immunities that other Towns within our Province by law exercise & enjoy & further that the said Town as soon as there shall be fifty Families resident And settled thereon shall have the liberty of holding two fairs, one of which shall be held on the ———— and the other on the ———— annually, which fairs are not to continue longer Than the respective ———— following the said ———— and that as soon as the said Town shall consist of fifty families a Market may be opened and kept one or more days in each week as may be thought most advantageous to the inhabitants: also That the first meeting for the choice of Town Officers agreeable to the laws of our said Province shall be held on the last wednesday in August next, which said meeting shall be notified by Mr John Baldwin, who is hereby also appointed Moderator of the sd first meeting which he is to notify and govern agreeable to the laws and customs of our said Province; and that the annual meeting forever hereafter for the choice of such Officers for the said Town shall be on the second Tuesday of March annually—To have and to hold the said tract of land as above exprefsed, together with all privilidges and appurtenances, to them and their respective Heirs & afsigns forever, upon the following conditions (viz)

First That every Grantee, his heirs or afsigns shall plant and cultivate five Acres of land within the term of five years for every fifty acres Contained in his or their share or proportion of land in said Township, and continue to improve and settle the same by additional Cultivation on penalty of the forfeiture of his Grant or share in the said Township & of its reverting to us our Heirs and Succefsors, To be by us or them regranted to such of our subjects as shall effectually cultivate and settle the same.

2ᵈ That all white and other pine trees within the said Township fit for masting our Royal Navy be carefully preserved for that Use, and none to be cut or felled without our special license for So doing first had and obtained, upon the penalty of the forfeiture of the right of such Grantee, his heirs & Afsigns To us our heirs and Succefsors, as well as being subject to the penalty of any act or acts of Parliament that now are or hereafter shall be Enacted.

3ᵈ That before any Division of the land be made to & among the Grantees, a tract of land as near the Center of said Township As the land will admit of shall be reserved and marked out for Town-lots, one of which shall be allotted to each Grantee, Of the contents of one acre

4ᵗʰ Yeilding and paying therefor To us our Heirs & Succefsors for the space of Ten years to be computed from the date hereof, The rent of one Ear of indian corn only in the twenty-fifth Day of December annually if lawfully demanded, the first Payment to be made on the twenty-fifth day of December 1762.

5th Every proprietor settler or inhabitant shall yeild and pay unto US. Our heirs and succeisors Yearly and every year forever, from and after the Expiration of ten years from the above said twenty-fifth day of December namely on the twenty fifth day of December which will be in the year of our Lord 1772 one shilling Proclamation money for every hundred acres he so owns settles or pofsesses, and so in proportion for a greater or lefser. Tract of land, which money shall be paid by the respective persons above said, their heirs or Assigns, in our Council chamber at Portsmouth, or to such Officer or Officers as shall be appointed to receive the same & this to be in Lieu of all other rents & service whatsoever

In testimony whereof we have caused the seal of our Said Province to be hereunto affixed witness Benning Wentworth Esq. Our Governor and Commander in chief, of our said Province the fourth Day of July in the year of our Lord Christ one thousand seven hundred and Sixty-one, & in the first year of our Reign—

By his Excellency's command
with advice of council

B. WENTWORTH

Theodore Atkinson Sec.ty

THE NAMES OF THE GRANTEES OF LEBANON

John Hanks
John Salter
Obadiah Loomis
Elijah Huntington
Huckins Storrs Jun
John Baldwin
Robbert Barrows Jun
Richard Salter
Constant Southworth
Thomas Storrs
Hobart Estabrook
Samuel Storrs
Charles Hill
Benjamin Davis
Joshua Blodgett
Joseph Turner
Josiah Storrs
Joseph Wood
John Storrs
Jonathan Murdock

Joseph Dana
John Swift
Daniel Allen Jr.
David Eldredge
Jesse Birchard
Nathan Arnold
Levi Hyde
John Birchard
Nathan Blodgett
Moses Hibbard Jun
John Allen
Robert Hyde
John Hyde
Lemuel Clark
Jefse Birchard
Daniel Blodgett 3d
Nehemiah Estabrook
Jonathan Martin
Nathaniel Porter
Jonathan Yeomans

INTRODUCTION.

Jabez Barrow	David Turner
Seth Blodgett	Daniel Blodgett
Joseph Martin	Jonathan Walcutt
Nathaniel Hall	John Birchard
Robert Martin	Judah Storrs
Thomas Barrows Jr	Edward Goldstone Lutwych

One whole share for the Incorporated society for Propagation of the gospel in Foreign Parts. One whole share for a Glebe for the Church of England as by law established—One whole share for the first settled Minister One whole share for the benefit of a school in said Town—his excellency Benning Wentworth Esq. a tract of land of five hundred acres as marked in the plan which is to be accounted two of the within shares

Jedediah Dana	William Dana
Mark H Wentworth	James Nevins Esq.
Jonathan Blanchard	Oneil Lamont
Clement Jackson Esq.	Hugh Hall Wentworth
Samuel Penhallow &	William Knight.

Province of Newhampshire July 5 1761
Recorded in the Book of Charters per
Theodore Atkinson Sec.ty

PROVISIONS OF THE CHARTER.

1. "That the town as soon as there shall be fifty families resident and settled thereon shall have the privilege of holding two fairs." These fairs were not unlike the agricultural fairs of the present day—except in this, that their main purpose was not the exhibition of products of the soil and of manufactures, but buying and selling—trade of any kind.

2. "A market may be opened and kept one or more days of the week." By the English laws the killing of animals for public sale was allowed only as a privilege at specified times. A man could not kill and sell any animal when it was most convenient for himself, but it must be done only on the specified market days. Similar laws prevail now in Canada. They, however, are often evaded, for though one may not *sell* meat on any day but the market day, yet he may kill upon any day for his own use and may *lend* to his neighbor, who in his turn may kill and return the borrowed meat on some other than the specified day or days.

In the Provincial Papers, Volume I, page 216, the following may be found:

31 October 1655

At the request of the towne of Hampton by their deputy itt is ordered that there shall be a markett kept there one day in every week, viz., on the fifth day which is *theire lecture day*

3 That all white and other pine trees within said township fit for masting our royal navy be carefully preserved for that use, and none be cut or felled without our special license

"As early as 1668 the government of Massachusetts, under which the province (New Hampshire) then was, had reserved for the public use all white pine trees of twenty-four inches in diameter at three feet from the ground. In King William's reign a surveyor of the woods was appointed by the crown; and an order was sent by the Earl of Bellemont to cause acts to be passed in his several governments for the preservation of the white pines. In 1708 a law made in New Hampshire prohibited the cutting of such as were twenty-four inches in diameter, at twelve inches from the ground, without leave of the surveyor, who was instructed by the queen to mark with the broad arrow those which might be fit for the use of the navy, and to keep a register of them. Whatever severity might be used in executing the law, it was no difficult matter for those who knew the woods and were concerned in lumbering, to evade it; though sometimes they were detected and fined. Great complaints were frequently made of the destruction of the royal woods—every governor and lieutenant-governor had occasion to declaim on the subject in their speeches and letters; it was a favorite point in England and recommended them to their superiors as careful guardians of the royal interest. On the other hand, the people made as loud complaints against the surveyor for prohibiting the cutting of pine trees, and yet neglecting to mark such as were fit for masts; by which means many trees which could never be used for masts, and might be cut into logs for sawing, were rotting in the woods; or the people who got them were exposed to vexatious prosecutions." Farmer's Belknap, page 188.

It is doubtful if any of the trees in the valleys and on the hills of Lebanon were ever marked with the "broad arrow" as fit for masting the "Queen's Navee."

The Persons.

The majority of the first proprietors resided in Connecticut. Many of them never came here, but sold or gave their rights to others. At that period many persons sought an interest in these wild lands merely as a matter of speculation, without any intention of ever occupying them as their homes. The following persons whose names are appended to the charter, became actual settlers:

Jedediah Dana,
Joseph Dana,
John Baldwin,
Charles Hill,
Joseph Martin,
Levi Hyde,
Nehemiah Estabrook,

William Dana,
Huckins Storrs,
Hobart Estabrook,
Joseph Wood,
Nathaniel Hall,
Moses Hibbard, Jun.,
Nathaniel Porter.

Clement Jackson was a physician at Portsmouth and, with his son, was surgeon to the troops gathered at Portsmouth and vicinity after the battle of Bunker Hill.

Mark H. Wentworth of Portsmouth was a merchant and a relative of the governor. At the commencement of the Revolution he was a Tory, refusing to sign the "Association Test;" refusing to sell rum for the use of the American army, the sheriff of Rockingham County was directed, February 27, 1777, to seize a certain number of hogsheads; September 12, 1777, he was required by the Committee of Safety to give his parole in writing for himself and family; also the wife and children of John Fisher, Esq., "that they do not leave the town of Portsmouth without permit from the Legislative authority of this state." These persons were held as hostages for Woodbury Langdon, Esq., a prisoner in New York City. He was the father of John Wentworth, the last royal governor; was appointed counsellor of the province, 1759; died at Portsmouth, December 19, 1785.

Hugh Hall Wentworth was another relative of the governor.

Jonathan Blanchard was of Merrimack, and seems to have been a speculator in wild-lands, as well as prominent in many affairs. He was interested in lands in Acworth and other towns.

Edward Goldstone Lutwyche was also of Merrimack, another speculator like Blanchard; the owner of a ferry about four miles below Read's Ferry. He was colonel of one of the provincial regiments. He was a Tory, fled from the state, and by act of the Legislature, 1778, was forbidden to return to the state under the penalty of transportation, and in case of a second return, he was to suffer death. His property was confiscated, but the franchise of the ferry was confirmed to Sarah Lutwyche, his wife, by the authority of the Legislature, 1776.

James Nevins was from Scotland, was counsellor, 1759; also collector of customs; and died at Portsmouth, February 6, 1769.

William Knight and Samuel Penhallow were of Portsmouth; their names appear as selectmen of that town, in 1760, in a petition against building a bridge in New Castle; in 1763, for a petition of Portsmouth for liberty to hold their town meeting in the state house, the holding of town meetings in the North meeting-house "having given offence to many of the Parishioners, who by means thereof have had their pews dirtied and spoiled, and who are also of opinion that the said Meeting house ought to be wholly set apart for the worship of Almighty God, and this hath lately produced no small contentions."

Oneil Lamont was also of Portsmouth; his name appears in a petition for a bounty on fish, wheat, hemp, etc., in 1763.

The Society for the Propagation of the Gospel in Foreign Parts was first formed in 1698, as a Society for Promoting Christian Knowledge; reconstructed in 1701, under its present name. Its design was the promotion of colonial churches, under the control of the Church of England. It still exists at London, England, having a large income.

RECORDS.

The proprietors' and the town records are here given to the close of the eighteenth century. The proprietors' records are in good condition in a copy made by Gideon Baker, proprietors' clerk, in 1806. The earlier town records are in a precarious condition, contained in leaves stitched together, with paper covers supplied by friendly hands.

At a meeting of the proprietors of the new incorporated Township of Lebanon in Newhampshire, legally warned, holden at the house of Amariah Storrs, inholder in Mansfield (ct) on the sixth day of October, A. D. 1761 the following votes were past (viz):

1st Made choice of Mr. Nehemiah Estabrook for moderator of said meeting

2nd Choose John Salter a Clerk for said propriety.

3d Voted to admit Mr. Moses Hibbard to vote as a proprietor, altho by mistake his name was left out of the Grant.

4ly Choose Mr. Jonathan Murdock collector for said propriety

5ly Choose Mr. Amariah Storrs Treasurer for said propriety

6ly The following persons chose for a standing committee for said Propriety (viz) Messrs Nehemiah Estabrook, Charles Hill, Joseph Dana.

7th Voted that the main street running through the Township of said Lebanon should be layed out ten rods wide.

This was the road known as the King's highway, but always appears in the records as the Enfield Road.

8ly That the committee hereafter to be chosen for the purpose of laying out the lots & roads in said Township make reservation of such Lands for roads in said Township as they shall Judge Necessary and convenient.

9ly Voted that the first Division after the one acre Division mentioned in the grant shall consist of fifty acres, being Proportioned according to the Quality of said land

10ly That the committee for laying out said lots shall proceed to the Business at or before the tenth day of October instant

11ly The following persons were chosen for a committee for laying out said Lots as above directed (viz) Capt. Nath Hall, Huckin Storrs Jun. Daniel Blodgett Jun. Charles Hill, John Hanks.

12ly Voted to allow the aforesaid committee 3/ per day while in said Service, & also to defray their expenses.

13ly Voted that the proprietors of the Township of Lebanon would choose a committee to Join a committee chosen by the proprietors of Enfield to receive and settle the accounts of Jedediah Dana, agent for the proprietors of said Townships, and that each committee make report to their respective constituents at their next meeting; and the following persons were chosen as a committee for the purpose aforesaid (viz) Mr Nehemiah Estabrook Capt. Samuel storrs, Mr. John Storrs

14ly Voted that a tax of ten Shillings, lawful money, be levied upon each proprietor to defray the expence of laying said Township, by the Committee chosen for that purpose, and that said tax be paid in by the first monday in January next

15th Voted that the money which was paid in by the proprietors of the Township of Lebanon to refund the expence of the Proprietors of the Township of Enfield, in case they had not Obtained a Grant, of a Township, shall be taken out of the hands of the former Treasurer (John Salter) by the present Treasurer of said propriety (Mr Amariah

Storrs) he giving a receipt therefor to the said former Treasurer & commit the same into the hands of the committee for laying out said township of Lebanon, and said committee to exchange the same (being paper bills) for silver to the best advantage, and render an account of their doings to the propriety.

16th That the committee for laying out said Township shall provide a surveyor for the purpose, & exhibit his account To the proprietors.

17th That the committee chosen by the proprietors of Lebanon to settle with the agent, shall be directed to motion to the proprietors of Enfield at their next meeting To direct their committee To Joyn them in considering the case of those persons who having paid their money towards procuring a Grant of a Township, were, notwithstanding, Deprived of the benefit of a right by reason of a surpluisage of proprietors who belonged to this Government, and to make report to said propriety—said meeting was then difsolved.

The foregoing votes attested and recorded
pr John Salter proprietors clerk

At a meeting of the proprietors of the new incorporated Township of Lebanon in the Province of Newhampshire legally warned and Convened at the house of Amariah Storrs inholder in Mansfield on the fifteenth day of December A. D. 1761. The following votes were past (viz):

1st Made choice of Mr Nehemiah Estabrook moderator to govern sd meeting.

2nd Choose the following persons as Aifesrors for said propriety (viz): Mr. Nehemiah Estabrook Capt. Samuel Storrs. Mr Thos. Storrs.

3dly Choose the following persons for a committee to join the committee chosen by Enfield proprietors to consider of the Business exprefsed in the eighth article of the warning (viz) To examine the state of the treasury of the proprietors of both townships as they stood before the separate grants, of said Townships To said proprietors (namely of Lebanon and Enfield) & to direct said committee to take such methods as shall be needful for settling the accounts of said proprietors of said Townships that were due and allowed before said Grants.—Capt Sam.l Storrs Thos. Storrs, John Salter.

The meeting was then adjourned to the 22d day of December inst. when the following votes were past viz:

4ly Voted to allow the accounts of Jedediah Dana agent for said propriety above what was before Granted £3. 11-7¾

5ly Voted to accept the doings of the committee for laying out the lotts with the alteration made upon their Plan

6ly Voted to allow the accounts of the aforesaid committee for laying out the lotts & to raise the sum £30.-0-0 Lawful money to make up the sum due to said committee—the same To be paid in by the first monday in March next

7ly Voted To postpone the payment of the money which was voted To be paid the second monday in January To the first monday in March next.

8ly Voted a lottery be made by Mefsrs Thos Storrs & Judah Storrs, and that Mefsrs Oliver Davidson & Ephraim Parker should draw the lotts

9ly Voted that the clerk procure a book for Records.

10ly Voted that Mr. Charles Hill be appointed to treat with the proprietors of the Townships between the old fort at No 4 (Charlestown) and said Lebanon Relative to a highway between said fort and said Lebanon.

11ly Voted that for the incouragement of the speedy settling said Township of Lebanon that those of the proprietors who shall settle upon said lands within the term of two years shall have the priviledge of cultivating and improving such a part of the intervale as shall best suit them with these restriction that the intervale so improved by them be in one piece or body & when said intervale shall be divided amongst the proprietors those persons aforesaid shall have their proportion of the aforesaid intervale so cultivated by them.

12ly The lotts drawn entered in the following Order

	No.		No
Daniel Allen Jun.	11	Nath. Hall	41
John Allen	62	Clement Jackson Esq.	23
Daniel Blodget	63	William Knight	26
Jonath Blanchard	47	Obadiah Loomis	48
Robt. Barrow Jun	61	Oniel Lamont	52
Jesse Birchard	17	Jonathan Martin	37
John Birchard	36	Jonathan Murdock	18
John Baldwin	10	Joseph Martin	45
John Birchard	4	Robert Martin	56
Seth Blodget	35	James Nevins Esq.	14
Joshua Blodget	49	Saml Penhallow	19
Jabez Barrow	54	Nath. Porter	40
Jesse Birchard	50	John Salter	55
Daniel Blodget 3d	31	Huckins storrs	22
Nathan Blodget	34	Constant Southworth	12
Thos. Barrow Jun	29	John storrs	43
Oliver Clerk	16	Thomas Storrs	24
Lemuel Clark	39	John Swift	46
Wm Dana	6	Huckins storrs Jun	44
Jedidiah Dana	1	Josiah Storrs	59
Benjamin Davis	51	Samuel storrs	57
Joseph Dana	30	Judah Storrs	28
David Eldridge	21	Joseph Turner	2
Nehemiah Estabrook	5	David Turner	25
Hobart Estabrook	42	Jonathan Walcutt	20
Elijah Huntington	7	Joseph Wood	60

John Hyde	58	Mark H. Wentworth Esq	15
Robert Hyde	8	Hugh Hall Wentworth	27
Moses Hibbard Jun.	6	Jonathan Yeomans	32
John Hanks	13	Edward Goldstone (Lutwych)	53
Charles Hill	38		
Levi Hyde	3	Minister's Lott	33

The above were the acre lots directed to be laid out by the charter "as near the center of the said township as the land will admit of for a town lot," but serious errors being found, the drafting was annulled. Page 1.

13ly Voted to raise a tax of £4.0.0 To be paid into the Treasury on the first monday of March next to purchase a right of land in The Township of Lebanon for Amariah Storrs in consideration of his being deprived of his right, his name through mistake being left out of the Grant, & if the mistake before mentioned should hereafter be discovered the money granted for the benefit of said Storrs to remain in the Treasury to be disposed of according to the Direction of the propriety.

14ly Voted to raise a tax of 10/ upon each right to be paid into the Treasury by the first day of December next ensuing and also a tax of 10/ more to be paid in by the first day of December 1763, to encourage Mr Oliver Davison to build a Saw-mill upon some suitable stream within the township of Lebanon, & if the said Davison should begin and compleat a good and sufficient saw-mill, as near the center of said township as shall be judged best within the term of two years, then the aforesaid sum & sums to be paid to the said Davison, at the several terms above mentioned & To direct the committee of the proprietors of said Township to take sufficient bonds for the performance [of the] premisies

15ly Voted to adjourn said meeting to the second tuesday of March next, when, at the said meeting so adjourned the following votes were past (viz):

1st That, whereas at a meeting of the proprietors of the township of Lebanon held by adjournment the twenty-second day of December A. D. 1761 The said proprietors voted to accept the plan drafted by Ebenezer Byles surveyor of said township, with some alterations made upon said plan, said propriety then proceeded to the drawing of the Lotts as laid out on said plan; since which upon examining and comparing said plan with said surveyors notes find a very Gross mistake in Running the lines upon said plan, and also in laying out said lotts, and that many inconveniances will consequently follow—we are therefore of opinion, that for the peace as well as interest of said propriety it may be best to reconsider and disannul those former votes relative to the laying out & drafting said lotts—Voted in the Affirmative.

2nd Voted that the first Division after the division ordered in the Charter of said Township consist of one hundred Acres, according To the Quality of said land

3ᵈ Voted That Mr. Oliver Davison have the priviledge of his first Division of one hundred acres to be laid so as to include the spot which shall be Judged convenient for erecting the sawmill reserving all other priviledges of the stream with a sufficiency of land for other Mills and necessary roads—Voted in the Affirmative.

4ly Voted that for the encouragement of the speedy settlement of said Township those persons who shall, within the space of two years, nextinsuing, proceed & continue to cultivate said land shall have the Benefit of their choice of their said Division of one hundred Acres of the Land of said Township in that part of said township as best suits them, with these restrictions that their said lotts be laid out so as not to encroach on the lott which shall be laid out to Mr. Oliver Davison & so as to prevent waste of land

5ly Voted to choose three men for propriety Surveyors for said Township, To lay out the lotts for the proprietors who shall enter upon and cultivate said lands as aforesaid & to make immediate return of the surveys aforementioned To the proprietors Clerk for said Township & that Those three surveyors aforesaid continue in their Busineſs for the space of two years next ensuing or untill the tenth day of March A. D. 1764

6ly Voted that Meſsrs Charles Hill, Levi Hyde, Jedediah Dana be chosen surveyors for said propriety for the purpose of laying out the lots in said Township.

7ly Voted that the surveyors aforesaid make reservation of a sufficient Quantity of land in said Township for the acre lotts as ordered in the charter of said Township

8ly Voted that at the expiration of two years said proprietors shall proceed To lay out the Acre lotts as mentioned in the charter of said township, and also the other Division of one hundred Acres of upland, to be laid out by a committee chosen by the proprietors for that purpose, To the Other proprietors who shall not enter upon said land within the aforesaid term of two years, and also their proportion of interval land in said Township exclusive of what shall be taken up within the aforesaid term of two years, agreeable to the former votes of said propriety for the encouragement of settlers.

9ly Voted to adjourn said meeting to the first monday in May next; When said proprietors met by adjournment and voted said meeting should be diſsolved.

At a meeting of the proprietors of the township of Lebanon in the Province of Newhampshire legally warned and convened at the house of Amariah Storrs inholder in Mansfield [Ct] on the first day of September A. D. 1762 the following votes were past (viz):

1ˢᵗ Said proprietors made choice of Mr Nehemiah Estabrook moderator for said meeting

2ⁿᵈ Choose Mr. Thomas Storrs collector in the room of Mr Jonaᵗʰ Murdock

3rd Choose the following persons a committe for clearing a road from the old fort at No 4 To said Lebanon. (viz) : Capt. Nathaniel Hall Mr. John Hanks, Mr John Birchard.

4ly Voted that the committee aforesaid proceed to clear a horse road from the old fort at No 4 to said Lebanon (& further if said committee Judge best) on or before the first day of October next ensuing & that said committee be ordered to use their interest with the proprietors of the Neighboring townships to join them herein, and render an Account of their proportion of the Charge to the proprietors at their Next meeting.

5ly Voted to raise a tax of 5/ Lawful money upon each of the proprietors of said township to be paid into the treasury on or before the first day of December next ensuing, to defray the charge of said road.

6ly Voted to adjourn said meeting to the second Tuesday in December next—

When said proprietors met by said Adjournment & past the following votes (viz) :

1st Said proprietors choose a committee of three men (viz) Capt. Samuel Storrs, Mr. Joseph Dana Deacon Nehemiah Estabrook, to Treat with the proprietors of the townships adjoining to or near the Township of Lebanon, relative to an encouragement for the preaching of the gospel in said townships, and make report of their proceeding as soon as the nature of the business will admit of.

2nd Apprehending it may serve to expedite the settlement of the Township to have the second division of one hundred acres to Each proprietor surveyed & laid out, sized and well bounded in due proportion to each proprietor by a committee appointed for that purpose; to be understood not to infringe or encroach in the least on the priviledge before granted to those who would first cultivate and improve said lands in said township; that is to say, all who have been or shall go and cultivate agreeable to the intendment of the former vote & before the expiration of said term may have the priviledge of taking up what lott they please, both upland and intervale, they making return thereof to the clerk of said propriety, previously laying out the more publick roads in the most convenient places; that a committee of three men be chosen for the purpose aforesaid & that they proceed upon that business as soon as the season will allow, & return a plan of their doings to the clerk as soon as may be.

3rd The following persons were chosen a committee for the purpose aforesaid (viz) :

    Deacon Nehemiah Estabrook
    Capt. Saml Storrs   } Committee
    Capt. Nath Hall

4ly Voted to raise a tax of twelve shillings upon each right to be paid into the treasury by the first day of February next to Defray the expense of laying out the lotts &c as aforementioned.

5ly Voted to adjourn said meeting to the second Tuesday in March next at one of the clock in the afternoon.

When said proprietors met by adjournment and voted to adjourn said meeting to the last Tuesday in March, instant at two of clock in the afternoon—when said proprietors met by adjournment & past the following votes (viz):

6ly Choose a committee of two men Mr Constant Southworth Mr. John Salter to join a committee of Enfield proprietors to examine into the state of the affair of Mr Jedediah Dana relative to the damage he sustained while acting in the capacity of an agent for the said proprietors, and make report at the next meeting

7ly Voted to accept the report of the committee appointed to treat with the proprietors of neighbouring townships for the encouraging of the preaching of the Gospel in said townships, in consequence of which said proprietors voted a tax of four shillings upon each proprietor for the purpose aforesaid,

8ly Voted to appoint Mr. Nehemiah Estabrook a committee to join a committee of the neighboring townships to make provision for the preaching of the Gospel in said townships the ensuing summer.

9ly Voted to appoint Mr Constant Southworth to go to Portsmouth To collect the rates due from the proprietors residing in those parts & to allow him 3/6 lawful money pr day for himself and horse & defray the expence of the Journey

10ly Voted said meeting be difsolved.

At a meeting of the proprietors of the Township of Lebanon in the province of Newhampshire legally warned and convened at the dwelling house of Mr. Amariah Storrs inholder in Mansfield on the ninth day of January A. D. 1764 the following votes were past (viz):

made choice of Mr. Nehimiah Estabrook for moderator for said meeting

2nd Voted to accept the doings of the committee in laying out three Divisions of land in said Township in May Last (viz) the one acre division & the division of one hundred Acres & also the intervale land,

3rd Voted that the encouragement given by the proprietors at their meeting in March 1762 (for the speedy settlement of the land in said township) should be continued untill March first A. D. 1765

4ly Voted to appoint Mr. Peter Aspinwall a committee To act in Conjunction with the committees of Hanover & Norwich in settling the accounts exhibited for laying out & clearing a road from the old fort No 4 to Lebanon & to direct said committee to commence an action at the next court against Capt. Thompson for breach of promise (provided the committees of the townships of Hanover and Norwich will join him in carrying on the action) wherein he engaged to pay the proportion of the expense, in laying out & clearing said road, for the township of Lime, which he now refuses to do.

5ly Voted to appoint John Salter, Peter Aspinwall and Oliver Clark a committee to settle the accounts of the committee for laying out three Divisions of land in said Township.

6ly Voted said meeting be adjourned to the last monday in January Instant.

The proprietors of the township of Lebanon met by adjournment and past the following votes (viz)

7ly Voted the sum of £45. 14. 0½ Lawful money to be paid to the Committee for their service in laying out the lotts in said Township.

8ly That the account of Mr. Experience Storrs be adjusted by the committee appointed for that purpose, and the balance added to the aforesaid sum of £45.-14-0½ allowed the committee.

9ly Voted to grant the sum of £29-6-7¾ for clearing the road from the old fort at Nº 4 to said Lebanon.

10ly Voted to raise £4-15. to pay the charge of a Journey To Portsmouth To collect the taxes due from the proprietors in those parts

11ly Granted the sum of one hundred pounds to be levied on the Rights of the proprietors to be paid by the first day of March next for the purpose aforesaid.

12ly Voted a committee of two men be chosen to prepare and draw the Lotts of the first Division of land in said township (viz) the one Acre Division & appointed Mr. Constant Southworth and Mr. Experience Storrs a committee for the purpose aforesaid.

13ly Voted to difsmifs the standing committee for said propriety (viz) Nehemiah Estabrook Charles Hill & Joseph Dana

14ly Choose Mefsrs Nehemiah Estabrook Constant Southworth and Peter Aspinwall a standing committee in the room of those dismifsed

15ly Voted to allow Mr Thomas Storrs three shillings per day & Defray his expenses in case he forthwith repair to Portsmouth To collect the taxes due from the prietors in those parts, said 3/ per day to be allowed only while said Storrs is actually in said service

16ly The following is a draft of the one Acre Division of land by the committee appointed for said purpose:

Mark Hunt Wentworth	20	Jabez Barrow	35
For the propagation of the Gospel	2	John Salter	7
Thos. Barrow Jun	57	Lot for the first settled Minister	11
Joseph Wood	5	Huckins Storrs Jun	61
Samuel Penhallow	59	John Hanks	21
Richard Salter	39	Joseph Dana	23
Josiah Storrs	46	Hobart Estabrook	1
Clement Jackson Esq.	64	Elijah Huntington	40
Constant Southworth	27	John Allen	60
Daniel Blodget	10	Samˡ Storrs	53
School Lott	22	Lot for the church of England	62
Jesse Birchard	17		

Jedidiah Dana	56	Robert Martin	13
Joshua Blodget	52	Nehemiah Estabrook	37
Robert Hyde	48	John Baldwin	42
Nath Porter	19	Joseph Turner	31
Jonathan Walcutt	18	Obadiah Loomis	26
Charles Hill	34	Robert Barrow Jun	14
Jonathan Martin	55	Wm Dana	16
John Hyde	24	Joseph Martin	9
Wm Knight	28	Lemuel Clark	58
Jonth Yeoman	50	Levi Hyde	29
David Turner	25	Nath. Hunt	54
Daniel Blodget	47	John Swift	33
Seth Blodget	41	Nathan Blodget	30
Judah Storrs	38	Moses Hibbard Jun	8
John Birchard	36	Nathan Arnold	51
Daniel Allen Jun	6	Benjamin Davis	12
Oniel Lemont	32	David Eldridge	63
Edward Goldstone Lutwyche	45	Thos Storrs	49
Hugh Hall Wentworth	4	Jonth Blanchard	43
John Storrs	3	John Birchard	65
Jonth Murdock	15	James Nevin	44

16ly Voted to adjourn said meeting to the second Tuesday in March next

The proprietors of the township of Lebanon met by adjournment the second tuesday in March A D 1764 and

17ly Voted to raise a tax of seven shillings upon each proprietors right To be improved in making and clearing roads in said Lebanon and appointed Mr Aaron Storrs a committee to receive and improve the same for the purpose aforesaid

18ly Voted to adjourn said meeting to the second tuesday in December Next—The proprietors of the township of Lebanon met by Adjournment the second tuesday in December & past the following votes (viz):

19ly Voted to raise a tax of eight shillings Lawful money on each proprietors right to support the preaching the gospel in said Township; said tax to be paid by the first day of May next

20ly Voted to appoint Mefsrs. Nehimiah Estabrook Capt. Saml Storrs a committee to provide preaching in said township the Ensuing Summer

21st Voted to raise a tax of ten shillings and sixpence lawful money on each proprietors right to be improved in making and clearing roads in said township, said tax to be paid by the first of November next

22nd Voted that the encouragement given by the proprietors at their meeting in March 1762 for the speedy settling the lands in said township should be continued untill the first day of September next ensuing

23rd Voted to appoint Mefsrs Nath Porter Silas Waterman and Wm

Dana a committee to receive & improve the aforesaid tax of 10/6 in making and clearing roads in said township

24th Voted to appoint Mr. Constant Southworth collector of rates in the room of Thos. Storrs & also directed Mr Southworth to go to Portsmouth To collect the taxes due from the proprietors residing in those parts & to allow him a meet recompence for the service

25th Voted to allow Mr Charles Hill liberty to keep up gates and bars at each end of his road running through his lot during the proprietors pleasure

26ly Voted to grant Mr. Charles Hill one Acre of the undivided land in Consideration of his deeding one acre of land to said proprietors on the south East part of his 100 acre lot for the use of a Burying place

This was the burying ground near Mrs. Alden's.

27th Voted to grant Mr John Bennet a priviledge of the stream Between Mr Oliver Davisons saw-mill & the mouth of the Mascomme River To erect a grist-mill, & liberty of pafsing to and from said mill, on the undivided land, provided said mill be completed by the first day of March A. D. 1766

The privilege here granted was between the Hubbard bridge and the mouth of the river.

29ly Voted to appoint Mr Levi Hyde clerk for said propriety
29ly Voted to difsolved said meeting

Lotts taken up by the first settlers of the township upon the Encouragement given by the propriety for the speedy settling said township.

The first column are the No of the 100 acre lotts the second column are the No of the intervale lotts

Jonathan Martin	22	19	John Birchard	23	2
John Allen	26	23	Asa Holgate & Joshua		
Nath. Porter	25	18	Blodget	1	9
Nehemiah Estabrook	16	39	Jedidiah Dana	3	32
Thomas Storrs	55	40	Charles Hill	4	30
John Salter	27	41	Huckins Storrs Jun	7	10
Nathan Arnold	52	44	Wm Dana	13	27
Nath Hall	8	11	Samuel storrs	14	3
Joseph Wood	9	13	Robert Barrow Jun	15	6
Robert Hyde	12	31	Joseph Turner	47	7
John Storrs	17	34	Daniel Blodget 3d	53	12
Robert Martin	21	28	Jonathan Murdock	24	17
John Birchard	28	15	Jessie Birchard	50	16
Jonth Blanchard	30	47	Levi Hyde	4	29
Nathan Blodget	38	4	John Dana	5	22

INTRODUCTION. 19

Thomas Barrow Jun	54	37	Joseph Dana	6	33
Minister Lott	56	36	John Hanks	49	38
John Swift	57	14	Jedediah Hibbard on		
Jabez Barrow	58	8	the right of Edward		
Richard Salter	59	5	Goldstone Lutwyche	51	49
John Hyde	61	24	James Hartshorn on		
Rufus Baldwin	62	25	the right of Prince		
John Baldwin	63	26	Aspenwall	60	50
Hobart Estabrook	64	42	Constant Southworth	65	45
Benjamin Davis	41	20	Seth Blodget right		
Josiah Storrs	20	1	taken by Charles Hill		20

The proprietors of the township of Lebanon in the Province of Newhampshire at a legal meeting held the twenty-second day of April A. D. 1765 and past The following votes (viz):

1st Made choice of Mr. Nehemiah Estabrook moderator for said meeting

2nd The question being put whether said propriety will affix any other time for the payment of that tax of 10/6, lawful money Granted the last proprietor's meeting to be paid in November next for making highways in said Lebanon—voted in the affirmative

3d Voted that the aforesaid tax of 10/6 lawful money be paid by the first day of May next.

4ly Voted to adjourn said meeting to the ninth day of May next.

The proprietors of the township of Lebanon met by adjournment and past the following votes (viz):

5ly That the committee appointed for making & clearing highways in said Lebanon be directed to receive & pais the accounts of Charles Hill and others for clearing a road from the house of said Charles Hill To the house of Oliver Davison in said Lebanon, and that the said Committee be further directed to improve so much of that tax of 10/6 granted the last proprietor's meeting as shall be necefsary to settle said accounts.

6ly Voted to allow the account of John Salter being the sum of twenty Shillings for a Book of Records & for his service in recording.

7ly Voted to allow Capt. Saml Storrs fifty shillings for five days Travel & expense to procure a sum of money for the service of said propriety & for the interest of £15–0–0 for two years lent said propriety.

8ly Voted to allow Thos. Storrs thirty-six shillings for service in Collecting rates for said propriety

9ly Voted to raise a tax of 3/ on each proprietor's right to be paid into the treasury of said propriety by the 15th day of May Instant to enable the committee to settle the accounts against said propriety

10ly Voted to appoint a committee of five men to draft the remainder of the lotts which shall not be taken up by the first day of September next.

11ly Appointed Mefsrs Nehemiah Estabrook Saml Storrs, John Salter

Constant Southworth and Nath. Hall a committee for the purpose aforesaid

12ly Voted to adjourn said meeting to the first tuesday of December next, at one of the Clock P. M.

The first town record extant was found by the writer years ago on a loose leaf, much worn and torn. It has been carefully preserved, and is here transcribed in its place by date.

TOWN

A True Coppy of ye Votes Passd at a Townmeeting Held at Lebanon On May ye 13th 1765 at the House of Mr Asa Killbourn (viz) After Chufing a Moderator Queryd

2nd Whether we Will Have a Minister This Summer or Will Not Voted the affirmative

3rd That We First Send Subscriptions To ye Neighbouring Towns and Get What we Can Subfcribed and What Remains Wanting To Supply the Pulpit Will Stand Sponsible For To Be Paid at ye End of s'd Six Month. Voted the affirmative.

4th Chose Aaron Storrs to carry a Subfcription To Take Care To Get as Much Subscribed In ye Neighbouring Towns as He Can

5th Voted that the Select Men take it Upon them To Seek Quarters for the Minister and to Provide For Him.

Lebanon New Hampshire Sept 12 1765

At a Town Meeting Legally Warned ware pafsed ye Following Votes. (viz) Jno Wheatley Chofen Moderator of Said Meeting

2d that the Highway through the Intervale in Said Township Lying on the Great River Shall be an Open Highway.

3d that the Selectmen of Said Town Lay out one Acre of Land for a Burying Place on the North Side of the Road that Leads to the Sawmill up on Mr Charles Hills Land

4th Voted That mr. Silas Waterman Purchafe a Town Book for Records.

Voted That Said meeting be adjourned to the twenty-Seventh Inftant.

Sept 27th 1765 at a Town Meeting held by Adjournment was then pafsed the following vote (viz) That Said Meeting be difmifsed.

PROPRIETORS.

At a meeting of the proprietors of Lebanon held by adjournment The second Tuesday in December 1765, the following votes were past (viz):

13ly Voted to raise the sum of 10/6 of lawful money upon each proprietor's right to be paid into the treasury by the first day of September next [1766] to be appropriated to the use of supporting the preaching of the Gospel in said township the ensuing Summer

14ly Choose Nehemiah Estabrook & Capt. Saml Storrs a committee for providing preaching as aforesaid

15th Voted to raise the sum of 10/6 lawful Money on each right for the use of clearing and making roads in said township of Lebanon to be paid by the first of September next

16th Chose Aaron Storrs & Jedediah Hibbard a committee for directing and ordering bufinefs of clearing and making roads in said Township

17th Voted that the aforesaid committee be directed to improve the aforesaid tax of 10/6 Lawful money in clearing & making roads in said township & also that they shall accept three days labour of each proprietor in full of the aforesaid tax from May untill the first day of October next, and from said first day of October to the tenth of November next four days labour shall be accepted as aforesaid

18th Made choice of Mr Aaron Storrs a committee to complete the Measuring of intervale lots not before measured.

19th Voted that Maj John Slapp shall have the privilege of Laying out a certain tract of undivided land in said township Bounded south on Mascomme river West on Jonathan Danas 100 acre lot north on Charles Hills 100 acre lot & east on Oliver Davison's lot, containing by estimation about thirty acres (except one acre to be taken up by Charles Hill in Lieu of one Acre taken from his lot to be improved for a burying place), and that said Slapp shall have the Liberty of improving the stream on Mascomme river below Davison's saw mill provided he erect and Complete a good grist mill on said stream on or before the first day of December next.

20th Voted to lay out a division of 100 acres of land in said township by the first day of October next, said lotts to be laid in due proportion to each proprietor according to quality of said land.

21st Made choice of Capt Nath Hall and Mefsrs Aaron storrs & Huckins Storrs Jun a committee for laying out the aforesaid division

22nd That the proprietors committee be directed to warn the next proprietors meeting without the Clerk being present.

23rd Voted to difsolve said meeting

TOWN

March 11 1766

At a Town Meeting Legally Warned Ware Passed The Following Votes (viz): Charles Hill Chofen Moderator for Said Meeting

Voted John Wheatley
Silas Waterman } Select Men
Charles Hill

Voted Silas Waterman Town Clerk

Voted Aaron Storrs Constable

Voted Jedediah Hibberb } Tytheing Men
Samuel Mecham }

Voted Charles Hill } Surveyors of ——.
Jedediah Hibberb }

Voted £1. 15s. Lawful Money to James . . For Land Taken off His Entervel .

Voted Selas Waterman £0 3s 8d Lawful Money for Purchasing a Book For To Reccord Town . .

Voted That Said Meeting be Difmifsed

at a Town Meeting Legally warned on April 24 1766 The following Votes ware pafsed

(viz) 1st Mr Charles Hill Chofen Moderator of s'd Meeting

2dly That warnings for Town meetings Shall Stand Eight Days before the meeting.

3dly That Warnings for Town meetings &c for the Future Shall be Set up in the most public place On the North & South Sides of the River Maskoma

4th Whither the Town would Grant a Tax for the Support of the Gospel the Enfuing Seafon

Refolv'd in the Negative.

5thly Voted to Defolve S'd meeting

Att a Town Meeting Legally Warned On Aug 25th Day 1766, The following votes ware pafsed

(viz) 1st John Wheatley Chofen Moderator of S'd meeting

2dly Whither it may be proper & Convenient under Our prefent Circumftances to purfue Such methods as may be Thought proper for the Obtaining of a Steady Gofpel adminiftration amongst us

Refolved in the Affir

3dly Whether The Towne will chufe a Comtee to Treat with Mr. Treadway now refident Amongst us in Order to his Steady Admr. in the Gospel ministry in S'd Town. Refolved in the Affirtive

4thly Chofe John Wheatley mr. Charles Hill and mr Jos Dana to be a Comtee For the purpofs a fore S'd

5thly Whether S'd meeting Shall be Adjourned to the 8th of Sept Next. Refolved in the Affirmt

Septr 8th 1766

Att A Town Meeting Held by Adjournment the Following Vote Was Pasd' (viz) that S'd Meeting Be Adjourned to the 8th of October next.

Att A Town Meeting Held By Adjournment October 8th 1766 Was Then Pafsed the Following vote that S'd Meeting Be Difmifsed

PROPRIETORS.

The following seems to have been the first meeting of the proprietors held in the town:

INTRODUCTION.

At a meeting holden in Lebanon in the province of Newhampshire at the house of Charles Hill [who lived on the river road in the south part of the village of West Lebanon] October the sixth 1766 the following votes were past (viz)

1st Voted Capt. John Wheatley to be moderator for said meeting

2nd Voted to adjourn said meeting to the thirteenth Instant at one of the clock afternoon

Met by adjournment the thirteenth of October & past the following votes (viz):

3rd Voted to raise a tax of twenty shillings lawful money on each proprietors right. to be paid by the first of October 1767 for the Settlement of the gospel in said Lebanon

4ly Voted to choose another committee man in addition to the former Committee for laying out the second division of hundred acre lotts.

5ly Choose Capt. John Wheatly to be committee man,

6ly That said committee shall proceed and lay out the second division of one hundred acre lotts Run the lines and make sufficient bounds on each proprietors lot also to size said lots according to quanty and quality, said committee to be sworn.

7ly Voted to adjourn said meeting to the first monday in may next one of the clock in the afternoon at the house of Mr Charles Hill

TOWN.

March 10 1767

At a Town Meeting Legally warned ware Paised the following votes. (viz) John Wheatly Moderator of S'd meeting

Silas Waterman Town Clerk

John Wheatly Joseph Dana Silas Waterman Select Men

Jefse Cook Conftable

James Jones Elijah Dewey Tything men

Charles Hill Hucking Storrs Afa Kilbourn Fence Viewers

Jos Tilden Jedediah Hebbard Surveyors of highway

Granted £3-18-0 Lawful Money For Laying Out Highways the Last year in S'd Town

Voted a tax to be Levied as the Law Directs For the Defraying Town Charges

Then S'd meeting Defolved

PROPRIETORS

Met by adjournment May the fourth 1767 and past the following votes (viz)

8ly Voted to reconsider a vote passed on a meeting held by adjournment The thirteenth of October 1766, the committee chosen for laying out the said division of 100 Acre lotts to proceed to lay out the second Division of 100 acre lotts, run the lines and making Sufficient bounds on each proprietors lot said lots to be sized according to quality & quantity and said committee to be sworn.

9ly That said committee proceed to lay out the second division of 100 acre lots upon the best of the undivided land in said Lebanon according to their Discretion.

10ly That the committee chosen to lay out the abovesaid division of 100 Acre lots, to complete their cost of laying out said division, Equally dividing the same to each proprietor & said cost to be paid To said committee by said proprietors by the first of May 1768, and those proprietors which shall pay their proportion of said cost to said committee within the above said term shall be entituled to a draft of said Lotts on their payment of the same. Said draft to be conducted by said committee: resolved in The affirmative.

11ly Voted to give said committee five shillings a day and they find themselves

12ly Voted Aaron Storrs seven shillings for his service laying out The aforesaid 100 acre lotts.

13ly Voted to choose another committee man in addition to the Aforesaid committee, that is a fifth committee Man.

14ly Choose Mr. Jedediah Dana to be the fifth committee man

15ly Choose Mr Charles Hill for the first afsefsor

16ly Chose Capt John Wheatley to be the second afsefsor.

17ly Choose Levi Hyde for the third afsefsor

18ly Choose Mr Aaron Storrs collector for said propriety

19ly Choose Capt. John Wheatley to be Treasurer for the proprietors of Township of Lebanon

20ly Voted to hold the proprietors meetings for the township of Lebanon in said Lebanon for the future.

21st Voted to difsolve said meeting.

TOWN

At A Town Meeting Legally Warned On May Fifth 1767 Ware Passed the Following Votes (viz) John Wheatley Moderator For S'd Meeting

Query Whither the Town will Be at the Expence of Supporting Mr Treadway on his Return to them Which is Daily Expected

Refolved In the Affirmt

Voted that the Select Men Provid For Mr Treadway at His Arival

Voted to Difsmis S'd Meeting

At A Town Meeting Legally Warned On May Twenty Fifth Day 1767. The Following Votes ware Pafsed (viz) Capt John Wheatley Moderator For S'd Meeting

To Refolve Whether S'd Town Will Do anything to have a Regular Candidate For the Gospel Ministry to Preach to them the Enfuing Season

Refolved In the Affirmt

OLD LAFAYETTE HOTEL.

Chose a Committee For the Purpos afores'd Namely Mr Aaron Storrs Mr Jos Dana Capt John Wheatley

Voted that the Select Men Provid For A Minifter Provided We Have One

Voted to Difsmis S'd Meeting

PROPRIETORS

At a proprietors meeting held June twenty-ninth 1767 at the house of Mr. Charles Hill the following votes were past (viz)

1st Choose Mr. Aaron Storrs moderator to govern said meeting

2nd Choose Capt John Wheatley for the committee man for to manage The prudential affairs of said propriety.

3rd Choose Mr. Nath Porter to be the second committee man

4ly Choose Mr. Aaron Storrs to be the third committee man

5ly Voted that the proprietors meeting be warned by the proprietors Clerk so ordered by the proprietors committee within the township of said Lebanon upon application of one sixteenth of said proprietors The warning to stand posted up in some publick place in said Lebanon, three weeks before hand with the particular articles to be acted on Inserted

6ly Voted that the proprietors committee should treat with Plainfield committee in respect to settling the town line between Lebanon & Plainfield & make return of their doings the first proprietors meeting

7ly Voted to choose a committee to treat with Mr. Joseph Tilden Respecting the service he has done on the highway

8ly Voted to choose three committee men for the above said service

9ly Choose Capt. John Wheatley for the first Committee man

10ly Choose Mr. Silas Waterman second committee man

11ly Choose Levi Hyde to be the third committee man

12ly Voted to omit the sixth article in the warning (viz) the raising a tax for supporting preaching the Gospel The ensuing year & likewise to see if said proprietors will raise a tax for making and mending highways in said Lebanon.

13th Voted to have but one committee man to settle with the Treasurer and others that the propriety are indebted to in Connecticut

14ly Choose Mr. Aaron Storrs to be said Committee Man

15ly Voted to difsolve said meeting.

At a meeting of the proprietors of the township of Lebanon July the 21st 1767 at the house of Mr Charles Hill the following votes were past (viz):

1st Choose Capt. John Wheatley to be moderator to govern said meeting

2d Voted to raise a tax of six shillings lawful money on each proprietor's right to support the preaching of the Gospel the Current year

3rd Voted to raise a tax of six shillings for making & mending highways in said town or two days work

4ly Voted to pay the abovesaid tax of six shillings for the support of the Gospel by the first Day of October ensuing

5ly Voted that the tax of six shillings lawful Money for the making roads & mending highways be paid by the first day of October next

6ly Voted Mr. Charles Hill a committee man for laying out the aforesaid money for making roads and mending highways in said Lebanon

7ly Choose Mr. Huckins Storrs second committee for the above said purpose of highways

8ly Voted that Maj. John Slapp should have all the undivided [land] Between the now travelling road to Mr Oliver Davisons and Mascomme river between Mr Joseph Danas 100 acre lot and Mr Davisons 100 acre lot provided the above Maj. John slapp. erect a good sufficient grist mill in said town of Lebanon by the first of January 1769.

9ly Voted that the committee should make Mr. Charles Hill what Restitution they shall think proper for a highway to the sawmill and things else whereby the lot is discommoded.

10ly Voted that Capt. John Wheatly and Mr Charles Hill should have twenty-eight shillings lawful money for the service they did the propriety the last winter in measuring the road from Charleston to Lebanon.

This measuring had reference to a dispute between Lebanon and Plainfield concerning town lines.

11ly Voted to suspend the drawing the second division of 100 acre lots in said Lebanon till such time as each proprietor has paid or secured the propriety for their proportion of taxes granted and those that shall be granted by virtue of this warning.

12ly Voted to difsovel said meeting

TOWN

At A Town Meeting Legally Warned On October 7th Day 1767 The Following Votes Ware Pafsed (viz) Capt John Wheatley Moderator For S'd Meeting

After Query Whither the Town would Have mr Wales to preach To them The Enfuing Season Refolved in the affirmative

After Query Whither The Town Wood Give Mr Wood an Equvalent For Land For High Way Taken of His Interval Lot. Refolved in the Negative

Voted to Difmiss S'd Meeting.

At A Town Meeting Legally Warned on Nov. 12th 1767 Ware Then Passed the Following Votes (viz)

1st Capt. John Wheatly Moderator for S'd Meeting

2nd Refolved to Chuse A man to meet the Convention as Cartified in S'd Warning.

3ly Chosen Mr Charles Hill To Attend S'd Convention

4ly Then Difsmifed S'd Meeting.

At A Town Meeting Legally Warned on Nov 20th Day 1767 Was then Passed the Following Votes (viz)

1st Mr. Charles Hill Moderator For S'd Meeting

2nd After Query Whither the Town Would Do anything To Support A School the Curant Year Refolved in Affirmative

3rd Queary Whither the town Would Reconsider the Vote as Above; Refolved in the Affirmative

4th Refolved To Do Something By Way of Subscription For the Support of S'd School

5ly Queary Whither thay Would Do any thing about A Highway. Refolved in the Affirmative

6thly To See Whither thay Will agree to Continue The Road alread Laid out from the Great River To the Great Entervale in S'd Lebanon Through S'd Lebanon To the East Line of the Town, and To have it Laid out as Soon as may be Convenient where it may best Accommodate the Publick & Least Difcommode the Inhabitants of S'd Lebanon Refolved in the Affirmative

Then S'd Meeting Difmifsed.

The Great River is the Connecticut; the Great Intervale is that lying north of the center village. The road was that passing by Mr. J. T. Pulsifer's and ran north of the Mascoma to Enfield.

PROPRIETORS

At a meeting of the proprietors of the township of Lebanon in the province of Newhampshire at Mr Charles Hills in said Lebanon February the 25th 1768 the following votes were past. (viz)

1st Choose Mr Charles Hill moderator to govern said meeting

2nd Voted to act upon the second article in the warning with respect To settling the town line between Lebanon & Plainfield.

3rd Choose Mr Charles Hill for a committeeman for the abovesaid purpose

4ly Choose Capt John Wheatly for the second committee man

5ly Choose Lieut. Nath. Porter for the third committee man

6ly Voted that the second article in the warning be the committee Instruction (viz) To hear Col. Atkinsons letter & to consider & act everything to the above mentioned difficulty that they shall think most conducive to the settlement thereof.

Colonel Atkinson was the Hon. Theodore Atkinson, the Secretary of the Province.

7ly Voted to raise a tax for laying out & making a road from the Great river to the Great intervale and so on to Enfield line.

8ly Voted to raise a tax of eighteen shillings lawful money on each proprietors right for the abovesaid purpose of making & clearing a road from the great river to the great intervale and so on to Enfield line

9ly Voted that the aforesaid tax be paid by the first of June 1768

10ly Choose Levi Hyde to be a committee man for laying out the abovesaid money for the above mentioned road

11ly Chose Mr. Huckins storrs to be the second committee man for the abovesaid purpose

12ly Choose Capt. John Wheatley to be the third committee man for The afore mentioned purpose.

13ly Voted that the committee chose for the aforesaid purpose should accept of one days work as 3/0 Lawful money.

14ly Voted to difsolve said meeting.

TOWN

At A Town Meeting Legally Warned on Feby 26th Day 1768 Ware Then Pafsed the Following Votes (viz) Capt John Wheatley moderator For S'd meeting. Silas Waterman Town Clerk; John Wheatley Silas Waterman Oliver Davison Select Men

Joseph Wood Conftable

Lt. Porter Lt. John Griswold Tythething Men

Oliver Griswould James Jones Surveyors of High Ways; Charles Hill Huckens Storrs, Asa Kilborn Fence Viewers

Queary Whither the Town Would Dow Any Thing about Bulding A meeting House For the Conveniency of Publick Worship in S'd Lebanon. Voted Negative

S'd Meeting Difsmised

PROPRIETORS

At a meeting of the proprietors of the township of Lebanon April 3rd 1768 The following votes were past, (viz):

1st Choose Capt. John Wheatley to be moderator to govern said meeting

2nd Choose Lieut. John Griswold to be a committee man for to view a certain Tract of land that Mr. Joseph Tilden requests for service done on the highway

3rd Choose Mr Huckins Storrs to be the second committee man for the abovesaid purpose

4th Choose Levi Hyde to be the third committee man for the above said purpose

5th Voted to adjourn said meeting to the third tuesday in May 1768, one of the clock afternoon

Met by adjournment May 17 1768 the following votes were past (viz):

1st Voted to accept of the doings of the committee chosen to settle the Dividing line between Lebanon & Plainfield

2nd Granted to Mr Joseph Tilden as a compensation for his labour done on The highway that leads to Hanover &c a tract of land as follows (viz) Beginning at the N. E corner of Mr Charles Hill's fifty acre lot thence running a perpendicular line to the North line of the Town, thence upon said north line westerly to said Tildens land, thence southerly upon the rear of said Tildens & Baldwins 100 acre lotts to the North west Corner of said Hills said fifty acre lot, thence to the first mentioned bound containing the whole of the undivided land between said Eastwardly line & said lotts—also to pay said Tildens proportion of taxes To the amount of four pounds by the first of June next

3rd Voted to difsolve said meeting.

At a meeting of the proprietors of the township of Lebanon in the Province of Newhampshire June the 8th 1768 the following votes were past (viz)

1st Choose Mr. Charles Hill to be moderator to govern said meeting

2nd Mr. Aaron Storrs reports the settlement to be made with the proprietors Committee, Collector, and Treasurer which he finds to be £34-11-4 due from the proprietors to the aforesaid committee collector & Treasurer. Granted to the aforesaid Aaron Storrs the above said £34-11-4 to settle with those the proprietors are indebted to

3d Voted that the above said sum of £34-11-4 be paid by the first of July 1768.

4th Voted that we would not reconsider the third article in the warning

5th Voted to difsolve said meeting

TOWN

At a Town Meeting Legally Warned on July 19th 1768 Ware Pafsed the Following Votes (viz) mr Charles Hill moderator of S'd Meeting

Query Whither The Spot of Ground Near the Burying place should be the place to set a meeting house upon Resolved in the Affirmative.

Voted to diffolve S'd Meeting

At a Town meeting Legally Warned on July 27th 1768 Ware pafsed the following Votes (viz): John Wheatley moderator for S'd meeting

After Query whether they would Give mr Wales a Call to settle in the ministry in This Town. Refolved in ye Affir.

Query whither they will agree to give mr Wales fifty pounds as a Salary for the first Year & to rife five pounds a Year till it arrive to seventy pounds, if he may be Obtained

Refolved in the Affirmative

Query Whither they will Do any thing to Render the Right of Land Devoted for the benefit of a School in s'd Town profitable for s'd purpofe Refolved in the Negtive

Voted to difsolve s'd meeting.

At a Town meeting Legally Warned on Sept. 7th A D. 1768 Ware Pafsed the Following Votes (viz) Levi Hyde moderator for S'd meeting

Query whither Thay Would Reconfider the Vote Passed on July 19th

1768 Relative To Setting the Meeting House on. Refolved in the Negtive

Query Whither Thay Will Do any Thing For the Support of a School In s'd Lebanon the Enfuing Season Refolved in the Affirmative

Then Voted Twenty Pounds to support s'd School A Committee Chosen Namely Lt John Griswould Asa Kilborn Joseph Wood, To Conducke s'd school

Voted to Difsolve S'd Meeting.

At a Town Meeting Legally warned on Sept. 30th 1768 The following Votes ware pafsed (viz) Capt. John Wheatly Moderator of S'd Meeting

After Query whither they would Accept of mr. Wales Verbal Answer (Sent by Deac Nehemiah Estabrook) of his Acceptance of, and Compliance with their call To settle in the work of the Gospel Ministry amongst them, Refolved in the Negative

Voted that said Meeting be Desolved.

PROPRIETORS

At a proprietors meeting of the township of Lebanon in the province of Newhampshire October 24th 1768 the following votes were past (viz):

1st Choose Mr Charles Hill moderator to govern said meeting

2nd Voted to adjourn said meeting to the first tuesday in December next at ten of the clock in the forenoon, at the house of Mr. Charles Hill.

met by adjournment the first tuesday in December 1768

1st Voted to choose a committee to lay out the governors lott in said Lebanon & to see what land it covers of lotted & improved Land & to make those persons a meet compensation out of the Undivided land

2nd Choose Mr Charles Hill to be a committee for the above said purpose

3rd Choose Levi Hyde the second committee man

4th Choose Lieut. John Griswould for to be the third committee man

5th Choose Jedidiah Hibbard to be the fourth committee man for the above mentioned purpose.

6th Voted to adjourn said meeting to the third monday in May next, 1769 at three of the clock afternoon.

The governor's lot was a tract of 500 acres in the southwest corner of the town, covering the farm of Mr. Bradley True and other land. He had a similar tract in the northwest corner of Plainfield, making a thousand acres in one body. The proprietors had divided this land among themselves, and occupied some portions of it. In 1766 Benning Wentworth had resigned as governor, and began naturally to look after his landed interests, and to claim the reservations made in the various townships. Hence the action of the proprietors.

TOWN

At a Town Meeting Legally warned on Tuesday the 14th Day of march 1769 the following Votes ware paſſed

1st Charles Hill moderator

2nly Joseph Wood Charles Hill & Silas Waterman Select men Silas Waterman Town Clerk. Jedediah Hibbard Conſtable Hucken Storrs Leather sealer Jonathan Dana and Saml Eſtabrook Tything men Nathiel Porter & Charles Hill Jun survayors of Highways, Benj. Fuller Pound Keeper.

3dly Whether they will agree to build two bridges Over the River Maſkoma, one at the ford way near Benj. Fullers (East Lebanon) and the Other near the mills in said Lebanon.

Reſolved in the Negative

Query whither they would agree to build one bridge Reſolved in the afftive

Query whether they would build a bridge at S'd fordway Reſolved in the Negtive

Query Whether they will build a bridge near said mills [Hubbard bridge] Reſolved in the Affive

4thly Whether they ment to be underſtood By their former Vote paſſed Sept 30th 1768 (wherein they manifeſted their Nonacceptance of mr Wales Verbal anſwer) thereby to Have Repealed or made void all their former votes paſſed by Them in favor of said mr. Wales Settling in the Gospel Ministry amongst them. Reſolved in the Affirmative

5tly To see if they will think proper (as a town) to make Mr Wales some Compensation for the Loss of his horſe ſuppoſed to be Gored to Death in Levi Hydes paſture ye Last year

Reſolved in the Negative

6thly Vote said meeting Diſolv'd

May 8th 1769 met and adjourned to May 22.

At A Town Meeting Held By Adjournment Ware then passed The Following (viz) Query the Town Would Do any Thing Relative To haveing a Gospel adminiſtration amongst Them the Inſuing Summer. Riſolved in the Affirmt Voted to Appoint A Committee For to Proqure a Minister The Inſuing Summer Charles Hill Capt. John Wheatley Joseph Wood Committee men

Voted To have s'd Committee To Applie To Mr Kenne and See if Thay Can Obtain S'd Mr. Kenne and if s'd Committe Should Be Disappointed of Him, Then Voted That s'd Committee Take the Best Method To Obtain a Minister Thay Could The Ensuing Summer

Voted To Have a Lawbook for the Use of the Town to Be Kept in the Clark's Office

Voted to Build a Cart Bridge at the Ford Way at masquom A Committe Chosen For that Parpose Namely Mr John Slap Charles Hill Silas Waterman Voted s'd meeting Difolved

At a meeting of the proprietors of the township of Lebanon in the province of Newhampshire at the house of Mr Charles Hill in said Lebanon October 23 1769 the following votes were past (viz):

1st Choose Mr Charles Hill moderator to govern said meeting

2nd Voted to choose a committee relative to the second article respecting laying out the governors lott & seeing what lotted and improved lands it covers & to make those persons a meet compensation that said Governor's lot covers.

3rd Choose Mr Charles Hill Lieut John Griswold and Levi Hyde for a committee for the above mentioned purpose.

4th Voted a tax of six shillings Lawful money on each proprietors right to be layd out for completing of the road that goes up and down the river between the great intervale & Plainfield line and if any of the aforesaid sum be left, to pay the proprietors debts

5ly Choose a committee to lay out the afore said sum (viz) Lieut Nath. Porter & Silas Waterman

6ly Voted that said proprietors should have 3/ a day for work if done To the acceptance of the committee chose for the aforesaid purpose

7ly Voted that the work should be done by the 23d of November 1769

8ly Voted to dismifs said meeting

At a proprietors meeting of the township of Lebanon in the province of Newhampshire held at the house of Mr Charles Hill insaid Lebanon March the 13th 1770 the following votes were past (viz)

1st Choose Capt John Wheatley moderator to govern said meeting

2ly To see if they will revoke the six shilling rate last granted; voted in the negative.

3d To see whether they will do anything relative to establishing bounds between Mr. Hebbard & Mr Hall Voted in the negative.

4th Voted to choose a committee to look into the circumstance of Mr Olver Davison, deceased, hundred acre lot

5ly Choose a committee for to look into the circumstances of the abovesaid Davison's lott & to lay out of the undivided land in said town a proportion of land to said hundred acres the same as they shall think proper. Mr Charles Hill Maj John Slapp & Levi Hyde be the above committee

6ly Voted that the proprietor's Clerk shall give Deeds in behalf of the proprietors To Mr Charles Hill & Maj John Slapp that is already Granted to them by the proprietors [To Charles Hill a tract for a part of his lot taken for a burying ground. To Maj Slapp of a tract for a mill site]

7ly To see whether they will give one thousand four hundred and forty-one acres of undivided land adjoining to Hanover line and adjoining Mr. Tilden's land, said tract to be laid one mile & half square

INTRODUCTION.

for the support of Dr Wheelocks school, upon condition that said school be erected in Hanover, and direct that the proprietors Clerk make a deed of said Grant upon the erection of said school as above said. voted in the affirmative

8ly Voted to difsmifs said meeting.

TOWN

At a Town Meeting Warned on Tuesday 13 Day of March 1770 Ware Passed the Following Votes (viz):

Charles Hill Moderator For S'd Meeting Silas Waterman Town Clerk, Charles Hill Silas Waterman Capt John Wheatley Select Men Nathaniel Hall Constable, Zacheus Douner Joseph Martin Tything Men, Levi Hyde Lieut. John Griswold Fence Viewers; Hucken Storrs Leather Sealer, Lieut. Nath Porter Rufus Baldwin Surveyors of Highways; Johnathan Dana Key Keeper of Pound; Maj. John Slapp Aaron Storrs Committee men To Examine the Select Men accounts Silas Waterman Town Treasurery

Voted S'd meeting Difsolved.

Att A Town Meeting Warned On the Fifth Day of November 1770 The Following Votes Ware Paised (viz) Charles Hill Moderator of S'd meeting

Queary Whither Thay Would Do any Thing Relating To the Second Article in the Warning S'd Article Was To See if Thay Would Build a Meeting House. Voted in the Affirm^{ty}

Query Whither Thay Would Build a Meeting House For the Convenancey of Publick Worship in S'd Town

Refolved in the Negative.

Queary Whither Thay Would Revive S'd Acct. of 60 £ For Erecting A Cart Bridge Near Maj Slaps Mills in s'd Lebanon Resolved in the Affirm^{ty}

Voted S'd 60 £ Be paid in the year 1772 by the 5 of Nov^b

Voted that the Select men Erect a Sine Pofts To Sit Up Warning On For the Futur One To Be Plasted at The Corner of The Road that Leads to Mr Wood And the Other att the Corner that Leads Out To Maj. John slaps. S'd Pofts To Be Set Upon the Town Costs.

Voted S'd Meeting Difsolved

Att A Town Meeting Warned On the 26th Day of November 1770 The Following Votes Ware paift (viz) Charles Hill Moderatorr of S'd Meeting. To See Whither Thay will Agree To Build a House For Publick Worship in S'd Lebanon Refolved in the Affirmative

Voted To have the Size of S'd House For Publick Worship To Be Thirty Foot Squair and Teen Foot Poft

Voted To Place S'd Hous Upon the Road that Leads Out To the Mills in S'd Town Upon A Peas of Flat Land East of Mr Charles Hills Barn

Voted S'd Meeting Adjourned To the 17 Day of December 1770

Met Dec 17 and adjourned to Jan 7 1771

At the Adjourned Meeting Held on Monday the 7th Day of January 1771 the following Articles ware paſsed In the Affirmative (viz)

1st Whether they would Go into the Reconſideration of The Votes Heretofore paſsed Relating to the Building of a Meeting house in said Lebanon Resolved in ye Afftve

2dly Whether they will Agree to build a House for publick worship In S'd Lebanon Reſolv'd in the Afftve

3dly Whether they would Have a Longer time to Complete Said Houſe in, then already Agreed upon Reſolved in the Afftiv

4thly Whether they would Have Said House Set upon Some Other Spot Than that already Agreed to Reſolv'd in ye Afftive

5thly Whither they will agree to Chuſe a Comtee to fix a Spot to Set S'd House upon and that said Spot agreed upon by said Comtee Shall be the place To Set Said Houſe Reſolv'd in the Affirmative

6thly made Choice of Saml Chase esq, Capt Hez. Johnson and Lieut. David Woodward to be a Cmtee To Affix a Spot to set said Meeting House.

Samuel Chase was a prominent man of Cornish, member of the Provincial Congress at Exeter, 1775.

Capt. Hezekiah Johnson was of Hanover.

Lieutenant, afterwards Capt. David Woodward, was of Hanover.

7thly Voted to Chuſe a Comtee to wait upon the above said Comtee when Convened.

8thly Made Choice of Mr Aaron Storrs Lieut. Porter Mr Charles Hill John Wheatley Eſq. and Mr Azariah Bliſs to be a Comtee for the purpoſe afore said

9thly Voted to Diſolve said Meeting

At a Town Meeting Legally Warned on Tueſday Day The 29th Day of Jany 1771 The following Votes ware Paſſed in the affirtve Mr Charles Hill Moderator of Said Meeting

1st Voted to Build a Houſe for Publick Worship

2dly Voted S'd Houſe shall be Thirty feet Square & ten feet poſts

3dly Voted that Maj. John Slapp Lieut. Nathl Porter and John Wheatley Esq be a Comtee to Conduct the Building of said House

4thly Voted that the Tax of 60 £ already Granted for the Building a bridge in said Lebanon be made as Soon as may be Convenient

5thly Voted to have a Tax Levied forthwith to Defray The Charge of The Comtee Choſen to deſign a Spot For the Setting a Meeting Houſe

6thly Voted To Clear and fence the Burying Yard Upon the Towns Coſt and Said Buſineſs to be Under the Direction of The Comtee Choſen to Conduct The Building of the Bridge in said Lebanon

7thly Voted to Diſolve said Meeting.

INTRODUCTION.

At a Town Meeting Legally Warned on March the 12th 1771 For the Choice of Town officers for the year Enſuing The following Votes Ware paſſed

1ˢᵗ Mr. Charles Hill Moderator of said Meeting Voted That John Wheatley Eſq Mr Charles Hill and Mr Silas Waterman Be Selectmen for the year Enſuing Mr Silas Waterman Town Clerk Oliver Griswold, Conſtable. Bela Turner and William Downer Tything— Lieut Porter and Lieut Griswold Surveyors. of Highways Charles Hill Lieut Griswold and Joseph Martin fence Viewers Huckens Storrs Leather Sealer.

Voted to Diſolve S'd Meeting

At a Town Meeting Legally Warned on Tueſday The 19th Day of March 1771 The following Votes Ware Paſſed Lieut. John Griswold Moderator of said Meeting

Voted to take into Confideration the Requeſt of Doc. Eleasor Wheelock Preſdt of Dartmouth College That one mile & half of Land in breadth and three Miles in Length of the Township of Lebanon in the North Weſt Corner thereof be incorporated with other Land into a Town or pariſh, Purſuant To Said Requeſt

Voted To Requeſt the General Court That the Lands Included within the following Lines (viz) From the N. W. Corner bound of Lebanon Running Eaſterly Upon the Town Line three miles; Thence Southerly a Perpendicular Line one mile and half Thence Weſterly a Parallel Line with the firſt Line to ye Great River, thence abutting Weſterly on Said River To the above mentioned Bound may be incorporated Into a Town or Pariſh

Voted Doc. Eleaser Wheelock To be an Agent to Repreſent the Town at the General Court In favor of the above Requeſt and for the obtaining of the same

After voting sums of money to various persons for services rendered the meeting diſolved

Doctor Wheelock, president of Dartmouth College, presented his petition to the governor and council, and on April 4, 1771, they recommended that the petition be granted. A tract of land three miles square, taken from Lebanon and Hanover, was for many years known as Dresden, and was called a town.

At a Town Meeting Legally Warned on Wedneſday the 21ˢᵗ Day of August 1771 The following Votes ware paſsed (viz) Mr Charles Hill Moderator.

2ᵈˡʸ Whither they will agree to give mr Isaiah Potter a Call to Continue in the work of the Gospel Miniſtry In order for Settlement in said work amongst them. Reſolv'd in the Affirmative

3ᵈˡʸ Made Choice of John Wheatley mr Charles Hill, and mr. Azariah Blifs to be a Comtee to Treat with Mr. Potter For the purpoſe afore said

4thly Voted that the Select men Should affefs the Inhabitants of said Lebanon for the Defraying all Necefsary Charges arifing on the acct of obtaining mr. Potter For His Labour and support for the time being amongst Them

5thly Voted to Enlarge the Meeting House already voted to be built from 30 feet Square & 10 feet posts to be 48 feet in Length Thirty-four feet in breadth & Twenty feet Post

6thly Voted to adjourn Said Meeting to the fourth Day of Sept. 1771. at said Meeting adjourned as above Said the above named Comtee made their Report to said Meeting of Mr. Potter's Acceptance of their motion made to him by said Comtee so far as to Return to them the Enfuing Spring. Extrordinaries Excepted Voted to accept S'd Comtees Report.

Voted to Remove the meeting House already Voted to be Erected near The Burying Yard in said Lebanon to the most Convenient Place in mr. Hills pafture Westerly Near the Road that Leads to the saw mill

Voted That Maj Slapp Mr. Silas Waterman and mr Huckens Storrs Be a Comtee to Build said Meeting House.

Voted That said Comtee Proceed to Erect and Enclose said Meeting House & Lay a Good floor in said House by the first Day Oct. which will be in the year 1772

Voted to Difsolve said Meeting

At a Town Meeting Legally Warned on Nov. 7th 1771 The following Votes ware pafsed (viz)

1st Mr. Charles Hill Moderator of said Meeting

2dly Voted to Transpofe the Meeting House. Voted to be Erected in Mr. Hills Pafture to The Clay pit about fifty Rods Westerly of said Spot before agreed to upon said Road

3dly Voted That Mr Azariah Blifs Maj. John Slapp & John Wheatley Efq Be a Comtee to over See and forward The Erecting & Enclofing and Laying a Good floor To said House By the first of October 1772

4thly Voted to Disolve said Meeting

At a Town Meeting Legally Warned on the Sec'd Day of Dec 1771 The following Votes were pafsed (viz)

1st Mr Charles Hill Moderator

2dly To Raise a Tax to Build a Meeting Houfe on Sawmill Road at the spot agreed to their Last Meeting, Nov. 7th 1771

3dly Voted To Disolve Said meeting

At a Town Meeting Legally Warned on Jan. 7th 1772 The following Votes ware Paifed (viz):

1st John Wheatley Efq. moderator

2dly To Raife a Tax to Build a Meeting Houfe on Sawmill Road at the spot agreed to their Last Meeting, Nov. 7th 1771

3dly Voted To Disolve Said meeting

At a Town Meeting Legally Warned on Jan. 7th. 1772 The following Votes ware Paifed (viz):

1st John Wheatley Efq. Moderator

INTRODUCTION.

2dly Voted to accept of the Spot Pitched By a Comtee in The Field of Jonathan Dana to Set a Meeting Houſe

3dly Voted to Tranſpoſe the meeting Houſe already Voted to be Built By a Tax near the Clay pitt, on Sawmill Road To the above Said Spot in S'd Dana's Field

4thly Voted that Maj. John Slapp Mr Charles Hill Lieut. John Griswold and Mr Silas Waterman Be a Comtee to Over See the Building of S'd Houſe

5thly Voted to Difsolve said Meeting.

At their annual meeting held March 10, 1772, they elected as their town officers:

Mr Charles Hill Moderator John Wheatley Esq Charles Hill, Silas Waterman Select Men for the Year Enfuing Silas Waterman Town Clerk Wm Dana Conſtable; John Hyde Jeſe Cook Tything Men Lt. John Griswold Joseph Martin Levi Hyde Fence Viewers, Oliver Griswold Leather Sealer; Jeſe Cook, James Jones Wm Downer Surveyors of Highways; Silas Waterman Sealer of Wates and Measures. Voted £40. Lawful Money For highway.

At a Town Meeting Legally Warned & Held on April 7th 1772 the following Votes ware paſsed (viz)

1st Mr. Charles Hill Moderator

2dly Reſolved to alter the Size of the Meeting Houſe to forty feet in Length, thirty in Breadth & ten feet poſt

3dly Voted to pay £5-10-6 for planks for Bridges

4thly Voted to pay the sum of £2-9-0 to Maj. John Slapp Comtee man for Clearing & Getting timber for a Meeting Houſe at the Clay Pitt

5thly Voted to pay Charles Hill, John Griswold & Silas Waterman £10-2-4 for Getting Timber for a Meeting House

At a Meeting Legally Warned & Held on April, 20th 1772. Voted Mr Charles Hill Moderator of S'd Meeting

Voted to Tranſpoſe the Meeting House from Mr. Dana's Field to Mr. Hills Paſture Near the House of Mr. Bela Turner

Voted that Azariah Blifs, Charles Hill Silas Waterman Maj. Slapp, Lieut. Porter and John Wheatley be a Comtee to oversee & forward the building of Said Meeting House

Voted To adjourn said meeting to the 27th inſtant, at which Meeting held by adjournment the following votes ware paſſed (viz)

Voted that above Named Comtee proceed to Erect & Encloſe said Meeting House as Soon as may be. Voted to Disolve Said Meeting

PROPRIETORS.

At a meeting of the proprietors of the township of Lebanon at The house of Mr. Charles Hill in the province of Newhampshire on the 26th of May 1772 the following votes were past (viz):

1st Mr Charles Hill was chosen moderator to govern said meeting

2nd Voted to choose a committee to make application to his Excellency to order the surveyor general to affix the S. W. corner and run the south line and Affix the south East corner of the Township of Lebanon, according to the charter of said township

3rd That Mr. Aaron Storrs & Capt. Elisha Sprague be a committee to make application to his Excellency for the granting the request in the above vote

4ly Voted to adjourn said meeting to the 29th of this instant at three clock in the afternoon at the house of Mr. Charles Hill

Met according to adjournment & the following votes were past, (viz):

5ly Whether the proprietors will agree to build a meeting house? past in the Affirmative

6ly Meſsrs Aaron Storrs Huckins Storrs & Jedediah Hibbard be a committee for the above purpose.

7ly Voted to raise a tax of forty shillings upon each proprietors Right to be paid in by the first of September next for the use of the afore mentioned meetinghouse

8ly Voted that the present proprietors' committee should be a Committee to receive & examine and pay out and to settle back, present and future accounts for the proprietors of the Aforementioned Township during the proprietors aſsignation, for the above said purpose

9ly Voted to raise a tax of twelve shillings Lawful money on each proprietors right to pay the aforesaid committee & to pay the outstanding Debts of said proprietors—to be aded to the forty shilling tax.

10ly Whether the said proprietors will appropriate the forty shillings Granted on each proprietors right, to the use of building a meetinghouse on such spot as may be hereafter, within one month from this 29 day of May, be affixed by an indifferent Judicious Committee of three men chose by the town of said Lebanon who shall be instructed to have regard to the general interest of the Township of Lebanon, & paid [the money] to the committee that may be appointed by said Town for building said house. Voted in the affirmative.

11ly Whether the proprietors will agree to build a meeting house in the Township of said Lebanon for the use of said town on the south side of the river mascomme, on the East side of the road which leads from the Sawmill late belonging to the estate of Mr Oliver Davison, deceaſ'd, into the road called Enfield road, near Lieut Nathaniel Porters dwelling hous (viz) at a certain beach tree marked on four sides & with the Letter M, standing on a small eminence, 100 rods from Enfield road & 112 rods from mascomme river, opposite Maj John Slapps Cornmill, of the following dimensions (viz) 44 feet in length and thirty-two feet in breadth, with 20 feet posts, and choose a committee of three men to accomplish the same as soon as the nature of said busineſs will admit. Voted in the affirmative.

12ly Voted to dismiſs said meeting

TOWN

At a Meeting Legally Warned & Held on June 8th 1772

Voted, Mr Charles Hill Moderator of S'd Meeting

Voted, That Azariah Blifs Charles Hill & John Wheatley be a Comtee to Receive mr. Potters anfwer to the propofals of said Town & to Make a Report thereof to Said Town

Voted to Adjourn Said Meeting to the first Monday in July next

at the abovesaid Meeting Held by adjournment on July 6th 1772, a Motion was made by S'd Meeting To Mr. Potter to Give his Answer to the Call Given To him by the people of said Lebanon to Settle in the Gospel Ministry amongst them. To which Call Mr. Potter was pleafed to Answer in the Affirmative.

Voted to give Mr. Potter thirty-Eight pounds in Addition to the Sixty-two pounds granted by the proprity of said Lebanon towards the settlement of the first Gospel minister settled in said Town (as a Settlement for Mr Potter) in cafe of His Settleing in the work of the Gospel Miniftry in Sd Town

Voted, To Give Mr Potter as a Salary fifty pound Lawful Money a year for the two first years & then to Rise Annually five pounds a year till it Shall amount to Eighty pounds; & that S-d Sum of Eighty pounds when attained to as above Said Shall be the Stated Salary for Mr Potter So Long as he Shall Continue in the Gospel Ministry in said Town

At a Meeting Legally Warned & Held the 10th Day of August 1772 the following Votes ware pafsed (viz) Mr Charles Hill Moderator of Said Meeting

Voted To Build a Meeting Houfe on the East End of Mr. Hills Pafture Near to Maj. Slapps

Voted That the former Comtee That was appointed To build a Meeting House Near to Mr. Turners be a Comtee to Build said House at the above said place, 48 feet in Length 34 in Breadth & 10 or 12 feet poft

Voted To Difannul and make void all former votes pafsed in said Town Refpecting a Meeting House, Excepting the timber procured for a Meeting House Heretofore

Voted to Difolve said Meeting

At their annual meeting March 9, 1773, they elected their town officers:

Jno Wheatley Efq be Modr of S-d Meeting Azariah Blifs. Maj. John Slapp Levi Hyde Select Men, Silas Waterman Town Clerk, Saml Bayley Conftable, Mefsrs Hezekiah Waters & Azariah Blifs Jun. Tything men Messrs Lieut John Griswold, Charles Hill & Joseph Martin fence Viewers; Mefsrs Wm Dana, Wm Downer, James Jones, & Jefse Cook Surveyors of Highways; Lemuel Hough Leather Sealer; Mefsrs Nathaniel Hall Nathaniel Porter Jr Deer Reeves

These were the officers to prevent the killing of deer out of season.

Among the papers of Nathaniel Hall the following complaint, under the statute, was found:

Province of New Hampshire SS. Plainfield March 22 1773.

Isaac Stephens of said Plainfield Complains & says that Alexader Brink of Hartford in the Province of Newyork & Sam^ll Meacham of Pelhan (Enfield) in ye Province of N. Hampshire & Joseph Martain of Lebanon in ye Provinc afores'd have in ye Months of February Last and March instant Hunted and Kill^d Deer kind within ye Bounds of ye Province of New Hampshire which ye s'd Isaac Stephens Stands Ready to prove, it being Repugnant to ye Laws of s'd Province, Expects to have said Breach or Breaches of law above mentioned Heard & Determined Before two of his Majesties Justices of ye Peace for s'd Province

Test.

After voting sums of money to various persons:

Voted to Submit the Laying out of a Road from Mafguama Bridge thro Jonathan Danas & Maj. Slapps Land to the Meeting House to the Discretion of the Select Men.

Voted to Raife a Tax of £20.-0-0 for the Support of a school in S'd Town the Current year.

Voted to Disolve S-d Meeting

Att a Meeting Legally Warned and Held on Sept. 7, 1773 The Following Votes Ware Pafsed

1st Voted Jedediah Hebbard and Jonathan Dana Grand Jurey men

2nd Voted that the Select men Provide a Box or Boxes on the Coft of The Town To Put the Names of the Inhabitants of the Town Qualified By Law To Be Draughted To Save as Pitet Jurey men

3^ly Voted That Warnings For Town meeting Be Set up on or Near the Meeting House in S'd Lebanon

4^ly Voted that John Wheatley Esqr, Capt Elijah Sprague Be Committee Men For To Rectifie any Mistakes Made By the meeting House Committee

5^ly Voted to Disolve S-d meeting

At a Town Meeting Legally Warned and Held on December 27th 1773. The Following Votes Ware Pafsed (viz):

1st Queary Whither the Town would Reconfider The Twenty pound Tax Voted att our annual meeting, held The 9th of Last March, Relating To the Support of a School or Schools in S'd Town

Resolved in Negative

2^ndly Voted that The Select men Take Back the Bill Committed To the Conftable To Collect For the Purpose above S-d

3^rdly Voted that the Select men Cros out Stephen Jewel Meeting House tax

OLD LEBANON BANK BUILDING.

4ly Voted that the Select men Rectifie the mistake made in Mr Levi Hydes Rate. S'd Rate was Thirteen Shillings Lawful Money.

5thly Voted That the Select Men Procure a Plan of The meeting Houſe Flower To Be Laid Before The Next Town Meeting in order To Erect Pues and Seets in S'd House.

Voted S-d Meeting Diſolved

At a Town meeting Legally Warned and Held on March 8th 1774 The Following Choices of Town Officers Ware made and the Following Votes Ware Pas^d (viz)

Voted That Dea Nehemiah Estabrook be Moderator of s-d Meeting

Voted Dea Nehemiah Estabrook John Wheatley Esq. and Mr. Charles Hill Be Selectmen; For y-r Ensuing

Voted Silas Waterman Town Clerk and Treasurer; Hezekiah Waters Conſtable; Azariah Bliſs, Joseph Martin James Fuller Samuel Estabrook Tything Men; Charles Hill John Griswold, Joseph Martin Fence Viewers; Lemuel Hough Leather Sealer; Lemuel Hough Jedediah Hebbard Oliver Griswold Samuel Eastbrook Surveyors of Highways. Charles Hill, Huckins Storrs Lt John Griswold Haywards

Sums of money were voted to different persons

At a town meeting held April 5, 1774, sums of money were voted for various purposes to purchase a set of "Wates and measures For S—d Town."

May 30, 1774, they declined to do anything to finish the meeting-house.

At A Town meeting Held on May 30th 1774 Ware Then Paſsed The 'Following Votes,

Deaⁿ Nehemiah Estabrook Moderator of S-d meeting

Made Choice of Lt Jedediah Hibbard Grand Juror To Serve At the — Superior Court To Be Held at Plymouth on the Second Tuesday of June Next

Query Whither The Town will Do Any Thing To Finiſh the meeting House—

Reſolved in Negative

Voted To Disolve S-d meeting

PROPRIETORS

At a meeting of the proprietors of the township of Lebanon in the province of Newhampshire held at the house of Mr Charles Hill in said Lebanon on thursday the 29th of September 1774 the following votes were past (viz):

1st Chose Deacon Nehemiah Estabrook moderator to govern said meeting.

2nd Voted to adjourn said meeting to the house of Capt. Bela Turner for half an hour

Met according to adjournment & the following votes were past (viz):

3rd Voted to pursue some method to afcertain the southwest corner of said town and south line according to the Charter of said town notwithstanding the former votes past in said propriety relative thereto.

4ly Voted and resolved to appoint a committee of five men to afcertain the southwest corner bound of the township of said Lebanon according to Charter it being 18 miles distant on a point from Charleston Northwest corner bound. Voted in the Affirmative

5th Voted & resolved Mefsrs Aaron Storrs Nehemiah Estabrook John Griswold Jedediah Hebbard & Nath Porter or the major part of them be our committee for the abovementioned purpose

6th Voted & resolved that the last mentioned committee or the major part of them be our committee to afcertain & mark the southern line of said township of Lebanon according to Charter, & to warn any person or persons whom they shall find trefspafsing on any undivided lands in this township immediately to desist & depart from said lands, and if they do not depart in consequence of such warning within a proper time the said committee or the major part of them are hereby authorized & empowered to proscecute them in law as treispafsers, and to take every legal method they shall Judge proper and necefsary to establish the southern line of said town-ship and vindicate said undivided land from such persons as have presumed To enter and make improvements on the same and so as to put a final end & close to any grounds of dispute which have subsisted respecting said southwestern bound & southern line of said township of Lebanon. voted in the affirmative

At a meeting held in Nov 1774

Voted to allow the accounts of Jonathan Freeman for runing The line from Charlestown Northwest corner to the southwest corner of Lebanon & planing the same and runing the South & East lines of said township, which is £2.-16-0

Jonathan Freeman was of Hanover, afterward a member of Congress.

2nd Voted to allow the accounts of Messrs David Woodward. James Hutchinson & Saml Haze for service done to said propriety as chainmen which account is £4.-0-0

3rd Voted to allow the account of Nehemiah Estabrook for service done to said propriety the sum of £2.-13-6½

4ly Voted To allow the account of John Griswold for service done To said propriety £1.-13-0

5ly Voted to allow the account of Jedediah Hibbard for service done to said propriety £5-4-5

6ly Voted to allow the account of Nath Porter the sum of £0-3-5.

At a meeting held the second Monday in December 1774

1st Whereas the committee appointed by this propriety at their meeting on the 29th Day of Sept. last report that they have employed Mr Jonathan Freeman to afsist them as surveyor in afcertaining the Southwest corner bound of said township of Lebanon according to Charter who has lodged a certificate of his doings therein with the Clerk of the propriety which is laid before them for their acceptance and as the acceptance or nonacceptance of said report is a matter of much consequence to this propriety, on which account a full meeting of the proprietors is greatly to be desired therefore voted that the final Consideration & determination of this propriety respecting said report be deferred to the next adjourned meeting. Paſt in the affirmative.

Met on the 10th of January 1775 and accepted the reports of Mr. Freeman

No further business of importance was transacted by the proprietors until March, 1778.

TOWN

At A Town meeting Held on Jany 15th 1775 Ware Then Paiſed the Following Votes Nehemiah Estabrook Moderator of S'd meeting

Query Whither The Town Would Build a gris mill in S'd Town Resolved In Affirmtive

Voted A Committee To Look out A Place To Sit S'd mill and make Report To S-d Town

The Committee Names are as Follows Namely Lt. John Griswold Mr Azeriah Blifs Enſ'n Hezekiah Waters

Voted The Sum of Thirty Pounds Lawful Money For the Support of Chools in S'd Town. A Comtee Chosen For the Above S'd Purpose Namely Capt Bela Turner Lt John Griswold Lt Jedediah Hibbard John Wheatley Esq. Maj. John Slapp

A Report of the Comtee Appointed by the Town of Lebanon to Divvide S'd Town into Districts For the benefit of Chools and to make an Equitable Distribution of £30. Granted By S'd Town For the Suport of of S'd Schools To the Several Districts aforesaid

We the Subscribers members of the aforesaid Comtee According to our Inſtructions Received From you have taken into our Conſideration the Bufineſs Afsigned To us & have mutually Agreed in the Following Diviſion & distribution aforesaid (viz.)

The first District To begin at the mouth of Enfield Old Road thence including all the Inhabitants on said Road To the North Line of Said Town & to Extend as far East as the East End of Capt Bela Turners meadow Lott on the N Side of the River Maſcoma.

The S. W. District To begin at the mouth of Enfield Old Road and to Extend East as Far as the S. W. Corner of Zalmon Aspenwalls First Hund1 acre Lott Lying on S'd Road, including Mr Joseph Wood Mr. Huckens Storrs and Deacon Nehemiah Estabrook & his Son Nehemiah

Estabrook Jun. Togather with all the Inhabitants South of S'd Road To the South Line of S'd Town

The S. E. District to Begin at said S. W. Corner of S'd Aspenwall Lott and include all the Inhabitants Living Upon Said Road North and E. & all South of Said Road To the E. Line of aforesaid South weftern District.

The Northeaftern District To Begin at the aforesaid E End of Capt. Bela Turners meadow Lott thence Southerly acrofs the River mafcoma So far as to include Hobart Estabrook Thence North eafterly to the Mouth of the South Branch of the aforesaid River Mafcoma So Far as to include all the inhabitants North of said River & said Branch and Wefterly as Far as the East Line of the First Mentioned District

We Then Proceded To make an Equal Distribution of the aforesaid Sum of 30 £ To the Several Districts as aforesaid according to The Laft years Lift of the Inhabitants of Said Town, Excepted. Which upon an Accurate Examination we find to be as Follows

To the First District	£11–18–6
Second Do	9–16–6
Third Do	5– 8–6
Fourth Do	2–16–6
	30– –0–0

We also Humbly offer to the Consideration of S'd Town Whither it may Not be for the Publick utility to Appoint Collectors In the Several Districts Aforesaid to Collect the aforefaid Sums Afsigned to Each District & Also to appoint a Com^{tee} To Manage the Affairs of the Schools in Said Districts with the Advice & Concurrance of the Inhabitants in them To which Com^{tee} or Com^{tees} the Aforesaid Collectors Shall be accountable for The Several Sums Committed To them To Collect For the Purpofe Aforesaid & also that Said Com^{tee} or Com^{tees} Render an account To Said Town at Their Annual meeting In march 1776. How and in What manner the aforesaid Sums of Money have been Difposed of By Them

John Wheatley Esq.
John Slapp
John Griswold   Com^{tee}
Bela Turner
Jed. Hebbard

The Aboe Report Was Excepted By the Inhabitants of S'd Town

Voted That The Coft of Mr. Bugbe's Sicknefs Tho Last year should Be Paid By The Inhabitants of S'd Town

At the annual meeting March 14, 1775 the town officers were chosen as follows—

Deacon Nehemiah Estabrook Moderator of S d Meeting

Selectmen Dea. N. Estabrook John Wheatley Esq Lt. John Griswold

Town Clerk and treasurer, Silas Waterman

Conſtable, Azariah Blifs

Tything men, Charles Saction John Lyman Abiel Wills, Nathaniel Porter Jr.

Surveyors of Highways Henry Woodward, Lt Sam¹ Paine Nathaniel Porter Jr. Zacheus Downer

Fence Viewers Lt. John Griswold Joseph martin Ens. Wᵐ Dana

Leather Sealer Capt Bela Turner

Haywards Joseph Wood James Jones Samuel Bailey Abel Wright Charles Hill

School Collectors, Nathaniel Storrs Silas Waterman Ebenezer Blifs, Jese Cook

School Committee Capt. Bela Turner John Wheatley Esq. Lt. Levi Hyde Lt. John Griswold Maj. John Slapp

Various sums of money were voted.

Voted £2.-0-0 L. M. to Defray the Expenses of the Comtee Appointed By The Province To attend The Continental Congress.

Difficulties with the mother country leading to the Revolution had already commenced. The Assembly of the province in May, 1774, had, by circular letters, requested the towns to send deputies to hold a convention in Exeter, in July, 1774, who should choose delegates to a General Congress of the colonies to meet at Philadelphia, and also to pay their proportion of the expense of the delegates. The above vote of the town is in answer to this request.

The time covered by the records already cited may be taken as the first well-marked period in the history of the town—the period of settlement. For this early period no history can be better than the records themselves. They were made from time to time, as they met to provide for their wants and further their enterprise of making for themselves homes in the wilderness.

A narrative of this first period will now follow, drawn from all possible sources.

THE TERRITORY OF LEBANON.

The territory included by the lines of the charter is characterized by two main valleys intersecting each other in the center village. One of these valleys extends easterly and westerly and is made by the Mascoma River; the other runs northerly and southerly and is formed on the south of the village by Great Brook and on the north by the hollow extending to Mink Brook in Hanover. Travel is easy along these valleys to surrounding towns, but steep hills hem them in on all sides. The center of the town is said to be near the foot of lower falls in the village. The rocks of the town are mainly mica slate abundantly supplied with iron pyrites. In the southwest part there is a large deposit of hornblende in the slate; the mass of Mount Finish is composed of this rock. It also makes its appearance in the eastern part of the Billings farm.

Colburn Hill and Rix Ledges are like islands of granite protruding through the slate rock. The granite is not found in places south of the river and does not appear except in boulders east of the valley which runs northward by Rix Ledges. A large vein of quartz runs along the eastern part of the town, a prolongation of the immense deposit of that material on Moose Mountain; it appears on the Cleaveland farm to the south, and extends into Enfield and Grantham. The rocks of the town give abundant evidence of glacial action in the scratches, grooves and furrows everywhere conspicuous on them. The granite boulders strewn over the region, some of which have been found on the summits of the Grantham Range, tell the same story. Now and then fragments of rocks have been found enclosing minerals, whose origin must have been on the hills of Lyme and Thetford. If many fragments of Colburn Hill have passed to the south in some of the mysterious movements of ancient times, places to the north have sent down their rocks, and there is no deficiency in the supply.

The Mascoma River must always be an object of interest to the people of Lebanon, because of its great usefulness as an unfailing and reliable source of power. It has also its beauties to commend itself to those who will study it with care.

Its ancient history is full of interest to those who have learned to read it, written plainly enough all along its course from the hills of Dorchester, Canaan and Hanover. There was a time when there was no river wending its way along this valley; but a chain of lakes occupied its bed. The most eastern of these filled the valley where the village of East Canaan now stands. Its western barrier was at Welch's Mills. It discharged its waters over the summit into the valley of the Merrimack. It was these waters tumbling over the rocky barriers which caused the potholes found at Orange Summit, so long the puzzle of geologists. After a time the western barrier was worn down and the waters were discharged towards the Connecticut. Westward was another large lake extending northward to Goose Pond and southward to Mud Pond and perhaps to East Pond. Still another filled the valley of Mascoma Lake, whose ancient shores are plainly visible at much higher points than it now reaches, so that the fertile lands occupied by the Shaker families were covered by its waters, which extended southward to Enfield Center. In these ancient times the lake discharged its waters a mile from the dam at East Lebanon, coming into a long valley at a point opposite the watering place at the turn of the road towards East Lebanon. Its ancient bed, worn into rocky chasms and wide, deep potholes, is still plainly discernible. Still another barrier was there at Chandler's Mills. A lake covered the meadows north of the village with its barriers at the falls by the sawmill. Below the falls was a long, narrow lake extending to the Hubbard bridge, where were the final barriers from the immediate valley of the Connecticut. In the course of time the barriers between these large bodies of water were worn away, the water drained into the Connecticut and in place of the chain of lakes we have the stream. Those who have seen the meadows of Canaan, and our own, in periods of very high water in the Mascoma, will not find it difficult to believe that this is a true history of the region, nor difficult to realize the appearance of the valley of the Mascoma in that early period. A few dams of no great length at several points in the course of the river would speedily fill these ancient lake beds. Doubtless these water basins were supplied and filled by the melting of ancient glaciers.

The soil of this territory has varying qualities. On the intervales loamy and rich; on the hills, stronger and more durable. The town was well timbered with beech, maple and other similar woods, while white pine and hemlock was abundant and of enormous growth.

Survey of the Town.

As already stated, the lines of the town had been run by the governor's surveyor before the granting of the charter. Immediately afterwards the proprietors took steps to ascertain the character of their grant, and to divide it into suitable lots, appointing as a committee for that purpose Capt. Nathaniel Hall, Huckins Storrs, Daniel Blodget, Jun., Charles Hill, John Hanks. This committee immediately came here from Connecticut in October, 1761, and commenced their work. Fortunately, from the records of the proprietors, the methods which they took to divide the land can be well ascertained.

"It being necessary to plan the Great River in Order to find the quantity of intervale in the town and also to lay out the hundred acre lots so as not to waste land, we proceeded to the northwest corner of the town to a hemlock tree mentioned in Mr. Boyles survey" where they commenced the survey of the Connecticut, running lines also around the intervale which they found, carefully computing its quantity.

They then commenced at the mouth of the Mascoma and surveyed that river towards the pond, carefully running lines around the intervale and computing its quantity. The close of the notes in the survey of the Mascoma is somewhat amusing. "Almost night; The committee been to the pond aforementioned out of which this River runs & concluding it run near the same course from the pond we stopt surveying said river"!

The following is their own account of their method of surveying the intervale: "The rivers being surveyed and a memorandum made for the beginning and ending of every piece, we began at a monument either at the upper or lower end & in running our courses where we made an Angle, we marked the tree or bush we ran to & when hened smooth made three hacks into it, to distinguish it from an angle, it being difficult to take account of every tree at every angle."

After having thus surveyed the intervale they prepared to lay out the upland. For this purpose it was convenient to have a well-defined base line. This base they laid out at the Enfield Road. Beginning near the house of O. L. Stearns they ran a line parallel with the south line of the town S. 72° E. straight through the town, turning out for neither hills nor valleys. This road was eight rods wide, and while known to the earlier settlers as Enfield Road, and later as the Old Enfield Road, is known to us

INTRODUCTION.

as the King's Highway, still existing in its original width, in some portions of it.

Upon the north side of this road there were laid out the acre lots, one for each proprietor. These acre lots now compose parts of the farm of N. B. Stearns and the Slacks.

They then began to lay out lots of an hundred acres from each side of this road. These lots were 100 rods on the road and 160 rods deep, with land reserved for highways and roads at suitable intervals. While these lots were nominally of the dimensions given, yet they were often made larger if the land was of a poorer quality. These lots were called the first division. Most of this first division were located south of the Mascoma, a few along the Connecticut north of the river.

They next proceeded to lay out the intervale, allotting nine and a half acres to each proprietor.

Next were laid out the second division of 100-acre lots. Commencing on the east line of the first division of 100-acre lots they run a line perpendicular to the Enfield Road, N. 18° E. to the Mascoma River. This line would strike the river east of the farm of Howard Benton. Then they proceeded up the river to Mascoma Lake and along the shore of the lake to the east line of the town. After having thus marked out this portion of the town they returned to the Enfield Road and laid out lots on both sides of the road.

In laying out the lots on the north side of the Mascoma they began on the river where the east line of the first division of 100 acres intersected it, and "let fall a perpendicular on the north line of the town N. 26 E.," and from the north line began to lay out lots of 100 acres each. The record states that this division was completed November 6, 1767. Aaron Storrs, Huckins Storrs, John Wheatley, Jedediah Dana, were the committee.

This second division of 100-acre lots were drawn as follows:

	No.		No.
Huckins Storrs,	43	Joseph Wood, right of J. Murdock,	34
Nathaniel Porter,	59		
Jedediah Dana,	44	Anderson Dana, Daniel Blodget,	24
Jonathan Walcott,	61		
Charles Hill,	7	Samuel Millington, R. Martin,	29
Richard Salter,	23		

HISTORY OF LEBANON.

	No.		No.
Jonathan Blanchard,	15	Capt. Joseph Marsh, Samuel Storrs,	4
Jabez Barrow,	38	Nathan Blodget,	66
Joseph Wood, by S. Waterman,	3	Josiah Storrs,	46
Joseph Dana,	5	Aaron Storrs, Jon. Martin,	21
Joseph Martin,	32	Nehemiah Estabrook,	41
John Swift,	9	Hugh Hall Wentworth,	63
Robert Hyde,	57	Mark H. Wentworth, Esq.,	63
Edward Goldstone Lutwyche,	36	School lot,	37
Lemuel Clarke,	48	Church of England,	58
David Turner, Joseph Tilden,	51	James Ticknor, right of Daniel Allen,	10
John Birchard, James Jones,	61	Huckens Storrs, Sr., right of Juda Storrs,	53
Daniel Ellis, right of Oneil Lamont,	31	Dr. Clement Jackson, Esq.,	14
Prince Aspenwall, right of Joshua Blodgett,	8	Elijah Sprague, right of John Birchard,	47
John Colburn, right of J. Yeomans,	26	Nathaniel Hall,	19
William Downer, Robert Barrow,	52	Ministerial lot,	17
N. Storrs, John Hanks,	12	Benjamin Davis, by Benjamin Fuller,	65
Oliver Griswold, J. Loomis,	28	John Allen, by Stephen Powel,	20
Samuel Estabrook, T. Storrs,	55	Jacob Benton, right of William Dana,	1
O. Davison, T. Barrow,	62	Jesse Birchard, by Rufus Baldwin,	40
John Griswold, Jesse Birchard,	25	William Knight,	54
Seth Blodget,	35	Samuel Penhallow, by Constant Southworth,	11
Thomas Storrs, John Storrs,	45	John Martin, right of Moses Hibbard,	13
Huckins Storrs, Sr., D. Eldredge,	60	Samuel Storrs, right of John Baldwin,	1
Amariah Storrs, J. Hyde,	2	Propagation of the Gospel in foreign parts,	30
Nathan Arnold, O. Clark,	49	John Salter,	50
Jedediah Dana, John Lasell, right of James Nevins,	56	Aaron Storrs, right of Joseph Turner,	39
Z. Downer, Gideon Peck, right of Constant Southworth,	6		
Zalmon Aspenwall, right of Daniel Blodget, 3d,	33		
Elijah Huntington,	18		

Following these there were divisions of fifty acres, of twenty acres, and smaller portions. By this time it is very difficult to locate the various lots. Many of the lots were laid out with some regularity, while others are irregular in their lines. There

INTRODUCTION. 51

are also records of alterations in boundaries, of changes of numbers, of mistakes, of the transference of lots from one division to another. At this date it requires the patient labor of months, great ingenuity to identify the different tracts laid out before the close of the eighteenth century.

It is very difficult to identify the ownership of these divisions of land. Most of the original proprietors mentioned in the charter never came here. They sold their rights to others, and they to others still. These lands being distributed by lottery, proprietors found themselves owners of land distributed in various parts of the town; this led to exchanges between them, each one seeking to have his land in one body.

Some of the lots were located on the eastern line in Enfield, others over the southern line in Plainfield; upon the settlement of these lines of the town the proprietors were obliged to find other lots within their territory to compensate for these losses. This complicated and confused matters very much.

At this time there are not more than two or three lots which have not been alienated from the descending of the original proprietors. Mr. Charles Dana occupies a part of the lot of an original proprietor of his name. Mr. John Hebard's farm has not been out of the family until recently. I think that a part of the farm of Abel Storrs shares in this distinction.

The mode in which they marked the lots may be seen from the following extract from their notes. They are beginning to lay out the second division of 100 acres: "Began to lott on Enfield road Continued said road from the east side of the first 100 acre Division 100 rods to a middling beach tree and numbered W $\frac{3\ 1\ 5}{4\ \ 6}$E thence 100 rods to a small beach tree and numbered W $\frac{5\ \ }{6\ 8}$E. thence 100 rods to a small beach and numbered W$\frac{7\ \ 9}{8\ 10}$E thence 100 rods to a hemlock which is the S. E corner of No 11 (afterwards divided) said lots to be known by lines running perpendicular to said Enfield road, &''

There still remain a few of these original marks upon trees which in some way have escaped the axe, and the tempests.

SETTLING.

The proprietors clearly saw that before their lands could be settled there must be some way of getting to them. At that time all roads stopped at No. 4, Charlestown. Beyond, to the north, along the valley of the Connecticut, there was an unbroken wilderness; no roads, no paths. The river was their only guide, but a safe one. Their first care was to clear some kind of a passage to their possessions. Hence at their meeting December 22, 1761, they appointed Mr. Charles Hill to treat with the proprietors of the townships between Charlestown and Lebanon concerning a road along the banks of the Connecticut. At their meeting September 1, 1762, they appointed as a committee to clear a road between Charlestown and Lebanon, Nathaniel Hall, John Hanks and John Birchard. This road was to be simply a bridle path, not a road for wheels, but such as a horse with packs might contrive to pass over. They were assisted in this work by the proprietors of Norwich, Hanover and Lyme, though the agent for Lyme seems to have refused to pay a proportion of the expense for that town. This path seems to have been completed some time in 1763.

Besides the surveying done in the town, work preliminary to a permanent occupation seems to have been done in the summer of 1762, most of the laborers, however, returning to their homes for the winter. Four men, however, are said to have passed the winter, 1762–'63, in the town, having with them some young cattle. The names of three are known: Levi Hyde, Samuel Estabrook and William Dana. The fourth may have been a hired laborer, but I conjecture that it was Charles Hill, who certainly was here very early. They had no house, but built themselves such a shelter of bark and boughs as they could. Tradition has assigned this camp to various localities, one of which was near the mouth of White River. I think this a mistake and that their camp was farther up the River Connecticut. When they made their survey of the Connecticut for the purpose of measuring and dividing the intervale they made the following note, "To the upper end of Camp Meadow." Then, after running several courses, they came to the "lower end of Camp Meadow." This is a piece of low land lying between the first and second falls on the Connecticut, going north from West Lebanon. This piece of land could only receive such a name from the fact that it had been a camping place. Tradition further states that they kept their stock

MAJ. WM. WILLIS BLISS.

at a beaver meadow somewhere in this vicinity. Now to the east of this locality, in the vicinity of the "Boston Lot," the early settlers found a natural meadow, a place on which no timber grew, and covered with wild grasses. It would be possible to collect enough of this natural grass during the summer to keep life in their stock. I have no doubt that this was the first spot occupied for a home within the territory of Lebanon. And what a long, lonesome winter that must have been! To the north they had no neighbors nearer than Haverhill and Newbury; to the south none nearer than Charlestown. They must go much farther east or west to find any friends.

It is a curious fact in the history of the town, one little known, that the first occupant of the soil within the boundaries of the town was not a living, but a dead man. A stranger to the town had found here his final resting place in 1762. Michael Johnston and John Pettie spent the winter of 1761–'62 at Haverhill, under the same circumstances as those of the four in Lebanon. In June, 1762, they left Haverhill in a canoe to go down the river to Charlestown, to visit their friends. "They made their way pleasantly till they came near the mouth of the White River, when they were drawn into a whirlpool, their canoe upset, and they plunged into the river. Johnston made every effort to reach the shore, but sank into the arms of death. Pettie being the better swimmer, gained the shore and bore the melancholy tidings of Johnston's death to his friends.

"Some time after this event a stranger passing up the river in a boat, discovered the body of a man lying upon the shore of a small island in the Connecticut between Lebanon and Hartford, Vt. Not knowing anything of Johnston or of his fate, and being far from any settlement, he performed the kindest office to a stranger corpse which remained in his power. He dug a grave in the best manner he could, interred the body and left it the sole proprietor of the island. It now bears his name, Johnston's Island (it has also been called Dead Man's Island). Col. Charles Johnston, after he came to Haverhill and learned the resting place of his brother, went down to the island, found the lonely grave, bedewed it with his tears, and erected a monument to his brother's memory."—Powers' "Coös County."

During the season of 1763 additions were made to the permanent inhabitants of the town. July 11, 1763, came William Downer with his wife and eight children. He had taken up lot 15, first division of 100-acre lots, which lies to the west of the house of Nathan Stearns, on the south side of the Enfield Road—or King's Highway. His intervale lot was No. 6, which lies upon the Connecticut south of the land owned by Jeremiah Wood.

A hard and toilsome journey this adventurous family must have had from No. 4, where all roads ended, to their home in Lebanon. From there onward there was only a "horse road;" no track for wheels, but only a path over which a horse might make his way. Fortunately a vivid sketch of this journey has been preserved for us by an adventurous settler of Orford, who two years later made his way over the same "horse road." "John Mann, Esq., and his wife came into Orford in the autumn of 1765, both from Hebron, Conn. They left Hebron on the 16 of Oct. and arrived in Orford on the 24th. They both mounted the same horse according to Puritan custom, and rode to Charlestown, N. H., nearly one hundred and fifty miles. Here Mann purchased a bushel of oats for his horse and some bread and cheese for himself and wife and set forward—Mann on foot, wife, bread and cheese, and some clothing on horse back. From Charlestown to Orford there was no road but a horse track and this was frequently hedged across by fallen trees; and when they came to such an obstruction as they could not pass, Mann, who was of a gigantic stature, would step up, take the young bride and set her upon the ground; then the oats, bread and cheese; and lastly the old mare was made to leap the windfall, when all was reshipped and the journey resumed. This was acted over time and again until the old beast became impatient of delay, and coming to a similar obstruction while Mann was some rods in the rear, she pressed forward and leaped the trunk of a large tree, resisting all the force her young rider could exert; and when Mann came up there lay the bride upon the ground with all the baggage resting upon her. The old cerature, however, had the civility not to desert them in their predicament, and as no bones were broken and no joints dislocated, they soon resumed their journey, Mann for the rest of the way constituting the van instead of the rear guard."—Powers' "Coös County."

This is the journey of a young and vigorous couple—how much more difficult the journey of a mother and eight children, some of whom must have been quite young. With only such a path to a new home how many things must be left behind. How slender must have been the furnishing of those early homes; how many comforts and conveniences must be wanting; how must their ingenuity be exercised to furnish rude substitutes for all household utensils. It is no wonder that about this time a traveler passing through a neighboring town found a wife declaring that she was "terribly" homesick and "that she would not stay there in the woods." Nevertheless there was in the wilderness a rude abundance out of which the patient and ingenious settler could extract substitutes for the luxuries and conveniences left behind, which would have their own wild charms.

In the fall of the same year, 1763, came Oliver Davison, James Jones, Elijah Dewey and their families.

Oliver Davison settled on land now owned by Mrs. Luther Alden. The proprietors were very liberal in their offers to him as a settler. At their meeting December 22, 1761, they voted a tax of ten shillings upon each right, to be paid in one year and an additional tax of the same amount to be paid in two years, to aid Mr. Davison to build a sawmill in the town, provided it should be completed within two years. They also voted to him 100 acres of land at any locality suitable for a sawmill. The mill was built near the Hubbard bridge, within the specified time. At that period it was a necessity to the settlers, aiding them greatly in providing for themselves homes. Mr. Davison died some time in 1769. Though he was not an original grantee, the proprietors allowed his heirs the same rights with themselves, and granted them a generous portion of land.

Elijah Dewey settled in what is known as Poverty Lane. James Jones settled on the King's Highway, near Mr. Foster's.

Charles Hill was among the first to take up his abode in Lebanon, in what is now the village of West Lebanon. His house and that of Oliver Davison are the first mentioned in the records. His lot extended from the river eastward to the old burying yard, which was originally the southeast corner of the lot. He was prominent in all the affairs of the town, frequently selectman, and on many of the important committees.

Asa Kilbourn took up one of the intervale lots on the Connecticut just south of the Mascoma. It was at his house that the first town meeting of which we have any record (May 13, 1765) was held. He afterwards removed to Canaan, and was a selectman in 1773.

Aaron Storrs settled on the river below Mr. Kilbourn and was frequently employed in the business of the town, moving finally to Hanover.

The Danas settled on the river, north of the Mascoma.

Nathaniel Porter settled on the place now owned by Nathan Stearns.

Nehemiah Estabrook on the farm owned by Mr. Slack. Samuel Estabrook on the Sweatland place.

The following persons are known, upon indisputable evidence, to have been in the town by 1767: Aaron Storrs, Charles Hill, Asa Kilbourn, William Downer, Levi Hyde, William Dana, John Wheatley, Silas Waterman, Jedediah Hibbard, Samuel Meacham, Oliver Davison, Joseph Dana, Elijah Dewey, Jesse Cook, James Jones, Huckins Storrs, Sr., and Huckins Storrs, Jr., Joseph Tilden, Joseph Wood, Sr., John Griswold, Jedediah Dana, Samuel Storrs, John Slapp, Nathaniel Hall, Nehemiah Estabrook, Samuel Estabrook, Nathaniel Storrs, Jonathan Dana, Zalmon Aspenwall, James Hartshorn, John Bennet.

There were others in the town, but I have not been able to recover their names.

In the year 1767 a census was taken of all the towns in New Hampshire. The return of Lebanon was as follows: Unmarried men from 16 to 60, 12; married men from 16 to 60, 30; boys, 16 years and under, 50; men, 60 years and over, none; unmarried females, 40; females married, 30; no slaves and no widows; total population, 162.

Mr. Powers in his history of Coös County, on the authority of John Mann, who passed through the town in the autumn of 1765, states that there were then but three families in the town: Charles Hill, son and son-in-law; yet we have it on record that

INTRODUCTION. 57

in May of that year there had been a town meeting whose object was to provide for preaching in the town. At the time of the census none were found in the town over sixty years of age, which shows that the population was made up of those in full vigor of life. The probability is that some of those who make up the above number were only hired laborers who had no intention of making themselves homes here.

The population of Hanover at the same time was 92, of Plainfield 112, of Cornish 133, Canaan 19.

It is evident that the people were busy in making themselves homes; that there were many openings made in the forests; that fields were prepared, planted and reaped. While they were busy in their arduous labors they were also thoughtful concerning those organizations, civil and religious, without which fertile fields lose their value and homes half their charms.

The people who came here from Connecticut had a hearty love for the institutions of religion. The thing which they would part with, with the greatest reluctance in their old homes, would be these institutions; about these they plan early in their new homes. At a meeting of the proprietors held September 2, 1762, they appointed a committee to join committees from adjoining townships to provide for preaching in the township. This was before there was an actual settler. This action was taken to encourage good people to make their homes in the wilderness.

At their meeting in March, 1763, upon a report of this committee, they voted a tax of four shillings upon each proprietor "for encouraging the preaching of the Gospel," and Nehemiah Estabrook was appointed their committee. At a meeting held in December, 1764, they voted a tax of eight shillings on each proprietor's right, to be paid by the first day of May, 1765, and Nehemiah Estabrook and Samuel Storrs were appointed a committee to provide preaching for that year.

In May of this same year the town takes action for the same purpose, appointing Aaron Storrs to circulate subscription papers and enjoining the selectmen to provide quarters for the minister when he should come.

There was undoubtedly preaching in the town during that

summer, but probably there was no permanent minister in the town. In the summer of 1766 we find by the records that a "Mr. Treadway was resident among them, and the town chose John Wheatley, Charles Hill and Joseph Dana as a committee to treat with him, in order to his steady administration of the Gospel ministry in said town." Mr. Treadway seems to have declined any permanent engagement.

The proprietors of the town at a meeting held October 6, 1766, voted a tax of twenty shillings on each right for "the settlement of the Gospel in said Lebanon." This certainly implies that the proceeds of the former taxes had been expended. A Mr. Wales was in town as a preacher in 1767 and seems to have been here some time previous. On July 27, 1768, they gave him a formal call to the ministry of the town, fixing his salary at fifty pounds a year, with the addition of five pounds per year till the sum should be seventy pounds. September 30, 1768, Mr. Wales sent a verbal answer by Dea. Nehemiah Estabrook to the call of the town, which they declined to accept; for what reason cannot now be known.

On the 22d of May, 1769, the town again took up the matter of preaching in the town and appointed Charles Hill, John Wheatley and Joseph Wood a committee, directing them to apply first to Mr. Kenne and if he could not be obtained, to do the best they could. Whether they were successful, there is no record.

The town seems to have taken no further action for the settlement of a minister till the 21st of August, 1771, when they resolved to give Mr. Isaiah Potter a call "to *continue* in the work of the Gospel ministry, in order to a settlement amongst us." From this it appears that Mr. Potter had previously preached in the town. The matter was not settled till July 6, 1772, when Mr. Potter accepted the call. They voted a donation of thirty-eight pounds in addition to sixty pounds granted by the proprietors to the first settled minister. His salary was to be "fifty pounds lawful money for the first two years and then to rise annually five pounds a year till it shall amount to eighty pounds, which was to be his stated salary." In addition, he came into possession of certain rights of land reserved by the proprietors for that

HON. EXPERIENCE ESTABROOK.

INTRODUCTION.

purpose—one of which was the farm where Mr. Albert Miller now lives, so long occupied by Mr. Potter and his family. All the above was the action of the town in its corporate capacity.

On September 27, 1768, the Congregational Church was formed, consisting of the following six members: John Wheatley, Azariah Bliss, John Slapp, Jonathan Dana, Joseph Dana, Zaccheus Downer. It was doubtless under the action of the church that Mr. Potter first came to the town. They also accepted him as their pastor, and he was ordained and installed as pastor of the church on the 25th of August, 1772. The ordination took place in the open air under a spreading elm standing on the banks of the Connecticut in the southerly part of the village of West Lebanon, Rev. Bulkley Olcott preaching the sermon.

The First Meeting-House.

The first public action concerning a meeting-house was taken February 26, 1768, when the question was proposed at their meeting. We cannot doubt that they felt the want of some place of meeting for civil and religious purposes. All their assemblies had been held at private houses; often at Charles Hill's, sometimes at Estabrook's, and often at Bela Turner's. But they were not yet ready for action, for they resolved to do nothing.

At a meeting held July 19, 1768, they decided the location of the meeting-house; that it should be upon a spot of ground near the "Burying Place," that is, near Miss Fanny Alden's. I suppose that they meant that when they should build a meeting-house, they would build it there, for they do not seem to have formed any plan concerning it since their meeting in February preceding.

At a meeting held September 7, 1768. it appears that some were dissatisfied with this location and sought to have the town reconsider their decision, but the majority were averse to any change, and the location of the future meeting-house remained fixed—for a time.

The affairs of a meeting-house continued to be warmly discussed in private, but do not appear in public for more than two years. At a meeting held November 5, 1770, they took up the matter again and voted to build a meeting-house—but they further voted that they would not build a meeting-house "for the convenancy of Publick Worship.'' The only explanation of this apparently contradictory action which the historian has to give is this: They resolved to build a house for civic purposes, what we call a town hall, but they would not build a house for religious purposes—a church. But they made no plans for building any house, only decided that they were going to build.

But they met again on the 26th of November and voted this time that they would build, not a town hall, but a house for "publick worship." They decided that it should be thirty feet square and "ten feet posts." They further decided (for the time) that it should be placed upon "the road that leads to the mills in said Lebanon upon a peace of Flat Land east of Mr. Charles Hills barn." This would be on the road to West Lebanon, near the southern portion of that village.

In the meantime they had been considering and discussing the matter, and came to the conclusion that they were not quite right; nobody was satisfied, and so at their meeting, January 7, 1771, they resolved to reconsider all their previous votes and to start anew, which they did in this way: They resolved that they would build a house for public worship; that they would take a longer time; that they would locate it upon some other spot; that they would choose a committee from out of town to "fix a spot to set said house upon and that said spot *shall be* THE *spot*."

They chose as their committee, Samuel Chase of Cornish, David Woodward and Hezekiah Johnson of Hanover.

It is not known what location this committee selected, but wherever it was the after action of the town shows that it was not satisfactory "to all concerned."

The following, found among certain old papers in the garret of Mr. George Hall, is the receipt of one of the committee:

Cornish March ye 7 1771

Then Received of Mr Aaron Storrs Nine shillings Being in full for my sarvice Going to Lebenon and assisting with ye Commity in prefixing ye place for seting a meeting house

Saml Chase

At a meeting January 29, 1771, evidently after the action of their committee, they voted to build a house for public worship, "that it should be thirty feet square and ten feet posts;" and that Maj. John Slapp, Lieut. Nathaniel Porter and John Wheatley, Esq., should be a committee for building. Nothing is said about the locality, so we are warranted in supposing that it is settled.

By this time they have the prospect of regular worship under the guidance of a settled minister. Upon thinking the matter over they see that the projected meeting-house will hardly meet their wants so they vote, August 21, 1771, to enlarge the meeting-house from "thirty feet square and ten feet posts to forty-eight in length, thirty feet in breadth and twenty-five feet posts."

But all this time there is dissatisfaction with the locality, and the spot that should be *the* place is not the place after all.

So, when they came together September 4, 1771, they voted to remove the meeting-house from near the burying yard westerly in Mr. Hill's pasture, near the road that leads to the sawmill. This, as I understand it, would be but a short distance, some rods, west of Mrs. Alden's. Major Slapp, Silas Waterman and Huckins Storrs were appointed a building committee, and were directed to erect, enclose and lay a floor in the house by the 1st day of October, 1772.

But at a meeting held November 7, 1771, they voted to "transpose" the meeting-house from Mr. Hill's pasture to the "Clay Pit about fifty rods westerly of the spot before agreed upon." This locality was on the north side of the Mascoma, near Hubbard bridge. Silas Waterman and Huckins Storrs are dropped from the building committee and Azariah Bliss and John Wheatley are put in their places.

December 2, 1771, they vote to raise a tax to build a meeting-house on the spot last agreed upon.

January 7, 1772, they vote to build on the field of Jonathan Dana, and to "transpose" the meeting-house from the "Clay Pit" to this new locality, which was, I think, on the river, below West Lebanon. Maj. John Slapp, Charles Hill, Lieut. John Griswold and Silas Waterman are the building committee this time.

They are not satisfied yet, and vote, April 7, 1772, to alter the size of the meeting-house to forty feet in length, thirty in breadth and ten feet posts.

In the meantime Major Slapp and other members of the committee had collected timber at the clay pit and cleaved the ground, for which the town paid.

At this meeting, April 20, 1772, the meeting-house is "transposed from Mr Dana's field to Mr Hills pasture near the house of Bela Turner." This was near the house of Richard Kimball, Esq. Azariah Bliss, Charles Hill, Silas Waterman, Major Slapp, Lieutenant Porter and John Wheatley are the building committee. At a meeting a week later the committee are directed to proceed with diligence to erect and enclose "said house."

The proprietors may be considered the conservative and aristocratic power of the town. Hitherto they have done nothing as a body, but doubtless have watched the strife, possibly have been able to keep track of the meeting-house in its numerous "transposings." They think the time has come for them to take some action, and attempt to pour oils on the troubled waters. On the 26th of May, 1772, they vote to build a meeting-house and appoint Aaron Storrs, Huckins Storrs and Jedediah Hibbard their committee. They vote a tax of forty shillings on each proprietor's right for that purpose.

This money is granted upon the conditions that the house shall be built upon such a spot as "may be within one month from this 29 day of May be affixed by an indiferent [impartial] judicious committee of three men chosen by the town of Lebanon, who shall be instructed to have regard to the general interests of the township of Lebanon."

Further: They agree to build a meeting-house for the use of the town on the south side of the Mascoma, on the east side of the road leading from Davison's mills to Nathaniel Porter's dwelling house, "At a certain beach tree marked on four sides, and with the letter M, standing on a small eminence 100 rods from Enfield road [King's highway] and 112 rods from Maj. Slapps corn mill."

This locality is on the road leading from Hubbard bridge to Nathaniel Stearns'. The letter M referred to is supposed to stand for meeting-house.

INTRODUCTION.

They further stipulate that the house shall be forty-four feet in length, thirty-two feet in width and twenty feet posts, which dimensions are different from any yet given—they appear like a compromise between contending parties.

The town appears to have paid little attention to the propositions of the proprietors for, August 10, 1772, they voted to build a meeting-house on the east end of Mr. Hill's pasture, near Major Slapp's. It was to be forty-eight feet in length, thirty-four feet in breadth and ten or twelve feet posts. They set aside all other votes and resolutions, reserving only the timber which had been collected.

This action seems to have been final, and the meeting-house was built on the south side of the road, a little to the west of Miss Fanny Alden's.

To us, at this day, this strife about the location of a meeting-house seems remarkable, and we are inclined to look upon the fathers of the town as a peculiarly obstinate, or "set" race. But we should do them injustice. They did not differ in this respect from their generation. The early records of the towns of the state show that the meeting-house was likely to be a bone of contention. In not a few towns the strife was so long and bitter, the interests or the tempers of the parties so irreconcilable that as a last resort they were obliged to appeal to the governor and council or to the Assembly. Not a few of the meeting-houses of this state in those early times were located by these high authorities.

It is not difficult to see some of the elements which would enter into the question of the location of a meeting-house in a community planted in a wilderness which they must subdue before they could gather around them the conveniences of civilization. Let us remember that the population is scattered,—an opening here and there in the primeval forest made for a home. Roads are few; none are good. From many a log cabin there would be only a rough path. Distance under such circumstances counts. A mile or a half mile is worth a struggle to avoid, when probably the whole family must go on foot "to meeting," or at best in the rudest vehicles.

And the location of a meeting-house in those days was not only a matter of convenience, but of interest. Wherever the meeting-house was placed, other things would gather around it. It would be a center, and making surrounding lands more valuable. They naturally expected that a village would grow up around the meeting-house, hence each would contend for a location which would be most to his advantage.

Yet when we remember that a radius of half a mile would cover all the localities chosen and abandoned so many times, we cannot avoid the impression that some of the people were "pretty set in their ways."

One cannot help feeling sympathy with the youthful pastor of the town, who was an eye witness of much of the struggle. A place of worship was so much needed, so desirable for his ministrations, and yet so hard to fix in any given locality. So much bitterness was engendered in the strife to stand in the way of that cordial union needful to their young enterprise of building up a church of Christ in the wilderness. He must have spent many days of anxiety while the strife was warmest, and he must have rejoiced greatly when the house was finally located and its doors were opened for the simple and earnest worship of the time. It is said that at one time when timber had been delivered on the river road "in Mr. Dana's field," a number of men with teams came to remove it. The young pastor made a warm appeal to them, assuring them that he could not remain unless they were more harmonious. His words had their designed effect and prevented a collision between antagonistic parties.

BOUNDARIES.

Very soon after the land of the town began to be occupied there arose a dispute between the proprietors of Lebanon and those of Plainfield concerning the boundary line between the two townships. A tree marked is mentioned in the charter as the southwest corner. Whether the tree could not be found as described, or whether there were two, I cannot determine, but it is plain that the lines claimed by Lebanon extended into territory claimed by Plainfield. The first formal action taken by the proprietors was on June 29, 1767, when they appointed a committee to confer with a committee of Plainfield concerning the matter. In the meantime there had been some communication with the

PROF. IRA YOUNG.

governor and council, and a letter received from Theodore Atkinson, which the proprietors considered at a meeting February 25, 1768. Of the tenor of that letter nothing certain is known.

The committee reported their action to the proprietors May 17, 1768, and it was accepted as satisfactory to them, but proved not satisfactory to the proprietors of Plainfield. A joint committee of the two towns was appointed upon the advice of Theodore Atkinson, or of the surveyor-general, to take the matter into consideration. The committee made the following report:

Sir:

With submission, these wait upon you with respect, and may serve to Inform, that we the subscribers Committees for the proprietors of Lebanon and Plainfield in pursuance of your advice, have established a bound between said towns and as near the center as possible, said bound being a large White Pine tree marked 3 and 4 and standing a little Below the Meadow called Hedge-Hog meadow in said lebanon, [a little north of Bradley Trues], just in the bend of the river, on the north side of a hill, on the east bank of Connecticut river

These are therefore to desire the favor of your Honr, if you, in your wisdom, shall judge our procedure in said affair to be Legal and Conclusive to certifie the same to his Excellency for his approbation thereof, that the same may be established as to law and custom doth appertain.

And we, as in duty bound beg leave to subscribe
  Your honors most obedient
  And very humble serv'nts

       John Wheatley
       Nathaniel Porter
       Charles Hill
       Thomas Gates
       Thomas Gallup
       John Stevens

Dated Lebanon
New Hampshire Oct 1768

The first three of the subscribers were of Lebanon, the others of Plainfield.

Four years later the dispute continues, and the proprietors vote to make application to the surveyor-general "To affix the South West corner and run the south line and affix the South East corner of the township of Lebanon." This application seems not to have had any effect, for at a meeting September 29,

1772, they are still seeking some method to settle the southwest corner of the township. They appointed Aaron Storrs, Nehemiah Estabrook, John Griswold, Jedediah Hibbard and Nathaniel Porter a committee to ascertain the southwest corner of the town and run the south line. They were also directed to give fair warning to all who were trespassing upon land which they claimed, to depart, and if they refused to do so, then to prosecute them to the extent of the law.

Now the charter fixes the southwest corner of the town at eighteen miles from the northwest corner of Charlestown. The committee resolved to measure from that monument to ascertain the southwest corner. They employed Jonathan Freeman of Hanover as a surveyor and David Woodward, James Hutchinson and Samuel Haze as chainmen. The measurement was duly made and Mr. Freeman returned the results to the proprietors who, on February 10, 1775, voted to accept the bound established by him. But the matter was not settled yet. Three years later, March 24, 1778, the dispute appears again, and now new parties appear,—Enfield and Grantham, all anxious to ascertain their true corners and lines. They appoint Elisha Ticknor, Jedediah Hibbard and John Griswold a committee to join committees from the other towns to settle the dispute. The report of the committee was adopted and the line between Lebanon and Plainfield established, September, 1778. Lebanon, notwithstanding the gallant fight made, lost in the battle. Land which the proprietors claimed and had occupied, fell into Plainfield, and they were obliged to make the occupants compensation for their loss.

Controversy with Enfield.

Though there are no references upon the records for about seven years to any further disputes about town lines, yet all the time the fires seemed to be smouldering, and burst out anew in 1785, when we learn that Nathaniel Porter had brought an action of ejectment against Joseph Johnson of Enfield. Johnson claimed territory which had been assigned to Porter as a part of Lebanon. The proprietors voted, January 11, 1785, that they would sustain Porter in his suit, and pay the expense. The suit was finally withdrawn.

State of New. Hamp
Grafton SS

Whareas, we the subscribers Being appointed a Com^tee by the Honble General Assembly of said State to Establish the boundaries between the towns of Lebanon and Enfield have met accordingly upon said towns and after Due Examination of the Bounds and lins of s'd of said towns of Lebanon and infield—Perceded as followeth, firstly begain at a white Pine tree on the easterly bank of Connect River which is called the agreement tree between Lebanon and Plainfield six mild to a stake and stones comonly known by the name of Sumner Bound—then examined the lins and records shown us Between s'd Lebanon and Enfield and find a bound standing on the Northeast Corner of s'd Lebanon comonally known by the name of the birch tree, but said tree being fell down, a stake and stones erected in the place where said birch stood, and we do establish the first said stake and stons called Sumner Bound to be a bound between said Lebanon and Enfield on the southerly side of said towns and the said birch tree (now stake and stons) to be the northerly Bound Between s'd Lebanon and infield, and Do order that a strat line Be drawn Between said Sumner Bound and said Birch tree or stake standing in place of said Birch tree, to be the Dividing line Between the said Lebanon and the s'd infield and have recommended to said Committee to settle with all parsons who are on land in either of said towns, which shall fall out of the town which he settled in, in the best way they can, according to ower order from said Genl Assembly

which is humbly submitted
Oct ye 23 1786.

Charles Johnson
Jeremiah Page
Moses Chase

State Papers

Condition of the Town—1775.

The records so far given, and the narrative, have given the chief incidents of the history of the town to 1775. New and exciting events lie in the immediate future—the Revolution and the Vermont controversy. Before entering upon these scenes let us seek to realize the condition of the people by such descriptions as are possible at this distance.

The number of the inhabitants has steadily increased with each year, after the first bold wintering here in Camp Meadow. By a return of a census ordered by Gov. John Wentworth in 1773, long supposed to be lost, but discovered in 1876 on file in the library of Congress by the Hon. A. H. Cragin, for many years an honored citizen of this town, and then of the United States Senate, we find the population of the town to be as follows: Unmarried men from 16 to 60, 44; married men from 16 to 60, 50; boys 16 years and under, 62; men 60 years and upward, 4; females unmarried, 79; females married, 54; widows, 2; slaves, none; total, 295; showing increase.

Population of Plainfield at same time, 275; of Hanover, 342; students at college, 90.

In 1775 another census was taken, with the following returns: Males under 16 years of age, 86; males from 16 years of age to 50, not in the army, 91; all males above 50 years of age, 13; persons gone in the army, 2; all females, 155; negroes and slaves for life, none; total, 347; increase in two years, 57.

We have, fortunately, a list of all the male inhabitants of the age of twenty-one and over, in the town in 1776. They are as follows:

John Wheatley,
John Slapp,
John Baldwin,
Samuel Bailey,
Jonathan Dana,
Eliezer Robinson,
William Dana,
Hezekiah Waters,
James Jones,
John Gray,
Jesse Cook,
Samuel Estabrook,
Samuel Paine,
Elijah Dewey, Jr.,
Huckens Storrs,
Joseph Tilden, Jr.,
Elkanah Sprague,
Daniel Hough,
Samuel Bailey, Jr.,
Daniel Bliss,
Joseph Tilden,

Nathaniel Wheatley,
Walter Peek,
Zacheus Downer,
Asa Colburn,
Constant Storrs,
Stephen Colburn,
John Williams,
Isaiah Potter,
John Wheatley,
Azariah Bliss,
Azariah Bliss, Jr.,
Stephen Bliss,
John Ordway,
Nehemiah Estabrook,
Rufus Baldwin,
Nathaniel Porter,
Nathaniel Porter, Jr.,
Elijah Dewey,
Phinehas Wright,
William Downer,
Barnabas Perkins,

Charles Tilden,
Oliver Griswold,
James Hartshorn,
Nathaniel Kidder,
David Colburn,
Moses Hebard,
Jeremiah Griswold,
Benjamin Fuller,
James Fuller,
Lemuel Hough,
Elisha Ticknor,
Isaiah Bliss,
Nathaniel Storrs,
Samuel Millington,
Solomon Millington,
Benjamin Write,
Hobart Estabrook,
Nathaniel Hall,
Jonathan Bingham,
Silas Waterman,
Jedediah Hebbard,
Joseph Wood,
William Radman,
John Colburn,
James Hebard,
Levi Hyde,
Elias Lyman,
Theophelus Barbrick,
Eleazer Woodward,
John Slapp,
Henry Woodward,
John Griswold,
Nathan Durkee,
Samuel Sprague,
Charles Sexton,
John Slapp, Jr.,
William Downer, Jr.,
Zalmon Aspenwall,
Joseph Martin,
Abel Wright,
Ebenezer Bliss,
Thomas Willes,
Jonathan Bettes,
John Hyde,
Shuman Lathrop,
Abiel Willes,
Joseph Dana,
Eighty-nine in all.

These are the names of the male inhabitants of the town in 1776. Of these family names only the following remain in the town at the present time, borne by descendants: Dana, Gray, Estabrook, Hall, Waterman, Hebbard, Wood, Peck, Storrs, Dewey, Hough, Bliss, Griswold, Ticknor, Durkee, Aspenwall, Lathrop.

By this time openings had been made in the forests in all parts of the town, and smoke arose above the tree tops from the settlers' rude cabins in all directions, except along the northern line of the town.

If the people wished their lumber sawed they could go to Davison's mills on the Mascoma, near Hubbard bridge, or to the sawmill of Huckins Storrs on Sawmill Brook, later known as Hinkley or True Brook. If they wished their grain ground they need not carry it down to No. 4, but they could take it to Maj. John Slapp's mills on the Mascoma, below Hubbard bridge. There were shoemakers in town. If they wished to build a house they could call upon Barnabas Perkins or Thomas Blake, joiners. I cannot learn that they had any store at this period. Their place of trade was No. 4, and "down country," though they might trade with Aaron Storrs of Hanover. They had a meeting-house for their civil and religious gatherings. No doctor, no lawyer, had as yet taken up their abode here, so far as known.

Roads sufficient to accommodate the people were built. A road ran through the town from north to south along the banks of the Connecticut, called the "Country Road," built not only for the accommodation of the town, but for those who went on beyond to settlements to the north. The river itself was also a highway on the ice in the winter; by rafts and boats in the summer. A road ran through the town east and west, the old Enfield Road part of the way, another keeping on the north side of the river by Edwin Perley's into the village by Jesse Cook's on Hanover Street, on across the meadows north of the village, up the side of Mount Tugg, through East Lebanon to Benjamin Fuller's, Zaccheus Downer's and Simon Slapp's, on to Enfield line. Roads led from the river road to Huckens Storrs' sawmill; they came from Poverty Lane and from the south part of the town where the Lathrops, Houghs, Hebards, Martins and Huntingtons had taken up their abode, to the same point, and to the King's Highway.

If they wished to go to law they could begin with John Wheatley, Esq., justice of the peace, and if their ardor for justice continued they could carry up their suit to the court of common pleas for Grafton County.

If they wished to give their children a superior education, as many of them did, they could send them to

"Dartmouth, happy in her sylvan seat."

For money, they had the currency of England with Spanish coin, having about this time many counterfeit "milled dollars" originating, it was supposed, "somewhere on the Connecticut River." They had also the paper money of the province, easily

INTRODUCTION.

counterfeited, and therefore subject to depreciation. They had also as a measure of value the bushel of wheat at six shillings, more or less.

They had been relieved some years before from the burdens of the Stamp Act, by its repeal.

They were marrying and giving in marriage. About this time Dea. Nehemiah Estabrook led to the altar Anna Bliss; Nathaniel Wheatley, Vinal Bliss; Simon Peter Slapp, Lucretia Wilson. Children were born and death claimed his victims.

Busy as they were in subduing forests, preparing virgin soil to bear for them food and the comforts of life, building homes and meeting-houses, and mills and roads, gathering for themselves conveniences and comforts, they nevertheless were compelled to think of other things, to take into their minds for solution the gravest problems.

THE REVOLUTION.

The gradually accumulating wrongs of the Mother Country had awakened, first the fear, and then the indignation of the colonies. Everywhere there was the same determination of resistance to any further aggressions upon their rights and privileges. It was also clearly seen that resistance, to be successful, must be united. It was therefore determined to call a Congress of the colonies. The Assembly of New Hampshire wrote a circular letter to all the towns of the state, requesting them to send deputies to meet at Exeter, July 14, 1774, and also to send their proportion of £200 to defray the expense of delegates to the General Congress. It was in response to this request that the town, at a meeting held in July, 1775, voted £2 as their share of the expense.

An order of the king in council had been passed, prohibiting the exportation of gunpowder and other military stores to America. The people of Portsmouth and vicinity, learning of this act, proceeded secretly, December 13, 1774, to Fort William and Mary and took possession of the powder and arms found there. April 19, 1775, occurred the battle of Lexington. All these things intensified the hostility of the people in the remotest towns and hamlets. The people of the province took up arms and hastened to the assistance of their brethren in Massachusetts. The battle of Bunker Hill had been fought and the tidings of it reached the people to make their course decisive.

Governor Wentworth had abandoned the province August 24, 1775, and all authority seems to have been passed by the Provincial Assembly to Conventions or Congresses made up of delegates chosen by the towns. These conventions made all possible preparations for the struggle which was near. They provided men and means to the best of their ability. They appointed a general Committee of Safety, with broad, but somewhat undefined powers. It was recommended that towns should appoint their own committees of safety. The town, at a meeting held July 17, 1775, appointed a committee of safety as follows: Nehemiah Estabrook, John Wheatley, Esq., Maj. John Slapp, Silas Waterman, Jedediah Hebbard, Azariah Bliss. Three of these were empowered to act upon any matter which might come before them; any one of them might issue a warrant and deputize an officer in case of necessity. They were also directed to confer with the committees of neighboring towns, that there might be uniformity of action. At the same meeting they appointed Nehemiah Estabrook, John Slapp and John Griswold to meet committees of neighboring towns to take action concerning the formation of regiments and their field officers.

The records of the town for this and the succeeding year, 1776, are very few, and recourse must be had to other sources of information. Swiftly following events had produced great excitement in the eastern towns and many were forsaking their employments and enlisting in the army or in local service. Farms were deserted, and it began to look to some of the more thoughtful as though food might fail the people. It was thought that the people in the Connecticut valley, at a distance from exciting scenes, might do good service to their country by remaining at home and raising food for others. Accordingly, Colonel Fenton, a citizen of Portsmouth, addressed a circular letter to the people in Grafton county, as follows:

To the people of the County of Grafton from a real friend who sincerely wishes their well being

For Gods sake pay the closest attention to the sowing and planting

CAPT JOHN BLISS.

your lands, and do as much as it is possible, not only for your own and families subsistence, but to supply the wants of your fellow-men down country, for you may be assured that every kind of distress, in the provision way, is coming upon them

Let nothing induce you to quit your farming business—mind no reports—there are enough without you—therefore your diligence in farming will much more serve your country than coming to assist us. Much depends on the Back settlement in raising grain

I am informed—that if the people in the Back settlements take up arms, a number of Indians & Canadians will fall upon them, but that if they remain quiet they will not. This I inform you of from the love I bear you, and give it you as a sincere friend should do

John Fenton

Portsmo 26th April 1775
Provincial Papers, Vol. 7, p. 480.

This advice, no doubt, was well meant, but had but little effect in keeping men at home, for this whole region was full of patriotism and well represented in the army.

In April, 1776, the committee of safety for the province sent to all the towns what is known as the Association Test. The selectmen of the towns were required to present it to all the male inhabitants of the town for their signature. The names of those who signed it and those who refused, were returned to the committee. The test was as follows:

We, the Subscribers, do hereby solemnly engage and promise, that we will to the utmost of our Power at the Risque of our Lives and Fortunes, with Arms oppose the Hostile Proceedings of the British Fleets and Armies against the United American Colonies.

This was practically the Declaration of Independence on the part of the people of New Hampshire. It was, in one view of it, treason to the king on the part of his subjects. Had the people failed to make good their pledge every signer would have been held as a traitor.

The following was attached to the list of names:

Lebanon July 4th 1776

These may Certifie that the within Resolve &c has been Presented to all the Inhabitants of Said Lebanon In manner and form as requested, who have freely and Chearfully affixed their several Names thereto. There being not one Dissentient therefrom in said Lebanon.

Test   Nehh Estabrook }
         Jno Wheatley } Selectmen
         John Slapp }

There is a very remarkable coincidence of dates in the history of the town. The charter was granted July 4, 1761. This most important paper bears date July 4, 1776. When on that day Dea. Estabrook, Major Slapp and 'Squire Wheatley affixed their names to this return, their brethren in the Continental Congress were doing a like act for the people of the thirteen colonies. Thus the sturdy declaration of independence in a little back settlement catches some of the beams of glory shining forever from the grander act.

There is one other thing worthy of notice in this list of names. In many of the returns from the towns of the state many of the signers were obliged to "make their mark." Not one name thus appears among the signers from Lebanon, indicating the education of the people in that early day.

In the spring and early summer of 1776 our army, weakened by diseases, smallpox and putrid fever, was forced to retreat from Canada before the reinforced armies of the British, to Crown Point. The news of this retreat raised great alarm in this region. There were no defences between these towns and their foes in Canada. The people feared and expected that they might be attacked, and their fields, beginning to smile with plenty, and their homes would be ravaged by an unpitying foe. Meetings of committees were hastily summoned by swift messengers. July 5, 1776, representatives from Lebanon, Hanover, Lyme, N. H., and Hartford, Norwich and Thetford, Vt., met at Hanover. Dea. Nehemiah Estabrook was chosen moderator of the convention. The purpose of their meeting was to plan some defences against the expected foes. They voted to raise fifty men to go to Royalton, build fortifications and scout towards Onion River, and thus defend one avenue of approach to their settlements.

Of this company David Woodward of Hanover was appointed captain, Joshua Hazzan of Hartford first lieutenant, and Abel Lyman of Lebanon, second lieutenant. They also appointed a committee of three to direct the fortification of Royalton, one of whom was Maj. John Slapp of Lebanon, an old soldier of the French and Indian wars.

To secure the other avenue of approach from Canada, the Connecticut River, they resolved to fortify and guard Newbury, Vt. For this purpose they voted to raise 250 men to be divided into four companies. Samuel Paine of Lebanon was appointed one of the captains. They were to serve three months. The convention after having pledged the pay of the soldiers was "dismist."

It was easy enough for these people, trembling for their safety, to vote to raise men for their defence. The men themselves would be readily found, but it was not easy to furnish them with arms, ammunition and military stores. In these days of rapid transportation we are likely to forget the difficulty of moving men or material in those early days. Now thousands of stands of arms can be made by machinery in a day. Then everything was made by hand, and a single gun was the work of time. Gunpowder was scarce and the people had not yet learned to make it, depending upon importations.

The following letter, written on the succeeding day of the convention by one whose name has become familiar to us, gives a vivid picture of the alarm of the people and the difficulties with which they had to contend:

Province of New Hampshire,
Lebanon, 6th July, 1776.

To the Honorable Assembly of the Province of New Hampshire:

May it Please your Honours,

The Necessitous and alarming circumstances the Inhabitants are under in these important Frontier Towns since the army have retreated to Crown Point out of Canada, leaving a Large Extent of our frontiers open to the Ravages of the Savage Indians, being almost Destitute of arms and ammunition & many of our Inhabitants Leaving their houses and fields for a prey to our Enemys:—We humbly trust your Honours will compassionate and afford us such Relief as you in your wisdom shall judge Necessary from time to time; Especially at this present time. We would inform your Honours that the Committees of several adjacent Towns met together & agreed to Raise three hundred men to build Garrisons and scout for our Defence as you will see by a coppy of the proceedings of s'd Committee, which I send you here enclosed. But as we are destitute of arms, ammunition & money, we are fearfull it will in a great measure prove abortive; and this only alternative left us; Either such as can to make escape into the Lower Towns, or fall a sacrifice to our enemies. We therefore pray your Honours would afford us imediate Relief in the premises, as it is of the utmost importance to us all; and we shall as in duty bound ever Pray.

In behalf of the Committee,
Nehemiah Estabrook

State Papers Vol VIII, p. 298.

These men deserve the noblest praise. In their dangers they do not begin by calling for assistance, but first do all they can and then ask help.

In answer to this request the Committee of Safety gave orders for raising and paying soldiers for this duty of guarding the frontiers. Men were enlisted from Lebanon and the surrounding towns. After a time, no enemy being discovered, these people recovered from their alarm and resumed their ordinary employments. Among those who contributed to this return of quiet was Captain Payne of Lebanon, of one of the companies stationed at Newbury. He went to Ticonderoga and had an interview with General Gates, then in command of the Northern Army. From Ticonderoga he went to Crown Point, from thence down the lake to Onion River, and then to Cohos on the Connecticut, finding no signs of the enemy.

At the session of the governor and council of Connecticut, July 2, 1776, "Maj. Griswold and Capt. Marsh, who were a committee for 12 towns in the Coös Country, were present and urged the governor and council for powder, and stated their apprehensions of an attack from Canada. The governor and council allowed them to purchase of Elderkin & Wales, 800. pounds at 5s 4d per pound, for cash or good security on short payment. Also to receive at the furnace at Middletown 1000 pounds of lead at 6d per pound." Minutes of governor and council, page 363 of "Revolutionary War in Connecticut."

Major Griswold was Maj. John Griswold of Lebanon, and Captain Marsh was Capt. Joseph Marsh of Hartford, Vt.

The inhabitants of this region were from Connecticut, and in their need naturally turned to their mother state for aid, which was always granted. "No state supplied more men, money and means of every kind, according to her ability than did Connecticut; or did more to hasten on the glorious issue of the Revolutionary War. Her troops were found in nearly every action in all the states." She was the great resource for supplies for all the states.

At the annual meeting March 11, 1771, they voted £5.3 to the Royalton company, and to eight soldiers from this town ten shillings each.

During this and the preceding year the smallpox had been

MAJ. JOHN GRISWOLD.

very prevalent, greatly weakening the army and preventing the success of its operations. We find that this year a pesthouse was established in town for the purpose of innoculation for that disease. This house was under the charge of Doctor Williams. The town voted, "that such of the people of the town as are Disposed to be innoculated shall have the preheminence before the people of other towns & in case there is sufficient room in the pest-house for others besides, that Doct. Williams has the Liberty to take in such a number as may be conveniently admitted without crowding said house." They further make stringent provisions concerning visits to the pesthouse.

Early in May, 1777, Maj. Jonathan Child of Lyme came to Lebanon and mustered in the following persons for service in the army: John Colburn, Jonathan Wright, Luther Wheatley, Nathaniel Bugbee, Edward Slapp, Jonathan Conant, Phinehas Wright. Each of these soldiers received a bounty of twenty-four pounds, raised by subscription in the town. They were members of Captain House's company, who was of Hanover.

July 10, Col. Elisha Payne wrote to Major-General Folsom at Exeter for 200 stands of arms and other material to be delivered to Capt. Aaron Storrs for the use of his regiment.

In the latter part of July the people in this region were again greatly alarmed. Ticonderoga had been evacuated and our Northern Army was in retreat before the forces of General Burgoyne. He sent strong detachments into Vermont to gather cattle and horses. A scouting party had captured a British scouting party and taken them to Charlestown. Upon these prisoners were found papers indicating that three detachments of British soldiers and Tories were to be sent to the Connecticut Valley, one to Charlestown, one to Royalton, and the other to Newbury, Vt. Warnings came from every direction. Bezaleel Woodward of Hanover writes at midnight, July 19: "As you regard the safety of this Frontier, for God's sake pray come forward without delay. Assembly at Exeter are earnestly requested to send forward arms and ammunition for people in this Country, as well as men. Capt Storrs returned home this day."

Maj. Francis Smith of Colonel Chase's regiment writes from Lebanon, July 20, 1777, imploring immediate assistance, in arms and ammunition. Lieut. Jonathan Freeman of Hanover was sent as a messenger to Exeter to hasten assistance. A large number of Tories had gathered in Strafford, Vt., and it was found that these had deserted to the enemy greatly increasing the fear of immediate attack through the whole region. Strafford was abandoned by the loyal inhabitants, they taking whatever they could to Thetford, and some crossing the river to Lyme. July 24, 1777, was observed as a day of fasting, humiliation and prayer, "on account of the distress of the war and the near approach of the enemy after Ticonderoga was given up."

Soldiers were hurried forward from all directions and opposed the progress of the enemy, who were finally met and defeated in the battle of Bennington, August 16, 1777, when the people were relieved of their fears and filled with great joy.

It seems that some of the inhabitants of the town, when drafted for the public service, failed to do their duty. Maj. John Slapp, Joseph Wood and Lemuel Hough were appointed a committee to examine into the matter, and if such persons had no reasonable excuse they were instructed to exact a fine from them, not exceeding ten pounds. "Said fines to be improved for the benefit or encouragement of such inhabitants of said Lebanon as have gone, or hereafter shall go into the publick service." Who these delinquents were cannot now be ascertained, even if it were worth while to inquire. While the ancient records give evidence that there were many Tories in the state, I do not find that any inhabitants of Lebanon bore that name. From another vote of the town it appears that fines imposed were remitted.

Beyond this there is no allusion in the town records to the war during the years 1778–'79. One reason is that the people were very much disturbed in their relations to New Hampshire, inclining to cast in their lot with the people of Vermont, who were struggling for recognition as a state. A special chapter will be devoted to this subject.

Early in 1780 the people were disturbed by alarms on the frontiers. All the histories are silent on these matters. There were no organized forces in the region, the war being transferred to the south. The only explanation of these frequent alarms and hasty raising of scouts and minute men is that the region was infested by bands of Tories and Indians under the command occasionally of British officers who made raids upon exposed frontiers.

January 26, 1780, the town recommended to the commissioned officers of the militia to select six men for a scouting party, in conjunction with other towns, in order to "make Discovery of the approach of the Enemy if any there be & to give timely Notice thereof to the Inhabitants."

Voted to recommend to said officers to Equip fifty-six men, to be ready at a minute's warning, to march against the Enemy, in case of an invasion, and also that they use their Endeavor to have the whole of their company put in the best posture of Defence that may be, in case of a Genl attack. Voted that the six men for scouting be Engaged till the first day of April next, unless sooner Discharged, and also that Each man receive 40s per month for the time being, as money passed in 1774. & also that the Town provide Each man with a blanket and a pair of Snow Shoes for their use for the time being, & then to be returned to the town. Voted that in case Lieut. Ticknor should fail of Going with s'd scout that s'd six men make Choice of such meet person as they shall chuse, to take Command of them in his Room. Voted that the authorities of this town stop the Transporting of all kinds of provision that may be attempted to be Carried away from or throo s'd town till the Danger of the Enemy be over, Excepting such as are purchased for the use of the Continent—

Voted that the authorities of the Town & all others the Inhabitants Be Directed to Examine all strangers supposed to be Spies & if need be Detain them, as the Exigency of the Case may Require.

Feb 4 1780, voted to raise four men in addition to the six men already Raised for a scouting party & that the Select men Do their Endeavour to furnish them with blankets and snow shoes on the same conditions as the other six. Voted that s'd Scouting party be paid at the Rate of 40s per month, for the time being, as money passed in 1774 by the first day of April next.

The vote above respecting the transporting of provisions was passed because it was suspected, with good reason, that Tories were furnishing these to the enemy.

The following letter seems to throw some light upon one of the causes of the constant state of alarm on the western frontiers of the state:

Exeter April 28, 1780

GENTLEMEN—The Indians drove from the Seneca County, having arrived in Canada, the winter past and the probability of their being inspired with sentiments of Revenge, have greatly alarmed the inhabitants of our Western frontiers, together with the likelihood of their being joined with a great number of Refugees from this and the neighbouring states. The Canada Indians & perhaps some of the British Troops, hath so intimidated them, that unless they are strengthened with more Troops to guard them than can possibly be afforded by this State, it is feared that the settlements on Connecticut River will brake up and perhaps fifty miles of Country the most fertile in this State left Desolate. Wherefore I am directed by the General Assembly to desire you to make application to Congress for such aid as they shall judge adequate to assist in Guarding our extensive frontiers, the situation of which you can give full information

P. S. Continued reports from Canada of the designs of the enemy against our frontier towns hath much added to the fears excited by the reasons above mentioned

Honr Messrs Peabody & Folsom at Congress.

The reference above is to the expedition of General Sullivan up the River Susquehanna into the territory of the Senecas in 1779. The forces for this expedition were New Hampshire troops, who proved both brave and hardy. "Their provisions falling short before the object of the expedition was completed, the troops generously agreed to subsist on such as could be found in the Indian country."

The state sent a few soldiers to assist those raised by the towns in guarding the exposed towns and repelling any attacks. The main stations were at Newbury, Vt., and Haverhill, from whence scouting parties penetrated in all directions.

Scouting in the winter when there were no roads and marches must be made on snowshoes, and camps formed wherever they chanced to be, was no holiday work, if the winter resembled that of 1880-'81. Such simple, unadorned records as these are very suggestive of the hardships of the fathers. They certainly paid a good price for the beautiful fields and homes they have left to their descendants.

June 26 1780. Voted to raise £10-0 (accounting wheat at 6/ per bushel) upon the present List forthwith to be paid to Capt. Paine as a bounty for Raising five men for scouting to the Northward For six months unless sooner discharged

That all this alarm and these preparations had some foundation was abundantly proved by subsequent events. For on August 9, 1780, the Indians appeared at Barnard, Vt., and took

RICHARD BURLEIGH KIMBALL.

three men captive. On October 16 they attacked Royalton, Vt., taking prisoners, burning the houses and killing some of the people. The alarm spread in every direction, arousing the inhabitants and calling out the soldiers. These were organized under Capt. John House of Hanover, who speedily turned the enemy back towards Canada.

At a meeting specially warned on account of this invasion of the savage foe the town

> Voted that they will assist the militia Officers in Raifing 12 men for one month. Voted to pay Each man, Serving as afore Sd, ten bufhels of wheat, or money Equivalent, by the 20th Day of Jany next also that the Sergt & Corpl be paid according to their Rank. Voted that Each man's pay shall Commence at the time of their Engaging in the service afore S'd. Voted that the Select men provide for the support of sd Twelve men for one month at the Expense of the Town & also that they supply them with Ammunition, in Cafe they are not supplied from the publick Stores.

The following circular letter was issued to other towns by the authorities of Lebanon:

> Lebanon New Hampshire Grants, 23d October 1780
> Whereas the present Day calls for every Exertion touching the publick Cause, that our Lives and properties may be safe & secure from Invasions of our natural and unnatural Enemies & that we have reason to believe, we have many of the most abandoned Wretches, that are lost to all the feelings of humanity among us, who do intend the Destruction of this flourishing Country if not prevented.—We, whose names are here inscribed, do request that no time be lost in taking up all suspected Persons that are Enemical to the Liberties of Country—That every Town would exert themselves for that purpose—That the Towns on this Frontier would form into some Plan for the Design and purpose of purging out this Detestable Leven. We desire the Committee & Selectmen & the Principal Inhabitants of the Neighboring Towns would attend at Mr. Bliss's, Inholder in Lebanon on Monday the 30th of October 1780 for this purpose
>
> Nehemiah Estabrook ⎫
> Elisha Lathrp ⎬ Committee of Safety
> Elihu Hyde ⎭
>
> Simeon Peck ⎫
> Theo—Huntington ⎬ Selectmen
> Nathl Stores ⎭
>
> A coppy of a Letter sent to adjacent Towns

November 9, 1780, the following votes were passed:

To keep Guard on the publick Roads as Long as it shall be tho't Necefsary. To Requeft the Military Officers to Clafs such men in s'd Town as are under their Command, as are fit for duty to attend upon Guarding as afores'd, & in Cafe of Delinquency, after due notice, Shall be Liable to a fine of one bushel of Wheat or the Equivalent in money— that Elihu Hyde Simeon Peck, Nathl Storrs & Theoph Huntington be a Comtee to Adjust the accts of provifion Expended in the Late Alarm [at Royalton] & also the Wages & Provifions of The 12 men that are Gone out upon the month's Service. That the Select men be Directed to purchafe one barrel of powder & Lead & Flints in proportion thereto & to render an acct. thereof to the Town. Voted a Tax of £82-0-6 to Defray the Expense the Town has been at in the Late Alarm, also the wages & the victualling of the 12 men Raifed by this Town for one monthf Service on the Frontiers. That Mr Huckens Storrs be appointed to Remove the Provifions from Strafford [Vt.] to Royalton, provided by this Town for the afores'd men, in Cafe that they Remove Thereto from Strafford afore s'd

Nov. 23 1780. Voted a tax of £114-19-7 To Defray the Expense of the Town of Lebn in the Late alarm. To Stephen Blifs £2.-18-9 for Sundries D—D by him to the soldiers Belonging to the several Regts Commanded by Mefsrs Col. Chafe, Col Bellows & Col. Ellis. Voted that this Town is willing to pay their Proportion with other Towns within the Limits of the afore s'd Regts of the 13 Galls of Rum D.—D out of Col. Chafe's store In sd Lebanon By Capt. Paine & By Col. Chafe's order To the soldiers afore's'd on their pafsage thro Lebanon in the Late alarm.

Few things gave the authorities of the state in these times more trouble than the supply of rum. The war rendered it both scarce and high in price, yet it was deemed a necessity, and many were the devices adopted to secure it.

What the town clerk meant by the D—D in his record above I do not know, unless it is an abbreviation for Delivered.

March 2d 1781 the town voted to Raise Six men for a Scouting party till the first Day of April next unlefs Sooner Discharged, to Give Each man that shall Engage in s'd service at the Rate of Eight bushels of Wheat per month—to provide for the s'd six men 1¼ lb of flour 1 Lb of pork & one Jill of Rum per Day. Voted a Tax of £25-1-8 to pay & Support s'd six men, to be paid by the first Day of April next.

May 7 1781 The town voted a Tax of £43-3-3 to Defray the Expense of the Late alarm to Newbury.

This alarm was occasioned by the following circumstances: There were residing at Newbury, Vt., and Haverhill, N. H., several prominent men whom the British were especially desirous of capturing. Among these were Col. Thomas Johnson and Gen. Jacob Bailey. The latter acted as quartermaster to the troops stationed at Newbury and vicinity. Heavy rewards were offered for his capture. Prowling about that region were many Tories who, concealing their characters under a mask of loyalty to the country, sought information to give to the British of any movements on the part of the colonies. Many plans were formed for the capture of these persons, but they were defeated by their caution. Finally Colonel Johnson, who was building a gristmill at Peacham, Vt., found, March 8, 1781, the house surrounded with foes. Many of them he afterwards recognized as neighbors and supposed friends. He was captured and taken into Canada, where he was kindly treated in hope that he would communicate valuable information, or be won over to the British side in the contest. He was finally released, on parole, with the hope that in some way he might be made useful to his captors. A determined but unsuccessful attempt was afterwards made to capture General Bailey.

Awhile after, a report was started in some way that a force was collecting at St. John's, Canada, for an invasion of the towns along the Connecticut River. This occasioned a new alarm to the state authorities and the towns. Preparations were hastily made to receive an enemy that never came.

During these times our armies were in great need of provisions. Congress called upon the states to furnish them. Cattle were driven out of the state to supply our forces in other states. Besides this, requisitions were made on the towns for provisions, each one to contribute an amount fixed by the value of his estate, to form a general fund. The following is the provision bill of Lebanon, which in some way has escaped destruction. It is endorsed as follows:

HISTORY OF LEBANON.

Lebanon Nov‹ 17. 1781

A PROVISION BILL FOR THE USE OF THE ARMEY FOR THE YEAR ENSUING.

	Pork		Beef		Wheat Flower		Rye		Salt		Bal	
	lb	oz	lb	oz	lb	oz	lb	oz	qts	jls	s.	d.
Zalmon Aspenwall	6	12	11	4	22	8	6	12	1	1	1	1
Zenas Alden	7	14	13	4	26	8	7	14	1	3	1	4
Daniel Alden	2	4	3	12	7	8	2	4	0	3	0	5
Thop. Barbrick	3	12	6	4	12	8	3	12	0	5	0	7
Isaiah Bliss	8	4	13	12	27	8	8	4	1	3	1	7
Sherbiah Ballard	3	12	6	4	12	8	3	12	0	5	0	8
Gedion Baker	7	2	11	14	23	12	7	2	1	2	1	5
Jonathan Bingham	9	12	16	4	32	8	9	12	1	5	1	8
Stephen Bliss	6	6	10	10	21	4	6	6	1	1	0	11
Azariah Bliss Jun	20	10	34	6	68	12	20	10	3	6	3	6
Samll Baley	4	8	7	8	15	0	4	8	0	6	0	10
Daniel Bliss	9	12	16	4	32	8	9	12	1	5	1	8
Stephen Billings	8	4	13	12	27	8	8	4	1	3	1	7
Ruffus Baldwin	18	12	31	4	62	8	18	12	3	1	3	2
Ruffus Baldwin Jr	6	0	10	0	20	0	6	0	1	0	1	0
Nathl Bosworth	2	4	3	11	7	8	2	4	0	3	0	4
Jonathan Bosworth	10	8	18	2	36	4	10	8	1	6	1	10
Lt Thomas Bingham	6	6	10	10	21	4	6	6	1	1	0	11
Saml Baley Jr	7	14	13	4	26	8	7	15	1	3	1	5
Ebenr Bliss	4	12	7	13	15	10	4	12	0	7	0	10
Asa Colburn	4	8	7	8	15	0	4	8	0	6	0	10
Stephen Colburn	0	12	1	4	2	8	0	12	0	1	0	2
Samll Crocker	2	4	3	12	7	14	2	4	0	3	0	5
David Crocker	2	10	4	6	9	12	2	10	0	4	0	6
James Crocker	10	2	16	4	33	12	10	2	1	6	1	10
Robert Colbourn	15	0	25	0	50	0	15	0	2	4	2	6
Jeremiah Conet	3	6	5	10	11	4	3	6	0	5	0	7
Jesse Cook	12	6	20	10	41	4	12	6	2	1	2	1
Isaac Corey	6	0	10	0	20	0	6	0	1	0	1	0
Jacob Colbourn	2	4	3	12	7	14	2	4	0	3	0	5
Israel Convers	2	10	4	6	9	12	2	10	0	4	0	6
William Chaplain	3	6	5	10	11	4	3	6	0	5	0	7
Samll Convers	3	6	5	10	11	4	3	6	0	5	0	7
Elijah Dewey	12	0	20	0	40	0	12	0	2	0	2	0
Saxton Dewey	2	4	3	12	7	14	2	4	0	3	0	5
Martain Dewey	3	0	5	0	10	0	3	0	0	4	0	6
William Downer	20	10	34	6	68	12	20	10	3	4	3	6
William Downer Jr	12	6	20	8	41	10	12	6	2	1	2	1
Nathan Durkee	4	8	7	8	15	0	4	8	0	6	0	9
Dea. Zachaus Downer	5	4	8	12	17	8	5	4	0	7	0	11
D'n Jonathan Danna	13	8	22	3	45	0	13	8	2	1	2	3
Capt William Danna	19	8	32	8	65	0	19	8	3	2	3	3
D'n Neh. Estabrook	4	2	6	12	13	12	4	2	0	6	0	6
Neh. Estabrook Jr	3	0	5	0	10	0	3	0	0	4	0	6
Saml Estabrook	15	12	26	4	52	8	15	12	2	5	2	8
Randol Evens	19	14	33	4	66	8	19	14	3	3	3	4
Edmund Freeman	25	2	40	14	83	12	25	2	4	2	4	3
John Fox	4	14	8	0	16	0	4	14	1	0	0	10
John Fenley	2	4	4	4	8	8	2	4	0	3	0	5
Benj. Fuller	4	14	8	0	16	0	4	14	1	0	0	10
James Fuller	7	14	13	2	26	4	7	14	1	3	1	4
Jer'h Griswold	12	12	21	4	42	8	12	12	1	5	2	2
Maj John Griswold	28	2	46	14	93	12	28	2	4	6	4	8
Joseph Griswold	8	10	14	6	28	12	8	10	1	4	1	6
Oliver Griswold	15	12	26	4	52	8	15	12	2	5	2	8
John Griswold Jr	3	6	5	10	11	4	3	6	0	5	0	7
John Gray	15	6	25	10	51	4	15	6	2	5	2	7
Leut Levi Hyde	13	8	22	8	45	0	13	8	2	1	2	3
Leut Jedediah Hebbard	23	4	38	12	77	8	23	4	3	7	3	11
Josiah Hovey	6	12	11	4	22	8	6	12	1	1	1	2
James Huntington	10	8	17	8	35	0	10	8	1	6	1	9
William Huntington	10	14	18	2	36	4	10	14	1	7	1	2
David Hough	7	8	12	8	25	0	7	8	1	2	1	3
James Hebard	8	4	13	12	27	8	8	4	1	3	1	5
Ensgn Nathl Hall	28	8	45	8	95	0	28	8	4	7	4	9

INTRODUCTION.

A PROVISION BILL FOR THE USE OF THE ARMEY FOR THE YEAR ENSUING.—Continued.

	Pork		Beef		Wheat Flower		Rye		Salt		Bal	
	lb	oz	lb	oz	lb	oz	lb	oz	qts	jl^s	s.	d.
James Harthorn	8	10	14	6	28	12	8	10	1	4	1	6
Widow Elesabeth Hyde	5	4	8	12	17	8	5	4	0	7	0	11
Daniel Hough	12	12	21	4	42	8	12	12	1	5	2	2
Hiraim Huntington	2	4	4	4	8	8	2	4	0	3	0	5
Thop Huntington Jr	3	6	5	10	11	4	3	6	0	5	0	7
Saml Huntington	2	4	4	4	8	8	2	4	0	3	0	5
Thop. Huntington	4	8	7	8	15	0	4	8	0	6	0	9
Jesse Heath	6	0	10	0	20	0	6	0	1	0	1	2
Elihu Hyde Esq	7	14	13	2	26	4	7	14	1	3	1	4
Oliver Hamlain	4	8	7	8	15	0	4	8	0	6	0	9
Doct. Ziba Hall	5	4	8	12	17	8	5	4	0	7	0	11
Lemuel Hough	20	10	34	6	68	12	20	10	3	4	3	6
Lt Charles Hill	12	6	20	8	41	0	12	6	2	1	2	1
Widow Jane Hill	12	6	20	8	41	0	12	6	2	1	2	1
Nathl Hall Jr	1	14	3	2	6	4	1	14	0	3	0	4
David Hinkley	3	6	5	10	11	4	3	6	0	5	0	7
Walter Harris	2	4	4	4	8	8	2	4	0	3	0	5
Moses Hebard	13	2	21	14	43	12	13	2	2	1	1	2
James Jones	34	2	56	14	112	12	34	2	5	6	5	9
Daniel King	2	4	4	4	8	8	2	4	0	3	0	4
Uriah Knight	2	4	4	4	8	8	2	4	0	3	0	4
Joiel Kilbourn	3	6	5	10	11	4	3	6	0	5	0	7
Elias Lyman	9	0	15	0	30	0	9	0	1	4	1	6
Joshua Lothrop	3	6	5	10	11	4	3	6	0	5	0	7
Saml Leach	2	4	4	4	8	8	2	4	0	3	0	4
Richard Lyman	2	4	4	4	8	8	2	4	0	3	0	4
Lt John Lyman	7	14	13	2	26	4	7	14	1	3	1	4
Sluman Lothrop	7	14	13	2	26	4	7	14	1	3	1	4
Lt Able Lyman	14	10	24	6	48	12	14	10	2	4	2	6
Maj. Elisha Lothrop	6	12	11	4	22	8	6	12	1	2	1	3
Capt John Lassell	11	14	18	12	37	8	11	4	1	7	1	10
Saml Lothrop	2	4	4	4	8	8	2	4	0	3	0	4
Josiah Lyman	3	6	5	10	11	4	3	6	0	5	0	7
John Martian	5	10	9	6	18	12	5	10	1	0	1	0
Joseph Martian	5	10	9	6	18	12	5	10	1	0	1	0
Dan Metcalf	2	4	4	4	8	8	2	4	0	3	0	4
Saml Millington	9	6	15	10	31	4	9	6	1	5	1	8
Solomon Millington	4	2	6	12	13	12	4	2	0	6	0	9
Timothy Owen	2	4	4	4	8	8	2	4	0	3	0	4
Nathl Porter	27	10	46	4	92	8	27	10	4	5	4	7
Ichabod Packard	2	10	4	14	9	12	2	10	0	4	0	6
Simeon Peck	19	8	32	8	65	0	19	8	3	2	3	3
Walter Peck	2	4	4	4	8	8	2	4	0	3	0	5
Ebba Peck	3	6	5	10	11	4	3	6	0	5	0	7
Estate of Eb Perkins	5	10	9	6	18	12	5	10	1	0	1	0
Goven Elisha Payn	16	8	27	8	55	0	16	8	3	0	2	9
Eliaz^r Robinson	13	14	23	2	46	4	13	14	2	3	2	2
Saml Richardson	3	6	5	10	11	14	3	6	0	5	0	7
Enoch Redington	3	6	5	10	11	14	3	6	0	5	0	7
Constant Storrs	10	2	16	14	33	12	10	2	1	6	1	9
Saml Sprage	19	2	31	14	63	12	19	2	3	2	3	2
Elkenah Sprage	6	6	10	10	21	4	6	6	1	1	1	1
Nathl Storrs	22	2	36	14	73	12	22	2	3	6	3	9
Maj. John Slapp	10	2	16	14	33	12	10	2	1	6	1	9
Clapp Sumner	9	0	15	0	30	0	9	0	1	4	1	6
Simon Slapp	5	4	8	14	17	12	5	4	0	7	0	11
Huckens Storrs	16	2	26	14	53	12	16	2	2	6	2	9
Josiah Sweatland	5	4	8	14	17	12	5	4	0	7	0	10
Joseph Tilden	15	12	26	4	52	8	15	12	2	5	2	8
Leut Elisha Ticknor	28	8	47	8	95	0	28	8	4	6	4	9
Barnabas Tisdall	5	10	9	6	18	12	5	10	1	0	1	0
Capt Bela Turner	19	8	32	8	65	0	19	8	3	2	3	3
Silas Waterman	24	12	41	4	42	8	24	12	4	1	3	7
Able Wright	10	14	18	4	36	8	10	14	1	7	1	10
Thomas Wells	8	4	13	12	27	8	8	4	1	3	1	5
Joseph Wood	34	2	56	12	113	8	34	2	5	6	5	9
Joseph Wood Jr	4	2	6	14	13	12	4	2	0	6	0	9

A PROVISION BILL FOR THE USE OF THE ARMEY FOR THE YEAR ENSUING.—Concluded.

	Pork		Beef		Wheat Flower		Rye		Salt		Bal	
	lb	oz	lb	oz	lb	oz	lb	oz	qts	jls	s.	d.
Benj. Wright	6	6	10	10	21	4	6	6	1	0	1	0
Ens Nathaniel Wheatley	14	10	24	6	48	12	14	10	2	4	2	6
John Wheatley Esq	6	12	11	14	22	8	6	12	1	1	1	2
Hez^k Waters	16	2	26	14	53	12	16	2	2	6	2	8
Abial Wills	5	4	8	12	17	8	5	4	0	7	0	11
Daniel Wills	2	4	4	4	8	8	2	4	0	3	0	5
John Woodward	2	4	4	4	8	8	2	4	0	3	0	5
Henery Woodward	12	0	20	0	40	0	12	0	2	0	2	0
Eleaz^r Woodward	7	14	13	2	26	4	7	14	1	3	1	4
Phinas Wright	3	6	5	10	11	4	3	6	0	5	0	7
Andrew Wheatley	2	4	4	4	8	8	2	4	0	3	0	5
Ephraim Wood	2	4	4	4	8	8	2	4	0	3	0	5
Asa Edgerton	12	0	20	0	40	0	12	0	2	2	2	3
Mary Bennet	1	2	1	14	3	12	1	2	0	2	0	2
Benj. Fuller J^r fourfold	33	0	55	0	110	0	33	0	5	4	5	6
Charles Saxton	4	8	7	8	15	0	4	8	0	0	2	9

Nathl Storrs
Hez^k Waters } Selectmen
Edmund Freeman

There are some things to be noticed in this bill of provisions. Each man's weight of pork and rye flour are equal, his wheat flour is double the weight of his beef. Of pork there is about 1.344 pounds and an equal quantity of rye; of beef 2.262 pounds, of wheat flour 4,524 pounds, equal to about 23 barrels; of money a little over £11. The largest assessments were upon James Jones and Joseph Wood, Sr., whose quantities are equal; the smallest, Mary Bennet.

REVOLUTIONARY PAPERS.

Losseses sustained in the publick service since the contest with Great Britain

May 1776 Taken by the Enemy at the Cedars in Canada from Noah Paine of Lebanon the following Articles, (viz.) 1 Coat 60/, 1 pr Dear skin Breeches 33/, 1 pr Rusia drabb'd Breeches 15/, 1 Beaver — Hat 24/, 5 pr of stockings 30/ 1 Cheque Wollen shirt 15/ 1 Linnen D^o 12/, 1 silk Handkerchief 8/. 1 pr mittens 2/6, 2 prs shoes 20/, 1 pr shoe buckles 2/6, 1 gun 72/, Blanket 18/, Cash 12/, Knapsack 3/6, Tumpline 2/

An exact account of the Losses Sustained By Lieut. Charles Hill. at the Cedars in Canada may 19, 1776

A new great Coat	£3—12
Strait bodied Coat fine Broad Cloth	4—10
Supatine Jacket	2. 2

Nankeen Jacket	1—	0
Beaver Hat	3.	6
Pocket Handkerchief	0—	3—8
English Blanket	1—	4
Knapsack	0—	4—
Fusee, Very neat	5—	0
Powder Horn		6—8
Guns D D to the Soldiers, of my own private Property, which I never rec'd pay for	12—	0—0
	£33—	8—4

The above acct. Charged as English goods ware sold for silver in A D. 1776.

The Cedars was an important post about thirty-six miles from Montreal up the St. Lawrence. The post was in command of Colonel Bedell, who, having information from two friendly Indians that a body of English and Indians were in the neighborhood, left his garrison to communicate the intelligence, instead of sending a suitable messenger, for which he was censured. The fort was unfortunately surrendered and the losses detailed above were in consequence.

A "beaver kitt" is a young beaver—a kitten. A tumpline is a broad strap passing across the forehead to aid in supporting the knapsack. D. D. probably is an abbreviation for delivered.

Lebanon Oct. 28th 1776

We whose names are hereunto Annexed, having rec'd of the Selectmen of said Lebanon the several Quantities of Gunpowder Ball and Flint Annexed to our several names. Do by these promise to be, and hold ourselves Accountable to the Select men of said Lebanon for the time being for the above articles Rec'd as aforesaid Excepting only such of them as may be spent in actual Service

Witness our hands

	lbs Powder	Lbs Balls	No. Flints
Zacheus Downer	1	2½	6
Abel Wright	1	2	6
Nathl Hall	½	2	6
Lieut Jed Hebbard	½	2	6
Abiel Willes	½	2	6
Isaiah Bliss	½	2	6
James Jones	½	2	6
Charles Tilden	½	2	6
Stephen Tilden	½	2	6

	lbs. Powder	Lbs. Balls	No. Flints
Stephen Colburn	½	2	6
Jer^h Griswold	½	2	6
Walter Peck	½	2	6
James Fuller	1	2	6
Elisha Ticknor Jun	1	2	6
Joseph Martin	½	2	6
Joseph Tilden Jun	1	2	9
Solomon Mellington	½	2	
Henry Woodward	½	2	
Elkanah Sprague	1	2	9
Eleazer Woodward	½		
James Hebbard	½		6
Daniel Bliss	¾	2	6
Oliver Griswold	½	2	
Moses Hebbard	½		
Jesse Cook	½		

Lebanon July 25 1777

Rec'd of Elisha Payne Leut Coll in Col. Chase's Reg't Ten fire arms, Belonging to the State of New Hampshire, and Sent by Them to and for the use of said Regt.—for the town of Lebanon; to be Returned to said Payne or any other proper officer, or accounted for at the price of five pounds ten shillings, besides the cost of Transportation when thereto Required—allso twenty pounds wt of powder, and twenty wt. of lead, and ten flints Belonging to said State as afore said. Rec'd p^r

Mr William Dana Leut.

Lebanon 25th July 1777

The proportion of arms and ammunition sent to Col^l Chase's Regt as follows

(viz)	Cornish	4 guns				4
	Plainfield	13 do	20 lb powder	25 lb lead	13 flints—13	
	Lebanon	10 do	20 lb powder	20 lb led	10 flints	10
	Hanover	12 do	20 powder	25 lb led	20 flints	12
	Cardigan	5 do	20 lb powder	30 lb led	15 flints	5
	Canaan	4 do	20 lb powder	10 lb led	4 flints	4
	Grantham	2 do				2
						50

One dollar to be paid on Each fire arm at time of Receiving them for the Cost of Transportation.

Lead 60 lbs powder 2 lbs town stock.

John Martin	1¾ do	Danl Hough	3 lb Do
Nath. Hall	1 lb Do 1 lb powder	Saml Paine	5 lb Do
Jed. Hebbard	1 lb powder	Abiel Welles	1 lb Do

An accompt of the time and Charges of my going to Royalton at the time of the alarm on the 16 Oct 1780 Myself three days; found a horse

PROF. CHARLES A. YOUNG.

INTRODUCTION. 89

to carry provisions from Lieut. John Lymans to the foot of Tunbridge mountains; necessary charges—eight dollars

Jeriah Swetland.

To the select men for the town of Lebanon; sirs. pleas to pay to Mr Daniel Hough of Lebanon the sum due to me from s^d town for my service A scouting in the year 1781 in Capt Charles Nelsons Company. Lebanon Dec ye 27 1784

pr me William Lathrop

Received of the Selectmen contents of the within order

Daniel Hough

May 6th 1777. Lebanon

We the Subscribers, whose names are hereunto annexed Hereby Certify & Declare that we have Rec'd of Nehemiah Estabrook & John Wheatley £24 Each Raised by subscription in the town of Lebanon, County of Grafton & State of New Hampshire for the Encouragement of such as should Voluntarily Enlist into the Continental Service for the Term of three years on Behalf of said Town.

Witness our hands and names as follows

    John Colburn
    Jonathan Wright
    Luther Wheatley
    Nathl Bugbie
    Edward Slapp
    Jonathan Conant
    Phinehas Wright.

Another ammunition list—date unknown:

Name	Amount	Name	Amount
Zacheus Downer	1 lb powder	Nehemiah Estabrook	1 lb powder
Saml paine	Do	John Martin	Do
Abell Wright	Do	Phinehas Wright	Do
James Gutter	Do	Abel Lyman	Do
Asa Colburn	Do	Jabez Baldwin	Do
Elias Lyman	Do	Charles Sexton	Do
Eleaz^r Woodward	Do	John Slapp Jun	Do
Tilley Kingsbury	Do	Thos' Blake	Do
Shuman Lothrop	Do	Hezeh Waters	Do
Danl Hough	Do	Oliver Griswold	Do
David Hough	Do	Elkanah Sprague	Do
Elisha Ticknor	Do	Levi Hyde	Do
Wm Dana	Do	Jos Tilden	Do
Jos Martin	Do	Saml Sprague	Do
Lieut Saml Paine	6 lbs lead	James Hebbard	4 lbs lead 1 lb powder
Oliver Griswold	4 lbs lead		
Wm Dana	1½ Do	Neh. Estabrook Jun	4 Do
Joseph Martin	1 Do	Thos Blake	4 do
		John Slapp Jun	¾ do

pr me Daniel Hough

HISTORY OF LEBANON.

An account of the Expense and losses sustained by the town of Lebanon, in the publick Defence since the contest with Great Brittain.

			£	s.	d.
May	1775.	Expense to Committee after and for ammunition	20	5	4
July	1776.	Expense to Committee after and for ammunition	29	0	0
July 25.		Rec'd of Col. Payne ten fire-locks, 20 lbs. of powder, twenty wt of Lead and ten flints which said Col. Payne obtained of the State of N. H. for the use of the Reg't commanded by Col. Jonathan Chase			
In the	1777	paid to nine men that join'd Col. Scilly's Reg't for three years service in the Continental Army £24 Each, silver, m .	216		
		By orders from Col. Chase an Express to Col. Paine July 3d, 1777, 22 miles—By another Express July 30th to Do. . .	1	16	
July 3d.	1777.	Express to Capt. Hendy, . . .		2	8
July 30th.		Express to Col. Morey, . . .		14	
May	1777.	Capt. Sam. Paine paid an Express to Col. Elisha Paine		18	
July	1777.	6 Pack horses, 3 days, 34 miles to Coffins	1	16	
		Man and horse two days to carry Packs		12	
		To Ferriage over Connecticut River .		10	2
Jule 30th	1777	to six Pack Horses to Otter Creek 70 miles to the Block House . . .	3	12	
		A man with the Pack Horses 7 days .	1	1	
Oct.	1777.	Paid James Jones for the use of his horse to Saratoga and for his bridle lost in s'd service	1	13	
		Committees Expense of Collecting and prizing horses for the service to Saratoga .	1	14	
		To 62 lbs. of lead; powder, 3 lbs . .	3	17	
July	1777.	Maj. Griswold's Express to Col. Paine		18	
July 18th.	1780.	By a journey of two horses and a boy two days to Orford to carry the baggage of a party of Frenchmen by order of Col. Chase		14	
	1780, 1781.	Two Expresses to Canaan on Publick service	1	5	8
Jan. 26,	1779	by six men as a Scouting Party for 1 month at 40s per month, as money passed in 1774	12		
Aug.	1780	by 60 men, one day, in the alarm at Barnard at 3s. per day		9	
	1780.	By Expence in the late Alarm Occasioned by the Enemy's destroying the Town of Royalton, &c	146	16	9

INTRODUCTION.

			£	s.	d.
	By paying and victualling 12 men Engaged for 1 month to scout upon the Frontiers at 48 per month, but as s'd men were in s'd service but three weeks their wages and victualling amounted to		41	4	6
March 2d.	1781.	To paying and victualling six men Raised for one month, to be under the command of Capt. Nelson to scout upon the frontiers, but as s'd men Continued in s'd service but three weeks, Expence	22	12	3
		Expence for transporting provision for s'd men to Newbury .	1	18	
March	1781	by Expence in the Alarm at Newbury	48	3	3
Sept.	1781	by expense in the Alarm at Corinth for 60 men	9		
		By Expence of the Selectmen in &c in procuring provisions and other necessaries for the soldiers in the several Services and Alarms inserted as abovesaid 50 Days a 6s per day .	15		
		Two barrels of Beef 2 hundred ½ per barrel for the troops at Corinth at £4. 10s per barrel	9		
	1781	By a bounty paid to Eleven men that engaged in the publick service for six months at £4 10s each	49	10	
		Additional pay advanced by the town to s'd men 24s per month for five months and ½	72	12	
	1780	For three men that 'Listed under Capt. Sam¹ Paine in the Public Service at Cohos —a bounty 40s each	6		
		For eight men under Capt Bush 1 month and ½ bounty and wages .	38	8	
		To Lieut Huntington 1 month and ½ at £5. 5 per mouth .	7	17	6
		Sum total	£770—	1—	1

Soldiers From Lebanon in the Revolution

The historian has found great difficulty, on account of the relations of the town to the state, in making a full and accurate list of these patriots. First, the names of those for whose connection with the army there is documentary evidence are given.

In Colonel Bedel's regiment were Charles Hill, ensign, Noah Payne, private, Eleazer M. Porter.

This regiment was raised to reinforce the army after its failure under Arnold to capture Quebec, and the death of General Montgomery. At a fort called the Cedars, above the City of Montreal the regiment was disgracefully surrendered by the major, Isaac Butterfield, Colonel Bedel being absent at the time. The surrender was in May, 1776.

Paine and Hill brought bills against the town for losses which they had sustained in the surrender.

COLONEL CHASE'S REGIMENT.

Isaiah Potter,* chaplain William Dana,* adjutant
Edmund Freeman, Capt.

CAPT. JOSHUA HENDEE'S* COMPANY.

Lieut. Zalmon Aspenwall*	Samuel McCluar
Ensign Nathan Aldrich*	Tim^y Owen*
Daniel Bliss*	Barnabas Perkins*
Jacob Colburn*	Phillip Paddleford
Sluman Lothrop*	Elisha Tickney*
Nath. Mason	Simeon Wheton
Peres Mason	Joseph Wood*
Solomon Millington*	Eleazar Woodward

The above discharged the 20th (1777) out 48 days each.

Lieut. Seth Martin	Eleazar Robbinson*
Serg^t Nathaniel Hall*	Simⁿ Ballock
Serg^t Nehemiah Estabrook*	Martin Dewey*
Cor^l Lemuel Huff*	Josiah Hovey
" Zacheus Downer*	Elias Limon*
" James Jones*	Mathew Peck*
" Joseph Loveland	Silvanus Wells

*Those marked * were of Lebanon.

Levy Hide*   Christopher Smith
Hezekiah Waters*   Joseph Sevey

The above dismissed the 18 of June. The above were in service 46 days.

Ensign Sim^on Duda (Derry)   Th's Ellis Barbaric*
Sergt. Henry Woodward   John Gray*
   "   Israel Winchester Peck Asa Williams

William Downer*
The above dismissed June 13 (1777)

John Grissel*   Charles Saxton*
Abel Right   Nathaniel Porter*
Joseph Hamelton
In the service 12 Days each, cauld 9 days.

In a roll found among the Hall papers the name of Walter Peck is found in addition to the above.

To carrying 45 Packs From Col. Chases to Mt. Independence, 100 miles £22-10-0

To Abel Lymon and Elish Tickney Ecabod Amsbery with There Horses five Days a fetching Baggage from Lebbanon to Col Chase's £2-2-0

To Ezra Percias? with one Hors assisting in gitting the sick along Home six days at £2-2-0

To three Hired Horses to assist in gitting the sick along Home 2 days, £0-12-0

                              Joshua Hendee Captain

Another roll of Colonel Chase's regiment contains the following names of officers from Lebanon:

Wm Dana, Adjutant   Isaiah Potter Chaplain
Samuel Payne Capt.   Jeddediah Hibbard Sergt. Major
John Lasel Capt.   Abel Lyman Lieutenant
Nathaniel Hall Lieut.

The above was copied from papers of Colonel Chase, now deposited in the archives of the New Hampshire Historical Society. The spelling is preserved and some of the names must be made out by the sound.

In the spring of 1777 there were great fears for the safety of Ticonderoga, when the militia was hastily ordered out, those in this region under the command of Col. Jonathan Chase of Cornish. The regiment marched to Ticonderoga, when, the alarms subsiding, they returned to their homes, in the latter part of June. From the names which appear above as of Lebanon, there could have been but few men left in the town.

They had scarcely been dismissed when a new alarm was raised, and they were again summoned to the field to meet Burgoyne and save Ticonderoga. The regiment marched under command of Maj. Francis Smith.

CAPTAIN HOUSE'S COMPANY IN COLONEL BALDWIN'S REGIMENT.

Daniel Hough	Sluman Lathrop
John Slapp jr	Ebenezer Bliss
William Downer Jr	

Col. Nahum Baldwin was of Amherst. His regiment was raised in accordance with a vote of a special convention of the Council and Assembly, September 17, 1776, for the purpose of reinforcing the army in New York. The regiment was in the battle of White Plains, October 28, 1776, and was dismissed in December of that year.

CAPTAIN HOUSE'S COMPANY IN COLONEL CILLEY'S REGIMENT.
Mustered March 17, 1777.

John Coleburn	Jonathan Conant
Edward Slapp	Phineas Wright
Luther Wheatley	Jonathan Wright
Nath. Bugbee	Jonathan Kingsbury
John Landee	Elisha Tilden
Stephen Tilden	Benj. Quin

COLONEL CILLEY'S REGIMENT.

John Colbarn	Edward Slapp
Jonathan Conant	Phineas Wright
Jonathan Wright	Josiah Magoon
Luther Wheatley,	Daniel Hough.
Thomas Blake, Ensign	Eben. Bliss
Nathaniel Bugbee	

These men were enlisted for three years in the Continental service in the spring of 1777.

This was General Stark's old regiment. The rendezvous of the regiment was Ticonderoga. When that fortress was abandoned this regiment fell back with the army to Saratoga; was engaged in the battle of Stillwater or Bemis Heights, and the battle of Saratoga. It passed the winter of 1777–'78 at Valley Forge; was present at the battle of Monmouth, N. J., was with Sullivan in the expedition into the Indian country, New York. It was stationed at West Point for a time.

Of those above named, Luther Wheatley, son of John Wheatley, a youth of seventeen, was mortally wounded in the battle of Stillwater, September 19, 1777, and died September 30.

CAPTAIN HENDEE'S COMPANY IN COLONEL HOBART'S REGIMENT.

Samuel Easterbrook Ens	Joseph Wood
Elisha Bingham	Zalmon Aspenwall
Jabez Baldwin	Jeremiah Griswold
Azariah Bliss	Josiah Bliss
Joel Tilden	Walter Peck
Jacob Colburn	Eleazer M. Porter

Colonel Hobart, called in the records Hubbard, was from Plymouth. He was present at the battle of Bennington with a part of his regiment, while the other part went on to Saratoga and Stillwater.

It has been said by several persons interested in such matters that there were soldiers from Lebanon at the battle of Bennington, which the historian would gladly believe if he could have reliable proof of the assertion.

When he first became a resident of Lebanon there were living those who could remember the battle; neither they nor any of their descendants made any claim of presence at that battle.

I find no proof of such presence in any document. There were soldiers from Lebanon in the field just before that battle and afterwards at the battle of Saratoga.

Colonel Chase's regiment, in which there were many soldiers from Lebanon, took the field May 7, 1777, but was discharged in July. See Revolutionary Rolls. Vol. II, pages 14 to 19. The regiment was called out to reinforce the army at Ticonderoga.

On page 138 of the same volume is a record of the discharge of sixty officers and men from Colonel Chase's regiment, June 11, 1777. Of these twelve, at least, were from Lebanon. The reason given for their discharge was that their crops needed their attention to provide food for their families and the army. On page 38 of Vol. II. Revolutionary Rolls, is another record of

Colonel Chase's regiment, under command of Maj. Francis Smith, which marched from Cornish to reinforce the army at Ticonderoga on the alarms of June 27 and July 4, 1777. There were nearly twenty of these soldiers from Lebanon in this regiment, comprising most of those whose discharge took place June 11, 1777. All received discharge before the middle of July of the same year.

Among those known to have been at Bennington was Colonel Hobart or Hubbard. Among the companies of his regiment was that of Captain Hendee, in which eleven men from Lebanon were enrolled, and it would seem probable that they were in the battle, but a careful examination of the official rolls leads to a different conclusion.

According to the official rolls (Revolutionary Rolls No. 2, pages 143 to 158), Colonel Hobart's command consisted of five companies, Captain Walker's, Captain Webber's, Captain Elliott's, Captain Post's, and Captain Hendee's. Nothing shows more certainly where soldiers have been than the pay-rolls, because they drew 2d. per mile for the distance they marched. Captain Walker's company is stated to have joined the Northern Army at Saratoga, No. 2, Revolutionary Rolls, page 143.

The same statement is made concerning Captain Webber's company, page 146, but their travel was from Stillwater. Captain Elliott's company was from Plymouth and towns adjacent. The roll does not state from what place their travel was allowed, but only "travel home."

Captain Hendee's company, page 155, was paid travel from Stillwater.

Captain Post's company was paid travel from Stillwater *and Bennington*, the only company of Colonel Hobart's command so distinguished. This company is known to have been at the Bennington battle in which Captain Post lost his life.

Out of the ten companies composing Colonel Stickney's regiment, only five drew pay from Bennington and Stillwater. Out of the ten companies composing Colonel Nichols' regiment, only three are distinguished as having been at Bennington. From all this the historian cannot resist the conclusion that Captain Hendee's company was not at Bennington.

MAJOR WHITCOMB'S BATTALION.

Major Whitcomb had command of a battalion of Rangers from 1776 to the close of the war. It was their duty to guard the upper Connecticut. In the roll of officers of the battalion as organized in 1780, is the name of Samuel Payne, as captain of a company. From the records we learn that three men enlisted under Captain Payne "in the Public Service at Cohos." Who they were the record does not state.

There were also eight men under Captain Bush a month and a half. Lieutenant Huntington was out for the same period. In 1781 eleven men "engaged in the public service for six months."

There were also others engaged for longer or shorter periods, called out at the various alarms in the closing years of the war; sixty men one day in the alarm at Barnard, August, 1780; twelve men scouting on the frontier three weeks; March, 1781, six men for one month under Captain Nelson to scout upon the frontiers.

To these the following names must be added: Nehemiah Estabrook 2d, who hastened to the front immediately after the battle of Lexington, and continued in the service to the close of the war. He was one of the body guard of Washington. He was undoubtedly one of the two reported by the selectmen as gone into the army. The other was probably Lieut. Thomas Blake.

What is said of Nehemiah Estabrook is traditional. The historian fails to find records to support it. His name is given in one of the lists of soldiers, but under different circumstances.

The following persons were engaged in the service of their country, who came to Lebanon after the close of the war:

Diarca Allen	Gideon Baker
Phinehas Allen	Zuar Eldredge
Jesse Cook	Nathan Durkee
David Millington	Enoch Redington
Nathaniel Storrs	

Edward Slapp, son of Maj. John Slapp, on the evacuation of Ticonderoga, was in the rear guard of the army and obliged to endure much fatigue and many hardships under the pursuit of the enemy, under which his health gave way and he was sent to the hospital at Albany, N. Y. In October, 1777, he obtained a furlough to return home. Ensign Charles Hill happened to be at Albany, and in a most friendly way offered to assist him in reaching home. Growing weaker on the journey, he was obliged to stop at Shaftsbury, about forty miles from Albany, where he died at the house of Ichabod Cross.

Nathaniel Bugbee contracted disease in the army and was a long time sick at Lebanon.

Ensign Thomas Blake was born in Dorchester, Mass., in 1752, son of Samuel and Patience Blake. He descended from William Blake, who came to Dorchester in 1630. In 1775 he purchased large tracts of land in Lebanon, and the sawmill by Hubbard bridge, known as the Davidson mills. He was a joiner and was at work on the college buildings when news came of the battle of Lexington. He immediately left and started, in company with some students and others, for Cambridge, and on the way was chosen leader. He immediately enlisted and was probably at the battle of Bunker Hill. He was first, ensign in Captain House's company, then lieutenant. and in General Sullivan's expedition he was appointed paymaster and continued such to the close of the war. He kept a journal which has been printed in Kidder's "History of the First New Hampshire Regiment." The first date is Lebanon. After the close of the war he traveled through the state, settling military accounts. He then went to Boston and established himself as a manufacturer of soap and candles, firm of Blake & Jackson. He died in Boston, February 18, 1840. He had the reputation of a most faithful and trustworthy officer.

The following is a transcript from the original in the Pension Bureau, Washington, D. C.:

We the subscribers Being a Draft from the Militia of the Regt. under the command of Col Jon^th Chase Do Acnolage we have Rec^d of him four pounds ten shillings each as one months advanced pay, agrable to a Vote of the Councel and assembly of the state New Hampshire

Lebanon

Zalmon Aspenwall	Isaiah Bliss
Joel Tilden	Joseph Wood Junr
Asa Colburn	Lem^l Fuller

SOLDIERS IN THE REVOLUTION.

Jabez Baldwin
Eleazer Mather Porter
Jeremiah Griswold
Jacob Colburn
Ensign Charles Hill
John Colburn
Jonathan Wright
Ensign Thomas Blake
Edward Slapp
Josiah Magoon
Ebenezer Bliss
Isaiah Potter chaplain
Lieut. Zalmon Aspenwall
Ensign Nathan Aldrich
Daniel Bliss
Jacob Colburn
Sluman Lathrop
Solomon Millington
Timothy Owen
Barnabas Perkins
Elisha Gecknor
Joseph Wood
Sergt. Nathaniel Hall
Sergt. Nehemiah Estabrook
Corp. Lemuel Hough
Corp. Zacheus Downer
Noah Payne private
Jonathan Conant
Luther Wheatley
Nathaniel Bugbee
Phineas Wright
Daniel Hough
William Dana Adjutant
Corp James Jones
Levi Hyde
Hezekiah Waters
Eleaser Robinson
Martin Deney
Elias Lyman

Azariah Bliss Junr
Walter Peck
Benj. Harris.

Matthew Peck
William Downer
Ths. Ellis Barbarick
John Gray
John Griswold
Abel Wright
Charles Saxton
Nathaniel Porter
Ensign Samuel Estabrooks
Capt Samuel Payne
Jedediah Hibbard Sergt Major
Abel Lyman Lieut.
Robert Colburn
John Slapp Jr
Nathaniel Wheatley
Silas Waterman
Elkanah Sprague
Stephen Colburn
Nathaniel Storrs
Jos. Gilden Jr
Nathaniel Porter Jr
James Hartshorn
Jabez Baldwin
Simon Porter Slapp
James Fuller
Moses Hibbard
John Fox
Asariah Bliss
Jeremiah Meachan
Benj. Fuller
Walter Peck
Eba Peck
Huckins Storrs
James Hartshorn
Nathan Durkee

The lists given on the preceding pages, probably incomplete, show nevertheless that the town did its part in the great struggle for independence. The lists have cost the historian months of perplexing labor, at great disadvantages, because of the attitude of the town towards New Hampshire in the Vermont controversy.

COMMITTEE OF SAFETY.

This body of men was a necessity of the times in which it originated. In the sudden breaking up of the royal authority before there was any organization to bind them together, and to be a channel for legitimate authority, this organization was devised. It seems to have had both legislative and executive powers. That of the state was only active when the assembly was not in session, as they had at the time no distinct executive body. The committees of the towns were appointed annually and were clothed with ample powers. To secure uniformity in their action, committees of neighboring towns consulted together and made rules for their government. The following are instances of their manner of proceeding:

At a meeting of the Commitees of Safety for the towns of Plainfield, Lebanon, Hanover Canaan & Grantham at the house of Mr Azariah Bliss in said Lebanon Aug 2ᵈ A. D. 1775 Chose John Wheatley Esq. chairman. Bezaleel Woodward Esq. clerk.

Voted that we will use our utmost Endeavorers as Committees of our respective Towns for the preservation of the Peace and suppression of Disorders among the people as Recommended by Congress

Voted that the laws of our Country ought and shall be our Rule of Proceedure in judging of the Qualities of Offences & punishing the same, only with such Variations as the Different Channel of Administration Requires

Voted that each Committee keep records of their Proceedure

Voted that this meeting be dissolved.

           Attest   Beza Woodward Clk.

At a meeting of the Committee of Safety for the town of Lebanon at the house of Mr. Azariah Bliss in said Lebanon on Wednesday the 2ⁿᵈ day of Aug. 1775 said Committee Chose Deacon Nehemiah Estabrook Chairman and John Wheatley Esq. Clerk

Voted that in Common Cases the Clerk of said Committee shall issue out proper precepts in behalf of said Committee for Conventing of Disturbers of the peace before said Committee

At a meeting of the Committee of Safety for the town of Lebanon Aug. 7ᵗʰ 1775 Tyxhall Cleaveland of Hanover and Zalmon Aspenwall of said Lebanon appeared before said Committee to answer to a Complaint Exhibited to s'd Comᵗᵉᵉ by Samˡ Paine a Grand Juror of s'd Lebanon against said Cleaveland and said Aspenwall for breach of peace & Disorderly conduct. When said Committee proceeded to an Examination of the Case which by the Confession of the parties above named, as well as by Evidence said complaint was judged to be supported, when upon the Submission of the parties and promises of Regular Conduct in the future said Com^tee Dismissed said Delinquents.

Also Hobart Estabrook & John Barbarick appeared before said Com^tee & were Examined Concerning their Labouring on the 20th day of July last being the day set apart by the Grand american Congress for publick fasting & prayer throughout the Continent—when the above named persons Confessed their fault, and being Duly admonished to a better Conduct in future (which they Engaged) were accordingly Dismissed by said Com^tee

Lebanon, Nov 25 1775

Jos Tilden of said Lebanon Husbandman appears before the Com^tee of Safety for said Lebanon & complains and says that he the said Tilden on the 23d day of this instant Was met on the Highway between the towns of piermont & orford By Capt. Bela Turner of said Lebanon and Was by him the said Capt Turner stopt and By Him Robbed of legal property.

Joseph Tilden

Lebanon Nov 27 1775

At a meeting of the Com^tee of Safety for said Lebanon the above complaint of Jos. Tilden aforesaid against Capt Bela Turner for Robbery was Considered & Evidences heard in form of both parties when said Com^tee took the matter of the aforesaid Complaint into Consideration & said Com^tee unanimously agreed that said Complaint is not Supported; and that him the said Jos. Tilden, the Complainant ought in Justice to make a proper Retraction to Capt Turner in a publick manner and pay all incidental charges.

'Test John Wheatley Clk.

Colony of New Hamp^r }
   Grafton County ss }

At a meeting of the Committee of safety for the town of Hanover in said County at the House of John Paine in-holder in said Hanover, March 23d 1776.

Present—Lt David Woodward Chairman
Capt. Aaron Storrs
Beza^l Woodward Esq Clk

Bezaleel Phelps of Norwich in the Colony of New York, yeoman, was bro't before this Committee by virtue of a warrant issued by Bezaleel Woodward and Aaron Storrs, two of the Committee, predicated on his having in his custody and detaining a certain Note of this Colony bearing the face of a six shilling Bill which is supposed to have been fraudently altered and increased as to the value or sum therein express'd by s'd Phelps, as by said warrant may more fully appear.

Respondent pleads not guilty

After a full hearing of evidences in said case said Phelps confessed that he had burnt said bill being conscious that it was altered, and that in case he may be excused from penalty in detaining said bill when he knew that it was counterfeit, he will disclose to this Committee the author of that and sundry other bills, and discover where some of said bills are—whereupon s'd proposal is agreed to, only that he pay costs hitherto made in the affair, till they can be regularly recovered of some other person. Costs taxed at forty shillings.

Said Phelps then desired Lemuel Paine of s'd Hanover to produce a certain forty shilling Bill which he received on the evening of the 15 inst. of Andrew Wheatley of Lebanon, which s'd Paine on request accordingly did, which bill is adjudged by this Committee to have been altered from a three shilling bill, and which s'd Lemuel on his oath declared he rec'd of said Wheatley as aforesaid

Committee adjourned to tomorrow morning, 9 o'clock March 24th Met according to adjournment.

Present—Lt David Woodward, Chairman
l t Aaron Storrs
Bez'a Woodward Esq Clk
} Committee of Hanover

John Wheatley Esq.
Major John Slapp
Major John Griswold
Mr Azariah Bliss
} Committee of Lebanon

1st Charles Hill of Lebanon in-holder is bro't before these Committees for putting off and passing counterfeit money at which time Solomon Cushman of Norwich produced a forty shilling Bill of the Colony of New Hampshire No 3260 emitted July 25th 1775 and payable Dec 20th 1779 which is adjudged by these Committees to have been altered, which bill said Cushman on his oath declares he re'd of said Charles Hill in payment for a silk Handkerchief, and s'd Hill is not able to inform us of whom he rec'd it. Whereupon it is considered and ordered that s'd Hill pay to s'd Cushman the value of s'd bill viz. forty shillings and costs.

Judgment satisfied

Beza. Woodward, Clerk.

The Committee then resumed the examination relative to the bill laid before this committee yesterday by Lemuel Paine, relative to which Charles Hill (being sworn) testified that being at this house on the evening of the 15th Inst. he saw Joseph Skinner (of Capt Greens company in Col Bedels Regt.) put a bill into the hand of Andrew Wheatley of Lebanon that he might get it changed

Bezaleel Phelps before named (being sworn) testifies That he he saw Andrew Wheatley give a forty shilling bill to Lemuel Paine to be changed, and afterwards as s'd Phelps was going to Dr Eager with s'd Skinner, s'd Skinner told this deponent that it was his bill with which Wheatley paid the reckoning at said Paine's and added *"And I made it myself, and I have altered a good many bills from three shillings to forty shillings, and I have Known many more altered both here and at Cambridge, and a person may make his fortune by it in a little time."* He also said all the money he spent at Cambridge he altered and further said to s'd Phelps that if he told anybody of it he would kill him. Said Phelps farther testifies that that he saw said Skinner cut certain peices from a certain book or pamphlet to use in altering bills, and s'd Skinner told him he had cut pieces from it before to use for that purpose, and that he would not take a thousand pounds for the book. Phelps described the book and informed particularly where he had left it (which being produced exhibited strong ground to apprehend from its appearance that it has been abundantly used for that purpose) Said Phelps further testifies when s'd Skinner had some paste to use in altering bills, Mrs Winton coming into the room asked what it was for? Dr. Eager replied *to paste books*—when he was sometimes in the room whilst Skinner was altering bills with the paste, both before and after Mrs Winton asked the question; said Phelps further testifies that he saw said Skinner alter a bill to a forty shilling last Sunday and this deponent observing Dr. Eager to be present part of the time, asked Skinner whether the Doctor knew of his altering bills, to which Skinner replied "Damn him, yes." Said Phelps further testifies [The remainder is wanting]—Prov. Papers, Vol. VIII, pp. 115, 116.

The Charles Hill mentioned above should not be mistaken for the Charles Hill who was one of the earliest settlers and was prominent in both town and church affairs. At this time he was dead. It was his son, Charles Hill, Jr.

Colony of New Hampshire. Grafton ss Lebanon March 25th 1776. At a meeting of the Committee of Safety for the town of Lebanon to hear and Consider of a Complaint Ehibited by Tyxhall Cleaveland of Hanover in said County, Trader against Robert Colburn of said Lebanon, yeoman, for that he the said Colburn being in company of Elijah King of Charlestown Doct. George Eager and Joel Foster of said Hanover on the 10th inst. (it being Lord's day) was aiding and assisting in Cutting and Causing to fall a Large tree on a certain frame (of a building) in said Hanover, belonging to said Cleaveland which frame was entirely moved by the falling of said tree.

Present at said meeting
John Wheatley Esq.
Maj. John Griswold
Maj. John Slapp
Mr. Azariah Bliss
Maj. John Slapp Chairman.   John Wheatley Clerk.

Said Colburn being brought by Virtue of a warrant from said Comtee before them, was Carefully Examined touching the aforesaid Complaint, when s'd Colburn Confessed that he was in Compy with the persons mentioned in said Complaint. Upon which Declaration of the Respondant the Com^tee proceeded to a Consideration of the point in Question & are of the opinion that him the said Robert Colburn is guilty of aiding and assisting in the fact Exhibited in the said Complaint & that the said Colburn ought in Justice to pay or secure to the satisfaction of said Cleaveland as a Compensation in Part, for the Damage done to said frame the sum of three pounds of Lawful money & as said Transgression was committed on the Sabbath or Lord's day, which in the opinion of the Com^tee Greatly Aggravated the offence that him the said Colburn be and is amerced the sum of five shillings for breaking the Sabbath and that he be held by Bond with one Sufficient surety for satisfying said judgment & paying Costs.

Lebanon, Dec 16 1776.

At a meeting of the Committee of Safety of said Lebanon Held at the house of Dea. Nehemiah Estabrook in said Lebanon

      Present Nehemiah Estabrook Chairman
         Azariah Bliss
         John Slapp
         John Griswold
         John Wheatley

Then appeared before said Com^tee Abel Wright of said Lebanon & made Oath that he Rec'd a certain Bill Emitted by the State of Connecticut, said bill Containing 10/6. of James Hebbard of said Lebanon ; said Hebbard also made oath that he Rec'd said bill of Saml Meacham of Relhan [Enfield] & said Meacham made oath that Jonathan Paddleford of said Relhan Delivered said bill to Phebe the wife of said Meacham.

The Committee Having Examined said bill are of the opinion that said bill is Counterfeit & that said Hebbard settle with the said Wright, & that said Meacham pay the contents of said bill to him the said Hebbard and that him the said Paddleford pay to said Meacham ten shillings and six pence & also the Costs necessarily arising in the Prosecution of the above premises

Bill of Tax on the within written premises

To James Hebbard for trouble and attendance	2/6
To Saml Meacham for travel and attendance	3/8
Costs of Committee	12/6
Total	£0. 18-8

Lebanon March 27-1778

At a Convention of the Com^tee of Safety for said Lebanon appeared Nathl Hall, Complain^t & Wm Downer Jr Defend^t. Then was Read in the Hearing of said Downer a Complaint Exhibited by said Hall against said Downer for Cursing & Swearing and threatening the Life of said Hall. Abel Lyman and Andrew Hall were produced by said Nathl Hall as Evidences to Support said Complaint

DR. CYRUS H. FAY.

The following is the original complaint, recently discovered among the Hall papers:

To the Com^{tee} of Safety for the Town of Lebanon in the County of Grafton on the N. Hampshire Grants
Gen^{tn}
Nathaniel Hall of s'd Lebanon complains and says that Wm Downer Junr of s'd Lebanon did on the 26th Day of this instant March in the Presence of Mr Abel Wright Lieut Abel Lyman and Mr Andrew Hall profanely Curse and swear and also threaten that on the morrow he would bring his gun and if s'd Nat^l Hall did tap trees on the North side of his Lot which Mr Wm Downer pretends to claim as part of his lot that by God he would shute s^d Hall, and Gentⁿ you are hereby desired to take immediate cogniciance hereof to prevent further evil
I am Gentⁿ
Your most obedient
& very humble servant
Nathl Hall.

The Commit^{ee} having heard the evidence are of the Opinion that said Complaint is well supported by s'd Evidences and that said Downer is guilty in manner and form as set forth in s'd Complaint. Wherefore the Com^{tee} judge that him the said Wm Downer be amerced in the sum of twenty shillings. L. M. as a fine to be paid into the treasury of the said town of Lebanon for three breaches of the peace (viz) Cursing, Swearing, and high-handed Threatening & that him the said Downer pay the Cost of this Court & stand bound with one sufficient Surety for the satisfying of the afore said Judgment
Signed by order of said Com^{tee}
John Wheatley Clk.

Bill of Costs—four Com^{tee} mens attendance half a day at
3/ each £0—12—0
Plaintifs attendance & evidences and other incidental Charges 0—16—0
Fine 1—0—0

£2—8—0

Lebanon June 22^d 1779

At a meeting of the Com^{tee} of Safety of said Lebanon at the house of Mr Silas Waterman in s'd Lebanon.
Present John Wheatley, Lieut. Elihu Hyde, Capt. Edmund Freeman & Mr Silas Waterman. John Wheatley Chairman P. T.
There appeared William Downer of said Lebanon, brought by special Warrant before said Committee to Answer to a Complaint Exhibited by Elkanah Sprague (one of the Tything men in s'd Lebanon) against said Downer for sundry breaches of the peace viz Cursing, threatening & strikeing; & also James Huntington for strikeing.

The Com^tee then proceeded on the premises & Having Read said Complaint in the hearing of the above named Delinquents & they being asked the Question, whether they acknowledged the facts Exhibited in said Complaint, the said Wm Downer Denyed the authority of said Court; and him the said Huntington acknowledged the fact as mentioned in said Complaint

Wherefore said Court proceeded to Examine the Evidences being Duly cited and sworn, and after hearing and Deliberating upon the Case find that him the said Wm Downer is fully Convicted by legal Evidence of a breach of the peace viz Strikeing the said James Huntington; & him the said James Huntington by Confession &c of striking him the said Wm Downer. Wherefore said Com^tee award that s'd Delinquents pay a fine of one dollar each and their proportion of Costs.

Lebanon March 6th 1780

At a meeting of the Committee of Safety of said Lebanon. Present Dea. Nehemiah Estabrook Chairman John Wheatley and Elihu Hyde members appeared Abigail Landee of said Lebanon to answer to a complaint Exhibited to said Com^tee (viz) Kicking and striking, which are open breaches of the peace of the Good people of this Town. Wherefore said Committee Do award that she the said Abigail pay a fine of ten Dollars and the Costs of Trial, & to stand committed till this judgment is satisfied.

Attest John Wheatley Clk.

The Committee of Safety having served its purpose during the Revolution and other disturbances, passed away. Probably no court ever administered more even-handed justice, so far as its action pertained to this town, than did this committee.

The following is a list of the persons who composed the committee at various times:

July 17, 1775.—Nehemiah Estabrooks, Maj. John Griswold, John Wheatley, Esq., Maj. John Slapp, Silas Waterman, Jedediah Hebbard, Azariah Bliss.

1777.—Deacon Estabrooks, John Wheatley, Major Griswold, Azariah Bliss, Jesse Cook.

1778.—Deacon Estabrooks, John Wheatley, Major Slapp, Azariah Bliss, Lemuel Hough.

1779.—Deacon Estabrook, John Wheatley, Elihu Hyde, Silas Waterman, Edmund Freeman.

1780.—Deacon Estabrook, Elihu Hyde, Elisha Lothrop.

1781.—Elihu Hyde, Deacon Estabrook, Major Lothrop. With this year the office ended.

In addition to the difficulties occasioned by the sundering of the relations of the people to the mother country, in civil matters another came up. They were free, as they held, from all obligations to England, but did not know how to dispose of themselves. They held that they had the right to form civil and political relations with any organization then existing, or create a new one. For various reasons they were dissatisfied with New Hampshire, and sympathized with the people of Vermont, and entered into civil relations with them. The history of this proceeding is now to be given.

The Vermont Controversy.

This controversy makes a singular chapter in the history of New Hampshire, New York and Vermont. Nothing like it is to be found in the history of any other part of the country. Until a recent period the acts of this controversy—it might, indeed, be called a drama—were little known and less understood. Doctor Belknap, writing of these times no later than 1784, being himself an observer of them, says in respect to them: "It is not easy to develop the intrigues of the several parties or to clear their transactions from the obscurity which surrounds them. He who looks for consistencies in the proceedings of conventions and assemblies which were involved in this controversy will be disappointed." Nevertheless, all human transactions have their principles and motives, and it is possible for the patient and persevering student to discover them and so arrive at an understanding of them. In this case it must be confessed that the task is a difficult one because of the number of the parties to the controversy, and because of the number and varying force of the motives and principles which governed the actors. There is not so much of obscurity as of complexity in these stirring events. The web is a tangled one, but the threads are whole, and with patience may be traced through to their ends. Inconsistencies are apparent only, and will in the end be found to be the natural results of well-known principles of human nature.

Before entering upon an examination of these extraordinary events, it may be well to mention the motives and principles governing the actors therein. They are these: 1. Grievances, real and fancied. 2. Neighborly sympathy. 3. Self-interest. 4. Patriotism. 5. Policy, American and British.

Many of the grants of land were made by the crown before much exploration had been made. There was profound ignorance of the interior regions—of their extent and boundaries. Under these circumstances it is not strange that grants of extensive territories should interfere with each other; that in some parts they should overlay each other, with the result that upon exploration and survey, different parties should appear to have a title to the same lands.

The Masonian grant, having its western line sixty miles from the sea, would not reach the Connecticut River. This western line, if *straight,* would commence in Rindge and run through Jaffrey, Peterborough, Greenfield, Francestown, Weare, Hopkinton, Concord, Canterbury, Gilmanton, across Lake Winnepesaukee, Wolfeboro, Tuftonborough, to Ossipee. If a *curve,* as some contended that it should be, then it would commence in Fitzwilliam and pass through Marlborough, Roxbury, Sullivan, Marlow, Washington, Goshen, New London, Wilmot, Orange, Hebron, Plymouth, Campton, to or near the south line of Conway.

Massachusetts claimed all the territory lying west of three miles north and east of the Merrimack River to the junction of the Pemigewasset and Winnipesaukee Rivers, "thence due north as far as a tree known as Endicott's tree, three miles north of the junction of the above rivers; thence due west to the South Sea." The states both claimed the same territory, and after many years of disputes and evasive decisions, the matter was finally referred to the king in council for his consideration. The final decision was: "That the northerly bound of the Province of Massachusetts be a curve line pursuing the course of the Merrimack River at three miles distance, on the north side thereof, beginning at the Atlantic Ocean and ending at a point due north of Pawtucket Falls, and a straight line drawn from thence due west till it meets with his majesty's other governments." 1740.

This decision established the boundary between Massachusetts and New Hampshire, greatly to the advantage of the latter, but at the same time it opened the way to another dispute of far greater consequences.

When in 1741 Richard Hazzen, surveyor, was instructed to run "the due west line till it meets his majesty's other governments," the question arose as to the western termination of this line. Connecticut and Massachusetts had established their western boundaries twenty miles east of Hudson's River, thus establishing the eastern line of the Province of New York. It was held that New Hampshire would meet "his majesty's other governments" on this line of the other provinces. Accordingly Surveyor Hazzen ran his due west line with an allowance of ten degrees for the variation of the needle, to a point twenty miles east of the Hudson River, thus annexing to New Hampshire the territory of Vermont. No serious attention was given to this claim of territory for awhile, because of the French and Indian wars, which rendered any occupation of them dangerous. During a short peace, Benning Wentworth, royal governor, relying upon a description of the bounds of New Hampshire and instructions contained in his commission, granted a charter for the township of Bennington, Vt., twenty-four miles east of the Hudson. 1750. He had written to Governor Clinton of New York, informing him of his intentions to make grants of the territory in Vermont, and requested of him a description of the bounds of New York, but made his grant before the receipt of any reply. When that reply came it claimed the Connecticut River as the eastern boundary of the Province of New York according to letters patent from King Charles II to the Duke of York, and so set up a claim to the territory of Vermont. Correspondence ensued between the governors of the respective provinces, when it was agreed between them that the matter should be submitted to the king for his determination.

Governor Wentworth continued to make grants, from time to time, in the disputed territory, till the close of the French and Indian wars, when in a single year, 1761, he granted fifty-nine townships, and a greater number in the two following years. New York was alarmed and "commanded the sheriff of Albany County to make a return of all persons who had taken possession of land under New Hampshire Grants and claimed jurisdiction to the Connecticut River." Governor Wentworth issued a counter proclamation, designed to quiet the people in their grants.

In 1764 the king determined the western boundary of New Hampshire and the eastern boundary of New York *to be* "the western banks of Connecticut River from where it enters the Province of Massachusetts, as far north as the forty-fifth degree of Latitude."

This decision, while it ended one controversy, opened the way for others. The words "to be" the boundary are capable of two quite different interpretations. New York took the words in this sense—that the Connecticut River had *always been* the boundary between the two provinces. Another party held that from the time of the decision onward the Connecticut was *to be* the boundary. It makes a great difference which interpretation of the words is adopted. If the first, then the government of New Hampshire had no right to make these grants west of the Connecticut, for the territory did not belong to her, and the people on those lands must seek a renewal of their charters at the hands of New York, with consequent expense and trouble. If the other interpretation is correct, then the people on the New Hampshire grants west of the Connecticut might remain undisturbed in their possessions as having received them by due authority.

Another opening for controversy for our own days was left in the words "western banks of the Connecticut." What is the exact line pointed out by those words? The meeting of the soil and the water? If so, whether at high, medium, or low water? It is a singular fact that this point, so likely to produce controversy, has never received an authoritative determination.

New York took the first interpretation of the words "to be," and required those who had received grants under New Hampshire to renew their charters, with new fees and a higher rate of quit-rent. The people resisted these claims, peaceably at first, and finally with force of arms. This is one element in the great controversy.

New Hampshire abstained from further grants, but turned an inquiring eye now and then upon the New Hampshire grants west of Connecticut River.

Soon the Revolution came and with it a dissolution of royal authorities and decisions, and involved new relations of the parties to the contest.

There had been a growing discontent in some of the towns on the east side of the Connecticut. The first public utterance of it took place in town meeting, February 1, 1776:

Qust. Whither this meeting will Resolve to pursue the Present Plan Proposed in warning for the Redress of their grievances and choose a Com^{tee} to Correspond with other towns on that subject

Resolved in the Affirm^{tive}.

What are these grievances? The warning is lost—and there is no further reference to them in the records.

From other sources we learn what these grievances are. The following towns met in convention of delegates at College Hall, Hanover, July 31, 1776: Plainfield, Lebanon, Enfield (alias Relhan), Canaan, Cardigan, Hanover, Lyme, Orford, Haverhill, Bath, and Landaff. Nehemiah Estabrook of Lebanon was chairman and Bezaleel Woodward, professor in Dartmouth College, was clerk. They issued an address, from which we learn the grievances of which they complained.

It should be remembered that New Hampshire had at this time declared her independence, and had assumed self-government.

After a reference to the subsisting struggle of the colonies with England, the address enumerates the causes of their complaints:

That a convention, elected, much as it chanced to happen, under our then broken and confused circumstances, assumed to determine how the present assembly should be elected, omitting some towns, uniting others, for the purpose of sending one only; granting to some the liberty of sending one and to others two representatives, and others three, limiting the choice of representatives to persons of £200 estate, by this means depriving many towns of any representation, and others so in effect.

In reply to objections to this complaint they say: That every town has a right to a voice in the formation of a government, whether it be large or small; "that no person or body corporate can be deprived of any natural or acquired right without forfeiture or voluntary surrender, neither of which can be pretended in this case;" that to unite a number of towns for the purpose of choosing a representative is as absurd as "to take the souls of a number of different persons and say they make but one, while yet they remain separate and different." To consent to be governed by a body elected in this way is, they say, to accept in their towns the very thing against which they are contending abroad—taxation without representation.

They further complain of the acts of the assembly: That they, thus unequally elected, had chosen from among themselves a certain number to be called a council, thus dividing the representative body into two parts, which was an act for which they had no instruction from their constituents.

That in future elections to the council, they direct that twelve persons shall be elected as follows: Five in the county of Rockingham, two in the county of Hillsborough, two in the county of Strafford, two in the county of Cheshire, and one in the county of Grafton, while they claim that the council should be chosen from the colony at large instead of apportioning them among the counties.

They complain that one portion of the state is seeking to aggrandize itself at the expense of the other; that their petitions and remonstrances have been treated with neglect and contempt.

These, then, were their grievances. Some of them were well founded, as to inequality of representation. It is to be noticed that up to this period, 1776, there never had been any representative to the assembly chosen from Lebanon. It appears, however, that Nehemiah Estabrook sat in the convention at Exeter, though I find no record of his choice by the town. Lebanon was classed, first, with Hanover, Enfield, Canaan, Cardigan [Orange], and Grafton. In 1776 it appearing that these towns had inhabitants enough for two representatives, Lebanon was classed with Enfield and Grafton. It does not appear that there was any inequality in the apportionment of the representatives according to numbers, but they contended that *every* town ought to have at least one representative.

In addition to these things there was little sympathy between the people in the eastern and western portions of the state. They were different in their origin, in their ways of thinking and acting. The eastern settlements were much older and somewhat aristocratic. The western towns, not without some show of reason, felt that they were despised, or at least not properly estimated.

This address and the action of many of the towns refusing to have any dealings with New Hampshire, produced some effect upon the assembly, and a committee was appointed to visit Grafton County and take under consideration their complaints and propose some measures to give them content. This committee reported conciliatory measures. But the attention of the people was suddenly diverted to other matters.

This state of mind of the people in the border towns should be kept in mind as a cause of their subsequent action. They were already disaffected towards New Hampshire for reasons altogether foreign to the Vermont controversy.

The people of Vermont would undoubtedly have submitted quietly to the rule of New York if they had been left undisturbed in their possessions. But that colony was not wise enough to pursue a conciliatory policy. The temptation to gain was great, and the authorities fell before it. They began to regrant land already held under grants from New Hampshire, demanding new fees and larger rents. This produced great excitement and distress. They remonstrated—the oppressions continued. They began to resist the authorities by force. They organized bands who administered summary punishment with beech rods to all who renewed their charters from New York. Various conventions of the towns were called, when finally, January 15, 1777, it was unanimously resolved that the district of land, commonly called and known as the New Hampshire grants, be a new and separate state. They immediately informed the Continental Congress of this action, gave their reasons for it, and asked for recognition as a sovereign state. New York remonstrated against any such recognition. Congress received the papers from both parties and "ordered that they lie on the table."

The new state proceeded with its organization, with a stern determination to maintain its independence. Congress would not recognize the new state, but did recognize some of its citizens so far as to appoint them to military commands, among them Col. Seth Warner, who had raised soldiers for the defence of the country. This gave great offence to New York. But both Congress and the state were doing better than they knew, for when Ticonderoga "was given up" and the whole region left open to the enemy, these companies of Vermont proved invaluable for the defence of that exposed territory.

The surrender of Ticonderoga and the invasion of Burgoyne's army, for the moment, arrested the action of the contending parties. All was alarm and confusion. The people of the new state saw their dearly bought and bravely defended homes desolated by a ruthless enemy. They must have immediate assistance or all must be lost. Detachments from Burgoyne's army were marching in all directions. Where should they seek assistance? Not from New York, who had claimed authority over them, for they were rebels against that jurisdiction. Besides that colony was fully occupied with its own dangers. Not from the Continental Congress, who had ordered their papers to "lie on the table," who were too far away and too slow. They had received their lands from New Hampshire; they never had any reason to complain of her rule over them, and to New Hampshire they naturally applied.

Ira Allen, secretary of the council for Vermont, wrote, July 15, 1777, from Manchester, Vt., to the Committee of Safety for New Hampshire, a most urgent request for assistance, vividly representing the condition of the people in the new state; that some of the towns were disposed to accept the protection of the British authorities, very freely offered, while the others must remain as captives to see their possessions destroyed or must forsake all and flee to other states.

This request was laid before the New Hampshire assembly, July 19, 1777, then convened at Exeter. What should be done? This people were in danger. It was best to help them. They had been formerly under the authority of New Hampshire; they were living in a territory which she had claimed, and so sympathy enforced their patriotism. If no assistance was granted, the people of Vermont would be driven away from their lands and New Hampshire would become a frontier and sustain all the resulting disadvantages of that position. New Hampshire had been deprived of this portion of her possessions by royal decree; that authority was now put in question, practically annulled; by this assistance a foundation might be laid to reassert her jurisdiction over this lost province.

Under the impulse of these mixed and powerful motives, the assembly took immediate and energetic action. The militia was called out and directed to rendezvous at Charlestown. They were placed under the command of General Stark, and marched to meet the invading forces. August 16, 1777, the battle of Bennington was fought, many of the invading forces captured, the rest driven away, and the threatened people of Vermont were left in possession of their homes, and had leisure to perfect their organization as a state and press their claims for recognition.

The managers of the infant state were very able and shrewd men, fully the equals, if not the superiors, of their contemporaries. Among them may be named Governor Chittenden, Ethan and Ira Allen. Disappointed in their hope of recognition from Congress, they began to take means to strengthen their own position. It was known that some of the towns east of the Connecticut were dissatisfied with their relations to New Hampshire. Communications were secretly held with them, and they were solicited and encouraged to cast in their lot with the new state.

The towns of New Hampshire, receiving no redress of what they called their grievances, soured towards New Hampshire, rejecting her jurisdiction, were just in the frame of mind to listen to these advances on the part of Vermont. That state took care that the people on this side the river should be supplied with information. Various conventions were held and the matter discussed thoroughly. We learn the attitude of this town in relation to the matter from the following action taken in town meeting, March 31, 1778:

A Pamphet Containing the constitution of the State of Vermont being Read in said meeting—Voted, unanimously, to accept thereof, with the several articles of alteration proposed to be made therein by the Convention of Com^tees from a Considerable Number of Towns on the Grants east of Connecticut river & to concur with such Towns as are Disposed, on said Easterly Grants, in the proposed union with the aforesaid state of Vermont.

That Deacon Estabrook & John Wheatley be a committee to Represent the town of Lebanon in the proposed Convention of Com^tees of a Number of towns on the Grants east of Connecticut River to be held in Lebanon in May next.

No records of the doings of this convention at Lebanon are now known, but events show that the sixteen towns of New Hampshire determined to connect themselves with Vermont, and appointed a committee to represent their wishes before the General Assembly of that state.

The General Assembly of Vermont, sitting at Bennington, June 11, 1778, having heard the representation of the committee from the New Hampshire towns . . .

that they are not connected with any State with respect to their internal police, and that sixteen Towns in the northwestern part of said Grants have assented to a union with this state agreeable to articles mutually agreed upon by this Assembly and a committee from the grants east of said river as by said Articles on file may more fully appear:

Therefore Voted and Resolved that the sixteen Towns above referred to—viz. Cornish, Lebanon, Enfield, Dresden [Hanover], Canaan, Cardigan [Orange], Lime, Apthorp [Littleton and Dalton], Orford, Piermont, Haverhill, Bath, Lyman, Gauthwaite [Lisbon], Morristown [Franconia], and Landaff, be and hereby are entitled to all the privileges and immunities vested in any Town within this state

They also voted to receive any other contiguous to these towns where a majority of the town should consent to the union.

After this vote of the Vermont assembly, a convention was held in Orford, June 25, 1778, to take final steps to dissolve their connection with New Hampshire, as appears from the following letter with its well-known signature:

Orford, June 25th 1778

Honble Sir—

The Convention of Committees from the several Towns mentioned in the inclosed Copies take this opportunity to transmit to you as President of the State of New Hampshire a Resolve of the Assembly of the State of Vermont relative to a union of the said Towns with them, by which you will be avail'd of the political situation of these United Towns and others on the grants who may comply with said Resolve. We hope that not withstanding an entire seperation has now taken place between your State and those Towns, an amicable settlement may be come into at a proper time between the State of New Hampshire and those towns on the Grants that unite with the state of Vermont relative to all civil and military affairs transacted in connection with the State of New Hampshire since the commencement of the present war to the time of union, so that Amity and Friendship may subsist and continue between the two States.

I am, Sir, in behalf of said Convention with respect,

Your most obedient Humble Servant

Nehemiah Estabrook Chairman

To the Honble Mesheck Weare Esq.
President of the Council of New Hampshire

At this point it is necessary to take notice of the reasoning by which these towns and others justified their bold step in severing their connection with New Hampshire.

From the time the colonies cast off the royal authority there had been much speculation and discussion as to the resulting state of the people in their political relations. How *far* were these relations affected by the severance of the tie which bound them to the mother country? They rejected all *authority* over their affairs. But were all former royal acts and decrees and grants made void? These are serious questions, deeply affecting the interest of the people, and difficult to determine. Upon the different opinions held in regard to these matters much of the action of the times was based.

Early in 1778 appeared a pamphlet, printed at Danvers, and signed a "True Republican," which discussed these questions in a very earnest way, and exerted a powerful influence over the minds of the people. The author is unknown and the pamphlet is a very rare one—only a single copy is known, found in the library of the Massachusetts historical rooms. Very likely other copies might be found by search among old papers in garrets.

The reasoning of this address is here given: That the grants and jurisdiction over them were created by royal authority, expressed through commissions; that they were maintained without the consent of the people, and that when the power which gave vitality to these grants is overthrown they no longer have any force; that lines and boundaries established by royal decrees were of no effect when the royal will could no longer enforce them; that jurisdiction over a people who had not been consulted, nor had consented thereto, must cease so soon as the force which maintained it was overthrown. He argues that the Revolution overthrew all royal authority and decrees; that power reverted to the people; that they went back into "a state of Nature." This last phrase had great influence over the minds of the people. It became a favorite phrase and seemed to them weighted with unanswerable argument. By this phrase they seemed to indicate the condition of a community who have no political relations to any sovereign power, but who are at liberty to choose under what government they will live; that until such a choice is made and guarded by mutual compacts they were entirely their own masters.

Others held essentially the same views with some important modifications: That while the Revolution overthrew most of the royal decrees, the town organizations were left intact, "which they received from the King as little grants or charters of privileges by which they were united in little incorporated bodies with certain powers and privileges, which were not held at the pleasure of the King (as those commissions were), but were perpetual." These primary organizations were to be considered as indestructible, unless voluntarily abandoned by the people themselves. It was contended that through these they might maintain order; that by a majority vote of the inhabitants they might connect themselves with any larger government which they might approve, or remain independent.

It was further asserted by those on the east side of the Connecticut that the towns which received grants of townships from royal governments were differently situated from those who were within the bounds of the Masonian grant. It was argued that authority over territory outside of the Masonian grant was wholly claimed by royal commissions; that the bounds of that authority were changed from time to time at the royal pleasure, as when he limited the Province of New Hampshire to the western banks of the Connecticut River, so that when the power which gave force and vitality to that authority was overthrown, the people became independent; that the people of the Masonian grant had erected themselves voluntarily into a distinct government, with prescribed bounds, by petitioning for a separate government, which the people on the grants had never done, and they, therefore, claimed the right to choose their own government—to give their allegiance where they thought fit.

Whatever may be thought of the soundness of this reasoning it was wonderfully effective in those days in the minds of many. They took their stand upon its soundness and by it were influenced to the boldest action.

It was this reasoning which led the people of the New Hampshire grants west of the Connecticut to cast off the authority of New York and declare themselves a free and sovereign state. First, they were placed under the authority of New Hampshire by the force of royal commissions; next, by royal decrees they were annexed to New York. In neither case were they consulted,—had no voice in their transfers from one to another authority any more than if they had been beasts or goods or chattels. The authority which had thus assumed to dispose of them had been overthrown and the right, which had always been theirs, of self-disposal came actually into their hands as towns, and they had the right to choose their future connections.

The sixteen towns, with others, taking this view of their condition after the Revolution, already dissatisfied by their grievances with New Hampshire, influenced by neighborly sympathy with the struggling young state, many of the inhabitants being old friends and neighbors from Connecticut, joined themselves with Vermont.

We find the town voting a tax of £8 as their share of "the public expense arising from the compleation of the union with Vt."

On July 7, 1778, "Voted that Maj. Slapp procure a coppy of an act passed by the State of Vermont for Regulating Taverns and preventing Tipling houses." These matters, from the frequent reference to them in the records, seem to have given the fathers a great deal of trouble.

At the same meeting, acting in their sovereign capacity as a town, they appointed John Wheatley a justice of the peace till the session of the assembly of Vermont, in October next.

Although there is no record of any choice, by the town, of representatives, it appears from other records that Nehemiah Estabrook and John Wheatley took their seats in the Vermont assembly October, 1778. The question came up what should be done with the towns which had united with the state from the east side of the Connecticut. The assembly voted on these questions:

Whether the counties in this state shall remain as they were established by this assembly at their session in March last? Yeas, 35; nays, 26.

Whether the towns east of the river, included in the union with this state, shall be included in the county of Cumberland? Yeas, 28; nays, 33.

Whether the towns on the east side of the Connecticut River, who are included by union within this state, shall be erected into a distinct county by themselves? Yeas, 28; nays, 33.

If the sixteen towns could not be included in any existing county, nor erected into a county by themselves, it was at least

WILLIAM P. GALLUP.

a hint that there was no place for them in the new state. The representatives from the sixteen towns so understood it, and after a manly protest against the action of the assembly, retired.

Lebanon, by a vote December 1, 1778, approved the action of her representative.

The people of these towns were evidently deeply disappointed by this action of the Vermont assembly. They had cut themselves loose from New Hampshire and their privileges under that jurisdiction, and united with Vermont in good faith, only to be summarily rejected. They had only a town organization— no place of records, no courts, no protection, except that furnished by themselves.

What is the meaning of this sudden change on the part of Vermont? They had at least encouraged this alliance, solemnly ratified it only in June preceding, had covenanted that these towns should have all the rights and privileges of the state, and yet deny them in such a way as to exclude them.

Self-interest is the key to this unexpected action.

Upon the report of the union of these towns, Mesheck Weare, president of New Hampshire, wrote, August 19, 1778, to the delegates in Congress from that state, protesting against the action of Vermont and of the towns east of the Connecticut, asserting that there was a respectable minority in the towns averse to any such transfer of their allegiance, and claimed protection from New Hampshire; that the proceeding had excited so much feeling that there was likely to be bloodshed, and requesting the delegates to secure the interference of Congress.

President Weare wrote also, August 22, 1778, to Governor Chittenden of Vermont, claiming the sixteen towns as an integral part of New Hampshire, and protesting against their reception by Vermont. He says further:

Were not those towns settled and cultivated under the grant of the governor of New Hampshire? Are they not within the lines thereof as settled by the King of Great Britain, prior to the present era? Is there any ascertaining the boundaries between any of the United States of America, but by the lines formerly established by the authority of Great Britain? I am sure there is not. Did not the most of these towns send delegates to the Convention of this state in the year 1775? Have they not, from the commencement of the present war applied to the state of New Hampshire for assistance and protection? It is well known that they did—and that New Hampshire, at their own expense, hath supplied them with arms and ammunition &c to a very great amount as well as paid soldiers for their particular defence and all at their request, as members of this state. Whence, then, could this new doctrine that they are not connected with us originate?

Here we have the argument on the other side. It is to be noticed that British authority is cited or denied as is most for the interest of the parties.

The president gives a diplomatic hint in the closing part of his letter far more effective than his argument:

When I consider the circumstances of the people west of the Connecticut River, the difficulties they encountered in their first settlement, their late endeavors to organize government among themselves, and the *uncertainty of their being admitted as a separate State*, I am astonished that they should supply their enemies with arguments against them, by their connecting themselves with people whose circumstances are wholly different from their own, and who are actually members of the state of New Hampshire.

The controlling aim of Vermont at this time was recognition from Congress as a sovereign state. The hint of President Weare, that her action in receiving the towns from New Hampshire might stand in the way of this recognition, produced its intended effect. The governor and council of Vermont were alarmed. They thought it possible that they had made a mistake in taking the New Hampshire towns into union with themselves. To be certain of this, Gen. Ethan Allen was dispatched to Philadelphia to ascertain what effect this action of theirs had produced upon Congress. Upon his arrival he found that the New Hampshire delegation had already introduced a protest against the action of Vermont in respect to the New Hampshire towns. He took pains to learn the general feeling of Congress concerning the proceeding and thus reports it:

From what I have heard and seen of the disapprobation at Congress, of the union with sundry towns east of Connecticut River, I am sufficiently authorized to offer it as my opinion that, except this state recede from such union, immediately, the whole power of the Confederacy of the United States of America, will join to annihilate the State of Vermont, and to vindicate the right of New Hampshire, and to maintain inviolate the articles of confederation which guarantee to each state their privileges and immunities.

This it was which caused that sudden change of disposition in the Vermont assembly towards the sixteen towns, so lately cordially received, and led to that rather unmanly way of informing them that their presence was not desired.

But the towns, though disappointed, were not discouraged. A convention was called at Cornish, December 9, 1778, to take into consideration their situation and to determine what action they would take. The convention was composed of delegates from twenty-two towns—eight of the towns were on the west side of the Connecticut River.

The convention seems to have finally adopted the proposals of a committee appointed to take into consideration the condition of the New Hampshire grants on both sides of the Connecticut. The majority of that committee were Jacob Bailey of Newbury, Vt., Elisha Payne of Orange, and Beza Woodward, professor of Dartmouth College. These proposals were as follows:

1. To agree upon and settle a dividing line between New Hampshire and the Grants, by committee from each party, or otherwise, as they may mutually agree.

Or 2, that the parties mutually agree in the appointment of a Court of Commissioners of disinterested judicious men of the three other New England states to hear and determine the dispute.

Or 3 that the whole dispute with New Hampshire be submitted to the decision of Congress in such way and manner as Congress shall prescribe;

Provided always that the Grants be allowed equal privileges with the other party in espousing and conducting their cause.

Or 4, if the controversy cannot be settled on either of the foregoing articles, and in case we can agree with New Hampshire upon a plan of government, inclusive of extent of territory, that we unite with them and become with them one entire state, rejecting the line arbitrarily drawn on the western bank of the Connecticut river by the King of Great Britain in 1764.

They further requested the towns of Vermont to withdraw the vote which cast out the towns from the east side of the river, and that all other towns join them in the foregoing proposition to New Hampshire.

Messrs. Marsh, Woodward, Morey, Child, Payne, Olcot and Bailey were appointed a committee to receive proposals from other towns.

There seem to be two main purposes in these propositions,

one to make a state out of the grants on both sides of the Connecticut, the other to make a state out of New Hampshire as limited to the Masonian grant and the whole of the New Hampshire grants. But there was undoubtedly a secret purpose in the minds of the chief actors underlying both propositions, and that purpose was that the *capital of the state, however constructed, should be somewhere on the Connecticut.* Ira Allen, who says he was providentially (?) at the convention, writes "at or near the college."

The following papers show the attitude of the people of Lebanon towards these propositions:

With Respect to the Question proposed by the Com^tee Chosen at Cornish in Dec. Last (viz) whether the people on the Grants or in this town are willing that the State of New Hampshire should Extend their Claim and jurisdiction over the whole of the Grants, N. H. at the same time submitting to Congress whether a New state shall be Established on the Grants—upon which motion we would observe

1st that New Hampshire Never had any Right of Jurisdiction (either by Charter or Compact) over the N. H. Grants (so called, therefore their attempting to Extend their jurisdiction over any part of s'd Grants, without the free and full Consent of the inhabitants on s'd Grants is such a stretch of arbitrary power, as we Conceive to be incompatable with the Natural and Just Rights of a free people

2nd And as the assembly of N. H. have not yet Determined to submit to Congress whether a N [new] state shall be Erected on the Grants or not, we think We Cannot Consistent with the principles held up to publick view by the Dissenting towns on s'd Grants Consent that the State of N. H. should Extend their Jurisdiction over the whole or any part of s'd Grants—Yet, Nevertheless

3dly if the State of N. H. are Desirous to Extend or set up their Claim over the whole of s'd Grants, in Opposition to the State of N. York in order to Facillatate the Establishment of a New State on s'd Grants we are free to Concede thereto, or

4thly if the state of N. H. will agree with the people on s'd Grants upon an Equitable plan of Government in which the Just and Natural Rights of the people shall be inviobly maintained & supported we are, on our part willing to unite with them and become one Entire state.

At a town Meeting of the Legal inhabitants of the Town of Lebanon Holden May 24th 1779 was taken under Consideration the Questions Purposed in a hand bill Published by a comitee at Dresden Apr 23 1779 and Resolved that the town Esteams no Consideration as an Equivalent to the Priviledg of an Equatable Representation—and not being favored with Gen. Bayleys Report are unable to pass any further Resolve upon said Question, it Being in our view foreign from the Prinsapel object in view under our Present Dispute With New Hampshire it being farther from our intention to Coaless with any state without our Inviolable Wrights and Privileges are made first Certain and as to advise New Hampshire concerning Extending jurisdiction—we look upon that to be a falacious Request—Calculated to Bring the Good people on the Grants into a Perpetual unrepresented situation that may be fattall to our Wrights and Liberties

According to votes of the convention a proposal to New Hampshire was made in March, 1779, to extend her jurisdiction over the whole of the grants on both sides of the river. The proposal met with ready acceptance on the part of the assembly, but in order to give time for due consideration it was postponed till the next session. June 24, 1779, the assembly voted that they would lay claim to the whole of the New Hampshire grants, so called, unless Congress should erect Vermont into a separate state. At all events, they would exercise jurisdiction as far as the Connecticut River.

Of course this action on the part of New Hampshire created fresh alarm and anxiety on the part of Vermont. Her difficulties were still further complicated by the action of towns in the southeastern portion of the state, who proposed to continue their allegiance to New York.

All these matters finally came before Congress for settlement. They appointed a committee to visit the disturbed region and report. A part of the committee came and made some inquiries, but seem not to have made any report. Congress heard and considered and delayed—and finally dismissed the whole subject for a time and left all parties in doubt and confusion.

On July 16, 1779, a convention was called at Dresden (Dartmouth College), at which the town was represented by Nehemiah Estabrook and Captain Turner. What was done at that convention does not appear from any records.

December 22, 1779, the town voted a tax of £200 to defray the expense of an agent or agents to represent the circumstances of the people on the New Hampshire grants before Congress on the first day of February, 1780.

Congress failed to do anything to give relief to the people at that time, but later in the year gave good advice, cautioning the people against disorders, and enjoining patience till all parties were prepared for a hearing. September 9 seems to have been appointed as a time for a final hearing.

Meantime all parties were making appeals to Congress and new projects discussed. Among them was one from Dresden, which seems to have been the birthplace of many projects, said to be the result of a convention held there. It is called the petition of the principal inhabitants on both sides of the Connecticut River, and is addressed to Congress. It sets forth the desirability of annexing Canada to the United States, and represents the project as feasible and not at all difficult!

At the same convention Colonel Olcot of Norwich, Vt., was appointed agent to represent the people on both sides of the Connecticut River from Charlestown upward. The sentiment of the people in this region on both sides of the river at this time seems to have been setting strongly towards union with New Hampshire.

In September, Congress took up these questions, and, as usual, delayed any decision. All parties became impatient, nearly to desperation. Vermont was determined to maintain her independence and secure a recognition. Since all previous arguments had failed, a new move of diplomacy was made. She began to coquette with the British authorities, intimating that as no place could be found for her in the Union, she might cast in her lot with her former sovereign. It is not easy to determine how far these intrigues were carried, but certainly to the very verge of discretion.

They awakened the gravest suspicions of fidelity on the part of the Americans, and created great alarm. The British authorities were led on with confident hopes of regaining that important territory. They made liberal offers, were careful to treat all captives with great kindness, frequently sending them back to their homes to speak the praises of their lenity. There is little doubt that those raids of Indians and others at this time, which made it necessary for Lebanon and the other towns to employ so many scouts, was another part of their policy. They designed to keep the inhabitants in such a state of anxiety and alarm, to put them to so much trouble and expense in guarding themselves, as to discourage and weary them, and lead them to conclude that it would be best for them to make peace with their enemies, and so gain opportunity to care for their fields and homes. There is no doubt but that the Allens were the leaders in these negotiations.

To complicate matters still more, another movement was made to form a new state, originating this time in the southern portion of the grants on both sides of the river. After several preliminary meetings a general convention of towns on both sides of the river was called at Charlestown, in January, 1781.

This town voted, December 25, 1780, "to accept of the motion made By the County of Cheshire. Voted that Lieut Elihu Hyde be a Delegate to attend the Convention at Charlestown, Jan. next."

The convention assembled at Charlestown, January 16, 1781. Forty-three towns from both sides of the river were represented. All the parties interested sent agents to watch, guide and control affairs, if possible, in their own interest. A large and able committee was appointed to prepare the business of the convention. That committee reported January 17 in favor of a union of all the towns on the grants with the state of New Hampshire, a result which was expected from the tone of the preliminary meetings. The agents of New Hampshire "were much pleased with their success and well enjoyed the night." The agents of New York were in no wise downcast, for it is suspected that there was a secret understanding between New Hampshire and New York that they would share the territory of Vermont between them, making the ridge of the Green Mountains the boundary of the two states.

But Vermont? It is manifest that this measure, if consummated, would be fatal to her interest. She could not afford to lose so many towns on her own side of the Connecticut. It was probable that many more towns would be persuaded to join the movement. Thus, shorn of so much of her domain, she could present her claims to Congress with little hope of recognition as an independent state. But what can be done to arrest the movement or to turn it in her favor? It seems a hopeless task. But one of her ablest sons is present at that convention, watching with eagle eyes its proceedings. He has come prepared for all emergencies, for he has the certificate of a delegate in his pocket, though he has not presented it. His skill has never forsaken him, he never loses heart. He is equal to the crisis in the fate of his beloved state. He inspires a motion that the report shall "be recommitted to be corrected and fitted for the press, as it would be a matter of public notoriety" and of great importance. The report is recommitted and Ira Allen does not sleep much that night. What arguments he uses, what considerations he presents, what motives he presses, cannot now be known. But when the next morning, January 19, at 10 o'clock, the report of the committee, "corrected and prepared for the press," is presented, behold, Vermont is substituted for New Hampshire and union with the first state instead of the latter state is recommended.

The report is adopted by a large majority. Eleven delegates from eight towns on the east of the Connecticut, most of them members of the New Hampshire assembly, dissenting and protesting.

The secret of this marvelous change of front is undoubtedly this: Certain prominent men in that convention had never abandoned the scheme of the capital of a state somewhere on the Connecticut River. When they planned for a union with New Hampshire they thought that they would so far extend her territory westward as to bring its center to the Connecticut. Just then, a suggestion is made to them that Vermont is willing to claim jurisdiction up to the line of Mason's grant. That suggestion is made by Ira Allen. It is now a question of probabilities, of the realization of their favorite scheme. New Hampshire has a capital already. Vermont has none, but is migratory. The large numerical majority of population in New Hampshire is in the eastern portion of the state and they would resist the removal of the seat of government so far to the west. Vermont has no concentrated population; it is more numerous in the Connecticut Valley than elsewhere—the balance of probabilities is with Vermont, and with her they would cast their lot.

Before the convention adjourned they appointed a committee to treat with the Vermont assembly and arrange for a union, and then adjourned, "to meet at Cornish N. H. Feb. 8 1781 opposite to Windsor Vt. where the Assembly would be in session."

February 10, 1781, Col. Elisha Payne presented to the Vermont assembly the request of the towns represented in the con-

HON. GEORGE S. TOWLE.

vention at Charlestown—Cornish to be received into union with that state. The assembly prepared the way for their reception by resolving that "in order to quiet the disturbances on the two sides of the river (Connecticut), and the better to enable the inhabitants on the two sides of the river to defend their frontier, the Legislature of this state do lay a *jurisdictional claim* to all the lands whatever east of Connecticut river, north of Massachusetts, west of the Mason line and south of latitude 45° and that they do not exercise jurisdiction for the time being." The latter is a saving clause, looking cautiously to future contingencies.

The terms of union were mutually agreed upon and confirmed February 22, 1781. By these terms the towns were to be received whenever they, by a majority vote, accepted them.

At a town meeting held March 13, 1781:

The several Articles of Union, Agreed upon By the Assembly Comtee of the state of Vermont & the Comtee of Convention from the County of Cheshire and Grafton &c being Read in s'd meeting was agreed to, Nem. Con. & Voted that Col. Elisha Payne and Lieut. Elihu Hyde Represent the town of Lebanon in the Assembly of Vermont to be Holden in Windsor the first Wednesday in April next.

Colonel Payne had from the beginning been a leader in all these affairs, being a resident of Cardigan (Orange), until this time, when he came to East Lebanon and built extensive mills there.

The following towns were formally admitted to union with Vermont at the session of the assembly at Windsor in April: Acworth, Alstead, Bath, Cardigan, Charlestown, Chesterfield, Claremont, Cornish, Croydon, Dresden, Enfield, Gilsum, Grafton, Gunthwaite, Hanover, Haverhill, Hinsdale, Landaff, Lebanon, Lempster, Lyman, Lyme, Marlow, Morristown, New Grantham, Newport, New Stamford, Orford, Piermont, Plainfield, Richmond, Saville, Surry, Walpole and Westmoreland.

But the measure designed "to quiet the disturbances on the two sides of the Connecticut river," resulted in anything but quiet. New Hampshire did not see her domain rent from her without vigorous protests and action. In many of the towns there was a strong minority who still clung to their former allegiance. As each state claimed jurisdiction over the same territory by the appointment of officers, institution of courts, and levying of taxes, collisions of a serious nature were inevitable. Vermont took possession of the records of the court of common pleas at Keene, N. H. New Hampshire protested and resisted. New Hampshire officers were arrested by Vermont officers and each was rescued by mobs of their friends. Vermont was charged with exchanging British soldiers taken in arms for private citizens. New Hampshire complained that in her dismembered condition she could not comply with the requisitions of Congress for soldiers and provisions.

The minority complained that they were not allowed to express their sentiments at the polls if in favor of New Hampshire. Some were threatened and insulted and forced to leave their homes and possessions because of their fidelity to New Hampshire. New Hampshire ordered the arrest of any person who took office under Vermont. Vermont imprisoned a New Hampshire sheriff. New Hampshire imprisoned a Vermont sheriff. New Hampshire ordered out the militia to release her sheriff. Vermont gave orders to Elisha Payne, as major general of her forces, to call out her militia and to resist force by force. Letters of remonstrances, protests and threats passed between the governors. Affairs were in as disturbed a condition as can well be imagined, and could not continue so without injury to the parties concerned and to the whole country.

While some of these collisions were of a serious nature and threatened bloodshed, others assumed a comical aspect, as in the following detailed experience of Colonel Hale, a New Hampshire officer. He had arrested a certain 'Squire Giles, who was rescued by the people at Charlestown. The sheriff shall tell his story in his own way:

> They son after held a Consultation for Taking and Carrying me to Bennington, but fearing that would not so well sute, they sent me their Judas to advise me as a frind to make my escape, immediately, to avoid Going to Bennington. I gave for Answer, if that was their intention I would Tarry all night. But in the morning I had a second message that they would be Ready for me in half an hower. I gave for Answer, that that would be time enough for me to take breakfast—which I then called for—and after breakfast I had another message that if I did not make my Escape they would Catch me before I got three miles, for

which I should be very sorry. I gave for answer that I should have the less way to come back—but that if I was not molisted I ment to set out for hom son, but finding that all their stratigems would not Prevent my Taking breakfast and leaving the Town in an open and Publick manner, they then Rallied all their forces that was Near at hand to the amount of about forty men and a Pretended deputy Sheriff at their head; but for a frunt Gard they Raised some of their most abeelist women and set forward with some men dressed in Women's apparill, which had the good Luck to take me Prisnor, put me aboard one of their slays and filled the same with some of their principal women and drove off nine miles to Williams tavern in Warlpole, the main body following after with acclimations of Joy—where they Regailed themselves; and then set me at liberty, nothing doubting but that they had entirely subdued New Hampshire! Prov. Papers, Vol X, pp. 481, 482.

Meanwhile all parties professed their willingness to submit to Congress all matters in dispute between them. Congress took up the matter, appointed committees to investigate and report, discussed and delayed, balanced between opposing interests. By August 20, 1781, it had proceeded so far as to declare by resolution that before they could recognize Vermont as a state they must "explicitly relinquish all demands of land and jurisdiction on the east side of Connecticut river, and on the west side of a line drawn twenty miles eastward of Hudson river to Lake Champlain."

Vermont assembly, sitting at Charlestown, October 19, 1781, declares that they were determined "to remain firm in the principles on which they first assumed government, and to hold the articles of union inviolate; that they would not submit the question of their independence to the arbitrament of any power whatever; but they were willing at present to refer the question of their jurisdictional boundary to commissioners mutually chosen, and when they should be admitted into the American union they would submit any such disputes to Congress."

The matter still lingered in Congress, when early in January, 1782, General Washington was prevailed upon to write a letter unofficially to Governor Chittenden of Vermont. In that letter Washington recommends a compliance with the requirements of Congress in abandoning all territory east of the Connecticut and west of a line twenty miles east of the Hudson; that only on that condition is there any prospect that the state will be received into the Union. He appeals strongly to their patriotism not to embarrass the United States in their struggle for independence, burdened already to the utmost; and finally intimates the disagreeable necessity of coercion on the part of Congress should the state continue to maintain its attitude towards the other states.

This advice was well received on the part of Vermont, and was effectual in composing the disputes about boundaries.

On the 19th of February, 1782, the Vermont assembly, being in session at Bennington, the whole matter of boundaries came up for consideration. Among other papers this letter of Washington's was read, having evidently a strong influence on their minds. On the 20th of February the assembly, being in committee of the whole, "Resolved, that in the opinion of this committee, Congress in their resolutions of the 7th and 20th of August last, in guaranteeing to the respective states of New York and New Hampshire all territory without certain limits therein expressed, have eventually determined the boundaries of this State," and they voted to relinquish the claims to the territory therein mentioned.

This action of Vermont virtually ended the great controversy, so far as boundaries were concerned.

But the towns on the east of the Connecticut must be disposed of. Vermont did not hesitate. The union was dissolved in the absence of the members from the east side of the river. Doctor Belknap says with admirable naïveté, "that when these members arrived and found themselves excluded from a seat in the Assembly, they took their leave with some expressions of bitterness."

Very likely that was the case; they certainly had some provocations for such expressions.

Probably Vermont was never very sincere in this union. Rather than lose her own towns in the movement towards New Hampshire, and see all her hopes of recognition as a sovereign state blasted, she consented to receive them with more diplomacy than cordiality. Probably "Honest deacon Moses Robertson" of Bennington unconsciously revealed the true feeling of many in Vermont when he said to General Folsom and others in an attempt to compose the dispute between the two states, "We never had it in view to take the East side of the River—only to get rid of them the first opportunity."

On the other hand there is as little doubt that New York and New Hampshire were secretly opposed to the recognition of Vermont as a state; that while they were intent in keeping their own domains from being absorbed by her, they were quietly obstructing her recognition in the hope that they might eventually divide her territory between them.

Vermont had to wait till February, 1791, before she was admitted to the Union.

This sudden secession of Vermont from union with the towns on the east side of the Connecticut left these towns in a sad condition. They had made many sacrifices and been at much expense to secure this union. They hoped for peace and prosperity under it; to be thus summarily dismissed from it while the echoes of the most solemn pledges of fidelity on her part had scarcely died away, was a sad blow to their expectations. With the burdens of the war pressing heavily upon them, with the distractions of a disputed jurisdiction, they had hitherto had little time and strength to devote to their own improvements in the surrounding wilderness. They hoped by this union to be released from one of these sources of trouble, but they are suddenly thrust back into their "state of nature," with nothing but their town organizations to rely upon for peace and order. They had rejected the rule of New Hampshire, for good reasons as they thought; pride, if nothing more, would make it difficult for them to return to that state. There was nothing left for them but to wait and watch, taking their stand upon their town organization.

It is necessary in a complete history of the town to notice their action when they were without any state connections. Of course it was necessary to have certain officers besides their usual town officers; they therefore appointed their own justices of the peace. Many of the duties of courts they committed to their committee of safety. They voted that this committee should take acknowledgments of deeds.

It was necessary that they should have laws to govern them in their daily transactions. They had rejected New Hampshire and its laws, Vermont had rejected them. They naturally turned to a code with which most of them were familiar, and which had no smell of bitterness about it—the laws of the state which held their well-remembered homes.

Voted, March 14 1780 that the Executive Authorities of the Town shall proceed in their Several Departments to persue and conform themselves to the Rules prescribed in the laws of Connecticut, Especially in those acts that more immediately refer to the preservation of the Peace and good order of the Towns, &c.

The following protest was made against the action of the town in certain matters:

Lebanon 31st March 1780

We the subscribers Inhabitants of the town of said Lebanon, who hold ourselves in duty bound to be the League Subjects of the State of Newhampshire—

Do hereby publickly remonstrate and protest against the Illegal proceedings of the Town of Lebanon (viz) the Town Voting to pay no regard To the Authority of the State of Newhampshire and that thay Would Yield no Obedience to any precept sent to them from the Authority of Said state for raising men for the defence of the United states or any otherwise—

The Town enacting Laws in town meeting repugnant to the Laws of the state and adopting the Laws of Connecticut to govern them Selves by in open violation of the authority of the state of Newhampshire. Altho they have Unanimously Acknowlidge themselves under the jurisdiction of Newhampshire by Vollentarily confiderating with said State, and the Town under a pretence of authority in a high handed manner frequently stop men in the highway Rob them of their property even when they have a Certificate from proper authority to pass unmolested and Blocking up the publick highway by falling Trees Across the path so as to Render it impractible for Travilors to pass Whereby Travilers have been much injured and to the disgrace of the Town and many Other Illegal proceedings inconsistant in themselves and injurious to the public peace of this and Neibouring Towns.—to be communicated to the Town forth with,

Saml Bailey	John Gray
Ebenr Bliss	Jabez Baldwin
Phinehas Wright	Gideon Baker
Solomon Millington	Charles Hill
James Jones	Wm Downer Jur
Elezer Robinson	Saml Millington
Joel Kilburn	James Feller
Wm Downer	Joseph Tilden
Jesse Heath	Wm Wakefield
Saml Millington	Nathaniel Hall Junr
Benga Fuller	

We are not for a moment to suspect these men of any want of patriotism in this act, for many of them had been in the army, only they thought that the town had no right to take such action without the sanction of a higher authority than the town itself.

Money was needed for public purposes—for building roads and bridges, for the support of schools, for raising soldiers for the public defense. Often they were at their wit's end to know how to assess the necessary taxes, and still more puzzled how to collect them, since there was no authority back of their own upon which they could rely. Of course there were some disposed to take advantage of this state of things and refused to pay their taxes and their debts. But they found means to enforce their payment. And yet we find them instructing their officers to exempt any who had placed themselves under the protection of the state of New Hampshire.

Let it be kept in mind that all these burdens of taxation for so many purposes were to be met by a depreciated currency, whose value was scarcely the same for two successive months. It was a hard problem to know how much money to raise in such a currency to meet their obligations and they were obliged to make a bushel of wheat their standard. Much of the time they could raise no money that had any fixed value, and were obliged to receive their dues in grain and provisions.

Men who, under such circumstances, could fight such sturdy battles for their preference for state affiliation, who could continually raise and equip men for their defense are worthy of all praise and honor. One other thing should be set down to their credit. However defiant they were of state authority, whatever expressions of bitterness they uttered at their betrayals by Vermont, they were always loyal to Congress. They heeded every command, they yielded to every requisition which came to them from that sacred source.

The following letter, addressed to Colonel Chase, indicates the position which they held:

Lebanon New Hampshire Grants July 7 1780

Sir As this Town hath been Repeatedly Called Together on account of orders Rec'd from you for scouting and other service, &c we haveing Collected the Sentiments of the Town with Regard to Raising men To Stand thus: that they acknowledge Subordination to you as a Colo. of their own Choice and ever will obey you as Such, But at the same time, think to obey you as haveing an authorative Power from the State of New Hampshire is Derogative To the Birth Rite of Englishmen, it Being a Tax Laid on us for men without being Represented &c. Sir, we wish fore the future you would Be Pleased To send a Request To us. We shall own the Power we Committed to you We mean not to Sett up an Allter in Deffiance To the Public Cause, & be Please, sir, to Excuse our Simplicity and Except this with our Sincere obedience from your Humble Servants.

       Simeon Peck   ⎫
       Theop Huntington ⎬ Selectmen
       Nath'l Storrs   ⎭

To Colo. Jona. Chase, Cornish

It was difficult in such circumstances to preserve peace and order. Some there would be ready to take advantage of the lack of organized courts and state authority to punish offences. Tippling houses, I judge, gave the fathers a great deal of trouble from the frequent mention of them upon the records and ordinances passed to regulate them; yet through their committee of safety they were able to control the disorderly elements. The people were determined to sustain their committees, and did sustain them, and there was very little serious disorder.

Having no place of records they experienced great inconvenience in the preservation of their deeds and other papers. Early in the war one Fenton, the probate officer for Grafton County, whose letter to the people of Grafton County has already been given, was suspected, probably with just cause, of too much friendship towards the king. The demonstrations against him were so violent that he fled from his home, leaving the important papers in his office in great disorder. Many of them were either carried away or destroyed, causing great perplexity and trouble among the people.

An old deed from Jane Hill, widow of Charles Hill, alludes to this event, reciting in a preamble:

& as said will was Lodged in the Judge of Probate of wills Office by said Judge's order (viz John Fenton Esq.) who has absconded himself and carried off or mislaid said will, so that it cannot be found, by reason of which the afore said estate has not yet been settled and there are several creditors who have demands on said estate, who want to have their accompts settled; in order for which there is an absolute necessity of disposing of some of said lands to answer the just de-

SALLY TRUMAN.

mands of said creditors, wherefore she, the said Jane as the sole Executor of the said last will and testament, &c.

The earlier deeds were recorded in the town, the acknowledgment being taken sometimes by a justice of the peace and sometimes by the committee of safety. Among those by whom these acknowledgments were taken are the following: John Wheatley, J. P.; Nehemiah Estabrook, chairman of committee of safety; Francis Smith, J. P., Plainfield; O. Willard, one of his majesty's justices of the peace for Cumberland County, province of New York-Vermont; Bela Turner, J. P.; Beza Woodward, Dresden; Peter Olcutt, assistant, Dresden; Elihu Hyde, J. P.; Eleazer Wheelock, J. P. Many of them are destitute of any acknowledgment. A large number were made and executed in Connecticut.

It is amusing to read the headings of these acknowledgements, showing as they do the changes in the connections of the town: State of New Hampshire, Grafton County, Lebanon; Province of N. H., Grafton County, Lebanon, on the New Hampshire Grants; State of Vermont, Lebanon; State of Vermont, on the Grants east of Connecticut River; State of Vermont, territory east of Connecticut River; State of Vermont, Windsor County, Lebanon. One officer determined to be right one way or the other, writes, "Lebanon, State of Vermont, alias New Hampshire."

At the time when the town was uncertain as to its allegiance—both as to which party it of right belonged, and where it was for the time being, some were disposed to take advantage of the circumstances and declare that there was no law that could be enforced, and that they would do as they pleased. But the people were generally, at heart, law-abiding and would not suffer any breach of equity.

The late Mrs. Truman, years ago, related to me the following incident as belonging to this period:

A certain man had bought some goods of his neighbor and refused payment, confidently declaring that payment could not be enforced. But he was mistaken. One night he found his dwelling surrounded by masked men, who led him out of doors and required him to pay his debts. He defied them. They then found an old horse, whose bony system was highly developed. They set him upon this horse in a position the reverse of that usnally chosen for equestrian exercise—facing the rear. They then ran a rail between the legs of the horse and tied the obdurate debtor by the feet to the rail and sat down on each end, which proceeding brought out an emphatic promise "to pay up." The crowd then marched him away to a distance, blowing horns and conch-shells and ringing bells.

Now on the way a couple were sleeping the sleep of the just (it is to be hoped). The wife was awakened and frightened by the noise, over which the horns predominated, which she, in her bewilderment, took to be the horn of Gabriel, when she gave a conjugal punch in the ribs of her spouse, crying out, "Wake up, husband, the day of judgment has come! Get up and put on a clean shirt."

The historian took this for a good story, which it is; but whether a tradition or myth, he knew not.

But a long time after, he discovered the following substantial verification of the whole matter:

Lebanon Newhampshire July 27 1779

To the Honble Meshack Ware and the Hon^{bl} Councel of the State of Newhampshire—

Gentlemen: your petitioners desire to inform your Honers of A late disturbance in this town: against all Laws both Humane and divine—and in defyance of the authority of the States a number of men went to the dwelling House of mr. Jams Joans in the evening of the 22^d inst. And by force and Violence toock him from his bed and bound Him on a horse with his face to the Horses tail: and he was obliged to ride in that maner four or five miles—to a tavern—they following him with Bells horns &c—at the tavern they abused him in a most Shocking maner with words and blows: then Returned about half a mile made a halt and abused him as before: Even threatening with death till He was obliged to Comply with their Ureasonable Demands, your petitioners are Very much threttened if we Say anything against Such Conduct. therefore we pray your Honers to take the mater into Considderation and Afford us Such assistance as you in your wisdom Shall think best

Jesse Heath
Saml Bailey } Com^{tt}
Charles hill

Some of the citizens of the town were far-sighted enough to understand how the conflict with New Hampshire must terminate, and to cast an anchor to the windward they presented the following petition:

To the Honble the Council & Assembly of the State of New Hampshire

We the Subscribers being Inhabitants of Lebanon in the County of Grafton and State afores^d Humbly Petition and give your Hon^rs to be Informed, that for Some Time past we have been greatly abused & harrassed by a Power, usurped without Right, to which we neither owe nor own Allegiance, and by which we have been prohibited, from Yielding that Subjection and Obedience to the State of New Hampshire which is justly due, and whereby we are deprived of those rights and Priviledges to which we are justly entitled as Subjects of s^d State, and are liable to many and great Evils and Burdens for want of that Protection, which we humbly conceive may be dutifully requested and demanded from the State of New Hampshire—

Wherefore we most humbly pray that your Hon^rs will take such Resolutions on the premises as may effectually redress the Grievances of your Petitioners and restore them to their Just Rights and & Priveledges & the Protection of said state, and may be duly represented in the Genl Assembly and have Justice administered under the Authority of the Same—

And your Pet^rs Shall ever pray &c
                    Lebanon 15th Decr 1778

Charles Hill	Benjam fuller
William Downer Jur	Simeon Hovey
Solomon Millington	Eliezer Robinson
Ebenezer Bliss	Phinehas Wright
Isaac Cory	Sam^ll Millington
Joseph Tilden Jr	Jesse Heath
Joseph Wood	Wm Wakefield
Sam^ll Bailey	William Downer
James Jones	Josiah Hovey
John Gray	James Fuller
Jabez Baldwin	

December 24 the petitioners voted to present their petition to the selectmen, and December 28 they voted

mr. william Downer their agent to pre sent S^d petition to the Honble Asembly of S^d State or in their reses to the Honble president and Council and Receive their answer

                            Jesse Heath, Clerk.

To the Honble the Gen^ll Assembly of the State of New Hamp^re To be Holden at Ports^mo in s^d State the third Wednesday of Decr Instant—

May it please Your Hon^rs

We the Subscribers Inhabitants of the Town of Lebanon in the County of Grafton in S^d State; having taken into consideration the

Several Resolves of the Honble the Continental Congress Respecting the Disputes that have Arisen about the Jurisdiction of the State of N: Hamp^re over the Hamp^re Grants (So Called) are of the Opinion that S^d Resolves implicitly declare it to be the Opinion of that August Body that that part of S^d Grants Lying East of Connecticut River (in which we are included) Should be under the Jurisdiction of the State of New Hamp^re; with which we Readily comply; and Acknowledge the same; Yet Nevertheless for us to be Obliged to pay the back State Taxes; for the time being that we have been unconnected with the State of New Hamp.^re in matters of Government, we Look upon it to be a Hardship, & Trust that your Hon^rs will Consider us in that matter, & as there is a Considerable Number of the inhabitants of this Town that wholly deny the Jurisdiction of N: Hamp^re,—if your Hon^rs should find yourselves Laid under the Disagreable Necessity of using Coercive measures, with Opposers, to your Authority we Hope that your Hon^rs will make a Specific Difference between them and Us, & we as in Duty bound Shall Ever pray

Joseph Tilden	Dan Metcalf
James Jones	Charles Tilden
Jesse Heath	Joseph Wood
Stephen Billings	Joseph Downer
Nathl Hall J^ur	Silas Waterman
Joseph Chamberlin	William Dana
Rufus Baldwin	David Hinckley
James Hartshorn	Solomon Millington
Joel Kilborn	Sherebiah Ballard
Barna Tisdale	Ziba Hall
Wm Downer	Heze Waters
David Crocker	Jno Wheatley
An^w Wheatley	Oliver Penneg
Saml Bailey	Stephen Tilden
Sam^el Millington	Thos Wells
Gid^n Baker	Phinehas Wright
Thos. Bingham	William Downer Jun
Charles Hill	Randol Evans
Simon Slapp	

SETTLEMENT OF THE CONTROVERSY.

On the 7th day of October, 1790, commissioners from the state of New York and Vermont, meeting in the City of New York, mutually agreed upon their boundaries, and other questions which had arisen, and the long dispute was terminated.

One of the conditions of their agreement was that the state of Vermont should pay to New York $30,000, to be paid to the inhabitants of New York who had suffered in their person and estate at the hands of the "Green Mountain Boy."

But this was a small compensation among the number who were to share in it, so the state of New York, taking the whole matter into consideration, passed the following resolution, introduced in the Senate and immediately concurred in by the assembly, March 1, 1786:

Resolved that the Legislature during their present meeting will make Provision for Granting to Col^o Timothy Church, Major William Shattuck, Major Henry Evans and about one hundred other Persons whom they represent, a Quantity of Vacant Lands equal to a Township of eight miles square.—Documentary History of New York, Vol. 4, p. 1017.

The township thus granted was situated on the Susquehanna River, and is now known as Bainbridge.

In closing the account of this remarkable controversy, loyalty to historical truth demands that certain statements should be made in behalf of the state of New York.

1. That the territory of Vermont was within the grant to the Duke of York, first made in 1663, regranted or confirmed in 1674, of which the Connecticut River was the eastern boundary.

2. If the validity of this grant be questioned, then by the decision of the king in council, in 1764, this boundary of the province of New York was made certain. New York had precisely the same title to the territory of Vermont that other colonies had to their territory—royal authority.

3. The province of New York made the following offers:

That all persons actually possessing and improving lands by title under grants from New Hampshire or Massachusetts bay, and not granted under New York shall be confirmed in their respective possessions

That where lands have heretofore been granted by New Hampshire and Massachusetts Bay or either of them and actually possessed in consequence thereof, and being so possessed, were, afterwards granted by New York, such possessions *shall be confirmed;* the posterior grant under New York, notwithstanding.—Documentary History of New York, Vol. 4, p. 953.

It is admitted in a proclamation of the state of New York that in some of the grants of that state as a province "the interest of the servants of the crown and of new adventurers was, in many instances contrary to justice and policy; . . . that many of the grantees labor under grievances arising from causes above mentioned, which, in some measure, extenuate their offence and which ought to be redressed."

4. While the inhabitants of Vermont suffered from the greed of some of the New Yorkers, the Vermonters themselves were unjustifiable in their opposition to the authority of the state of New York, because the soil belonged to that state.

The Vermonters treated with great harshness and cruelty the subjects of New York. They speak with apparent gaiety and glee of applying the Beech Seal to those who took grants from New York. What the beech seal was, and its mode of application, may be gathered from the following statements, made under oath.

Benjamin Hough, a magistrate under the authority of the state of New York, under the authority of a self-constituted court of Vermonters, was sentenced to be

> Tyed up to a tree, and receive two hundred lashes upon the naked Back . . . that thereupon the Deponent immediately had his Clothes taken off and he was stripped to the skin and four persons being by the said pretended Court appointed to carry the said sentence into Execution This Deponent accordingly received the two hundred lashes on his naked Back with whips of cords.—Documentary History of New York, Vol. 4, p. 896.
>
> Daniel Walker being duly sworn on the holy Evangelists of Almighty God deposed in part that a few days afterwards he met with the above said Hough. That the said Benjamin Hough showed him his naked back, which was then sore and appeared to have been much cut and wounded and the waistcoat which he then wore was stiff with Blood.

Another part of the sentence of this Hough was that "as soon as he should be able, should depart the New Hampshire Grants, and not return again upon pain of receiving five hundred lashes."

One of the offenses charged against this man was that "he had taken a commission of the peace under the government of New York and exercised his office as a magistrate for the County of Charlotte alleging that this deponent well knew that they did not allow of any Magistrate there." They did not charge him with any injustice in the exercise of his office. His offense was that he had accepted a commission from the state of New York.—Documentary History of New York, Vol. 4, p. 896.

For some time after the dissolution of the union with Vermont the town remained independent. They were not ready to return to their allegiance with New Hampshire; not until they could make acceptable terms with that state.

Aug 12 1782. Query whether they will Raife the Nine men sent for by the State of New Hampshire to Join the Continental Army? Refolv'd in the Negative

3rd Whether they will Raife one man for The Defence of the Frontiers to serve as a Soldier till Novr. next? Refolv'd in the Negative

4th Whether they will Raife the sum of £914-13-4 Demanded by the State of New Hampshire? Refolved in the Negative

5th Whether they will Choofe one or two men to Set in Convention at Concord in the afore S'd state to affist In forming a Constitution for S'd State of New Hampshire? Resolvd in ye Affir

6th Chofe John Wheatley to Reprefent The town of Lebanon in s'd Convention for the purpofe aforesd

The sum demanded by New Hampshire was arrearage of taxes. This they declined to pay, on the ground that they did not belong to that state, and also because all this time they had been raising and paying soldiers at their own expense.

They were willing, however, to send a delegate to the convention for forming a new constitution, because some of the provisions of the constitution under which the state had been acting since the Revolution was one of the grievances which had first alienated them from New Hampshire. If things could be made better for them, they were willing to assist.

But apparently affairs did not proceed to suit them, for at a meeting September 24, 1782, they voted to recall their representative chosen to represent the town in convention at Concord, in the state of New Hampshire. Ten days later they reconsidered this last vote.

By November the town had received the constitution and appointed a committee to examine and report upon it. November 26, 1782, they voted to recall their representative from the convention, the proposed constitution not appearing satisfactory to them.

The town, after many delays, after conventions of other towns held at Hanover, after sending agents to the assembly, after remonstrances and petitions, finally took its place as a town in the state of New Hampshire.

Development of the Town.

During all these years of disturbance and distraction concerning its state relations, the town has been steadily improving. Old roads were made better, new roads were laid out and built, bridges were built over the Mascoma at various points, one in this village, one near Walter Peck's, another at Davison's mills, another still on the river road.

All this time the town had been gaining in inhabitants. The close of the Revolution brought many accessions of the best material. New names are found upon the records, and prominent in town affairs—the Allens, Phinehas and Diarca; Gideon Baker, the Huntingtons, Stephen Billings, Thomas Blake, Walter Hains, Arad Simons, Zuar Eldredge, Nathan Durkee. Col. Elisha Payne, coming here from Orange, was a valuable acquisition to the town. The proprietors made him valuable grants of land in the east part of the town in 1778, "on conditions that the said Payne, his heirs or assigns shall build and erect a good sawmill & gristmill on the Mascomne river near to the place where said river empties out of the pond, within two years from the first day of April next [April, 1778] except the publick commotions and present wars shall render it impracticable, in which case they shall be built as soon as the publick affairs will admit of."

In this same year the proprietors voted to consider the propagation lot and the church glebe and a part of the governor's lot as undivided land. They also proceeded to lot all of the undivided land, making this generous, and it may be presumed acceptable provision, "to allow the committee and surveyor five gallons of rum while laying out said undivided land."

The proprietors also gave liberty to Colonel Payne to erect "a dam across Mascomme river at the mouth of Enfield pond in order to raise said pond sufficient for the use and benefit of the mills which he has undertaken to build."

The undivided land had been laid out into fifty-acre lots and

DIARCA ALLEN.

November 8, 1779, at the house of Nehemiah Estabrook, was drawn as follows:

	No		No
Thomas Barrows Jun	1	John Swift	12
Elijah Huntington	38	Daniel Allen Jun	34
Huckins Storrs Jun	6	Robert Barrows Jun	19
David Eldridge	42	Jefse Birchard, by John Griswold	48
Hobart Estabrook	15		
Daniel Blodgett 3d	14	John Allen	37
Thomas Storrs	3	Joseph Wood	5
Charles Hill	18	Moses Hebbard	7
Joshua Blodgett	11	Joseph Turner	51
Nathaniel Porter	9	Jefse Birchard	40
David Turner	33	Jonathan Murdock	36
Joseph Martin	2	John Birchard	16
Robert Martin	25	Daniel Blodgett	8
School Right	20	Minister Right	4
James Nevins	32	Mark H Wentworth	10
Hugh Hall Wentworth	41	Clement Jackson	39
John Hyde 30 acres	54	Seth Blodgett 30 acre	53

N. B. The lot No 24 is taken out by Mr. Joseph Wood on the original right of Robert Hyde

N. B. When the draught of the fifty acre Division was drawn in Lebanon, through mistake there was no lott in said division drawn to the original right of Richard Salter, wherefore the proprietors Committee ordered that the lott No 35 in said division be afsigned to said right   Attest

Gideon Baker, Proprietors Clerk

At the same time the proprietors granted a tract of land in the southwest part of the town to "David Hinckley Clothier as an encouragement to him the said David to set up his trade as a Clothier in said Lebanon."

In March, 1780, the proprietors appointed a committee to revise the field books of the several divisions of land, and to procure a plan of the township. This plan was made by Lieut. John Payne, "and being duly examined was accepted as correct in general." This plan still exists; that is, the parchment on which it is made does, the lines being faded and in many places entirely defaced. It is endorsed as follows: "This plan is laid down to 100 rods to an inch by John Payne Jun—surveyor."

In 1781 the proprietors made a division of twenty-acre lots, and assigned them by lottery.

June 26, 1780, the town appointed John Wheatley, Elisha Ticknor, Major Griswold, Deacon Estabrook and William Dana a committee "to adjust and put in proper order all the publick expense that the town has been at since the Contest with Great Britain." See page —

At the same time they voted "to lease for nine hundred and ninety-nine years the whole of the sequestered right of land for the benefit of schooling in said town."

The town in 1779 had voted three gallons of rum for the raising of a bridge over the Mascoma, this being the only business transacted at that meeting. It appears that in 1781 said rum had not been paid for and hence the selectmen were instructed, March 31, 1781, to include said rum in the taxes to be raised.

May 30, 1781, the town voted to build a pound (the first) near Esquire Hydes, and that Henry Woodward be pound keeper. This pound was on the hill where Henry Farman now lives.

Something of the condition of the town and their way of doing business may be gathered from the following vote:

To raise ten hard dollars, immediately, to bear the Expence of an Agent now going to the Assembly of New Hampshire. Accordingly the following collection was made for the aforesaid purpose. viz:

Gov payne	£1-6-8
Nathl Storrs	0-6-0
Maj. Griswold	0-6-0
Jesse Cook	0-3-0
Doct Hall	0-3-0
Abel Wright	0-1-6
David Hough	0 1-2
Saml Lothrop	0-0-3
	2-7-7

The hard dollars were specie—at the time exceedingly scarce—and probably hard in another sense.

April 8 1782 Voted that the select men take into their care the money of Vermont Emission now in the town treasury & make the best thereof for the benefit of the town that lyes in their power.

This was a relic of their union with Vermont.

November 26, 1782, there came before the town a proposition which gave them some anxiety. Colonel Payne and some others proposed to take parts of Lebanon, Enfield and Hanover

DEVELOPMENT OF THE TOWN.   147

and make them into a town. The town appointed Captain Freeman, Lieutenant Ticknor and Captain Dana a committee to "examine into the matter and report." That report was adverse to the plan.

The following, recently discovered among the papers in the state house, sets forth this plan for a new town:

The petition of Elisha Payne, and others inhabitants of the towns of Lebanon, Hanover Enfield and Canaan humbly shew that their local situation is such, being in the four adjoining corners or parts of said towns, and so remote from the center of the respective towns to which they belong, and the places of holding their town and other publick meetings, that renders it very inconvenient and almost impossable for them to attend, especially on the Sabbath or Lord's day; that the territory of land hereafter described, being about four miles square, is so situated, and the laying of the rhodes through the same such, that it makes it convenient for them to be a district or town by themselves and will not hurt nor injure the respective towns from which they may be taken off. Your petitioners, therefore, humbly pray your honors to take their case into your wise consideration and grant them relief by allowing them an incorporation with town privileges agreeably to the following limits and boundaries Beginning at the N. W. corner of lot No 50 of the village lots & so called in the line between said Lebanon and Hanover, from thence running south 23° West by the westerly line of said village lots until it comes to the Masquome river then turning and running up said river and crossing the same to the S. W. corner of lot No 26 on the southerly side of said river; from thence southerly on a strate line to the South West corner of lot No 9 on the Northerly side of Enfield Rhode; thence S. 72° E by said Enfield Rhode to the east line of Lebanon called the Freeman line and to continue the same course in said Enfield one mile and a half thence turning off and running N. 36° E. parilel with the town line until it comes to said river; thence up said river till it comes to the bridge standing on said river in Canaan from thence N 36° E so far as one mile and a quarter from Enfield north line; thence turning off and running N 64° W through part of Canaan and into the town of Hanover to the N E corner of lot No 13, and by the northerly line thereof and by the northerly line of three lots till it comes to No 17; thence turning off by said lots No 17, 18, 19 and to continue the same course till it comes to the line between Lebanon and Hanover and thence by said line to the bound begun at

Walter Peck	Daniel Swetland
Ebba Peck	James Bellows
Nathan Blodgett	Jonathan Bingham
David Hinkley	Abiel Willes
Edm'd Freeman	Elisha Payne
Gid. Baker	Ephraim Brown

John Crowell
David Stoddard
Leonard Hoar
Daniel Alden
Enoch Reddington
Dearca Allen

Samuel Karr
Daniel Willes
Jeriah Swetland
Clapp Sumner
Phineas Allen

The tract described above commenced on Hanover line, about a hundred rods westerly of the farm buildings of George Blodgett, striking the Mascoma a little west of Howard Benton's buildings; thence it passed up the river about a hundred rods, and from thence a straight line to the Alvah Bosworth farm, now occupied by Warren Daniell, intersecting the broad road laid through the town; thence on the line of that road to Enfield line, and the same course a mile and a half into the territory of Enfield; thence a northeasterly course, striking the Mascoma again in Canaan.

It will be seen that these lines would include East Lebanon and the village of Enfield. It should be remembered that at this time there were few buildings in the center of the town, and that the meeting-house was then in the neighborhood of Mrs. Alden's, while there was a large business done at East Lebanon. There is no doubt that Colonel Payne was the originator of this movement.

The Legislature refused to grant the prayer of the petitioners.

About this time there was another plan to divide the territory of Lebanon. The authorities of Dartmouth College wished to have entire control of the territory around the college and sought to have the territory granted by the proprietors of Lebanon, and a similar territory in Hanover, erected into a town or parish to be called Dresden, a name which Hanover Plain bore for many years.

The following papers have reference to this plan:

Objections against the incorporation of a part of Lebanon & Hanover in the county of Grafton into a distinct town.

1. The Freeholders of that part of Lebanon which is subject to taxation, proposed to be taken into said corporation are unanimously opposed to such an Incorporation, that is those of them who reside in said Lebanon. Fourteen hundred and fifty acres are all the land exclusive of College Lands Lying in said Lebanon proposed to be taken in—thirteen hundred acres of which are owned by said resident Freeholders, and a

LUCINDA HOWE STORRS.

From painting by J. J. Jennys, June, 1802.

considerable part of one hundred forty acres remaining are owned by a Minor.

2 That the said resident Freeholders have done already their proportion for building up Dartmouth College, and they can see no reason why they should be subject to the authority of said College and their dependants. They have given one hundred and fifty acres of land, and in money and labor to the amount of fifteen pounds, altho but eight in number, and subject to those difficulties which generally attend those who settle a new country; and if such an Incorporation should be made every vote would be carried according to the inclinations of the said authority; who will always have a sufficient number of Dependants, to assist them in carrying any point, whereby the situation of said resident owners would be exceedingly uncomfortable

3 By such an Incorporation the said Freeholders will be excluded from all benefit of public rights, and ministerial and school privileges in said Lebanon. The public rights in s'd Lebanon are so far improved and disposed off that a considrable sum accrues to Lebanon from such improvements A minister is settled, a meeting house and several school-houses are built. From which benefit the said Freeholders would be excluded by such an Incorporation.

4 Many new roads must be built to accommodate such a town as is desired, whereas if the said Freeholders remain as they are in conjunction with Lebanon, the expense of said new roads will be saved.

5 That the said Incorporation will ever be greatly burdened with poor to maintain Dependants must be introduced and not warned out till they become a town charge

6 That the expense of maintaining town order will be great, & a very large part of that expense will fall upon the said Freeholders in proportion to their interest. The said Freeholders and the owners of double if not treble the land in said proposed township which will be subject to taxation, and the College will ever own stock and other ratiable property—whereby the s'd Freeholders are apprehensive that they shall be obliged to do a great, if not the greatest, part towards supporting the poor, and discharging other town expenses, which they feel unable ever to perform

7 That it would be unprecedented to separate [them] from a particular corporation they had joined, without their consent either explicit or implicit.

to the Speaker of the house of Representatives of the state of New-hampshire now seting att Concord. Sir. Should thare be any moshun thursday Nex to see if the a Sembly will in corporate in to a Destinct town a Sarting track of Land Lying on Conocticut River so cauled Being part of Hanover and part of Lebanon by the name of Drisden. I Beg Sir you would in forme the Honorabel House that thare is a potishon or praer to s'd house not to encoporate in to a Destinct town the Lands potishiond for, last seting of a sembly—those that signed a gainst in coperation owne more than one half the ratabol land contand in the potishion for in corperation—yea, sir, and the house in generol are sensobel the coledg lands and   of coledg are not taxt sir there is not much, if any more one hundred and seventy acers under Emprovement taxabel Lands in s'd tract potishond for incorperation. Sir we heard thare was an order of cort upon thare potishon that the matter should be heard and Reson shone if any why it should not be incorperated and that the order of cort should be published in the publick papers we have no knoledg of the orders being complyed with— Sir the Reson of my troughbling you with this letter was I was Desired to a tend cort and see that the potishoners protest a gainst in corperation Lade before the Honorobel House when I set out better than a fortenate a go from home expected to a Returned home time enough to a ben Down by the Day and Left the potishon with the signers—being wether bound find I cant comply with thare request. I feare they will have no opportunity to send thare potishon on with thare resons why they would wish not to be incoperated in to a Distinct town.

Sir tho yeu are a Stranger to me the stashon or place yeu stan in is sofishont Evedenc to me that yeu are a gentleman of vorosity and must feale for every Ingured Sufforer in the state in which asembly that you are the Speaker of that Body that we under God have no whare els to look for help in matters of this nature

Sir if you think that we are not to poore to be Notist, having but small intrest Liabol to pay what ever is put upon us without Ever having a voice in Representation liabol to make and mend the Rodes threw all the coledg land without thare help which Rods are very bad and the few and poor inhabitans will be oblig to make and mend or suffer the penalty of Law for Not doing it that you will at least Continue our trial or Delay incoperating said town untill the next Seshon att which time Hanover and Lebanon will be represented, as they are not know [now] as they consider it

If a Sembly under the consideration that we cant by Reson of the rods being Bloct and some other matters that the house ought to know upon oure trial that cant be Laid before the a sembly this seshon, if they in thare wisdom would give us heare ing att the nex seting we should think ourseves in Duty bound to pray

Gideon Tiffane { in behalf of signers a gainst in coperation of Dresden

Decemb'r 20th 1783.

The "a sembly" very properly denied the petition for the "incoperation" of Dresden. Whether because the House was convinced by the reasonings of the remonstrance or because the Hon. John Dudley, then the speaker of the House, being carried away by his compliment as a "gentleman of vorosity," threw his influence against it, is not known.

Feb 24 1783 Voted that Elijah Dewey Jun, Esq. Hyde and Maj Griswold be a committee to Draw a Letter in the name of the town, to be sent to Mr Aaron Hutchinson & be signed by the Town clerk, in behalf of the town.

The next reference to this matter is in May, 1783.

Voted to sit on that Clause in the warning respecting Aaron Hutchinson. chose Messrs Elisha Ticknor Maj. John Griswold and Nathaniel Hall committee to make report.

The historian is unable to say what these records refer to. He *guesses* that it was a negotiation for Mr. Hutchinson to take up his residence in Lebanon as a lawyer.

March 11, 1783, after electing town officers for the year:

Voted to build a new Meeting House—that a Committee be chosen to draw a plan for the bigness of s'd House and compute the quantity of stuff sufficient to cover s'd House and lay the under floor Chose Maj John Griswold Hezekiah Waters David Hough committee for the purpose above said

March 26 of same year:

Voted to build a Meeting House near the Dwelling House of Elihu Hyde Esq. by the first day of Sept. 1784. Voted to build a Meeting House 60 feet in length 40 feet in breadth with 24 feet posts—that Simeon Peck Lemuel Hough and Hezakiah Waters be a Meeting, House committee and that they perfix a perticular spot for s'd House agreeable to above vote.

The spot pointed out above is on the hill where Henry Farnam now lives.

The first meeting-house was at this time only about ten years old. But the southwestern portion of the town had increased more rapidly in numbers and demanded a location nearer to them, opposed, of course, by those in other parts of the town.

May 6 1783 Voted to Chefe a Member to attend the General Afsembly in June Next, with Inftructions, if our Grievances be taken of, then to take a Seat in S'd House otherwife to Return. Col. Elifha Paine was Chofen a Member to attend the Generl Afsembly in New Hampfhire in June next. A committee was Chofen to draw Inftructions for the Member for the Afsembly & Report to the meeting

May 19 1783. Voted to Release Col Elifha Paine as a member of Afsembly. They then Chose Col Elifha Payne and Elihu Hyde as Agents to the Afsembly and raised a tax to defray their expense.

The grievances noted above were the arrearages which New

Hampshire demanded of the town, arrearages which had accumulated while the town was in union with Vermont and independent.

Later in November, Capt. Edmund Freeman was "chofen agent of the town to wait on the General Afsembly of New Hampshire at their nex Sefsion to Lay before them the affairs of S'd town." The town claimed a set-off against the demands of the state for expense incurred in providing soldiers, bounties, equipments, etc., which the state was not willing to allow.

February 25, 1784. Beza Woodward of Hanover was chosen agent "to take Care of the affairs of the town Refpecting the Expenditures of the war & other matters already laid in Before s'd Afsembly."

March 7, 1784, town officers were chosen, and Col. Elisha Paine was elected as representative of the town at the General Assembly in June next.

Messrs. Major Griswold, Lieut. Elisha Ticknor, Abiel Wills, Silas Waterman, Samuel Sprague and Rufus Baldwin, howards, or hog constables. This was the first recognition of this ancient and honorable institution in the town. It was also voted that the yards of the constables should be held as pounds.

March 22, "Voted that those persons That Have paid a Provifion Tax in the year 1781 shall be Repaid in the Prefent Town Tax and 10^d Be paid pr lb for Pork & six Pence for Beeff."

"That a Charter be Requested of the afsembly for the feries all them that shall be wonted over the Great River."

Votes for Prefident [of the state]
George Atkinfon	39
M Weare	7
Elisha Paine	1

Votes for Senator
Elifh Paine	43
Mofes Dow	1

This was the first state election in which the town had taken any part since its settlement nearly twenty years before. All the time it had its grievances, part of the time it was classed with other towns, part of the time it was connected with Vermont. The form of government adopted at the beginning of the Revolution had expired by its own limitation—the proclamation of

HIRAM A. SIMONS.

peace—a new constitution had been adopted and Lebanon took its place among the towns of the state, ably represented by Colonel Payne.

EIGHT SCHOOL DISTRICTS.

Dec 6 1784 Voted to accept the following Divifion of school Difricts

1st Diftrict Beginning at the North west corner of the town thence Runing on the Great River to North west Corner of the River Lott Latley owned by Deacon Jonathan Dana thence East To the Bend of the River south of John martins thence up Mascoma to the North End of maj Slapps Intervale thence east 72 Degree North—(N. 18° E) To Hanover Line.

2d Diftrict—Beginning at the North west corner of Decon Dana's River Lott bounded on Conectcut River to Plainfield and on Plainfield Line so far as To Include the Dwelling Houfe of Thomas Wright & Jofiah Hovey thence northerly to the Center of Jedidiah Hebbards Lott thence Northerly To the River Mascom

3d Diftrict to begins at the North easterly corner of the second Diftrict thence extends southerly upon the Line of said Diftrict till it Strikes Plainfield Line, thence Easterly on Plainfield Line opposite to the school Lott Latley owned by Samuel Huntington on the East Line of said Lott; thence on a North Line till it Strikes Mascoma River at the North East Corner of Hubbard Estabrook Lott [which would be on the farm now owned by Charles Gerrish]

4th District To Begin at the North East Corner of Hubard Estabrook Lott, thence up Mascoma River To the mouth of Great Brook [which is the brook coming in from the south] thence on a Direct Line To the north easterly corner of John Fox's Lott thence south To the south easterly corner of Mr James Perkins Lott, thence westerly to the South west corner of Zalmon Aspenwall's Lott.

5th Diftrict Begining at the North East Corner of John Fox's Lott thence a strait Line To the Brige Near John Porters Houfe thence up Great Brook To the Brige Near David Blifs' thence South To Plainfield Line, thence on Plainfield Line To the south East corner of the third district and bounded Westerly on said Diftrict and northerly on the forth Diftrict To the firft mentioned Corner

6th Diftrict begins at the South East Corner of the 5th Diftrict thence on Plainfield Line To the South East Corner of Lebanon thence northerly on the town line till it Come Due East of the North Line of Wetherill Hough Lotts thence Weft to the North Weft corner of said Houghs west Lott thence on a Line To John Fox's North East Corner of his Lott Leaving John Porter [Howe Place] in Esq. Wheatley's Diftrict.

7th Diftrict Begins at mr Witherrill Houghs North West Corner thence To the South east corner of mr Parker's Lott [Packard?] where he Now Lives thence Northerly to Hanover Line then Westerly on Hanover Line To the bound of the firft Diftrict thence on the east line of firſt Diſtrict to mascoma at the North End of maj Slapps Intervale Thence To the mouth of Great Brook ; thence up Great Brook To John Porters Brige, Thence To Witherill Houghs North Weſt Corner

8th Diſtrict from Witheril Hough's north west corner Due East to Enfield Line; thence north on Enfield Line To the North East Corner of Lebanon Thence Westerly on the Town Line Till it come where the 7th Diſtrict Strikes Hanover; thence on the Line of the 7th Diſtrict Till it comes To Witherill Hough's North west corner.

Some of these lines are evidently somewhat uncertain and difficult for us at this distance of time to retrace. East Lebanon was in the eighth district. The center village in the seventh and extended north to Hanover and south to the Howe farm and west beyond Scytheville. West Lebanon was in the first district. The families on the Great River, south of the Mascoma, were in the second district. Poverty Lane was in the third district. John Hebbard's farm would be in the fourth district. Dea. E. Cole's farm would be near the easterly line of the fifth district, and the sixth district took in the southeast corner of the town.

In this year William Dana presented the following petition to the Legislature :

Petition

Humbly shows William Dana of Lebanon, Grafton County, that he was one of the first settlers in said Lebanon, that he has suffered greatly by the passing of persons through his land in going over Connecticut river to Hartford in the State of Vermont (so called) that the privilege of a ferry on said river has not been granted, but the profit of assisting to cross said river has been engrossed by those that live not in the state of N. H. and have no estate therein, and can easily evade any laws of said state for the regulation of ferries; your petitioner therefore prays, that granting to him and his heirs the privilege of a ferry, beginning at the northwest corner of his home lot in s'd Lebanon, thence extending across said river in a direct line with the north line of said lot to the western bank of said river; thence south on said bank one mile and a half; thence east across said river to the north bank of the river Mascom, thence north on the easterly bank of the first mentioned river to the first mentioned bound

Wm Dana

Evidently they have not yet settled their affairs with the state, for January 31, 1785, "Voted that the Selectmen be directted not to make up a tax on the Town for the old Demands of the State of Newhampshire"

DEVELOPMENT OF THE TOWN.

The following indicates that there was discontent in the town concerning the place of meeting on the Sabbath. "Voted that the meeting on the sabbath be Held one Half the Days at Constant Storrs or Nathaniel Storrs." This would take the people on the hill in the neighborhood of Abel Storrs.

At the "anuail meeting," March 8, 1785, Elisha Payne was chosen representative. I suppose this to have been Elisha Payne, Esq., not the colonel.

<small>Voted to move the meeting House Near to Elihu Hydes Dwelling House & set up as soon as possible & begin next Monday.—that Constant Storrs Nathl Porter David Hough Hez^{ah} Waters and Elias Lyman be a Comitte to move said House & set it up at said place.

At a special town meeting warn'd by the Constables & Held at the meeting House March 15 1785, voted to Build a meeting House in the center of the town, and Desolved said meeting.</small>

So "next Monday" has come and gone and the meeting-house yet stands. The folks in the center and eastern parts of the town have rallied and at this meeting have carried their point.

At the annual meeting it is recorded that George Atkinson had seventy-six votes for the president of the state and Col. Elisha Payne eighty-two votes for senator.

A Stray colt.

<small>Taken up by Maj Elisha Lathrop of Lebanon august 16, 1785 a Stray mare Colt, one year old, of a Pail sorrel Colour, four white feet & Legs up to his knees & hams—white face, both Eyes white

Lebanon Aug. 22 1785

the Above Stray Colt was Prized by Daniel Hough & Stephen Colbarn at £3-15 they being under oath

Elihu Hyde Town Clerk

Fees: for entering /6; for attending and Giving oath to the above persons 2/; to the aprisers 1/3.</small>

The town was still in trouble with the state and conventions of towns were held at Hanover on their affairs, at several different times, and a petition to the assembly on their grievances ordered, and agents appointed to *wait* on the assembly.

<small>Dec 22, 1785 Voted to direct the Selectmen to Procure a part of the Extent in the sherifs hands and pay the same to him by the Time the Extent is out</small>

An extent as here used was a writ to a sheriff for the valuation of lands and tenements, to be followed in a specified time by an execution. New Hampshire had issued a great many of these writs against delinquent towns.

Still further action was taken in this matter at a meeting January 17, 1786:

Voted to direct the Selectmen to Hire the £50 they have Borrowed To Pay the sherif in part of the Extent against the town for Deficiency of men on the best terms they can and they will Indemnify them

Whereas the Town have this Day Directed the Selectmen to Hire £50 to Pay the £50, Borrowed To Pay the sherif Towards his Extent for Deficiency of men Do therefore vote, To Prevent Cost, that any Gentlm that will Pay in any sum or sums to the selectmen, that the Same shall be allowed them on any State Tax that shall be made up in the Town, with Intereft Till the same Bill be made up

This action of the town indicates unmistakably that the people were poor—not that they did not own valuable lands and good homes, and had good crops, with horses and cattle—but they had no money. To understand their condition, their trials and straits, we must take a view of the condition of the wider community of which they were a part.

The War of the Revolution had imposed heavy burdens upon the states and the people. The real money of the country was soon exhausted, and there was no other way to continue the struggle but by the emission of paper money by Congress and the states. The length and expenses of the contest soon made it manifest that these bills would never be redeemed. Besides this they were printed with so little skill that they were easily counterfeited. They soon began to depreciate in value and depreciated more and more, till their purchasing power was reduced to zero in many cases. As the paper money depreciated, silver and gold disappeared; they were hoarded up by those who could get them, because their value was substantial and continuous. New emissions of bills were made from time to time, with the attempt to give a higher value than the old, but they shared the same fate of rapid depreciation. The extent of this depreciation may be seen by some tables compiled by authority of the Legislature from time to time:

Continental Paper

Feb.	1777	£104	equal to	£100 silver
Jan	1778	325	do	do
Jan	1779	742	do	do
Jan	1780	2934	do	do
Jan	1781	7500	do	do

ORREN HUBBARD.

By this time the Continental was practically worthless and useless.

The state emissions were a little better, but were insufficient for the wants of the people. If new emissions were made they would depreciate the more. The state was, therefore, forced to receive its demands in silver or its equivalent. But where were the people to get silver? It had hidden itself, as it always will, in the face of unredeemable paper money. During the war the people could meet the demands against them in beef, pork and grain to feed the army. But the war was over and the Congress and the state had no use for these articles. Both states and individuals were at their wits end to meet their just obligations. The state must receive its dues in gold or silver. The people had none. Just then some wise people thought they had found a way out of the difficulty. It was this: The Legislature must make money. They must issue bills and make them a legal tender for all debts due itself and individuals. It was said "that the people had a right to call upon their representatives to stamp a value on paper, on leather or any other substance capable of receiving an impression; and that to prevent its depreciation a law should be enacted to punish with banishment and outlawry every person who should attempt by any means to lessen its value."

To this it was answered that if the state must receive these bills for its dues, it could never redeem them, having no specie, and if these bills were never to be redeemed they could not pass for money.

Many other extravagant plans were proposed for the relief of the people. The Legislature was wise and stood fast by the first principles of finance. Conventions of towns were held and petitions poured in upon them for relief. Finally the Legislature, sitting at Exeter, September 20, 1786, was visited by a mob, clamorous for relief.

The president, General Sullivan, addressed them and explained the reasons why their petitions could not be granted. But they were not satisfied. They placed sentries at the doors and held the Legislature as prisoners. They went on with their business till evening, when the president, in attempting to pass out, was hedged in by the crowd. He attempted to reason with them.

and warned them of the fatal consequences of their conduct. They only replied with cries for paper money, an equal distribution of property and a release from debt. Just at this moment a drum beat at a distance and a cry was raised for the artillery by some of the citizens of Exeter. At this the mob was panic stricken and dispersed in all directions.

Now it was in this condition of things that the town was called upon to meet the demands of the state for deficiencies. Their action under the writ of the sheriff shows how hard it was for them to raise so small an amount as £50. As a town they could only do it by borrowing of some one who was the fortunate possessor of so much gold or silver.

By a census taken by a law of the state in the year 1786, we again learn the number of the people.

Pursuant to a Resolution of the Honble the House of Representatives of the state of New Hamp^r & read and Concurred in the same day by the Honble Senate: that the Selectmen of the several Towns, districts & parishes within the said State make a Return of all the Inhabitants within their respective districts to the Secretary of s^d State on or before the sec^d Wednesday in June nex. viz. the whole number of white & other free citizens, inhabitants of every age sex and condition, including those bound to servitude for a term of years & also all other persons not Comprehended in the foregoing description except Indians Not paying Taxes. Wherefore in conformity to said Resolve we, ye subscribers, have taken an exact account of the inhabitants of the Town of Lebanon in the County of Grafton in s^d state Which is as follows, viz.

Whites &c included in the foregoing description	841
Persons not included in s^d description	2
	843

                  Nathl Wheatley
    Attest   James Crocker   Selectmen
                  Nathaniel Hall Jun

Dated in said Lebanon, May 23 A. D. 1786

In 1773 the number was 295, gain in thirteen years of 548. Most of this accession of numbers was after the declaration of peace.

At the annual town meeting, March 14, 1786, Maj. Edmund Freeman was chosen representative, John Sullivan had 118 votes for president of the state and Elisha Payne, Esq., had 118 votes for senator.

At the same meeting, "Voted that Rept. Colburn Thomas Wells & Charles Tilden be a Commi^{tee} to look up 3 or 4 men to ansur for this town To Compleat their Quota of Continental men."

About this time it was discovered that the charter of the town was in a dilapidated condition. The following deposition accounts for it:

Levi Hyde's Deposition.

I, Levi Hyde, of Lawful age, Testify and Declare that in the year 1765 (I being Clerk to the propriety of the Town of Lebanon) at that time had in possession the Charter of s^d Town and the Records of said propriety, the s^d Charter was Repositated in a Chest that stood in my house and was stuffed full of Clothes, & by some means (but how I know not) some mice got into s^d chest and Eat, not only some of the Clothes, but the said Charter also, which was doubled together (& the Varmin, as I believe, & have sufficient ground therefor) Did eat out the middle of s^d Charter as it was folded or Doubled together, as may appear by s^d Charter to the satisfaction of any person upon View thereof; & as proof that said Charter was Defac^d as aforesaid I found two mice dead in s^d Chest, which had been lockt up therein for a time but how long I know not

Levi Hyde

State of New Hampshire, Grafton s.s. Lebanon June 8th 1886

Personally Appeared the above named Levi Hyde & being Duly cautioned to speak the Truth made Solemn Oath to the truth of the above Written Deposition.

Attest   John Wheatley Just. Peace

Lebanon June 8th 1786 These may Certifie that I the Subscriber was Resident in said Lebanon & at the Dwelling House of the above Deponent when the Charter mentioned in the above Written Deposition was first Discovered to be Defaced as above Described & am fully pesuaded of the truth of the above Written Deposition.

John Whealley

Oct 20 1786 Voted to accept the offer of made by Mr Lemuel Hough & Mr Robert Colburn.

Voted to raise the sum of one thousand pounds in order to pay arrearage taxes demanded by the State of New Hampshire to be paid in Beef, Pork, Flax, Wool, neat Stock, Butter & Cheese & Wheat, said articles to be paid in at the rate of Wheat at five Shillings per Bufhel agreeable to an offer made by Mr Lemuel Hough & Mr. Robert Colburn for paying said Taxes to the state for the aboves^d sum of one thousand pounds in the above said articles, s^d Hough & Colburn to have the profits of the Demands of the Town upon the state said Hough and Colburn to become obligated to clear the town from Cofts.

Voted that the Tax be made up and collected forthwith.

Voted that the Selectmen be directed to make up two Rate Bills for sd purpofe, one Bill for the nominal sum Demanded by the state, the other Bill to be made up for the sum of one thousand pounds in the articles before mentioned

This, then, was their way out of their difficulties. They had no money to meet the demands of the state, but they had the above mentioned articles. These they raised on their lands and could spare. Messrs. Hough and Colburn thought they could take these articles, turn them into money, and pay the demands of the state, and, using the set-off which the town pleaded against the state for expenses during the war, have something over. They were willing to take the risk, and bound themselves to save the town from loss. Each tax-payer's proportion of the one thousand pounds was to be ascertained first, and then he was to turn over to Mr. Hough enough of beef, pork, flax, wool, neat stock, butter, cheese, or wheat to meet the demand, supposing wheat to be worth five shillings a bushel in prices—a good arrangement for the people and the only one open to them in their condition. It is to be wished it could be added that the arrangement was a good one for Messrs. Hough and Colburn. They certainly deserved a handsome profit as a reward for their energy and public spirit, but they did not attain it. It is understood that they lost, and lost heavily. They could not make ready sale of the afore-mentioned articles. The town saw and sympathized with their misfortune, but voted that they could do nothing to relieve them.

John Wheatley, Esq., died July 30, 1786, in the sixty-seventh year of his age. His final record as town clerk was made 28th of March, 1786. The records of the annual town meeting of 1787 are not found.

Dec 3d 1787 Voted that the spot to set a Meeting House on be as near the Centre of the Town & Travel as any Judicious man shall judge reasonable.

Voted a Comtee of five men to pitch on the spot to set a Meeting House on. Chose Aaron Hutchinson Esq. Mr. Wm Huntington, Capt. David Hough Col. Elisha Paine & Deacn Thoph. Huntington for the abovesaid purpose. Committee to report near the first of January next.

Jan. 10, 1788. Voted that the place for a Meetinghouse to stand on, be near Mr. Abbotts [at the head of School Street].

JAMES HUBBARD.

Voted to build a meeting House near to Mr. Abbott's—to raise a sum of money for the purpose of Building a meetinghoufe,—to raise the sum of three hundred pounds for the purpofe of Building a Meeting House & that s^d sum be raifed by the first of January next—a committee of five men to view the Roads and accommodations respecting the particular spot to erect the Meeting house on. Chase Aaron Hutchinson esq. Mr. Wm Huntington Capt Daire Hough Col. Elisha Payne & D^n Theoph Huntington committee for s^d purpose.

Chose Col. Elisha Payne, Maj Math Wheatley, and Mr Lemuel Hough a Committee for Building the Meeting House.

Chose Capt. David Hough a Delegate to attend the Convention to be holden at Exeter respecting the Federal Constitution & Voted a Com^tee of nine men to give Instructions thereon Viz Col. Elish Payne, Mr Const Storrs, Aaron Hutchinson Esq. Maj John Griswold Col. Edmund Freeman Lt. Elisha Ticknor Maj Nathl Wheatley Capt. David Hough & Deac^n Theoph Huntington Comm^tee

Subsequently Captain Hough declined the office of delegate and Col. Elisha Payne was chosen.

The confederation of the colonies was a work of haste under exigencies, and during the Revolution its defects became manifest and embarrassing in the extreme. These defects were as follows: There was not coercive power in the Continental Congress. It had no power to punish individuals for any infraction of its land; it had no power to levy taxes or to collect revenue for the public service; they could apportion among the states the necessary sums, the states might raise them or not, according to their pleasure; it had no power to regulate either foreign or interstate commerce. Each state framed its own regulations of these important matters and they were often antagonistic. The want of uniform laws in these affairs left the Confederation at the mercy of foreign powers.

Besides these defects there were others of less serious nature, but which yet stood in the way of national prosperity.

In order therefore "to form a more perfect union, establish justice, insure domestic tranquility, promote the general welfare," a convention of the states assembled in Philadelphia to frame a new constitution. After months of labor and discussion, the present constitution was finished and sent out to the states for their approval.

It was during these discussions that the people formed themselves into political parties. Questions were then raised which survive to our own times, views upon which have had a controlling influence upon the course of our affairs.

One part of the people wished to give a certain supremacy to the general government over the state governments. These took the name of Federalists. Another portion of the people believed that no state should part with its sovereignty. It might delegate its powers for certain objects and ends, but never beyond recall. It was held whatever the state might give up, it should be able to resume at its pleasure. These were called Anti-Federalists.

Upon these grand points the people took sides and carried their discussions, not merely to warmth, but to bitterness. They rightly deemed these matters of the utmost consequence, and met them with a corresponding degree of feeling.

When, therefore, a convention was called of the people of New Hampshire to sit in judgment upon the new constitution, they felt the importance of the work before them. We need not be surprised that the town thought it proper that their delegate should have the advantage of the deliberate judgment of her wisest citizens framed into instructions for his guidance.

Another thing which made this convention important was the fact that eight states had already taken action upon it, and stamped it with their approval. The action of New Hampshire would be decisive, this being the ninth state to vote. If New Hampshire approved of it, its adoption is made certain.

The convention met at Exeter in September, 1788. John Sullivan was president. The provisions of the constitution were warmly discussed, and it was immediately manifest that some of its provisions would meet with strong opposition. The friends of the constitution feared the result, and an adjournment to a future day was proposed and carried. February 22, 1788.

The convention met again at Concord, June 18, 1788. A committee was appointed to prepare and recommend certain amendments. The convention reached a final vote on its adoption, Saturday, June 21, when the yeas and nays were called. While the secretary was calling over the names of the members and recording their votes, there was a death-like sllence, every bosom throbbed with anxious expectation.'' We listen for the name of Colonel Payne and his answer—it is yea. The vote stood fifty-seven in favor and forty-six against the adoption. The voting was conducted in silence, followed by intense excitement. Messengers started in all directions to announce the result. The vote of New Hampshire gave vitality to a government which later generations have held worth living and dying for.

The closeness of the vote shows how nearly equally divided the people were upon the great questions of the constitution. We learn from the elders that they were most warmly discussed in this town. There were here Federalists and Anti-Federalists, who had their arguments and their arguments, at many times and "in divers places."

It is said that the word Federalist came to a novel use. The pronunciation of it was made a test of soberness. If one in attempting to pronounce it rendered it *Fetherlist*, it was certain he had a "drop too much." Oftentimes accuser and accused both proved to be *Fetherlists*, not withstanding their party differences.

At the annual meeting, March 11, 1788, we find an office filled for the first time—Joel Gilden and Sluman Lathrop, Surveyors of Lumber. This, after a time, became a prominent business in the town. Many of the magnificent pines "fit for masting the royal navy" found their way down the Connecticut to "Old Harford" and intermediate points.

Capt. David Hough was chosen representative to the General Assembly. Votes for president of the state: Hon. John Sullivan, Esq., 82; John Langdon, Esq., 1; Beza Woodward, 3. For senator for Grafton County, Elisha Payne, Esq., had 57 votes; Jonathan Freeman of Hanover, 12.

December 15, 1788, the town held its election for representatives to Congress. The state then had no congressional districts, as now, but each town voted for the three members to which the state was entitled, as many then, it will be noted, as we have now. The vote was as follows:

Benj. Bellows Esq.	29	Elisho Payne Esq.	32
John Sullivan Esq.	20	Simeon Olcott Esq.	15
Saml Livermore Esq.	22	Beza Woodward Esq.	7
Benj. West Esq.	17	Moses Dow Tsq.	3

At the same time the town voted for the first time for five presidential electors, with the following result:

John Dailey Esq.	21	John Sullivan Esq.	14
John Pickering Esq.	22	Simeon Olcott Esq.	2
Joshua Wentworth Esq.	20	Timothy Walker Esq.	1
Samuel Sherburne Esq.	21	Elisha Payne Esq.	5
Nath'l Adams Esq.	23	Moses Dow Esq.	3
Benj. Bellows Esq.	16	Sam'l Livermore Esq.	5
Charles Johnston Esq.	13	Francis Smith Tsq.	1
Beza Woodward Esq.	16	Peter Green Esq.	1
Moses Chase Esq.	10	John Stephens	1

February 2, 1789, the town met again for the choice of representatives to Congress. Benj. West had 23 votes, Saml. Livermore 23, Abiel Foster 23. Samuel Livermore, Abiel Foster and Nicholas Gilman were elected, the last not among the candidates voted for in this town. The smallness of the vote shows that little interest was taken in this election.

At the annual meeting, March, 1789, for president of the state, John Sullivan, Esq., had 80 votes, John Pickering, Esq., 2, Benj. Bellows 2.

For senator from Grafton County, Jonathan Freeman had 65 votes, Elisha Payne, Esq., 16.

Capt. David Hough chosen representative.

The following is an instance of a proceeding common at the time, but not known in our day—the binding out of a boy:

This indenture made the sixth day of August anno domini 1789 Between Jesse Cook, Stephen Billings and Gideon Baker, Selectmen of Lebanon in the county of Grafton and state of New Hampshire of the one part and Samuel Weathers of Woodstock in the county of Windsor and state of Vermont, Husbandmen of the other part witnesseth—that the said Selectmen, by and with the Consent of two of the justices of the peace for the said county of Grafton have by these presents put, placed, and Bound John Patrick Juner, of the age of twelve years on the twelfth day of Dec. last, a poor boy belonging to Lebanon whose parents John Patrick and Molly his wife are not able to maintain him, to be an apprentice with him the said Samuel, and as an apprentice with him the said Samuel to dwell from the date of these presents untill he, the said John Patrick Juner, shall Come to the age of twenty-one years, according to the law in such case provided, by and during all which time and term the said John Patrick jjuner shall the said Samuel his said master well and faithfully serve in all such lawful business as he, the said John Patrick juner, may be put to by the Com-

ABEL STORRS.

mand of his said master, according to the wit, power, and ability of him the said John Patrick juner & honestly and obediently shall behave himself in all things towards his said master, and honestly and orderly towards the rest of the family of the said Samuel,—and the said Samuel doth hereby covenant for his part, with the said selectmen for them and their successors in office and for the said John Patrick jun. that he, the said Samuel, shall teach and instruct him the said John Patrick jun. in the mistery and occupation of Husbandry and also shall learn him to read and write, and shall also find him with sufficient meat drink apparel and other things needful for an apprentice, so that the said apprentice shall not dureing said term be a charge to the said town of Lebanon, and shall at the expiration of said term dismiss the said apprentice with two new suits of Cloths, one suitable for Sabbath days, the other for other days

In Witness whereof the Parties hereunto have set their hands and seals the day and the year first above written

Signed sealed and delivered

In presents of   Samuel Mathews
  John Colburn Jr
  Aaron Hutchinson   Jesse Cook
                                    Stephen Billings
                                    Gid. Baker

We Elihu Hyde and Aaron Hutchinson two of the justices of the peace for the County of Grafton within mentioned do hereby declare and assent to the binding of the within named John Patrick Juner an apprentice to the within named Samuel Weathers according to the form & effect of the within written Indenture. Given under our hands the sixth day of August Anno Domini 1789

                                    Elihu Hyde
                                    Aaron Hutchinson

A New Meeting House.

For some time past, a meeting-house has appeared upon the records. Several votes indicated that the matter was settled and the meeting-house built long before this. Not by any means! So far they have been only thinking, planning and voting. As yet there has been only some preliminary skirmishing between the parties, now and then a *reconnoisance*, sometimes "in force," to feel each other's strength. But the real battle is now at hand, and the historian will devote himself to this one subject until the meeting-house is located and built. The records supply the best history and become quite dramatic in their interest.

April 9 1789 Voted to build a Meeting House near to Mr Abbotts [head of School Street] where a former Com[tee] stuck a stake for that Purpose, by a majority of eighteen votes.

So once more the people of the center and eastern parts of the town have prevailed. By no means. For there is debate and discussion and next:—

Voted to reconsider the matter respecting building a meeting house, near to Mr Abbotts and it is accordingly reconsidered!!

Voted to choose a committee of four men to find the center of this Town. Chose Col. Elisha Payne, Aaron Hutchinson Esq. Deac[n] Theophilus Huntington, and Capt. David Hough a committee for s[d] purpose

A good committee of the first citizens of the town.

This was in April. In June we make a new acquaintance, the shadowy form of the present town hall rises before us. There has been much talk and planning between the afternoon of the 7th of April and the 22nd of June. A new object is presented for the suffrages of the people—for a "majority of eighteen votes," more or less.

Voted to Build a TOWN HOUSE on some convenient spot of ground that shall be agreed on by this Town and that the Society (religious) have Liberty to add to s'd house to make it convenient for Public Worship & make use of it for s'd purpose as they shall see fit.

Voted to raise two hundred pounds for the purpose of building a Town House—that the Selectmen be directed to measure from the center tree to the several spots proposed to set a Town House and report the distance to each spot at an adjourned meeting

This now is the problem whose solution we watch with intense interest—Whether a town house with a meeting-house attached can be more readily located than a meeting-house, pure and simple.

Oct 1. 1789 met and heard the report of the Select men respecting the distance from the center of the Town to the several spots proposed to set a Town House on. Adjourned for one quarter of an hour. Probably at the suggestion of the Leaders of various parties who wish time to consult, possibly to look at the different "spots."

Met according to adjournment and voted to build a Town House on Mr Peck's land, northerly of the Road about six rods easterly of a green pine tree standing in his field—that the Selectmen be a committee to lay out the spot of ground for to set s'd House on & also a parade sufficient to answer said purpose as they shall judge necessary—that Capt. David Hough, Ensign Hez[h] Waters and Lt. Conslant Storrs be a Com[ttee] to draught the fashion of s[d] House. Voted that Col Elisha Payne be a Com[tee] man to assist in s'd draughts, Adjourned for four weeks.

The committee this time are all military men, bristling with titles. Something may be expected from the well-known energy and efficiency of that class of men.

Oct 29. 1779. Met and voted to accept the draught of s'd House as exhibited by the Com^tee. Adjourned for 15 minutes. Met and Chose a Com^tee to forward the building of s'd House. Chose Mr Simeon Peck. Maj Nathaniel Wheatley & Capt. David Hough Com^tee for said purpose.

By this time the town house is so assured that it is time to think of disposing of the old meeting-house standing on its original location, so they vote that the selectmen be empowered to dispose of it, exclusive of private property, after said house is not wanted for public use.

The "spot" selected for the town house as above was near Scytheville, probably in the vicinity of S. A. Peck's. The exact place is uncertain, for the "Green Pine Tree," is no longer visible.

Still farther:

Voted that the several Surveyors of highways be a Com^tee to collect the votes of every legal voter in Town respecting the spot to set a Town House on, in order to accommodate the whole Town, and make return to the adjourned meeting.

Nov 27th Met and adjourned to Dec 4. Met at the house of Mr. Simeon Peck and adjourned for half an hour. Met and adjourned till the second Tuesday in March, and the fore named Com^tee be directed not to proceed in matters respecting s'd House till s'd time of adjournment.

March 9 1790 Met and Adjourned till March 25 inst. Met according to adjournment and voted to reconsider all the votes respecting s'd Town House. Voted to dissolve s'd Meeting

Spring came and ripened into summer, summer faded into autumn, and autumn sank into bare and leafless winter. Several town meetings were held during the season, but not one word concerning either meeting-house or town house.

Suddenly, in a gloomy day of December, it was the 20th day A. D. 1790, like thunder out of a clear sky, comes this vote:

Voted that the place to set a Meeting-house on (it is to be a meeting house after all) be near Mr. Abbotts. Voted to choose a Com^tee of 8 men to choose a com^tee respecting s^d meeting house (the town clerk uses no capital this time, as though he had little faith in it). Chose Capt Human Lathrop, Capt David Hough, Mr Clap Sumner, Maj. Wheatley St. Constant Storrs Ens. Hez^h Waters Col. Edmand Freeman.

Mr Simeon Peck. Adjourned 15 minutes Met. Committee recommend that Lt. Constant Storrs Mr. Simeon Peck Capt. Hough & Ensign Waters be a Com^tee to prepare a plan and devise measures for the building s'd Meeting House, and report to ajourned meeting

Dec. 27 1790 Voted to reconsider the former vote respecting building a meeting House near Mr Abbotts. And so closed the year 1790

The records for the year 1791 are missing. The subject of a meeting house seems to have come up during the year, for at the annual meeting, March 13, 1792, "Voted to reconsider a former vote to build a meeting house," by Mr. Simeon Peck.

About this time the old meeting house, which had patiently waited the decision of the town, whether it should be supplanted by another, and wondered whether the adventures of the new would equal those of the old, suddenly disappeared. It was on the long contested spot in the early evening. It was not there in the morning. "A company of young men, headed by one 'Captain Stubbs' *alias* Comfort Allen, gathered in the night and proceeded quietly to remove the bone of contention, and before the morning light, the house of worship was levelled to the ground. The timber was bought by private persons and the house rebuilt on the hill near H. Farnam's, and continued to be used for meetings for several years."—Dr. Allen's Centennial.

It appears that the house was not wholly torn down, but some part of it remained, for with a sort of grim humor, the warning for a meeting immediately after calls upon the legal voters to meet in town meeting "at the standing Part of the old meeting house in said Lebanon." The town also took measures to punish those who had assaulted the old house.

It is not difficult to ascertain the motive for this destruction of the old house. It was not, probably, mere wanton mischief, such as young men will sometimes indulge in, but had a bearing on the great controversy. Judging from some of the votes passed, and other circumstances, a division of the people was impending, and there was a threat of two meeting houses. One party, the west and southwest of the town, were satisfied with the old location and proposed to keep the old house. The center and east saw that they must either go there, or else assume the expense of a new house. It was considered that if the old house was out of the way, there was small probability that those in that part of the town would build alone a new house.

COL. CONSTANT STORRS.

From painting by J. J. Jennys, June 23, 1802.

It is only in the light of such conjectures that this vote, passed April 26, 1792, can be understood:

Voted to *unite* and build *one* meeting house for the town.—to Build a meeting house on or Near the old meeting house spot.—To Choose a Comm^tee to Build s'^d house viz Lemuel Hough, Capt. David Hough, Hezekiah Waters, Aaron Hutchinson. Esq., Lt Constant Storrs, Voted that the above Comm^tee set a stake where the house shall stand—that they Draw a Plan for s^d house and lay it Before our Next meeting, and Draw a subscription to Raise money to Build s'^d house

At this meeting the west and southwest people prevailed. It was probably a reaction in their favor from the destruction of the old house. But

May 7. 1792 Voted to Reconsider a former vote of uniting and Building a meeting house for the town altogether.—To releas the above Commit from Building a meeting house—that the Town will Except of the money subscribed of those that tore down the old meeting house if there is suficient subscribed to sattisfy the agents.

Besides Comfort Allen, who was the leader in the raid on the old house, it is more than probable that the following persons were "there or thereabouts," Eliel Peck, Jonathan Quimby, James Ayers, Nathaniel Kimball, Moses Persons, Joseph Lathrop, Gordon Lathrop, Joseph Byington, Enoch Worthen, Urban Lathrop.

May 17 1792 Voted to choose a Committee to set half an hour to see if they can agree on a Place to Build a meeting house Committee— Capt Nathl Hall, Capt David Hough, Clap Sumner. Adjourned for half an hour. Met and Committee report that the westerly side of the Plane on which Robert Colburn now lives is the Place for a meeting house about 25, or 30 rods southerly from the School house on s^d Plains

Voted to form the meeting into a Committee of the whole and go out and Vew the Spot Reported by s^d Committee for the meeting house

Voted to Except the Report of the Comm^t which was to Build a meeting house on the s'^d Plain within 25 or 30 rods of a school-house. S^d vote carried By a majority of 104 to 41

Voted to reconsider a former vote for Building a meeting house By Esq. Elihu Hydes, s^d vote passed the 26th of April Last.

Voted to go on and Build a meeting house on or Near the Stake which the committee of the whole stuck; Not more than 25 or 30 rods from s^d stake.

Capt. David Hough, Lieut. Constant Storrs, Mr. Stephen Billings, Lieut. Robert Colburn, Capt. Nathaniel Hall, Mr. Clap Sumner were chosen a committee to build said house. The committee was instructed "to make out a subscription and Raise as much money as they can and sell the Pew ground, and finish s^d house; and when finished, if money remains in their hand Raised by subscription and sail of Pew ground, to be Refunded Back to the subscribers; s^d Committee to Build according to the old Plan." Also the committee are instructed to "look out all Necessary roads Leading to s^d meeting house spot."

The meeting house is located finally by this decisive vote. Though it does not appear in the records, the decisive consideration was a generous offer by Robert Colburn to give to the town what is now the park, if they would locate the house upon it. The park was then a field under cultivation, hence the direction to the committee "to look out roads to the meeting house spot." That spot was some distance inside the present fence and a little to the west of its present location as a town hall, for that is the building where fortunes were so raised.

Though the above vote for the location of the meeting house seems a very decisive one, there was dissatisfaction. The defeated party did not lose heart, and made another trial to have the location changed.

A special meeting was called for the 11th of September, 1792, at eight o'clock a. m., "to see if the town will agree upon some just Plan of measuring, whereby they may find a spot to set a meeting house upon that may Do Equal justice to the whole of the Inhabitants of s^d Lebanon and do any other Business Relative thereto that they shall think propper. Voted to Chuse a comm^t to Propose a Plan of measurement to find where the center of Travel is in s^d Lebanon. Chose Nathl Porter Danl Alden, Capt Danl Phelps Capt David Hough for above said Purpose Adjourned for half an hour"

Met and the committee reported "that a former Plan of measurement to find the center of Travel should be the Present Plan." Voted not to accept said plan.

The 12th day of November, 1792, they voted "to choose a Comm^t to set with the old meeting house comm^t to see if they could agree on Sumthing that should make harmony and union in said town in Regard to meeting house affairs. Chose Jesse Cook, Aaron Hutchinson Nathl Storrs Robert Colburn"

The following is the report of the committee:

SETH BLODGETT.

Nov 16 1892. Agreed that the Revd Isaiah Potter's Hearers Shall be considered as one Family, and that there be an Indifferent Com^{ee} from out of Town that shall take Mr Potters rate bill View it, and have the Hired men and those that aint a going to live in Town not reck^d and the rest reckon^d as in said family and the said Com^{ee} shall ride into Each and Every part of this Town and view Every Circumstance of said Family as to Attendance on Publick worship, and say whether the said Family shall meet all the Time at the repaired Meeting-house, or all the time at the new Meeting-house, or whether at each of said houses part of the time, and if so, then in what Proportion at Each of said Houses so as to do Equal justice to Each member of said Family, as to attendance and Publick worship

Jesse Cook
Robert Colburn
Cook Papers

Nov. 22 1792 Voted that a disinterested Com^{ee} be chosen to Determine a center spot for a meeting house for Publick worship, which Comm^{tt} shall consider the travel as it Respects quality and quantity and actually measure to find the same and say where in Justis it ought to be Erected upon the consideration of Every Circumstance of the Present and future Inhabitents—Provided measures are taken to Prevent injustis in the Respect to Subscriptions for work Done on the house already raised.

Nov 26. Voted to Reconsider the last claws in the last vote (viz) Provided measures are taken to Prevent injustis with Respect to Subscriptions and work Done on the meeting-house already Raised. Chose a comm^t in town to measure s^d town. Chose a comm^t to nominate a Comm^t, viz Nathl Porter, Lemuel Hough Clap Sumner Dea^n Downer Charles Saxton. Adjourned for $\frac{1}{2}$ an hour. Met and Comm^t report that Stephen Billings Lt. Joseph Wood. Danl Hough Capt. Asher Allen be a comm^t to measure s^d town and are accordingly chosen with the substitution of Samuel Estabrooks for Stephen Billings who declined

December 24. 1792. the committee reported as follows:

Lebanon Dec 17 1792

To the Inhabitants of the Town of Lebanon—Greeting!

We, the subscribers that were appointed By s^d Town as a committee to measure & find where s^d Town could get together with the Least Travel—have accordingly Gone and measured & calculated to Different Spots and Beg leve to Report.

In the first Place we calculated the said Travel to the New meeting house & secondly to the mouth of the Lane Between Mr James Jones & Mr. Nathaniel Storrs and found that there was 215 miles & 29 rods less Soul Travel to s^d lane than to the New Meeting house—Likewise we found the land Travel to the aforesaid spots to Be 37 miles & 246 (rods) the least Travel to the New meeting house Reconing one travel from

Each habitable Hundred acre Lot. Likewise we found it to Be 52 miles & 303 Rods more Land Travel to Mr Peck's spot than to the New meeting house.

Samuel Estabrook
Dan'l Hough
Asher Allen
Joseph Wood Jr
} Committee

In the above report the "land travel" means the distance to the specified points from each inhabited house in town. By "soul travel" is meant this distance multiplied by the number of persons living in each house. From the report it appears that the meeting-house on the Plain was nearer a geographical center of the town than the other localities, but that the *center of population* was at the "mouth of the lane between James Jones and Nathaniel Storrs," which was in the neighborhood of Abel Storrs'.

This report seems to have been final. The meeting-house, which had been already raised and work done upon it, stood its ground. We at this day see that the location was wisely chosen. The village is both the geographical and the natural center of the town.

Various papers relative to this meeting house are here given. The people had little money to vote or give for the expense of building, but they had material and labor. The following is the subscription of the inhabitants:

Coppy of Subscription Paper for the Purpose of raising money for Building a Meetinghouse on the plain by Robert Colburns.

GEORGE BLODGETT.

DEVELOPMENT OF THE TOWN. 173

	Wheat £	Cash shillings		Wheat	Cash
Stephen Billings	3 -0 -0	6	Stephen Bliss	£3 -0 -0	6
Simeon Peck	20 -0 -0	12	James Hartshorn	0-15 -0	
Isaiah Potter	15 -0 -0	10	Phinias Parkhurst	5 -0 -0	6
Isaac Walbridge	3 -0 -0	6	Hezekiah Waters	3 -0 -0	6
Josiah Cleaveland	5 -0 -0	6	Aaron Hutchinson	15 -0 -0	20
Jabez Kellogg	2 -0 -0		Clap Sumner	10 -0 -0	12
John Colburn Jun	9 -0 -0	20	Reuben Putnam	1 -4 -0	
Beriah Abbott	10 -0 -0	20	Andrew Aldrich	0 10 -0	
Elkanah Sprague	5 -0 -0		Fredrick Cook	0 -5 -0	
Withiral Hough	7-10 -0		Pelam Cook	0 -5 -0	
Johatham Hamilton	5 -0 -0	10	Joseph Basford	0 -5 -0	
Roger Hebbard	0 -6 -0		Simeon Cook	0-10 -0	
Zenas Alden	4 -0 -0		David Stoddard	1 -0 -0	
Asa Woodward	1-10 -0		John Payne	2-10 -0	
Daniel Cushing	1-10 -0		Noah Powers	1-10 -0	
Benjamin Gary	2 -0 -0		James Bellows	1-10 -0	
John Andros	3 -0 -0		Phineas Allen	3 -0 -0	
Elial Peck	1 -0 -0		Alexander Cambell	3 -0 -0	
Jahleel Peck	4 -0 -0		Nathan Blodgett	3 -0 -0	
Sam¹ Estabrook	9 -0 -0		Abial Wills	1-10 -0	
Ziba Huntington	2 -0 -0		Cady Allen	3 -0 -0	
Sherekiah Ballard	5 -0 -0		Walter Peck	6 -0 -0	10
Jesse Cook	15 -0 -0	20	Diarca Allen	5 -0 -0	12
Charles Saxton	2 -0 -0		Enoch Redington	1-10 -0	
Nath¹ Bidwell	3 -0 -0		Elisha Payne	10 -0 -0	12
Daniel Barker	2 -0 -0	6	Jeriah Sweatland	1-10 -0	
Robert Colburn	20 -0 -0	40	Benj. Fuller	1-10 -0	
Andrew Wheatly	3 -6 -0		David Whitmore	3 -0 -0	
Asa Fitch	1-10 -0		Zacheus Downer	8 -0 -0	15
Ashur Allen	1 -5 -0		Richard Aldrich	6 -0 -0	
Daniel Wills	1 -0 -0		John Chapman	2 -0 -0	2
Ebba Peck	2 -0 -0		Oliver Ellis	2 -0 -0	
Arad Simons	4 -0 -0		Gideon Baker	4 -0 -0	
Abijah Chandler	2 -0 -0		Andrew Baker	1 -0 -0	
Richard Corning	2 -0 -0		Gideon Baker Jun	2-10 -0	
Ebenezer Bliss	2 -0 -0		Richard Lyman	4 -0 -0	
David Hough	15 -0 -0	12	James Hibbard	3 -0 -0	
Nathan Durkee	4 -0 -0		John Porter	5 -0 -0	
Lemuel Hough	15 -0 -0	18	Daniel Hough	4 -0 -0	
Sluman Lathrop	5 -0 -0		James Ayers	2 -0 -0	
Samuel Lathrop	4 -0 -0	12	Enoch Freeman	1 -0 -0	
Zure Eldridge	2 -0 -0		Richard H Little	1 -0 -0	
Daniel Bliss	4 -0 -0		Daniel Alden	7 -0 -0	12
Jonathan Quimby	2 -0 -0				
Constant Storrs	20 -0 -0	24	Total	£398 -5	353 S.
Nathaniel Storrs	10 -0 -0	18			
Jonathan Bosworth	2 -0 -0				
Nath¹ Bosworth	1 -0 -0				

Whereas the Town of Lebanon Did on the seventeenth Day of May 1792 vote to Erect a Meeting-house near the western part of the plain on which Robert Colburn lives in s'd Lebanon, And whereas David Hough Constant Storrs, Robert Colburn, Stephen Billings, Nath¹ Hall and Clap Sumner are A committee appointed for that Purpose and whereas the said Com^tee have undertaken to lay out money or certicutes that may be subscribed towards Erecting said house the Subscribers in Consideration of said undertaking do Each one promise the said Com^tee to pay them the sum or sums Set against our Respective names in the Articules specified at or before the 25 day of Dec next in witness of our hands
    Lebanon 21st May A. D. 1792 the above is a coppy
                Stephen Billings s'd Com^tee & Clerk

Floor Plan of the Meeting House on the Common, now the Town Hall.

A debit and credit account was opened with each one of the subscribers and others, of which a few examples are added showing the condition of things in those days:

	£	s.	d.	Money
Aaron Hutchinson Cattle or Grain	15			£ 1
To A Pew on the floor of the house No 21	17	10		
Contra Cridet by Cash Laid out for rum	1			
Oct. 1792 by a yoak of Oxen and one Cow	15			

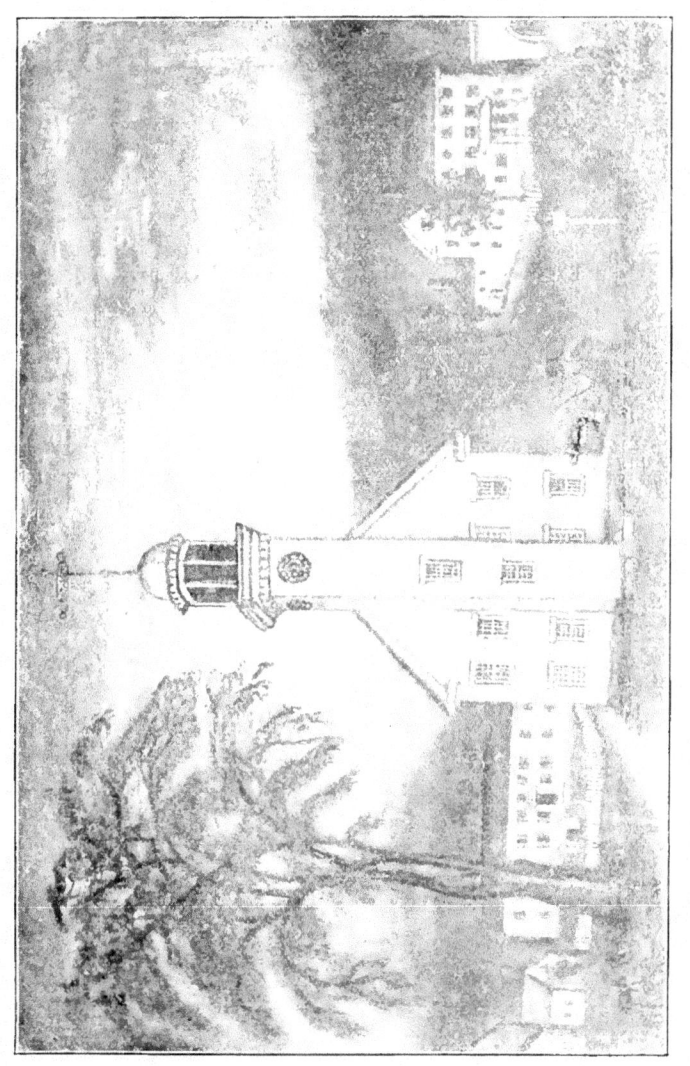

THE OLD MEETING HOUSE ON THE COMMON. PRESENT TOWN HOUSE.

Photographed from a Painting.

	£	s.	d.	Money
By two cows	10			
By a note of hand against Joel Tilden	4	8		
Samuel Estabrooks in stock or grain	9			
20 Decr 1793 by one half A. Pew on the floor No 10	11	10		
Contra Cridet				
By an order from Thos Hough		17		

	£	s.	d.
By Robert Colburn	2	3	0
By a yoake of steers	8	0	0
By one yearling Hiffer	1	17	6
By a Pr of two years old stears	9	0	0

Nathaniel Storrs Subscription	10			18s
19 Dec 1793 by one half of A Pew on the floor No 32	20	5		
To his Pew in the Gallery No 13	15	5		
	45	0		18s
Contra Cridit				
Feby 9 1793 By his acompt this day exhibited	4	10		
Also by cash				18s
By 6 thousand 10′ Nails at 15/	4	10		
By one Hogshead & 1/3 of Lyme at 45/	2	15		
by an order from Thomas Hough	4			
by flax & flax-seed & Cash		16	9	
1. Oct.r 1793 Cr By three Creatars	14	10		
19 Decr Cr By two Due Bills	13	18	3	
	£45			18s
John Porter	£ 5			
17 Dec 1793 By a half of a Pew on the floor No 44				
Bid of By Richard Lyman	11	5		
	16	5		

	£	s	d
Contra Cridet			
Jan 1793 as by his acct this day exhibited		10	6
By eight Bushels of Wheat	2		
Oct. 1793 By pr of two years old stears	7	5	
By his Due Bill	6	9	6
	16	5	0
Levi Webster Dr			
By Sundrys	16	0	0
Contra Cridet			
By himself and Son framing Meeting house thirty day	16		

It will be seen that the amount of cash in the subscriptions was small, £17, 13s. The remainder was paid in various articles and ways—in produce from the farm, in lumber and labor. A few of the articles turned in were the following: "A yearling Hiffer," a "pair of two year old stears," "Belfry Job," "3 creatars," "1 Gal rum" by three different persons; seven and one half gallons by one person. These, to us, are novel contributions to a meeting-house, but they gave what they had.

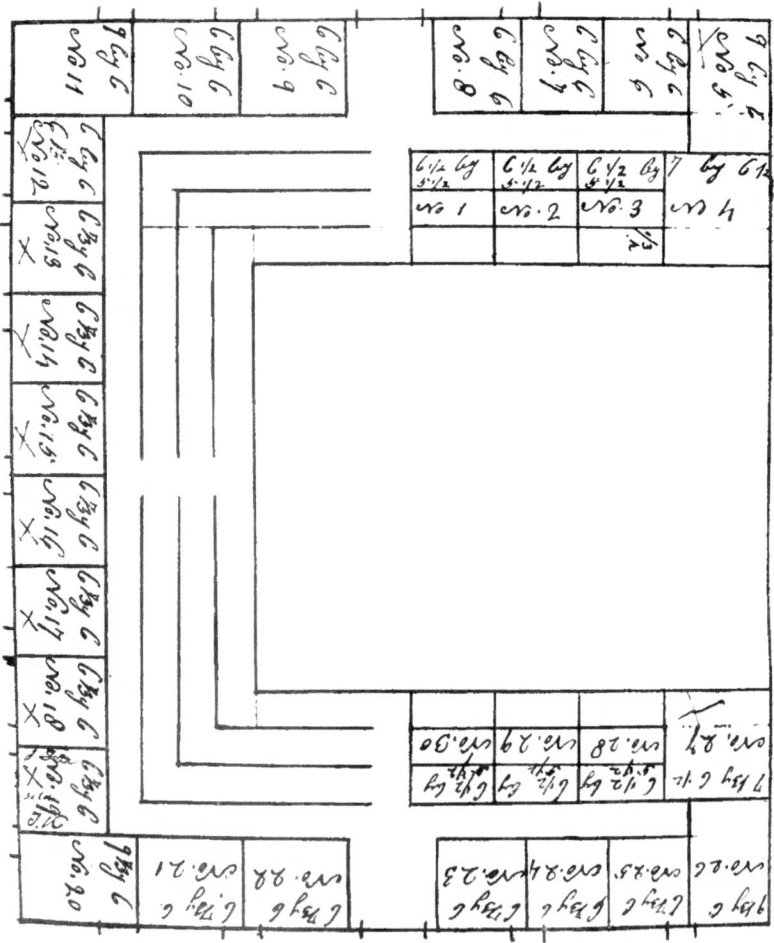

Gallery Plan of the Meeting House on the Common, moved in 1850.

OLD VIEW OF THE COMMON.

After the house was enclosed and the pew ground laid out the committee proceeded to sell the pews according to the following advertisement:

Advertisement

Lebanon 10th January 1793 to be sold at Public Vendue to the highest Bidder or Bidders the Pews in the New Meeting house at Lieut Robert Colburns Dwellinghouse in Lebanon on thirsday the thirty first day of Jany instant at nine o'clock in the forenoon. One fourth part of the pay to be made this Winter, and the remainder Next Christmas in wheat at five Shillings p^r Bush or Neat Stock equivalent

By order of the Com^{tt}

Stephen Billing Com^{tte} Clerk

N. B. if the Stock is paid in the Last Payment it must be by the first of Octr next

Lebanon Jan. 31st A. D. 1793 the Vendue was opened agreeable to the above advertisement and the No^s pew was sold to the following Persons (viz)

	£	s.		£	s.
No 7 to Jesse Cook at	14	....	No 31 to Simeon Peck	32	....
No 8 to Sherekiah Ballard	17	10	No 4 to Simeon Peck	16	....
No 32 to Nathaniel Storrs	40	10	No 42 to Lieut. Samuel Lathrop	33	10
No 1 to Capt. Daniel Phelps	41	....	No 28 to Lieut Robert Colburn	20	....
No. 25 to Jesse Cook	21	10	No 10 to Lieut Saml Estabrook	23	....
No 2 to Deaⁿ Zacheus Downer	40	....	No 29 to Clap Sumner	23	....
No 9 to Stephen Billing	18	10	No 11 to Deaⁿ Zacheus Downer	39	10
No 30 to Richard Corning	20	....			
No 41 to Daniel Hough	22	10			

Jan. 31st 1793 this Vendue is adjourned to the twenty fifth of Feby 1793 Stephen Billing Com^{te} Clerk

Feb. 25 1793 Met according to adjournment and opened the Vendue and proceeded to sell and accordingly we sold the following Pews to the following person (viz)

Attest. Stephen Billing Clerk

	£	s.		£	s.
No 18 to Cady Allen	13	10	Fifteenth of March 1793 met according to adjournment opened the vendue and sold the following Pews to the following persons (viz)		
No 17 to Beriah Abbott	18	....			
No 40 to Oliver Ellis	18	....			
No 16 to Zenas Alden	20	....			
No 15 to Phineas Allen	20	10			
No 14 to Col^l Elisha Payne	40	....	No 6 to Asa Woodward	14	5
No 43 to John Colburn Sr	32	....	No 22 to Joel Tilden	25	....
No 44 to Richard Lyman	22	10	No 34 to Capt David Hough	34	5
No 36 to Capt. Josiah Cleaveland	20	....	No 3 to Capt Arad Simons	24	....
No 33 to Lieut Robert Colburn	40	....			
No 24 to Lemuel Davenport	32	....	15 March 1793 This Vendue was adjourned from time to time &c and the remainder part of the pews was sold		
No 23 to Moses Persons	26	....			
No 21 to Aaron Hutchinson Esq	17	10			
25 Feb. 1793 this Vendue is adjourned until the fifteenth day of March next					
			No 19 to Capt Shuman Lathrop	15	....
			No 47 to Richard Aldrich	26	10
No 20 to Capt. Asher Alden	15	....	No 46 to Capt Joseph Wood	27	....
No 37 to Jacob Ela	15	....	No 35 to Abijah Chandler	22	10
No 45 to Jonathan Quimby	16	10	No 5 to Capt Constant Storrs	16	....
No 48 to Jonathan Bosworth of Enfield	15	....	No 12 to Simeon Peck	37	15
			No 27 to John Baswell	14	15

Sold the Town Nos 26, 38, 39.

The following are the Pews set to the several Persons as sold in the Gallery of the house.   Attest Stephen Billing

	£	S			
No 16 to Capt Daniel Phelps	16	....	No 20 to Abial Wills	10	....
No 15 to Urial Huntington	16	1	No 21 to John Colburn Jr	8	10
No 14 to Capt Sluman Lathrop	14	....	No 4 to Capt Joseph Wood Jr	13	15
No 5 to Capt. Constant Storrs	9	....	No 3 to Daniel Alden	12	15
No 17 to Capt Constant Storrs	16	6	No 2 to Witherell Hough	12	....
No 13 to Nath¹ Storrs	14	15	No 1 to Noah Powers	15	10
No 18 to Capt David Hough	14	10	No 11 to Rev. Isaiah Potter	10	....
No 27 to Jesse Cook	13	11	No 8 to Daniel Stickney of En-		
No 19 to Lemuel Hough	13	....	field	9	5
No 12 to Thomas Hough	12	12	No 7 to Lieut Sam¹ Estabrooks	11	....
No 30 to William Corning	13	....	No 26 to Jesse Cook	9	....
No 29 to David Whitmore	13	5	No 24 one half to Benjah Abbott	4	10
No 28 to John Porter	13	5	No 22 to the town	....	....

The net sum realized from the sale of the pews seems to have been £1449, 19s., 7d., which was more than enough to cover the expense of building. Accordingly the amount of each man's subscription was refunded to him, for which he gave a receipt as follows:

Lebanon 30th Dec 1794

Rec'd of the Comte for erecting the New Meeting house in Lebanon five pounds twelve shillings being in full for my subscription, and I promise said Comtee to repay a part back if wanted to compleat sd house in a maner agreeable to the vote of s'd town Respecting subscriptions for said house

By me Diarca Allen.

The way in which this repayment was managed seems to have been this: When a subscriber bought a pew he was credited the amount of his subscription on the price of the pew, paying the balance. Thus Diarca Allen's subscription was five pounds and twelve shillings. He bought one half of No. 15 on the floor at £10, 5s., which, less the amount of his subscription, would leave £4, 13s., as the amount to be paid for the pew.

The house thus built was originally fifty feet front and sixty feet rear. It was moved from its original position in 1868, enlarged and remodelled and is now occupied as a town hall.

In February, 1895, the historian became the fortunate possessor of a little volume, "Early Lebanon." The Lebanon is in Connecticut. In this book there is a chapter, "The Meeting House War," the substance of which is here given:

When the settlement of Lebanon began, 1697, a broad avenue, thirty rods wide, was laid out and upon each side home-lots of forty-two acres were staked out. About midway of this broad avenue a place was selected for a meeting-house, "fixed and established forever," to prevent any future controversies as the town became more populous.

In 1700 two of the settlers bought a large tract of land north of the town, which they desired to have annexed to Lebanon. To this the proprietors of Lebanon objected, having, it seems, a prophetic discernment of a meeting-house controversy. The purchasers of the new tract answered that their land was large enough for a society of its own, and that they would reserve thereon a location for a meeting-house, and that the first should never be in any way disturbed. Upon this condition the annexation took place.

In 1724 the society voted to build a new and larger meeting-house on the old location, but so much opposition developed that nothing was done. In 1724 the society of Goshen was set off from the southwesterly part of the town, resulting in this: that the first house was no longer in the geographical center of the town, putting a new argument in the mouths of those desiring a change of place. Appeal was made to the General Assembly, which in 1731 appointed a committee to visit the place and determine the matter. After hearing the parties the committee fixed upon the original location, that being the agreement of the first settlers *that it should remain forever on that spot.*

The fires burned higher and hotter. The reply was that the original agreement was only a vote and, therefore, repealable; that if originally binding, the bonds were broken, because one of the parties had gone out—the Goshen society—and they protested more fiercely than ever against being compelled to pay their full share of the expense of the new building, whose location was so inconvenient for them, and that they were expecting soon to form a new society and build a house for themselves.

Upon their application another meeting was called and held in 1732, when it was voted that within eighteen years thereafter, but not before six years, there should be set off a new society in the northern part by a dividing line agreed upon and described in the vote; that until the new society should be so set off the northern settlers should continue to pay their share towards the building and keeping in repair a meeting-house on the old site; that a separate account of all the moneys so paid by the people north of the line described should be kept, and that when the new society was formed, and had built a meeting-house of their own, all the money so paid by them should be refunded to them by the old society, to be applied toward the building of their own meeting-house; and that application should be made to the General Assembly for an act ratifying and confirming this agreement. The application was made and the General Assembly sanctioned, ratified and confirmed it.

Certainly an eminently fair bargain, which restored peace to the contending parties. The new meeting-house was built by the parties in common, and the cost to the northern settlers was carefully kept, and all was quiet until 1767, a period of thirty years. The eighteen years passed away without any movement to build among the northern people.

By this time repairs were needed upon the central house, and the question arose who should pay for them. The first society voted that if the northern people should within a reasonable time procure an act of incorporation, then the old society would pay back the sums paid by the others.

Still nothing was done by either party. The question was raised whether, since the eighteen years fixed and sanctioned by the General Assembly had long ago expired, the first society were bound by their new vote, and whether it might not be repealed at any future meeting. This was a matter of many discussions, until 1772, when at the request of the northern people, a society meeting was called, at which it was voted, by a majority of two, to take down the central house and build farther north, at the then center of population. But this would remove the house to the great inconvenience of the southern part of the town. They remonstrated and petitioned the General Assembly for their further interposition in the affair. The assembly at its October session, 1772, appointed a committee to examine the matter and report to the assembly in May, 1773. That report was in substance as follows: That there was an ancient agreement that the meeting-house should stand upon Meeting-House Hill, its first site; that this agreement was made for good reasons, and ought to be held sacred and inviolable; that it was then expected that the northern people would have a society of their own, and a dividing line was agreed upon and provisions were

CLEMENT HOUGH.

made to reimburse them for whatever sums they might pay to the ancient society, and that the building should remain in its first location, and that the new society, when it should build, should have the money contributed by them refunded.

The General Assembly approved the report, fixed the location on the spot it had always occupied, ordered that it should be kept in repair by the whole society, and that if the northern people should form a new society within five years then all the money they had paid in should be returned to them.

Then it was said that the assembly had neither ratified nor disallowed the votes of the old society, and they did not know whether those votes were legally binding or not. The northern people, not feeling able to build without the certain return of the advancements which they had made to the first society, took no steps to form a society.

For a time something like harmony prevailed between the factions, but it was the calm before the cyclone.

By 1802 the meeting-house again needed repairs, and at a meeting called to consider the subject, a vote was passed by a majority present, refusing to repair it. Some of the southern people again appealed to the General Assembly, reciting the facts and asking relief. After a hearing the assembly authorized and empowered the inhabitants south of the proposed dividing line for a new society, to tax themselves for repairs, to call meetings, choose certain officers, to lay and collect taxes for such purpose, and to make future repairs, exempting all the inhabitants north of the line from any liability for such taxes or repairs, but saying nothing of the legal rights, privileges or franchises which the northern people held in common with the whole society.

Under this instruction of the assembly, the southern voters met, taxed themselves, raised about $600, appointed a committee which expended the sum in repairs.

But this did not give peace. At a meeting of the whole society, March 27, 1804, it was voted by a large majority, upon a proposition made by Daniel Tilden, Israel Loomis, John Davey, Samuel Bailey, and John Hayward, that the society would relinquish all its right and interest in the meeting-house and consent that the materials thereof should be used in the construction of a new one, upon conditions, that the said Tilden and others, as a committee, would give sufficient bonds that they would build a good commodious meeting-house for the use of the society at or near the then center of the whole society (about one mile northerly) within one year from the first day of April next at their own sole expense, and give full title thereof to the society without any cost, and that the people living north of said center would fund their proposition for the support of the ministry forever.

The committee accepted the conditions of the above note, executed a bond in the penal sum of $10,000. The bond was accepted by the society and deposited with the clerk, and the whole matter seemed to be settled.

Twenty days afterward the contractors, with their workmen, peaceably began to take down the old building to obtain materials for the construction of the new. But when the people saw their familiar house of worship in which they and their fathers and mothers had met for a century to offer their prayers and praises, to receive consolation in their bereavements and trials; when they saw this building around which so many associations clustered, in the process of destruction, their hearts burned within; they could not endure the sight, and their indignation at what seemed to them as sacrilege threatened violence. Writs were sought and obtained and several of the workmen were arrested. The work of destruction was suspended. Soon other writs were obtained, protecting the contractors and workmen and the house was leveled to the ground. But bitterness filled the hearts of the contending parties. Men of the highest standing were arrested and without bail. Among these was Hon. William Williams, a signer of the immortal Declaration of Independence, a man venerable by age and honored for his distinguished services throughout the land, and at that very time himself a judge of the County Court. He feels the touch of the town constable upon his shoulder, and is marched off a mile away and placed under a keeper, submitting quietly to the indignity. The only ray of light visible in this unseemly strife is the loyalty of the people on both sides to the forms of the law.

The house, so beloved by one party, whose distinguished materials were so coveted by the other party, lay upon the ground, now a new cause of contention. The southern people were determined they should not be removed; the northern people were determined to have them. The contractors thought of the heavy bond resting upon them. Open violence was threatened, which the local authorities were powerless to suppress, for they differed among themselves.

But wiser counsels prevailed. Leading men on both sides advised that resort be had to the higher courts. Suits in trespass were brought by the southern people against Daniel Tilden and the others of his committee for damages in demolishing the meeting-house, and the people quietly awaited the action of the court. At the trial many issues were raised, but the issue turned mainly upon the question whether the ancient agreement that the first place selected for the locating of the house "to be fixed and established forever" was still valid. The court affirmed that it was. On a further hearing upon the question of damages, the case went against the contractors for removal of the old church.

Of course a bill of exceptions was filed and the case went to the Superme Court of Errors. The whole case was gone over from the beginning, and the court affirmed the decision of the court below, and so ended the long controversy of one hundred years, involving the comfort and wishes of three generations. All parties gracefully submitted to the judgment of the court. A new meeting-house was built upon the first location, and in due time the northern people built a house of their own.

Now, most of the early settlers of this town came from the very scene of this "Meeting-house War," or its vicinity and were, therefore, thoroughly qualified to carry on a dispute about the location of a meeting-house in a different locality. The proclivity must have been inherited, fed in their childhood by constant hearing and interminable discussions, participated in as soon as they were made freemen. They knew the value of all manner of obstructions; how to vote and how to get votes repealed and annulled. They knew what things to let alone—excellent knowledge in all quarrels—hence they would have nothing to do with writs and counter writs, nor with appeals to the General Assembly, which, as is often the case, left their affairs worse confounded than before. Lebanon, Conn., is justly proud of the multitude of eminent men born on its soil. It was the home of the distinguished Trumbull family, the pastorate of President

Wheelock, the founder of Dartmouth College, the birthplace of Jeremiah Mason, one of the profoundest lawyers of the country, and of a host of others, yet the fathers of our own Lebanon in their wilderness home devised and executed a measure beyond the genius of all these great men of the old town. For not one of them thought of finding where the meeting-house ought to stand by measuring the land and soul travel and finding thus the equity of the whole matter.

The following transaction, common enough in those times, is found, happily, but once on our records:

Nov 27 1789 Voted to set up the maintenance of Mr. Patrick and his wife for the term of one year to the lowest bidder and that the moderator [Lemuel Hough] be Vendue Master, for s^d purpose—to set up and make sale of said persons' maintenance—being bid off at twenty-nine pounds by James Fuller in behalf of Lemuel Hough aforesaid

Very justly they seem to see the unseemliness of such a spectacle and immediately vote to build a workhouse or houses for the use of the poor, thirty-six feet by eighteen; that the selectmen be directed to pitch upon a spot to set said house upon and agree with some person or persons to build said house on the best terms they can.

At a meeting held June 22, 1789, to choose a representative to the Congress of the United States of America, Elisha Payne, Esq., had fifty-three votes. Benj. Bellows, Esq., and Simeon Olcott, Esq., one each.

March 1790 For President of the state John Pickering Federalist had 63 votes and Benj. Bellows 18

For State Senator Jonathan Freeman had 79 votes Edmund Freeman and Aaron Hutchinson one each.

Elisha Payne *Esq* was chosen representative

March 25 1790. Where as it is found detrimental to the increasing of that necessary and useful animal of sheep for the Rams to run at large in the fall of the year therefore to prevent the same

Be it enacted by the Inhabitants of the town of Lebanon in Town meeting assembled that no Sheep Ram shall be suffered to go at large out of the owners enclosure from and after the first day of September annually to the twentieth day of November; and if any ram shall be found going at large as aforesaid the owner thereof shall forfeit and pay the sum of ten shillings Lawful money, the one half to the treasurer of said Town for the use of the poor of s^d town, and the other moity to the person who shall sue for and prosecute the same to effect, together in the cost of suit.

CLARK HOUGH.

Aug 30 1790 Voted to direct the Selectmen to examine into the request of Messrs Robt. Colburn, & Lem. Hough with respect to their Losses in paying the arrears of Taxes for the Town to the State Treasury.

No action of the town seems to have been taken in this matter.

Voted for representatives to Congress with the following results. Abiel Foster had 2 votes Sam¹ Livermore 32 John Sam¹ Sherburne 26 Elisha Payne *Esq.* 20, Jonathan Freeman 11, Aaron Hutchinson 10, Elisha Ticknor 1. Elihu Hyde 1.

Of these candidates Samuel Livermore only was elected.

At a meeting in October they again voted for members of Congress, when Jeremiah Smith had 55 votes, John S. Sherburne 43, Abiel Foster 13. Jeremiah Smith was elected.

The following shows to what extent one branch of manufactures was pursued in the town:

This certifies that Daniel Robinson of Lebanon in the County of Grafton and State of New Hampshire has made or caused to be made three hundred thousand of wrought ten penny nails between the eighth day of Feby Anno Domini 1789 and the twentieth day of Jany current.

In witness whereof the selectmen of said Lebanon hereunto set their hands and seals and the nearest justice of the peace countersigns, this 28th day of —— 1791

           Jesse Cook [SEAL]
           Stephen Billings [SEAL]

Attest
  Aaron Hutchinson Jus. pacis

Endorsed Rec'd an order on the treasurer for fifteen pounds.

This was in accordance with an act passed 1787 to encourage the manufacture of nails in the state, repealed in 1805.

Records for the year 1791 are not to be found.

The state constitution of 1784 provided for a revision after seven years. A convention was called for the purpose in 1791 to meet at Concord, and Elisha Payne, Esq., was chosen the delegate from Lebanon. The convention met September 7, and began its work of revision. Various amendments were proposed, some to be accepted, while others were rejected. September 16 the convention appointed a committee, of which Elisha Payne, Esq., was a member, "to take into consideration the Constitution and the Resolutions passed at this session and the several motions made for alterations that have not been acted upon and prepare and report to the Convention at the adjournment alterations and amendments to be submitted to the people."

The convention met again February 8, 1792, heard and considered the report of the committee, when it was ordered that the amendments proposed should be printed and sent out to the people for their approval, returns to be made on the last Wednesday in May.

April 26, 1792, the town chose as a committee to take into consideration the revised constitution, Col. Elisha Payne, Aaron Hutchinson, Esq., and Capt. David Hough.

May 7 the town met "at the remains of the old meeting house," to act upon the amendments of the constitution. The above committee probably made some report and recommendations. They then proceeded to vote upon the seventy-two amendments proposed. One of the proposed amendments was promptly rejected, Article VI. which would allow anyone to be free from the support of the minister of a town upon his filing his dissent with the town clerk within certain specified times. Nos. 37 and 43 were also rejected. The latter required a property qualification of five hundred pounds.

When the convention re-assembled at Concord in May, it was found that some of the amendments had been accepted and others rejected. Other articles were, therefore, prepared and sent out to the people, to be considered by them on the twenty-seventh day of August, when the town voted unanimously for the acceptance of the constitution. When the returns from the state came in it was found that the amendments were accepted by the people.

A Coppy of Ye Inventory for 1792

Below is the earliest inventory of the town which is to be found among the town papers. Its items furnish interesting information concerning the condition of the town at that time:

No. of Polls from Eighteen to Seventy years of Age	236
No. of Acres of Orchard Land	
No. of Acres of Arable or Tillage Land	467½
No of Acres of Moing land	883
No of acres of Pasture land	1148
No of Horses and Mares	144
No of oxen	177
No of cows	277

DEVELOPMENT OF THE TOWN. 187

No of Horses and Cattle three years old 115
No of Horses and Cattle two years old 182
Yearly rent of mills wharves and Ferries repairs being deducted £69—8
Sum total of the Value of all Real Estate improved owned by the inhabitants £5520—
Sum total of the Value of all Real Estate not owned by the Inhabitants 234
Sum total of the Value of Stock in Trade
Sum total of Money in hand or on Interest £450
No of Horsis & Cattle one year old 299

      Jesse Cook ⎫
      James Crocker ⎬ Selectmen
      Stephen Billings ⎭

August 27, 1792, the town voted for six presidential electors, with the following result:

John Pickering Esq.	56	John White Esq	56
Elisha Payne *Esq*.	51	Benj. Bellows Esq	56
Joseph Badger Esq.	55	Jonathan Freeman Esq	1
——— Barret Esq	55		

The above record indicates the singular fact that the town clerk did not know the Christian name of one of the candidates. In these days if the votes were cast as recorded above, it might defeat a president. It should be Charles Barret.

At this same meeting the town voted for representatives to Congress, with the following result:

Payne Wingate Esq.	55	Jeremiah Smith Esq	59
John Sherburne Esq	48	Elisha Payne Esq	49
Beza Woodward Esq	2	Jonathan Freeman Esq	7
Abial Foster Esq	10	Timothy Walker Esq	2

John S. Sherburne, Payne Wingate and Abiel Foster were elected.

Now and then during these years there appears a vote directing Rev. Mr. Potter where to preach on the Sabbath. Upon the question whether he should preach a part of the time at the old meeting-house, the vote was affirmative 32, negative 55. The town meetings this year were held generally at "Robt Colburn's New Barn," which was on the ground where H. W. Carter now lives.

For some reason they voted again for presidential electors, November 12, 1792, and Josiah Bartlett, John Pickering, Thomas

Coggswell, Timothy Farrar, Benj. Bellows, and Jonathan Freeman each had 52 votes. They also voted again for representative to Congress, when Payne Wingate had 53 votes.

March 12, 1793, at the annual meeting the vote was as follows: For governor, Josiah Bartlett, 59; senator for the 12th district, Samuel Emerson, 59; Col. Elisha Payne, 7. Col. Elisha Payne was chosen representative to the Legislature. Jonathan Freeman had 85 votes for councillor.

This was the first time the town voted for governor of the state, the title having been changed under the revised constitution from president to governor. It was also the first time the town voted for a councillor. This was the first town meeting in the new meeting-house.

To show the ancient manner of calling a town meeting, the general form is here given for the annual meeting March 11, 1794:

State of New Hampshire) To Ephraim Wood Constable in
Grafton ss (and for the town of Lebanon
Greeting.

You are hereby directed and required to warn all the Legal Voters in the town of Lebanon to meet in town meeting at the New Meeting house in said Lebanon on Tuesday the 11th Day of March Next at nine o'clock A. M. on s'd Day to act on the following articles:

Given under our hand and seal in said Lebanon this 20th Day of Feby A D. 1794

Nath¹ Porter
Asher Allen } Selectmen
Dan¹ Phelps

hereof fail not and make Return of your Doings to the town clerk of said Lebanon by the 11th Day of March Next at Nine o clock in the morning on s'd Day.

In Pursuance of the above Warrant I have Posted up a true coppy of the above Warning on the 24th of Feby 1794

Attest Ephraim Wood Constable

At this meeting votes for governor were: John S. Gilman, 99; Elisha Payne, 16; Benj. Bellows, 2; Jonathan Freeman, 1; Nicolas Gilman, 1; Elihu Hyde, Esq., 1.

This is the largest vote cast to this date.

Votes for councillor: Jonathan Freeman, 53; Beza Woodward, 8; Elisha Payne, Esq., 11; Robert Colburn, 1.

For senator for 12th district: Jonathan Freeman, 5; Elisha Payne, Esq., 76; Moses Dow, 6.

REV. STORY HEBARD.

Maj. David Hough was chosen representative.

For the first time the selectmen presented a detailed account of their doings and the affairs of the town.

August 25, 1794, the town was called together to vote again for representatives to Congress, there being no choice at the previous election.

December 8, 1794, the town again met to choose a representative, their ballots being limited to Payne Wingate and Abiel Foster. Abiel Foster had 32 votes, but Payne Wingate was elected.

The years which follow, to the close of the century, were years of quiet, so far as the affairs of the town were concerned. They regularly elected their town officers, voted for representatives to Congress, for governor and other state officers. They were busy laying out new roads, improving the old, now and then symptoms of a contest appearing. These years will, therefore, be passed over without particular mention. Some things which are new in town affairs, or which may have special interest, will be noted.

March 10, 1795, Pelatiah Buck was appointed fish inspector. March, 1796, Jude Bailey was appointed inspector of the fishery, and again in March, 1797.

When the country was new and the Connecticut poured its floods into Long Island Sound unrestrained by dams, its waters were the resort of a multitude of salmon and shad. They came up as far as Lebanon, the salmon turning up White River and the shad up the Mascoma to deposit their spawn. Great numbers of these fish were taken by the early settlers for their own use and for sale to the people not so happily situated. It is with these matters that the inspector of fish was concerned.

The old people used to say that they had seen the clear waters of White River blue and almost solid with the shoals of salmon struggling up its current.

Two weeks in June, 1795, must have been full of interest to the people here, for at that time the Legislature was in session at Hanover. Most of the people saw their law-makers at work for the first and only time. Whether it increased their respect for, and confidence in, that august body tradition does not say. The place of meeting was very convenient for Colonel Payne, the representative of the town. John G. Gilman was governor, Russell Freeman of Hanover speaker of the house, and Ebenezer Smith, president of the senate.

The name of Stephen Kendrick, for many years town clerk and prominent in all affairs, makes its first appearance in the records March, 1796, when he was chosen sealer of weights and measures.

November, 1796, voted to procure two palls, one large and one small one, and to be kept at Mr. Simeon Peck's.

In March, 1797, the town, by vote, established prices for work on highways as follows:

Laboar from the first of May to the first of August 3/6 per day; from the first of August to the first of October 3/ per day, and 2/6 per day the rest of the season.

Oxen carts and plows to be one half the price of Man's labor at each of the afore said times.

During this year the cemetery in the center village was purchased of John and Benjamin Kimball for $66.66, and also the cemetery near Ebenezer Cole's.

The year 1798 might appropriately be termed the bridge year, for it was a year in which large sums were spent in building and repairing bridges. Among the charges for this work are the following, which read strangely to this generation: For rum at the lower bridge, $.57; for rum for two bridges, $18.76; for rum at the bridge, $3.75. Here are similar charges for 1799: For liquor for venduing bridge by Col. Payne's, $1.36; for rum to work on the road, $.75; for rum used at the bridge, $6.00; for rum and wine for Barbrick family, $2.00; for rum for his family, $.50.

THE TOWN IN 1800.

Before entering upon the events of another century, let us try to realize the condition of the town at this period. It is about thirty-six years since the first settlements were actually begun. What progress has been made? How much has been done towards subduing the wilderness? Who are living here now? Who of those who began with the early days of the town have passed away? What improvements have been made in roads, in the comforts and conveniences of life? What are the people doing—what are they talking about?

The town is settled and quiet in its state relations, which in the years past occupied so much of time, thought and expense. The town is not connected with Vermont nor planning any union with that state. It is not in a "state of nature"; that is, independent and sovereign, but is connected "with respect to its internal police" with New Hampshire and contented. Its large arrearages of taxes have happily been paid, though Messrs. Hough and Colburn are still a little sore on that point. We learn who were living here at that time from the following list of tax-payers:

Asahel Abbott
Beriah Abbott
Josiah Adams
Andrew Aldrich
Andrew Aldrich, Jr.
Clark Aldrich
Elisha Aldrich
Richard Aldrich
Abijah Allen
Asher Allen
Diarca Allen
Joseph Amsden

John Andrews
Cyprian Andrews
Daniel Alden
Zenas Alden
Zalmon Aspenwall
Cady Allen
William Avery
Solomon Abba
Richard Andrews
Daniel Abbott
Joseph Abbott
John Abbott

Judah Bailey
Andrew Baker
Gideon Baker
Gideon Baker, Jr.
Nathaniel Bidwell
Stephen Billings
Alfred Bingham
Azariah Bliss
Asel Bliss
Daniel Bliss
Ebenezer Bliss
Isaiah Bliss
Widow Anna Blodgett

Edward Bosworth
Pelatiah Buck
Richard Buswell
Stephen Bliss
Samuel Barker
John Buswell
Jacob W. Brewster
George Booth
Pelatiah Bugbee
Wm Burbech
Stephen Barker
Justis Bruce

Abijah Chandler
Waters Clark

Samuel Crocker
Joshua Cushing

Aaron Cleaveland
John Colburn
Robert Colburn
Stephen Colburn
Giles Cook
Jesse Cook, Jr.
William Corning
James Crocker

William Dana
William Dana, Jr.
Joseph Downer
Martin Dewey
William Downer
Zacheus Downer
James Duncan, Jr.
Nathan Durkee

Jacob Ela
Joseph Ela
Zuar Eldridge
Oliver Ellis
Aaron Estabrooks
Hobart Estabrooks
Rhodolphus Estabrooks
Benjamin Ela

Moses Farnam
Humphrey Farrar
Barnabas Fay
Asa Fitch
Asa Fitch, Jr.
John Fox
Edmund Freeman
Edmund Freeman, Jr.
Roger Freeman
Enoch Freeman

Elijah Gould

Asa Colburn
Roswell Clark
Jonathan Conant
Seth Convers
Colton Center
Jonathan Colby
Daniel Castet
Joseph Castet

Samuel Dustin
Timothy Dudley
Daniel Demon
Joseph Dodge
Rufus Durkee
Timothy Darling
Silas Downer
Andred Downer

Theodore Ela
Samuel Estabrooks, Jr.
Joseph Evans
James Ela
Oliver Edwards
Phineas Elkins
Joseph Ellis

Otis Freeman
Nathaniel Freeman
Benj. Fuller
Benj. Fuller, Jr.
James Fuller
Nathan Flanders
Abraham Forster
Caleb Fellows
Joseph Flint
Jedediah Freeman

Oliver Griswold

ABRAM PUSHEE.

Samuel Gage
Joseph Goodridge
John Gray
David Gray
Joseph Griswold

Dan Hall
Orla Hall
Nathaniel Hall
John Hewet
Jonathan Hamilton
James Hartshorn
Aaron Hebbard
James Hebbard
Moses Hebbard, Jr.
David Hinkley
Daniel Hough
David Hough
Lemuel Hough
Thomas Hough
Witherel Hough
James How
Elias Huntington
Miller Huntington

John Jeffers
Nathan Jewett

Thomas Kirshaw
Stephen Kendrick
John Kimball
Benjamin Kimball

Wm Loomer
Denison Lathrop
Elijah Lathrop
Samuel Lathrop

Nathaniel Mason

Joseph Garland
Ezekiel Gove
Joseph Giles
Comfort Goff

Uriel Huntington
William Huntington
William Huntington, Jr.
Ziba Huntington
Joseph Huntington
Aaron Hutchinson
Asaph Hyde
Elihu Hyde
Elihu Hyde, Jr.
Silas Hyde
Guy Hough
Widow Hannah Huntington
John Houston
James Hebbard, Jr.
James Huckins
Joseph Hill
Daniel Hinkley
Silas Hebbard

James Jones
Joel Joslyn

John Kile
Ephraim Kile
Aaron Kinsman

Sloman Lathrop
Richard Lyman
James Little
Ebenezer Lewis

John Martin, Jr.

Joshua Markham
Bela Markham
Elam Markham
John Martin
Jonathan Martin
Joseph Martin

Joseph Martin, Jr.
Elias Marsh
Reuben Mason
Jesse Morse
Jeremiah Marston
Parly Mason

Wm. H. Packard
David Packard
Ichabod Packard
Nathaniel Packard
Nathaniel Packard, Jr.
Phineas Parkhurst
Elisha Payne, Jr.
John Payne
William Payne
Simeon Peck
Eliel Peck
Walter Peck
Ebba Peck

Jahleeb Peck
Turner Peterson
Daniel Phelps
John Porter
Nathaniel Porter
George W. Post
Noah Powers
Howard Phelps
Elisha Payne
Arnold Porter
Luther Pyke
Absalom Packard

Jonathan Quimby

Cephas Robinson
Elijah Reid
Enoch Redington
James Ralston
Daniel Richards

William Rowland
Micajah Rowell
Noah Read
Amos Robinson
Thomas Ray

Ebenezer Simon
Arad Simons
Abner Smith
Alpheus Smith
Asa Smith
Daniel Smith
Elijah Sprague
Elkanah Sprague
Widow Deborah Sprague

Constant Storrs
Constant Storrs, Jr.
Jesse Storrs
Nathaniel Storrs
Phineas Strong
Clap Sumner
Jeriah Swetland
Roswell Swetland
Orsemus Strong

Elijah Sprague, Jr.
William Spring

Benjamin Taylor
Elish Ticknor
John Ticknor
Paul K. Ticknor
Charles Tilden
Joseph Tilden, Jr.

Nathan Upton

John Walton
Thomas Waterman
Hezekiah Waters
Luther Waters
Joseph Weed
Thomas Wells
Eliphalet Wells
Andrew Wheabley
David Whitmore
Daniel Willes
Roger Willes
Ephraim Wood

Samuel Young

Daniel Strong
———— Sexton

Osgood True
Jesse Tibbets
James Ticknor
Joseph Tilden, 3d
James Trussel
Joel Tilden

David Underhill

John Wood
Joseph Wood
Luther Wood
Roger Wood
Abel Wright
Francis West
Abel Wright, Jr.
Jocob M. White
Isaac Warren
Ebenezer Whitmore
Jonathan Ware

The names of forty-one of those who signed the "Association Test," in 1776, appear in this list. Of the eighty-seven names appended to that test, more than one half have either died or left the town.

THE PROPERTY IN TOWN, 1800.

There were about 300 polls, indicating a population of over twelve hundred; twenty acres of orchards. In 1792 none are returned.

Tillage, about 442, which is less than in 1792.

Mowing, about 1,164, a gain of nearly 300 acres.

Pasture, 1,674 acres, a gain of about 500 acres.
Horses, 211.
Oxen, 248.
Cows, 405.
Cattle, four years old, 152; three years old, 223; two years old, 362.
Value of buildings and improvements, $13,370.
Stock in trade, $950.
Money at interest, $1,143.

In estimating quantities of land, the law of that period established the following rules: "Accounting so much orchard as will in a common season produce ten barrels of cyder or peavey, one acre; so much pasture land as will summer a cow, four acres; what mowing land will commonly produce one town of good English hay yearly or meadow hay in proportion, one acre; and what arable and tillage land will commonly produce twenty-five bushels of corn, one acre; in which is to be considered all land planted with indian corn, potatoes and beans and sown with grain, flax or peas." Laws for Inventory, 1797.

In inspecting the foregoing returns of the land, the reader will please keep these rules in mind.

In the number of polls the following are not included:

"Those from eighteen to twenty-one enrolled in the militia; instructors and students of colleges; ordained ministers and preceptors of academies, paupers and idiots."

The inventory shows that the town has made rapid progress in population and improvements. The following are the town officers for the year 1800:

Moderator, Col. David Hough.
Town Clerk, John Colburn.
Selectmen, Thomas Waterman, Gideon Baker Jr., Jonathan Hamilton.
Tything men, Abel Wright, Barnabas Fay, Nathan Jewett, and Ephraim Wood
Highway Surveyors, Joseph Downer, Hubbard Estabrook, James Crocker, Paul N. Ticknor, Maj Constant Storrs, Nathan Durkee, Andrew Baker, Nathan Jewett Pelatiah Buck, Clap Sumner, Enoch Freeman
Fence viewers, Joseph Martin, Jr., John Payne, Zuar Eldridge, William David, Jr.

SIMEON S. POST.

DEVELOPMENT OF THE TOWN.

Hog-rieves Theodore Ela, Daniel Bliss, William Loomer Zalmon Aspenwall, Clark A. Aldrich, Nathaniel Freeman

Surveyor of lumber, Thomas Hough.

Representative, Col. Elisha Payne.

Constable and collector, Edmund Freeman

No sealer of leather, or of weights and measures chosen

Votes for Governor, Hon. John Taylor Gilman   156
                Timothy Walker Esq.   3

Councillor David Hough
Russell Freeman   54
Senator for 12th District David Hough   106
Constant Storrs

Voted to raise two hundred dollars for the use of the town the year ensuing

Voted to raise five hundred dollars for the use of the highways the ensuing year.

Roads and Bridges.

An inspection of the records shows that the town was well supplied with roads in all directions, and that they were diligently improving them. About this time there were movements throughout the state to improve the means of communication with the different portions of the state. The people were prospering and had a surplus from their farms seeking a distant market. Bridges over the Connecticut were planned and chartered. Turnpikes had already been built in some portions of the state and others were projected, and among them the fourth New Hampshire turnpike, having its northern termination at West Lebanon, to connect by Lyman's bridge with a turnpike through the valley of the White River. The Connecticut River was at this time the channel of transportation. Farm products were carried in boats down the river to "Old Har'ford," which returned laden with salt, sugar, molasses and other supplies.

The boats floated with the current downward, assisted by poles, and sails when the wind served. Their return was more difficult, as they had the current against them, and were obliged to gain every foot by the exertion of strength. This transportation gave employment to a large number of men. What is called the "Point" on the opposite bank of the Connecticut was a harbor for these boats. Sometimes a hundred would be tied to the banks at the same time.

To improve the navigation of the river, locks were built and canals cut. Among them those at Olcott's Falls were chartered a little before this time. They had already been built at Bellows Falls and a charter had been sought for locks at Water Quechee, in Hartland. Much of the pine lumber found in this and the surrounding towns was floated down the river in rafts to older towns in Massachusetts, but chiefly to Hartford, Conn. From there it could be readily sent to New York by water.

In this region there were no public conveyances. If any one

ROADS AND BRIDGES.

wished to take a journey he must go on foot or on horseback, or in his own carriage. A large part of the journeying was on horseback. Mail facilities were few and far between. During the Revolutionary War a post rider started from Portsmouth once a fortnight, rode to Haverhill, from thence down the river to Charlestown and back again to Portsmouth. In 1791 there were four post routes over which the post-rider went once a fortnight. Postoffices were established in ten of the principal towns and postmasters were allowed two pence on every letter which passed through their hands. By 1800 there had been some improvement in this system, but chances to send letters were still few and far between, except by private conveyance.

At this period the business of the town was mainly farming. Cattle and horses were raised for market, pork to a limited extent. Flax was cultivated, dressed and spun and woven into garments. Oil was pressed from the seed. People made their own cloth, which was dressed by David Hinkley, clothier, whose mills were on True brook. The trees which they were obliged to cut down to prepare their land for cultivation, such as were not fit for lumber of the first quality, they burned, and from the ashes made pot-ash in large quantities. There were several tanneries in different parts of the town. Lumber was manufactured largely at Payne's mills, at other points on the Mascoma. Almost every brook had its temporary sawmill.

Of stores there were many. The Lymans on the Point did the heaviest business, taking in exchange for sugar, molasses, salt, nails, etc., beef, pork, etc. James Duncan had a store near the new meeting-house. He was also licensed to retail "speritous liquors" and wines. Turner Peterson on the river road had a store and he is licensed to sell "foreign distilled liquors." Joel Tilden, merchant, on the river road, was approbated to sell liquor. Uriel Huntington had a store west of where E. Cole now lives, and was licensed to sell "foreign Distilled Speritus liquors." Winneck & Ralston had a store at Payne's Mills (East Lebanon).

Taverns were plenty. Samuel Gage on the south side of the Mascoma, Sumner Clap on the county road from Concord to Hanover, Beriah Abbott at the head of School Street, Capt. Joseph Wood on the river road, Theodore Ela on the river road,

Enos Kellogg in the east part of the town, Ephraim Wood in the south part of the town, Rodolphus Estabrooks on the river road, all licensed to sell liquor. In the year of 1800 there were at least fifteen places where liquor was sold according to law, which is significant enough of the customs of the times.

What were the people thinking and talking about in those days? They had their own immediate concerns, improvements in their farms, new comers to be discussed and estimated, marriages, engagements, births, deaths, now and then a choice bit of scandal; politics there were, Federalists and Republicans, and party spirit ran high in those days; theology, the doctrines were warmly discussed from morning to night, and late in the night, discussed with loud voices, sometimes with quickened temper. Upon these great themes the people thought more and thought deeper than nowadays. One sad event was prominent in their thoughts and conversation. A stranger had come among them, sickened and died; none knew his name or whence he came. The record concerning him is brief, but pitiful; it runs thus in the accounts of the selectmen:

Paid Luther Waters for digging a grave for Traveler who died in town 0.50.

Paid W. Clark for making a coffin for do $1.33.

About this time there was much talk and wonder about strange reports brought from Orford. They heard that a man living there had invented a boat in which he could sail against wind and current, a boat which he called a steamboat. It is now well established that Capt. Samuel Morey of Orford constructed, as early as 1793, the first boat propelled by paddle-wheels under the power of steam. It is now known that Robert Fulton visited Captain Morey and saw his boat, and that he adopted some of the features of this Orford invention in his own larger and successful enterprise.

There was one sad event which filled the thoughts and conversation of the people that year, the death of Washington at the close of 1799. Most sincerely was he lamented by the whole people, who first began to see the true proportion of his greatness as they looked upon his receding form through the mists which gather over the dark river. Many of the inhabitants had been soldiers under him and mourned him as a father lost.

HALSEY R. STEVENS.

What did the people do for amusements in those days? They had their "logging bees," their "raisings," their huskings. The woods were full of game, even bears, deer and wolves were not wanting to test the courage and try the skill of the hunters. The streams and ponds were full of "speckled beauties," upon which no one was forced to try the foot rule to see if they were beyond the legal four inches before he could decide whether to keep the victim or restore it to the waters to die. Such strings of trout as Ephraim Wood used to take as he came down Great brook to "the Meetin' House" will not be seen in our day, even after re-stocking from the fishing houses and five years' protection and careful spying of fish wardens. For the boys, besides fishing and hunting, there were orchards to visit. There is a wonderful affinity between boys and apples which grow upon other people's land; it is hard to keep them apart. The same apples are sour when given to him, but of wonderful flavor if stolen. In those days apples were not plenty; there were only twenty acres of orchards in the whole town. I have no objections to telling you *now* the best places to go. If in the center village and vicinity, go by all means to Constant Storrs, for he has the largest orchard in town, six acres. There is small chance for those in the eastern part of the town, unless they go to the same place. If you start from West Lebanon, try Deacon Porter's. He has a good orchard, but don't let the old gentleman catch you, for his "eyes are very black." If in the region of Poverty Lane, try Nathaniel Hall's, not many trees but very good. You might go to James Jones', but I should not advise it.

Amusements? How could they be wanting when they had "training days," and general musters. Trainings meant something in those days—no mere half day job for officers and men, but they began soon after twelve o'clock midnight and lasted as long as the next day—in effects. Then there were Fourths of July to be observed with patriotic ardor unknown to the present generation.

But probably the greatest days of the year, the days most anticipated and enjoyed, were those of Commencement Week at Hanover, where all sorts of things and people were gathered from far and near.

LYMAN'S BRIDGE—FOURTH NEW HAMPSHIRE TURNPIKE.

At the beginning of the present century the people of the Connecticut valley had so far conquered the primeval forests as not only to satisfy their own wants, but to have something to spare for others. The Connecticut River had been the natural outlet of the surplus products of the land. But this outlet only touched the western borders of New Hampshire, so that a large portion of the products of the most fruitful portion of her territory passed over this watery way to distant cities and towns, to the loss of trade and commerce to her own citizens. At that period supplies could be received at less cost from Hartford and New York City, by way of Long Island Sound and the Connecticut River, than from Portsmouth or Boston. Sagacious men in Portsmouth, then a flourishing seaport, and in Boston saw this large trade diverted from their cities with anxiety, and sought a remedy. At that day there could be but one way—to build better roads. Hitherto roads had been built so as to secure communication between towns only. There had been no thought of them as highways for trade and commerce between the seaports and the distant hills and valleys of western New Hampshire and Vermont. Hitherto they had been sufficient if they could be passed in safety for local purposes. Now it was sought to so improve them as to make it easier to reach the sea by the shortest path than by the longer but cheaper waterway.

The petition for the Fourth New Hampshire Turnpike states clearly its purpose: "The petition of Elisha Payne [Lebanon], Russell Freeman [Hanover], and Constant Storrs [Lebanon], humbly shows that the citizens of this State experience great inconvenience from the badness of the roads between Merrimack river and the towns of Lebanon and Hanover; that the trade of the western parts of this state & and of the northern parts of the state of Vermont is of course turned from our own seaports and our most commercial towns, to those of Connecticut and New York, that the natural impediments between the aforesaid places and said Merrimack river render the provisions by law for making & repairing public roads wholly inadequate to the purpose of rendering communication easy, convenient & safe; that a plan for opening and extending a communication from Lake Champlain to the Mouth of White River in Vermont, by means of a turn pike road from said lake to the head of said 1 river [White] is contemplated by several enterprising citizens of that state & is encouraged by their government, under an expectation that the interests of our citizens will induce them to meet and extend a plan so well calculated to invite and facilitate an intercourse which would by highly beneficial to both; wherefore your petitioners pray that they and such others as may associate with them may be incorporated into a body politick, with such powers and under such limitations as may be thought fit, to build and keep in repair a turnpike road."

These were far-reaching views for the times. The purpose of the Fourth New Hampshire Turnpike was not simply to collect toll and pay stockholders a fair interest on their investments, but a link in a well-devised system to bring the products of distant fields to seaboard markets. Lyman's bridge was another link in this system. On the west side of the river commenced the White River Turnpike, extending up the valley of that river and connected with others to Lake Champlain.

It is to be noted that these links constitute the route today occupied, substantially, by one of the great highways, Central Vermont and Northern railroad, from the vast interior of our country to the seaboard, a most striking testimony of the sagacity of these Vermont and New Hampshire farmers.

LYMAN'S BRIDGE.

The following action was taken in the New Hampshire senate, January 9, 1794: A vote granting the prayer of the petition of Ebenezer Brewster for the exclusive privilege of building a bridge over the Connecticut River anywhere between the mouth of White River and two miles north of Mink brook, was brought up, read and concurred in.

October 21, 1795, the Vermont Legislature passed an act incorporating Ebenezer Brewster, Rufus Graves of Hanover and Aaron Hutchinson, Esq., with those who should become proprietors with them, a corporation under the name of The Proprietors of the White River Falls Bridge, by which act they were invested with the exclusive privilege of building a bridge or bridges over the Connecticut River anywhere between the mouth of White River and the lower part of White River Falls on the Connecticut River.

The above-named persons conveyed all their interest in this corporation to Elias Lyman of Hartford, Vt. Brewster, January 21, 1801, Graves, same date, Hutchinson, January 29, 1803, to Elias and Justin Lyman, who had then become associated in business.

A bridge was built over the Connecticut by the Lymans on the site of the one now known as Lyman's bridge, about the year 1802 or 1803. No reference whatever is found on the town records relative to this bridge.

FOURTH NEW HAMPSHIRE TURNPIKE.

Upon the petition of Elisha Payne of Lebanon, Russell Freeman of Hanover and Constant Storrs of Lebanon, the New Hampshire Legislature granted, November 25, 1800, a charter for a turnpike road, "four rods wide from the east bank of Connecticut river in the town of Lebanon, nearly opposite the mouth of White river eastwardly to the west branch of Merrimack river in the town of Salisbury or Boscawen also to survey lay out, make and keep in repair a turnpike road four rods wide from the east abutment of White River Falls Bridge in Hanover, southeastwardly till it intersects the road first mentioned, and to be a branch thereof."

Some of the provisions of the charter are as follows: For every mile of said road, and so in proportion for a greater or less distance, or greater or smaller number of sheep, hogs or cattle, viz., for every fifteen sheep or hogs, one cent; for every fifteen cattle or horses, two cents; for every horse and his rider or led horse, three fourths of one cent; for every sulkey, chair, or chaise with one horse and two wheels, one and a half cents; for every chariot, coach, stage-wagon, phaeton or chaise with two horses and four wheels, three cents; for either of the carriages last mentioned with four horses, four cents; for every other carriage of pleasure, the like sums, according to the number of wheels and horses drawing the same; for each cart or other carriage of burthen with wheels drawn by one beast, one cent; for each wagon, cart, or other carriage of burthern drawn by two beasts, one and a half cents; if by more than two beasts, one cent for each additional yoke of oxen or horse; for each sleigh drawn by one horse, three fourths of one cent; if drawn by two horses,

OLIVER LATHROP STEARNS.

one and a half cents; and if by more than two horses, half a cent for every additional horse; for each sled drawn by one horse, half of one cent; for each sled drawn by two horses or a yoke of oxen, one cent; and if by more than two horses or one yoke of oxen, one cent for each additional pair of horses or yoke of oxen—provided that nothing in this act shall extend to entitle the said corporation to demand toll of any person who shall be passing with his horse, team or cattle, or on foot, to or from any mill, or on their common or ordinary business of family concerns within the town where such person belongs.

The proprietors were empowered to purchase and to hold in fee simple so much land as will be necessary for said turnpike road.

"If said turnpike shall in any part be the same with any highway now used, it shall not be lawful for said corporation to erect any gate or turnpike or across said part of the road that now is used or occupied as a public highway, anything in this act to the contrary notwithstanding."

It is further provided that at the end of every six years an account of the expenditures and profits of the road shall be laid before the legislature—"that whenever the neat income of the toll shall amount to the sums which the proprietors have expended on said road, with twelve per cent on such sums so expended from the times of their actual disbursement, the said road with all its rights, privileges, appurtenances shall revert to the State of New Hampshire, and become the property thereof to all intents and purposes."

The first meeting of the corporation, warned by Elisha Payne, was held March 24, 1801, at the dwelling house of Clap Sumner, innholder, near where Richard Walker now lives, in Lebanon. Elisha Payne, moderator; Benj. J. Gilbert was chosen clerk. The meeting then adjourned to meet at the same place April 14, 1801. At this meeting the rights of the proprietors were divided into four hundred shares and numbered from one to four hundred, inclusive, Elisha Payne to have the first hundred, Russell Freeman to have the second hundred, Constant Storrs to have the third hundred, and Benj. J. Gilbert to have the fourth hundred.

An assessment of one dollar and fifty cents was voted upon each share, to be paid before the first day of September next.

Maj. Constant Storrs chosen as treasurer.

FIRST SHAREHOLDERS.

Those in Lebanon were the following:

No.				Name	No.		Name
No. 1	to	10		David Hough	No. 45		Edward Bosworth
"	31	"	2	Samuel Lathrop	" 46		Oliver Ellis
"	32		33	Simeon Peck	" 47		Elijah Reed
"	34			Hobart Estabrooks	" 48		David Hough
"	35			Ephraim Wood	" 59		James Ralston
"	36			Zenas Alden	" 62,	63	James Little
"	37			Richard Aldrich	" 65		Nathan Jewett
"	38			Edmund Freeman, Jr.	" 66		Clark Aldrich
"	39			James Crocker	" 67		Abijah Chandler
"	40			Stephen Kendrick	" 69		Thomas Hough
"	41			Joseph Wood	" 82		Daniel Hough
"	42			Ira Gates	" 84		Beriah Abbott
"	43			Thomas Waterman	" 98 to 107		Richd & Ebenezer Kimball
"	44			Stephen Billings			

The location of this road was a difficult affair, because of rival claims. The corporators sought to avoid all complications, charges of partiality and subjection to undue influences by the selection of a locating committee outside of the state. Accordingly at a meeting held May 29, 1801, voted that Gen. James Whitelaw of Ryegate, Gen. Elias Stevens of Royalton and Major Micah Brown of Bradford, all of Vermont, be a committee to survey and lay out the route for the Fourth Turnpike road in New Hampshire, if the sum of three hundred dollars be raised by voluntary subscription to pay the expense of laying out the same.

The first action taken by the town in relation to the proposed road was November 24, 1801, when they declined to appoint a committee to confer with the proprietors in relation to the necessary bridges through the town.

January 2, 1804, the following action was taken:

Considering the decayed state of the bridges over Mascoma river, and the repairs necessary soon to be made on said bridges and also on the road easterly and westerly thro said town—

Will the inhabitants of said town tax themselves, assess and raise the sum of six hundred dollars, to be made up with the next tax or taxes which may be assessed by said town and to be paid into the hands of the selectmen of said town, by the first day of September next and to be at the disposal of the proprietors of the Fourth N. H. turnpike road, provided the said proprietors shall by their agents specially empowered assure the said selectmen (in behalf of s'd town) the performance of the following—namely:

1. That the said proprietors shall make and compleat their Turnpike road and bridges from Doctor Parkursts to Ichabod Packard's mills in said Lebanon in the rout last established by them, and from thence thro' the easterly part of s'd Lebanon to Matthew Stanleys in Enfield in the rout which the committee last appointed by them may report as being the best all circumstances duly considered the whole to be compleated by the first day of December next.

2. The said proprietors or their agents shall assure the s'd selectmen in behalf of s'd town, that the said road and bridges within s'd town shall at all times be kept open and in good repair from and after the first day of December next, free for the use and occupancy of s'd inhabitants of s'd Lebanon, as well before as after they may erect gates for collecting toll; it is not however understood by anything before mentioned that after s'd turnpike road shall be compleated that the town retains any special privileges not secured to them and other towns by the act incorporating said Proprietors.

Passed in the affirmative.

Some of the citizens resisted the collection of the above tax of six hundred dollars for the benefit of the proprietors of the turnpike road, as appears from the following record:

In the warning for a town-meeting to be held May 14 1805 were these articles. 2 to see whether the town will save harmless Diarca Allen, Joseph Wood and Thomas Wells, the present select men of s'd Lebanon from all damages, costs and charges which have or may accrue to said Allen Wood and Wells, in an action of trespass commenced against them by David and William Packard of said Lebanon to be heard and tried before James Wheelock Esq. on the eleventh day of May next, in consequence of an assessment made on the polls and rateable estate of the said William and David of their proportion of the sum of six hundred dollars, as voted to be raised and paid to the proprietors of the Fourth Turnpike road corporation in said state, at a meeting of the legal voters of said town holden on the second day of January 1804.

3. To see whether they will save harmless the said Allen Wood & Wells in all cases in consequence of said assessment made on the polls and rateable estate of said Town.

4. To appoint an agent or agents on the part of said town to defend in all cases which may happen by reason of said assessment.

At the meeting the articles 2, 3 were passed over. On article 4, Voted to appoint two agents to assist the selectmen to defend in all cases which may happen by reason of the assessment of six hundred dollars, as set forth in the warrant calling this meeting. Chose Aaron Hutchinson Esq. and Nathaniel Porter agents for the town as aforesaid.

The suit seems to have failed, as nothing farther concerning it appears upon the records.

At a meeting of the corporation July 6, 1801, "Voted that Col. Elisha Payne, Col. Aaron Kinsman, Col. David Hough and Capt. Asher Allen [surveyor] a committee to survey the different proposed routes and report at a future meeting." This committee reported by their chairman, Colonel Payne, at a meeting held in Lebanon, September 24, 1801, as follows:

From the mouth of White River to Mr. Simeon Pecks [Solon A. Peck's] by Mascoma River we surveyed two routes, and find by all measurement the northern to be 1010 rods; the southern is 908 rods, which is 102 rods the shortest: Your committee recommends the southern (provided the town of Lebanon will support a reasonable part of the bridges). From Mr. Simeon Peck to Packard's bridge but one route which is 634 rods; from said Packard's bridge to Enfield two routes, the northern is 990 rods, the southern 816 rods which is 174 rods the shortest. We are of the opinion that the southern is the best.

The northern route spoken of above would pass by J. T. Pulsifer's to the village on to Chandler's mills, thence keeping the north side of Mascoma River over Mount Tugg to East Lebanon, crossing the river and along the shore of the pond.

The southern route crossed the Mascoma at the Hubbard bridge, passed by Breck's, through the village to Chandler's mills, then crossed to the south side of the Mascoma, continued over the hill by the Cleaveland place to the shore of the pond.

The stockholders voted to accept the southern route from the Connecticut to Simeon Peck's and Packard's bridge, "on condition that the town of Lebanon will build support and keep in repair all the bridges necessary to be supported over Mascoma river on said rout and westerly of said Packard's."

The report of the committee continues thus:

From the college bridge we surveyed three routes; the old county road, which intersects by the pond is 9 miles 116 rods; the route through the great valley which intersects near Aldens bridge, continued to the pond is 9 miles 64 rods, which is 52 rods nigher than the county road ——the route over Mount Support and intersects by said Aldens bridge continued to the pond is 8 miles 220 rods, which is 216 rods nearer than the county road. The committee think the center or valley road will be levellest and best for the publick.

DR. PHINEAS PARKHURST.

ROADS AND BRIDGES.

This part of the committee's report concerns the branch road to the bridge between Hanover and Norwich.

The county road was the road which passed from Mink brook in Mill Village over the hills by the Blodgett and Walker farms, to East Lebanon. There can be no question that this was *not* the levelest route, yet it was much used in early days.

The route through the "great valley" was the present road to Etna Village, on the east of Rix ledges. The Mount Support route is plain. Alden's bridge was the first bridge east of the center village.

The stockholders, in acting on this part of the report, selected the route by the old county road by a vote of 206 yeas to 191 nays.

They also voted that the road from Packard's mills [Chandler's] should be on the north side of the river.

Thus both the longest and most difficult route was selected, an indication that some other influence than good judgment influenced the action of the stockholders.

The location of this part of the turnpike did not satisfy all parties. At a meeting held at Clapp Sumner's, Lebanon, July 1, 1802, the above votes were reconsidered:

Voted that the turnpike road from near the mouth of White river be laid out made and established by Doct. Parkhursts & Lebanon Meeting house to near Packards mills.

Dr. Parkhurst then lived at the Luther Alden place, and this vote established the southern route to Chandler's mills.

Voted that the Turnpike road from White River Falls Bridge [Hanover] be laid out, made and established from said bridge by College Plain over Mount Support [so called] till it intersects with the part established from the mouth of White River [which was near Howard Benton's].

Voted that Asa Hazen Isaac Partridge & Joseph Loveland be a committee, who are hereby authorized and empowered to examine the different routes proposed from Packard's mills in Lebanon to the westerly line of Enfield near the pond and decide whether the road shall be laid on the north or south side of Mascoma river, and the determination of said committee, or either two of them, shall be final and conclusive; and in case either of the persons before named should fail of attending, that Arthur Latham be appointed to join the two who may attend to the business as a substitute for the one who may fail.

Colonel Hough and Colonel Payne were appointed to wait on the committee who were appointed to establish the route from Packard's mill to Enfield line when they shall come out on the business of their appointment.

This committee "determined that the turnpike road from Packard's mills should be laid on the north side of Mascoma river to near Payne's mills (so called), thence across said river to Enfield line."

There was evidently a warm contest over the location of the road from Packard's mills to East Lebanon. That the route on the north side of the river across Mount Tugg was not the best, probably, was as apparent at that time as now. There must have been some strong personal interest which gave that direction to the road. At this distance of time it is difficult to ascertain with certainty what that interest was. But the following is probably not far from the truth: At that time Mr. Clapp Sumner was a prominent man in the town, and in the corporation. He was also an innholder, living at the Richard Walker place on the old county road. The establishment of the route on the south side of the river would be fatal to his tavern. Besides it was for the interest of that whole neighborhood to have the turnpike laid by their doors.

At a meeting of proprietors held at the house of Abijah Chandler in Lebanon, October, 1803, all former votes, "so far as said votes established that part of the route of said road which extends from the bridge near Zenas Aldens over Mascoma river in Lebanon to Matthew Stanleys in Enfield," were reconsidered.

Voted that the directors be authorized and directed to proceed to lay out a rout from for the turnpike from the bridge near Zenas Aldens in s'd Lebanon to Matthew Stanleys in Enfield crossing on to the south side of Mascome river so as to pass near by Capt Aaron Cleavelands dwelling house, in such place and course as the said directors shall think best.

At a meeting held at the same place, December 6, 1803, another committee was appointed to reëxamine the route between Dr. Phineas Parkhurst's and Enfield line—Joel Marsh, Elias Stevens and Jesse Williams, committee.

At a meeting held the first Tuesday in February, 1804, this committee reported:

That in the town of Lebanon from or near Packards mills to the end of the road made by the Shakers we are of opinion that said road ought to be made on the south side of the river provided that three or four sharp ridges westerly and near Aaron Cleaveland's should be taken down in the road so that in no place they rise no more than one foot in sixteen. If not we are in favor of the route on the north side of the river from Packards mill to Payne's mill, notwithstanding the great rods in the distance. We have likewise viewed the route from Dr. Phineas Parkhursts to Packard's mill on the northerly side of the river are of the opinion that a good road can be made to the satisfaction of the public

The inhabitants of the easterly part of Lebanon take the liberty of submitting the following proposals for the consideration of the gentlemen composing the said commitee viz

1st That in consideration of said road being laid out made and completed on the north side of Mascoma river in Lebanon from Ichabod Packard's on or nigh the route of said road as it is already staked out to the lower end of Enfield pond by Payne's mills (so called) and from thence to Enfield town line that the proprietors aforesaid shall be exempted from the payment of all damages which they might otherwise have been subjected to on account of said road passing through lands belonging to the several owners thereof from said Packards to where said road may cross said Mascoma river at the lower end of the pond before mentioned

2d. That upon the fulfilment of the consideration above mentioned the proprietors aforesaid shall be paid the sum of two hundred dollars by the inhabitants aforesaid.

3d That one or more surety or sureties shall become obligated to the proprietors aforesaid for indemnifying them against said damages and the payment of the sum above specified.

This was manifestly a deliberate bid on the part of the inhabitants of the easterly part of the town for the location of the road on the north side of the river.

On the other side:

The said committee further represent that they are informed by David Hough, one of the selectmen of the town of Lebanon, that the town of Lebanon has voted to raise the sum of six hundred dollars to be paid said proprietors if said road should eventually be made to cross Mascoma river at Dr Pheneas Parkhurst's and twice more before it arrived at the meeting house [at staple bridge and at Coles foundery] and by said meeting house to Ichabod Packards, thence on to the south side of Mascoma river as now laid to Enfield line

The proprietors voted that in case the six hundred dollars shall be paid by the town of Lebanon, and the corporation be secured from all land damages, then the road should be laid on the south side of the river, otherwise the road should be laid on the north side of the river, provided the inhabitants of the easterly part of the town comply with their promise of two hundred dollars.

After many discussions and various negotiations, the turnpike received a final location, keeping mainly on the south side of the river. After crossing Stony brook, instead of following along the banks of the river, it passed by the Cleaveland place and kept on by Manchester's, across the point of the ridge westward of the Floyd or Gile buildings. The house which was occupied for a tavern by —— Barnes stood on the road as thus laid, and was moved to its present location when the road was changed about 1826.

The following are the courses and distances of the road through the town as they are found upon the old records:

Beginning in Enfield near the Shakers Thence by the side of the pond 330 rods to a hemlock tree or stump Marked XVII; thence north 45° west 92 rods to a maple stump XVIII thence north 20 west 40 rods to stake and stones marked XIX; thence north 33 west 66 rods to Houstons barn, southwest corner; thence north 48 west 88 rods to stake and stones marked XXI; thence north 55° west, 122 rods to a beech tree marked XXII; thence north 82° west 10 rods to a beech tree marked XXIII; thence south 63° west 48 rods to stake and stones marked XXIV; thence south 42° west 36 rods to a maple tree marked XXX; thence south 40° west 60 rods to stake and stones marked XXVI; thence south 77° west 14 rods to Capt. Aaron Cleaveland's horseshed; thence north 89° west 68 rods to a stake and stones marked XXXIII; thence south 80° west 136 rods to a stake and stones marked XXIX; thence south 65° west 64 rods to the stone causeway built by Peter Miller at the north end; thence north 68 west 160 rods to a birch tree marked XXXI; thence north 50° west 40 rods to a white birch marked XXXII; thence north 80° west 66 rods to the southeasterly corner of Packards bridge [Chandler's]; thence north 20 west 12 rods across the river to stake and stones marked XXXIV; thence west 32 rods to a great rock with stones on the top; thence north 38 west 40 rods to stake and stones marked XXXVI thence north 50 west 37 rods to a pine stump marked XXXVII; thence north 65° west 24 rods to a pine stump marked XXXVIII; thence north 45 west 71 rods to a white maple tree at the crotch of the roads [Howard Benton's] marked XXXIX

Thence on the main road towards the mouth of White River north 64° west 67 rods to a stake and stones marked I; thence south 82° west across the river 31 rods to a stake and stones marked II; thence north

65° west 42 rods to a cherry tree marked III; thence south 83° west 28 rods to a stake and stones marked IV; thence south 73° west 52 rods to a stake and stones marked V; thence south 85° west 118 rods to the south end of Houghs horse-shed [old Lafayette hotel]; thence south 80° west 44 rods to a stake and stones marked VII; thence north 71° west 71 rods to a rock with stones on the top; thence south 81 west 90 rods to a maple tree by Mr Pecks house marked IX. [This tree stood until a few years ago, when, giving signs of decay, it was reluctantly cut down.] Thence south 87° west 156 rods to a stake and stones at the west end of Mr Peck's bridge [staple bridge]; thence west 100 rods to the north abutment of a bridge by Mr Gates [Moses Perley's]; thence north 71° west 38 rods to stake and stones marked XII; thence north 85° west 14 rods to stake and stones marked XIII; thence south 78 west 70 rods to stake and stones marked XIII; thence north 87° west 130 rods to the north corner of the bridge called Doct. Parkhurst's bridge [Hubbard bridge]; thence south 62° west 14 rods to stake and stones marked XVI; thence north 75 west 13 rods to an oak tree marked XXII; thence north 46° west 98 rods to Mr Waters well [on the Richard Kimball place]; thence north 35 west 78 rods to a pine bush marked XVIII; thence north 33° west 98 rods to a stake one rod south of Hubbards store, thence north 170 west 22 rods to Esq Hutchinsons office; thence north 8° west 76 rods to stake and stones marked XXII standing north from Dana's [Southworth's] tavern; thence north 46° west 54 rods to a pine stump marked XXIII; thence south 65° west 15 rods to the north end of Lyman's bridge at or over Connecticut river.

The road was divided into sections and that is the reason of the change in the Roman numerals. The last section commenced by Howard Benton's and terminated at Lyman's bridge. A surveyor would look in vain at this day for the various beech, maple and pine trees or stumps, or "the great rocks with stones on the top" mentioned. Perhaps only two of the marks mentioned through the town remain unchanged, one is "Mr Water's well" and the other the "stump of the maple tree by Mr. Peck's."

The following persons of Lebanon were officers of the road at various periods:

David Hough, director, to 1803.
Joseph Wood, director from 1806 to 1809, from 1810 to the abandonment of the road.
Stephen Billings, director, 1809.
Ziba Alden, director from 1817 to 1827.
James Ralston, clerk from October, 1801, to July, 1802.

Rev. Isaiah Potter, clerk from 1806 to 1815, when he resigned. Thomas Waterman, clerk from 1815 to the end.

The toll gate was placed where Colonel Hoffman lived.

Gatekeepers, ——— Woodbury, Zenas Alden and Col. William Hoffman.

Commencement in those days was attended by great multitudes from all surrounding regions. Many of those coming from Enfield and Canaan used to save their toll by passing over the old county road by George Blodget's. Whether their horses climbing those steep hills commended the economy of their drivers is doubtful.

At the annual meeting March 10, 1801, Maj. Constant Storrs was chosen representative.

Voted that the selectmen have four shillings per day for their services as selectmen.

The town was divided into nine school districts.

The center village under this division was in the sixth district, whose dimensions were as follows: On the west the farms of Mr. Breck and Edwin Perley; on the north Hanover line; on the east Howard Benton's; south, the Porter farm, occupied by ——— Howe, and contained the following families: Rev. Isaiah Potter, Hobart Estabrook, Samuel Estabrook, Abner Smith, Walter Peck, Simeon Peck, Eliel Peck, Jahleel Peck, Joseph Abbott, Roger Freeman, Luther Pike, Joseph Weed, John Kimball, Benj. Kimball, Guy Hough, Charles Toothaker, Enoch Freeman, Jacob W. Brewster, John Colburn, Nathaniel Bidwell, Zenas Alden, Robert Colburn, Jacob Ela, Asahel Abbott, Thomas Hough, Barnabas Fay, Stephen Kendrick, Jon. Quimby, John Walton, Samuel Young, Beriah Abbott, Elkanah Sprague, John Porter, Jesse Cook, Stephen Billings, Jesse Cook, Jr., Samuel Niles, Andrew Wheatley.

At the annual meeting March 9, 1802, Col. David Hough had 151 votes for councillor, there being only one vote cast for any other candidate, and was elected.

Aaron Hutchinson, Esq., was chosen representative.

August 28, 1802, the town voted for five representatives to Congress, with the following result:

Samuel Tenney,	88	Silas Betton,	85
Clifton Clagget,	85	Samuel Hunt,	81
David Hough,	81		

Who were elected; Capt. David Hough was of Lebanon and was reëlected. Besides these Constant Storrs, Moody Bedel, Nahum Parker, Thomas Cogswell, Jonathan Smith each had 11 votes, and Aaron Hutchinson had 6.

At the annual meeting March 8, 1803, Aaron Hutchinson was chosen representative.

March 25 the town took the following action:

> Voted to choose a committee to form a vote in regard to the small Pox matter. Chose Rev. Isaiah Potter Stephen Kendrick Col David Hough for the committee, who reported as follows:
>
> That the town consents that the Innoculation for the small Pox be carried on agreeable to Law in said town for the term of six months from the 20th day of Sept: next, under the Direction of the Selectmen in some one Place or Places, not exceeding three, whare the selectmen shall think most proper, under the following conditions and regulations, that is to say—that the individuals who are to be innoculated shall pay all the Expense of erecting any building or Rent of any already set up, and Compensate the selectmen for their attendance, and fully indemnify the town from any Expense in consequence thereof, and duly conform in all respects to the law in that behalf provided. But no liberty is hereby granted for any innoculation until sufficient surety is made to the selectmen that the above conditions shall be observed
>
> Voted to except the report of the committee.

At the annual meeting March 13, 1804, Stephen Kendrick was chosen for the first time town clerk. Clapp Sumner chosen representative.

November 1, 1804, the town voted for presidential electors with the following result:

Oliver Peabody	112	Robert Wallace	113
John Prentice	112	Benj. West	113
Timothy Farrar	113	Charles Johnson	113
William Hale	112		
John Goddard	35	Timothy Walker	34
Levi Bartlett	35	George Aldrich	34

| Jonathan Steele | 35 | William Tarlton | 34 |
| Robert Alcock | 34 | | |

The first names of this list constituted the electoral ticket of the Federalists, whose candidate was C. C. Pinkney of South Carolina.

The second list of names constituted the ticket of the Republicans, whose candidate was Thomas Jefferson. This was the successful ticket in both the state and nation. The vote shows that the town was strongly Federalist in its politics.

At the annual meeting March 12, 1805, the vote for governor was as follows:

John Taylor Gilman, 174; Col. John Langdon, 80. Gilman was the Federalist candidate and Langdon the Democratic. The latter was successful; his election marks the beginning of Democratic rule in New Hampshire. The elections this year show one of the sudden changes of parties. Governor Gilman was first elected in 1794, and reëlected each year till 1805. The vote given above shows a great gain in the Democratic vote of the town. In the presidential vote it was a little more than one-quarter of that of the Federalists. In this vote it lacks only fourteen of being one-half.

Voted that the selectmen procure a work-house for the use of the poor.

Aaron Hutchinson chosen representative.

At a meeting held Feb 22d 1806 Maj. Thomas Waterman was appointed an agent for the town to remonstrate to the Hon. Court of Common Pleas, against the acceptance of the doings of sd Courts Committee relative to the alteration of the River road through this town.

This is the first instance on the records of any outside action in the roads of the town.

At the annual meeting March 11, 1806, the vote for governor was as follows:

| John Langdon R | 83 | John T. Gilman F | 74 |
| Jeremiah Smith F | 14 | Elisha Ticknor | 1 |

John Langdon was elected by a large majority.

Maj. Thomas Waterman chosen representative.

The vote for a work-house was renewed.

At a meeting April 22, 1806, upon a report of a committee chosen for that purpose the town was divided into fourteen districts. During this and preceding years the town was largely occupied in making new roads, in altering and discontinuing the old.

On October 28, 1806, a town meeting was warned at the old meeting-house. The object in holding the meeting at that place was that the people might view a piece of road from Poggem.

At the annual meeting March 10, 1807, the vote for governor was as follows: John Langdon, R., 71; John S. Gilman, F., 55, which means that the town had become Democratic.

Major Thomas Waterman chosen representative.

Upon the question, Is a revision of the constitution necessary? yeas 1, nays 65.

During the year there seems to have been much dissatisfaction with the bounds of the school districts and the division of the school money, but the town at various meetings held during the year refused to take any action in the matter.

At a meeting held September 7, 1807:

Voted that the Selectmen make such suitable provision of meat and drink and powder for soldiers on Battalion and Regimental Muster days, as may be done in *cheapest* manner to answer the law.

The law was as follows: "That the selectmen of the several towns and unincorporated places within this state shall furnish suitable meats and drinks for the refreshment of all non-commissioned officers and soldiers within their several towns and places, or thirty-four cents in lieu thereof for each man, on regimental and battalion musters which may be in the months of September and October, and also one-quarter of a pound of powder to each non-commissioned officer and soldier; at the expense of said towns and places; and it shall be the duty of each soldier *to consume said powder* when directed by his commanding officer; the meats and drinks to be furnished on the parade where such regimental or battalion musters are; the number of men ascertained by a roll certified by the commanding officer of the company to which they belong. And if the selectmen of any town or place, after proper notice of such muster shall neglect or refuse to furnish the supplies aforesaid, they shall forfeit and pay the sum of fifty cents for each non-commissioned officer or soldier whom they shall neglect to furnish, to be recovered by the commanding officer of the company which shall be so regulated, in any court proper to try the same, to be appropriated towards defraying the expenses of said company."

The amount paid according to law for the year 1807 was as follows:

Stephen Kendrick for powder and rum for field day	$23.20
Jonathan Hamilton for provisions and transporting Do	23.30

Another account of this year placed by the side of one for 1881 will show the changes of time:

1807

Gideon Baker for service as comtee man in selling with the selectmen	$0.34
Ephraim Wood, Do	0.34
James Howe Do	0.34
	1.02

1881

For auditing Selectmen's accounts	$15.00

At the above meeting the selectmen were directed to purchase the cemetery at East Lebanon of Benjamin Fuller.

At the annual meeting March 8, 1808, Voted to procure one scraper for each highway district. There were nine districts.

Voted that the town will pay for Ringing the Bell on all public meeting days, and on funeral occasions

This is the first mention of a bell in the town. It was procured some time in 1807 by subscription. Nothing is now known of its weight or character. This was the third bell to send its peals through the valleys and among the hills of this region. The first was for the use of Dartmouth College, brought by General Eaton in a horse-cart from Hartford, Conn., 1790. It reached Hanover on the afternoon of the day before commencement. "It was immediately suspended from a tree and made the welkin ring with a new sound, to the great joy of all the inhabitants and of all the visitors of that occasion," many of whom had never heard a bell before.

The second was a bell at Meriden, procured about 1798. It is said to have excited so much envy among the neighboring towns, and so much boasting among the people that it was called the "Meriden Idol."

The first bell-ringer was Jacob C. Richardson, who was paid for that service and for sweeping the meeting-house $17.

The Federalists of the town seem this year to be demoralized, as indicated by the vote for governor: John T. Gilman, F., 18; John Langdon, 75.

Major Thomas Waterman, representative.

But in the election for presidential electors November 4, 1808, the Federalists recovered their strength. Their electoral ticket had 156 votes, the Republicans 67. The candidate of the Federalists was C. C. Pinkney; of the Republicans, or Democrats, James Madison, who was elected, though the majority was against him in the state.

At the annual meeting March 14, 1809, the votes for governor were: Jeremiah Smith, F., 190; John Langdon, R., 74. Jeremiah Smith was elected by a small majority.

Col. David Hough was chosen representative.

The town voted not to lay a road from Lebanon city to the mouth of the White River. This road was designed to be in competition with the Fourth New Hampshire Turnpike.

Guideboards are mentioned this year for the first time.

Paid Downing Amsden for Gide boards $3.75
" Thomas Hough for lumber for gide Posts $1.24
" James Hutchinson for Lettering Guid Boards $5.00

Here is another sad account:

Paid Elijah Rowell for Horse and journey to Orange in Vermont in search of the Stranger's friends that died at Mr. Aldens $1.80

1810.

Town officers, Capt. Joseph Wood, moderator.

Town clerk, Capt. Jesse Cook.

Selectmen, David Hough, Capt. Diarca Allen, Hobart Estabrook.

Tything men, Aaron Hebbard, Runa Hall.

Hog reeves, Ephraim Wood, Jr., James Crocker, Jr., Bracket Greno, Josiah Magoon, James Ralston, Harry Wheatley.

Collector and constable, James Willis.

Fence viewers, Aaron Hutchinson, Esq., Jonathan Hamilton, Silas Waterman.

Poundkeeper, Eliel Peck.

Sealer of weights and measures, James Howe.

Sealer of leather, Osgood True.

The town voted that the selectmen should visit the schools, and that Rev. Mr. Potter should assist them.

For some time this and surrounding towns had been greatly disturbed by reports of the disappearance of dead bodies from the cemeteries. The vicinity of the Medical College established at Hanover near the close of the last century gave sufficient ground for these reports. There is no doubt that the graves were sometimes disturbed. The selectmen were accordingly directed to enforce the law passed June, 1810, against "digging up the bodies of dead people." The penalty for this offense was severe, namely, "a fine not exceeding two thousand dollars to be publickly whipped not exceeding thirty-nine stripes, or be imprisoned not exceeding two years." The same penalty was also enforced against any person who should knowingly receive any such body.

At a town meeting held September 10, 1810, James Hutchinson was appointed agent of the town to carry on a suit against the White River Falls Company.

At a meeting held on the 27th of August to choose representatives to congress, the Federalist candidates were George Sullivan, William Hale, James Wilson, Roger Vose, who each received 151 votes, and Daniel Blaisdell, who received 149.

The Republican candidates were Josiah Bartlett, John A. Hooper, D. L. Morrill, Samuel Dinsmore, Obadiah Hall; each received 62 votes.

1811.

Diarca Allen, David Hough and Hobart Estabrook, selectmen; Jesse Cook, town clerk.

Vote for governor: John Langdon, R., 104; Jeremiar Smith, F., 175. Langdon was elected.

William Hale, George Sullivan, Daniel Blaisdell, Federalists, representatives to congress, had 156 votes.

John A. Harper, Obed Hall, Republicans, had 82 votes.

From the record it appears that there had been a freshet lately, as Selden Freeman asks the town to make him some consideration for brick destroyed by water—which they declined to do.

This year one of the citizens of the town received the reward of patience and perseverance. James Crocker, who lived at the place now occupied by the widow of Sam'l B. Gerrish, had asked the town annually for nearly ten years to grant him a road from his house to the meeting-house by way of Deacon Huntington's, Howes' and Mr. Peck's bridge. The town had directed the selectmen and appointed committees to examine and report upon the proposed road, but somehow he did not get the road. He did not call out the commissioners or the court's committee, but reposed confidently upon the justice of his fellow-citizens and continued his applications. When we learn the route he had to go to get to the meeting-house, west of Frank Peabody's on to Horace Storr's, and then by an old road to the bridge at Scytheville, it seems tardy justice when his request is finally granted. The road is the one now traveled to the John Ela farm.

War of 1812.

As early as 1806 England began proceedings which gave offense to the United States, and finally culminated in war. England and France were at war with one another. By an order in council the whole coast of Europe from the Elbe to Brest was declared to be in a state of blockade. Napoleon retaliated by declaring a blockade of all the British islands. Another order of England forbade all coast trade with France. Under these orders English and French cruisers seized and condemned American vessels without scruple, and without fear, so small was our navy. American commerce under the action of these powerful nations was swept from the seas. In addition England claimed the right to search American vessels for suspected deserters from her navy, a right exercised in the most offensive manner and resulting in the impressment of many native-born citizens into the British navy. Remonstrances were of no avail.

In November, 1807, another order in council was issued, forbidding neutral vessels to enter French ports, unless they had previously entered a British port and paid a duty. Napoleon retaliated by a decree confiscating every vessel which should submit to British search or pay any duty to Great Britain. In the view of these haughty nations no other people had any rights which they were bound to respect.

In December, 1807, congress laid an embargo which held all vessels, foreign or American, in our ports, and ordered all American vessels to return home immediately. On all sides the commerce of the United States suffered. If any of her vessels ventured abroad two powerful nations were ready to seize their cargoes, and one of them scrupled not to seize both cargoes and crews. Finally their own government shut them up in their own ports. The natural, inevitable result was great discontent. The people were divided into two great parties, the Federalists and the Republicans. The Federalists were apologists for England and opposed to the measures of the government. The Republicans (the Democrats of the period) resented the conduct of England and favored war. Controversies between these parties were exceedingly bitter. Each condemned what the other proposed or did. Negotiations were entered into, but they came to nothing. England thought she had nothing to fear from the United States, and if they did not like her orders in council, or the proceedings of her cruisers, what difference did it make to her? She persistently adhered to her policy.

There was nothing left to the United States but to declare war against her oppressor, which was done June 18, 1812.

To the Federalists the act savored of the ridiculous. For a country impoverished, with an empty treasury, with a navy comprising only eight frigates, two sloops and five brigs to take up arms against England, the mistress of the seas, they said and felt, was the height of folly. The Republicans, on the other hand, gloried in the courage and faith of the act. Little was done on either side for a time. On the land defeats exceeded successes on our side. But victories were gained on the seas and lakes. Though England at first despised our navy, she soon learned to respect it. Many of her haughty cruisers were forced to strike their flags to the courage and skill of the despised Yankees. Besides, a vast swarm of privateers scoured the ocean in every direction and preyed upon British commerce, with such success, that in a single year they captured more than three hundred vessels. Fourteen of these privateers sailed from Portsmouth the first year of the war, commissioned by the United States "to take, burn, sink and destroy the enemy wherever he could be found, either on high seas or in British ports."

As time passed away without any substantial successes to our arms by land, and the burdens of war pressed more heavily on the people, discontent and complaint increased. "Agriculture mourning, Commerce in tears." New England was opposed to the war, because her interests suffered. Her commerce and fisheries were extensive and profitable; the war destroyed them. Some of her wisest men denounced the war as suicidal; they whispered first and then talked openly of resistance. They went farther and recommended and planned a dissolution of the Union. The discussions of the parties were fierce and bitter.

Men in their party zeal became unjust and refused to recognize any merit, however conspicuous, on the other side. Mr. G. W. P. Curtis in an oration exclaimed: "Perhaps some fearless sailor now climbs the shattered mast to nail the flag of my country to the stump—my life on it, that fellow is a Federalist." Another, in view of the great naval victories, said: "It is worthy of remark that Hull, Jones, Decatur, Bainbridge and Lawrence are all Federalists."

In the war New Hampshire bore an honorable part. Her soldiers and sailors were conspicuous by land and sea. In the bloody battle of Chippewa, Colonel McNeil showed all the bravery and coolness of a veteran and was promoted by congress for his gallant conduct. Later, at the fierce battle of Bridgewater, when McNeil was disabled by a wound in the knee, Colonel Miller of Peterboro came forward with his memorable "I'll try, sir," and led his regiment to the most brilliant success.

LEBANON IN THE WAR OF 1812.

If the historian depended upon the town records alone, the history of the town in the second war with England would be as brief as a chapter in the history of Ireland, which was to the following effect:

"There are no snakes in Ireland." For there is not the slightest reference in the records of the town to this war. The town seems to have taken no action, whatever, in relation to it. There are no resolutions, no directions to the selectmen, no offers of bounty, no provisions for drafts—the records are wholly silent as to the contest. The business of the town went on in its ordinary channels. This silence of the records, this non-action of the town, in so important a matter can only be accounted for from the fact that the majority of the inhabitants were Federalists, and as such bitterly opposed to the war, and would have nothing to do with it. While the records are silent, tradition is nearly so. It is not difficult to learn who of the early inhabitants took part in the Revolution from tradition, but very few are spoken of as in the war of 1812.

The historian has resorted to the best means at his command to learn who of the inhabitants of the town took any active part in that contest.

Early in the summer of 1812 the people in the north of the state were fearful of attacks from Canada, and upon their representation that much smuggling was carried on in that region, Governor Plumer reported the facts to the general government, and General Dearborn made a requisition for a company of militia, to be stationed in that quarter, with their headquarters at Stewartstown. This company was commanded by Capt. E. H. Mahurin. Their time of service expired January 27, 1813, when Capt. Edmund Freeman, son of Colonel Freeman of Lebanon, was ordered to occupy the post March 11, 1813. In the roll of his company occur the following names credited to Lebanon:

Elias H. Blodgett, corporal	Silas Curtis
Amasa Blodgett	Joseph W. Green
Ebenezer Brainard	John Holbrook
Peter P. Payne	John Perry
Eli Wood	

Their time of service was six months.

In Captain Courson's company of the Third Regiment of detatched militia are the following credited to Lebanon:

Moses Abbott, sergeant major	Isaac Allen
Amasa Blodgett, sergeant	Josiah Magoon, 1st lieut.
William Clifford	Lathrop Hamilton
Sherburne Hutchinson	Zaran Haven
William Lothrop	Elisha Paine
William Redington	Moses Seaven
Lambert W. Cushing	John Wright

In Capt. John Willey's company of the Third Regiment:
Mark Horsom.

The above were enlisted in the fall of 1814 for sixty days and were stationed at Portsmouth in anticipation of an attack by the British naval forces.

In Capt. Benjamin Bradford's company of the Forty-fifth Regiment, U. S. Infantry:

William Cole.

Capt. Joseph Griswold, Eleventh Regiment of U. S. Infantry.
In Capt. Richard Bean's company, Eleventh U. S. Regiment, Edmund Freeman, 3d fifer.

The following is the best account which can be given of the above persons:

Corp. Elias H. Blodgett was the son of Nathan and Anna (Perrin) Blodgett, born in Lebanon, April 22, 1786, and a brother of Seth Blodgett; married Sally Dustin, December 3, 1809; died at Alden, N. Y.

Sergt. Amasa Blodgett, brother of the preceding, was born in Lebanon, February 23, 1794. Both of the above left Lebanon and died in the West.

Peter Pratt Payne was the son of Elisha Payne, Jr., grandson of Col. Elisha Payne; born November 22, 1795.

Lathrop Hamilton, son of Jonathan and Polly (Payne) Hamilton, and brother of Ziba Hamilton, was born in Lebanon, April 3, 1797; died March 25, 1827.

Isaac Allen, quartermaster's sergeant, son of Isaac and Joann B. Allen; born in Lebanon, October 30, 1792; lived for a time at Crown Point; removed to Lebanon again in 1822, then moved to Wayland, Mass.; died in Boston while on a visit June 14, 1861.

William Lathrop was the son of Capt. Samuel and Lois (Huntington) Lathrop; born April 15, 1796, and was a brother of Mrs. Truman. After the war he went into the state of New York and after a time was never heard of again.

William Cole was the son of Timothy and Tabitha (Downer) Cole. He enlisted for the war in Captain Bradford's company of the Forty-fifth U. S. Regiment, March 10, 1814, when he was about sixteen years old. He was at the battle of Plattsburgh when he assisted in destroying a bridge to prevent the passage of the British troops. He resided for a short time at Colebrook, whence he returned to Lebanon where he died.

Elisha Payne, 3d, was a brother of Peter P. Payne; born January 15, 1793.

William Redington, son of Enoch and Huldah Redington; born February 14, 1793, at Lebanon; died March 5, 1828.

Moses Seavey.

Moses Abbott, sergeant major, son of Beriah and Polly Abbott; born April 21, 1787; moved to Pomfret, Vt., and died there.

Capt. Joseph Griswold was the son of Maj. John and Elisabeth (Porter) Griswold; born August 2, 1776. He was of the Eleventh U. S. Regiment, and was employed for a time in the recruiting service. Mrs. Truman remembers that he and his company appeared on the common one Sabbath morning about the time for service, when Mr. Potter was escorted from the church to the company, when he offered prayer, and was then escorted back to the church door. He afterwards removed to Paulet, Vt., and in his later years became blind.

Capt. Edmund Freeman, Jr., was the son of Col. Edmund Freeman, formerly of Hanover, and the first settler of that town. Captain Freeman, after the war, lived in Lebanon many years where Samuel Wood now lives. Afterwards he removed to Hartland, where he died September 26, 1854.

Edmund Freeman, 3d, son of Capt. Edmund and Zilpah (Poole) Freeman, enlisted in Capt. Richard Bean's company of the Eleventh U. S. Regiment, January 8, 1713, for five years. After the war he went West and after a time he was never heard from again. It is supposed that he died in Canada.

Of the other persons named no account can be given. They probably were never permanent residents of the town and may have been substitutes for drafted men.

Tradition, so far as Lebanon is concerned, has preserved very few incidents connected with this war. A small boy at the "nooning" one Sabbath happened to stray away from the meeting-house to some distance, when he caught sight of a soldier; he followed on and found "the fields full of them." He lingered around their camp during the afternoon service, and when he reached home he had to render a strict account of himself for thus breaking the Sabbath, and we may suspect that the reprimand was none the less painful from his grandfather's being a minister and a Federalist. Later in the day the boy had the mortification of seeing the soldiers pass by his house on their way to Burlington, and reflected that he might have seen the soldiers without incurring quite so much pains. The boy of that day is Capt. Edward A. Howe of the present.

It is hardly possible for us to understand the bitterness of feeling between the parties of that day. There are a few lingering still, old enough to remember that war, and to have imbibed something of the spirit of the times. You are pretty sure to see a flashing of the eyes and a quickening of the blood when the affairs of that period are alluded to.

Mr. Potter was an ardent Federalist and preached a sermon upon General Hull's surrender which, while it gave satisfaction to perhaps the majority of his hearers, awakened the strongest indignation in the breasts of the Republicans of the time. They denounced him with unsparing bitterness and pronounced his discourse treasonable and he worthy of death.

Whether the war was just and wise or not, it came to an end to the great joy of all. A treaty of peace was signed at Ghent, in Belgium, December 24, 1814. Before the news of peace reached the United States the battle of New Orleans was fought, and the war ended in a blaze of glory for the Americans.

The war certainly resulted in good to the country. The United States won the respect of other nations and her vessels were no longer liable to be annoyed and plundered on the seas. American naval victory enabled Mr. Webster to insert, without a word of opposition, in the Ashburton treaty the proud and essential declaration—"the American flag shall protect all that sail under it." To the energy and bravery displayed in that war we owe our exemption from any important acts of hostility on the part of foreign nations for a period of sixty-seven years, and our ability to enforce reparation for minor acts done to our injury.

State and Town Officers, Etc.

1812.

Diarca Allen, Stephen Kendrick, Esq., Col. Thomas Waterman, selectmen.

John G. Gilman, Federalist, had 162 votes for governor; William Plumer, Republican, had 97, elected by the legislature. Col. Thomas Waterman chosen representative.

The selectmen were directed to fence the several burial grounds.

Mr. Potter, Samuel Selden and James Hutchinson appointed a committee to visit the schools.

At a meeting to vote for representatives to congress in November, the following persons on the Federalist ticket each had 197 votes: Daniel Webster, Bradbury Cilley, William Hall, Samuel Smith, Roger Vose, Jeduthan Wilcox.

On the Republican ticket each of the following had 98 votes: John F. Parrott, Josiah Butler, John A. Harper, David L. Morrill, Jesse Johnson, Samuel Dinsmore. The Federalist ticket was successful.

The vote for presidential electors was the same, namely, Federalist ticket, 198; Republican, 98. The Federalist ticket was successful in the state, but failed in the country. James Madison was chosen president.

1813.

Diarca Allen, Thomas Waterman and Stephen Kendrick, selectmen. James Hutchinson, town clerk.

Vote for governor: John G. Gilman, F., 179; William Plumer, R., 94. John G. Gilman elected.

Col. Thomas Waterman chosen representative.

Nothing beyond the routine business of the town was done at the annual meeting.

1814.

Thomas Waterman, Diarca Allen, Stephen Kendrick, selectmen. Stephen Kendrick, town clerk. Col. David Hough, representative.

For governor, John G. Gilman, F., 213; William Plumer, R., 115. John G. Gilman elected.

On a vote for a revision of the constitution, yeas 6, nays 105.

In the fall elections for representatives to congress the Federalist ticket had 200 votes and the Republicans 101. Federalists elected.

The town voted seventy-five dollars to William Payne as some "farther compensation for the great trouble, cost and loss of time by him sustained in consequence of his agreement to support Cuff Searle."

1815.

Col. Thomas Waterman, Jonathan Hamilton, Samuel Selden, selectmen. Stephen Kendrick, town clerk. Dea. Nathaniel Porter, representative.

Vote for governor: William Plumer, R., 103; John Taylor Gilman, F., 200, who was elected.

At a town meeting held November 13, 1815, it was voted that it was "the wish of the town to make provision for effecting a settlement with the Rev. Mr. Potter."

Voted not to choose a committee to confer with him on the subject.
Voted that it is not the wish of the town to settle a colleague with the Rev. Isaiah Potter.
Voted to reconsider the first vote that was passed.

In the town meetings of those days a reconsideration of a vote was understood to annul it.

Early in this year the war with England closed. It seems hardly possible that a war which pressed so heavily upon the people in all directions, which almost destroyed all industrial and commercial operations, which demanded money and men, whose beginning and progress provoked so much angry discussion and bitterness of feeling; it seems hardly possible that such a war should begin and find not the slightest recognition in the action of the town from first to last. Impossible as it seems, such is the fact.

1816.

Thomas Waterman, Jonathan Hamilton, Samuel Selden, selectmen; Stephen Kendrick, town clerk; Samuel Selden, representative.

Vote for governor: James Sheafe, F., 170; William Plumer, R., 129, who was elected.

The vote of the town shows a marked change of feeling, if not of principle in the loss of the Federalists and the gain of the Republicans, and the same change prevailed through the state. The war, which had met such fierce opposition, had been marked with such brilliant victories on the seas and lakes, had closed in such a blaze of glory at New Orleans, and was followed with such conspicuous benefits to the standing of the United States among foreign nations, as to cause men to doubt the wisdom and justice of their opposition.

At a meeting held September 9, 1816, "chose a committee to confer forthwith with the Rev. Mr. Potter relative to a settlement, and report to this meeting where upon the Rev. Mr Potter appears in meeting and offers in writing the same proposals as were offered by him to a collection of individuals of s^d town under date of July 8th last [and this meeting now request their said committee to coöperate with the said Rev. Mr. Potter, and obtain his terms without any condition of settling a colleague and this meeting is adjourned till Thursday the 19th instant at two o'clock in the afternoon at this place to hear the proposals of the s^d Rev. Mr. Potter through their said committee]."

A pen has been drawn through the matter enclosed in brackets.

Voted that Capt. Joseph Wood, Enoch Freeman and Capt. Giddings Whitmore be a committee to confer with the Rev. Mr. Potter, on terms of settlement without any condition of settling a colleague.

At a meeting held September 19, 1816:

Voted that the salary of the Rev. Mr. Potter be continued and paid to him until the 22^d of August next [1817] and that the said Potter be excused from performing any ministerial services from and after this time, upon condition and in consideration that the said Potter relinquish (as he now agrees to do) all claim for any salary from the town, or individuals from and after the said 22^d of August

Voted that the selectmen assess on the inhabitants of Lebanon, upon the last invoice a tax to pay the Rev. Mr. Potter his salary for the year past.

In November the town voted for representatives to congress and for presidential electors, when the Federalist ticket had 130 votes and the Republicans 94. The Republicans were successful in the state and nation. James Monroe was elected president.

The year 1816 is known as the cold year. There was frost every month of the year, except August. In some portions of the state there was frost every month. Snow fell on the 9th of June, the famous cold Friday, when people were obliged to work in winter clothing and with hands covered with mittens. Most of the crops were destroyed. In the southern part of the state the mean height of the thermometer was 43°, while the average was about 46° in that region. This season so discouraged and disgusted the farmers of the state that many of them began to look for a more genial climate. From about that time emigration to the West commenced, which has steadily depleted New Hampshire, let us hope.

Colonel Hoffman says that there was only six bushels of sound corn raised in the town that year, and that was raised on a small piece of land near Olcott's Falls, where it was protected from the frosts by the spray from the water. There was a good crop of wheat and rye. Corn sold at three dollars a bushel.

1817.

Thomas Waterman, Jonathan Hamilton, Samuel Selden, selectmen; Stephen Kendrick, town clerk; Samuel Selden, representative.

Vote for governor: Samuel Sheafe, F., 154; William Plumer, R., 115, who was elected.

At a town meeting held December 24, 1917, "Voted not to appoint an agent or attorney to defend in the suit of Barrett Potter against said town." Barrett Potter was the son of Rev. Mr. Potter, and the suit was for arrears of salary.

In the summer of this year (1817) the people of this vicinity had their first sight of a president of the United States. President Monroe entered the state and proceeded as far north as Hanover. At Enfield, coming by the Fourth New Hampshire Turnpike, he stopped at the habitation of the Shaker community. The elder came forth from the principal house in the settlement and thus addressed the president: "I, Joseph Goodrich, welcome James Monroe to our habitation." The president then offered his hand to the eldress, when she said: "I respect thee, but I cannot take thy hand." The president examined the institution and their manufactures for about an hour and was highly pleased with the beauty of their fields, their exemplary habits, their improvements in agriculture and the neatness of their substantial but plain buildings.

He passed from thence through Lebanon to Hanover, where he unexpectedly met an old acquaintance in the widow of the late revered and lamented President Wheelock. This lady was a native of New Jersey, was at Trenton at the time of the battle in which he was a lieutenant of a company. He was wounded in the battle and she dressed his wound after he was conveyed to the house where she then was. The president did not remember her at first, but as the past came to his mind the interview became peculiarly affecting to the two individuals and highly interesting to the large circle of ladies and gentlemen. In a letter from Hanover it was said: "We were delighted with the short visit of the president. For his sake the hatchet was buried for at least twenty-four hours; a short truce, but a merry one." This was said in view of the bitterness existing between the political parties of the day.

1818.

Aaron Hutchinson, Diarca Allen, William Benton, selectmen. Town clerk, Stephen Kendrick. Representative, Stephen Kendrick.

Vote for governor: Jeremiah Mason, F., 140; William Plumer, R., 115, who was elected. The Federalist vote in the state was divided nearly equally between William Hale and Jeremiah Mason.

On the 19th of October the town voted that the selectmen and a committee of three examine and determine a route for a road from the turnpike road through the great hollow to Hanover line, and cause the same to be surveyed. Chose Col. David Hough, S. Kendrick and S. Selden for that committee. This was the road by Rix ledges to Mill Village.

1819.

Col. Thomas Waterman, Ziba Alden and William Benton, selectmen; Timothy Kenrick, town clerk; Col. David Hough, representative.

Vote for governor: William Hale, F., 103; Samuel Bell, R., 76, who was elected.

Voted to accept the report of the committee on the new road through the Hollow to Hanover.

The record does not say whether the report was in favor or against the building of the road, but probably in favor, as the road was built soon after.

1820.

For the purpose of comparison with the former lists, and as a matter of interest, the list of taxpayers for 1820 is given.

Abbott, Beriah
Abbott, Moses
Allen, Parthenia
Allen, Susan
Allen, Abner
Allen, Isaac
Allen, Diarca
Amsden, Benj.
Amsden, Downing
Amsden, Joel
Amsden, Joseph
Amsden, Uriah
Anderson, David
Alden, Luther

Alden, Phelps
Alden, Ziba
Alden, Zenas
Alden, Ezra
Alden, Julius
Aspenwall, Eleazar
Aldrich, Clark
Aldrich, David
Aldrich, Milton
Aldrich, James
Aldrich, Richard
Aspenwall, Horatio G.
Amsden, William
Allen, Joshua

Baker, Abel
Baker, Jabez
Baker, Alpheus
Baker, Dorothy
Barnes, Silas
Barnes, Samuel S.
Brewster, Amos A.
Blodgett, Seth
Buswell, Richard
Burns, Josiah
Buck, William
Buck, Cyrus

Bliss, Isaiah
Bliss, Daniel
Bowen, Josiah
Brinks, William
Benton, William
Benton, Calvin
Billings, Stephen
Billings, William
Bosworth, Edward
Bosworth, Dan
Bosworth, Jesse
Brown, Ira A.

STATE AND TOWN OFFICERS, ETC.

Buck, Pelatiah
Bellows, Josiah 2d
Blanchard, Stephen

Bugbee, Amos
Bunker, John
Bosworth, Alva

Colburn, Stephen
Colburn, Benjamin
Colburn, John
Cook, Bathsheba
Cook, Jesse
Cook, Giles
Cook, John
Crocker, Charles
Crocker, David
Crocker, Joseph
Crocker, James
Crocker, Samuel

Carr, Thomas
Cushing, Joshua
Cleaveland, Aaron
Cleaveland, Zenas
Clark, Francis
Chase, Harvey
Carpenter, Thomas D.
Cutting, Isaac
Champion, John
Chandler, ———
Cotton Factory Co., Lebanon

Dana, Jedediah
Deman, Thomas
Downer, Erastus
Downer, Jason
Downer, Joseph
Downer, Elisha
Downer, Silas
Dewey, Martin
Dewey, Grenville

Delano, Luther
Delano, Zenas
Dustin, Samuel
Dustin, Daniel
Dustin, Daniel, Jr.
Dutton, Zachariah
Durkee, John
Davis, William A.

Ela, Benjamin
Ela, Jacob
Ela, James
Eldridge, Polly (widow)
Ellis, Oliver

Estabrook, Aaron
Estabrook, Hobart
Estabrook, Rodolphus
Elliot, Samuel

Freeman, Enoch
Freeman, Erastus
Freeman, Daniel
Freeman, Joseph
Fitch, Asa
Fitch, Isaac

Fox, John, Jr.
Foord, John
Foord, Joseph
Foord, Hezekiah
Freeman, Otis
Freeman, Jesse

Flood, Nathaniel
Flood, Benjamin
Freeman, Nathaniel
Fuller, James
Fox, John

Goold, John
Goold, Elijah

Gray, David
Gray, John
Gray, Samuel
Goff, Frederick
Green, Henry
Griffin, Jacob
Griswold, Ahira

Hall, Nathaniel
Hall, Dan
Hall, Araunah
Hibbard, Aaron
Hibbard, Moses
Hinkley, Daniel
Hubbard, George
Huntington, Elias, Jr.
Hutchinson, Aaron
Hutchinson, James
Hubbard, Orrin
Hubbard, Josiah
Hebbard, John
Hall, John
Hall, Daniel
Hamilton, Jonathan

Judkins, Stephen
Jones, David
Jewett, Haynes

Lyman, Elias
Lathrop, Shuman

Fay, Barnabas
Fay, Winslow
Flanders, Moses
Frary, Elisha
Fifield, Calvin

Gallup, Benjamin A.
Greenough, Bracket

Greenough, Moses
Grimes, Alexander
Gates, Ira
Gates, Laban
Gates, Paul H.
Gillet, Ahira
Gage, Jesse E.

Hardy, Daniel
Hardy, Oliver
Hardy, Johnson
Huntington, Ziba
Hough, David
Hough, David, Jr.
Hebbard, Silas
Hough, Asel
Hough, Clement
Hough, Daniel
Hough, Clark
Hough, John
Hough, Witherell
How, Elisabeth
Hubbard, Benj. T.

Kendrick, Stephen
Kendrick, Stephen, Jr.
Kenrick, Timothy
Kimball, Willis
Kimball, Elisha

Lull, Frederick
Lathe, Joshua

Lathrop, G. H.
Lathrop, Elijah
Lathrop, William
Lathrop, Samuel
Leach, James
Leach, Isaac
Livermore, Absalom R.

Lathe, Sylvanus B.
Liscomb, John
Loomer, William
Low, John
Low, Edward
Laughton, David

Mason, Joseph B.
Mason, Marshal
Morse, Wareham
Merret, Henry

Marsh, Zebinah
Martin, Joseph, Jr.
March, David
Marden, Joseph

Nelson, Charles
Parkhurst, Phineas
Parkhurst, Calvin
Parkhurst, Asa
Peck, Eliel
Peck, John
Peck, Azel
Peck, Walter, Jr.
Porter, Arnold
Porter, Nathaniel
Porter, Nathaniel, Jr.
Post, Andrew
Post, George W.
Perkins, Enos M.
Purington, Mark
Packard, Anna (widow)
Packard, Zadoc

Packard, Holden
Packard, Ichabod
Packard, Asahel
Packard, Wm. H.
Packard, Nathaniel
Payne, John S.
Payne, Zenas
Payne, William
Peabody, Thomas
Pierce, Isaac
Pierce, Zephaniah
Plastridge, Caleb
Plaistridge, Charles
Potter, Thomas
Pritchard, Dexter
Picket, John
Percival, James

Risley, Roswell
Rea, Thomas
Richardson, Jacob B.
Richardson, William

Robinson, Lake
Ralston, James
Redington, Constant
Redington, William

Slapp, John
Slapp, Simon P.
Stephens, John

Sanborn, William
Selden, Samuel
Storrs, Constant

Stanley, Abijah
Sargent, Ezekiel
Sargent, Aaron
Smith, Daniel
Smith, Edward
Sartwell, Roswell
Smalley, Lyman
Strong, Orsemus
Stephens, Isaac

Ticknor, Elisha
Ticknor, William
Ticknor, Isaac
Ticknor, Paul K.
Ticknor, John
True, Osgood
Truman, Thomas
True, George

Walling, Baker
Walling, Benj.
Waterman, Thomas
Waterman, Silas 2d
Wood, Henry G.
Wood, John
Wood, John, Jr.
Wood, Joseph
Wood, Roger
Wood, Samuel
Wood, Ephraim
Wood, Benjamin
Wright, Abel
Wright, Abel, Jr.
Wood, Ephraim, Jr.
Wood, Jesse
Whitmore, Ebenezer
Whitmore, William
Watson, French

Young, Samuel

Storrs, Constant 2d
Storrs, Dan
Storrs, George
Storrs, William
Storrs, Ziba
Simon, Arad
Sevey, Moses
Sevey, William

Taylor, Daniel
Tucker, Samuel
Tibbetts, Jesse
Tilden, Joseph
Tilden, Joel
Tilden, Joseph, Jr.
Tilton, Henry
Ticknor, Paul

Wells, Thomas
Wells, Eliphalet
White, Fanny
Williams, Orville
Winneck, John
Wilson, Thomas
Wells, Reuben
Whitmore, Clapp S.
Whitmore, David
Whitmore, David, Jr.
Williams, Robert
Woodbury, James
Woodbury, John
Woodbury, Leonard
Wallace, Joseph
White River Falls Co.
Woodward, Isaac
Warner, Caleb

Young, Ammi B.

TIMOTHY KENRICK.

It may be interesting to recall the condition of the town at this period of its life. Its population is given as 1,710, about one hundred less than in 1810. This decrease was undoubtedly owing to western migration. Number of polls, 199; of horses over four years old, 164; of oxen, 158; of cows, 407. Sheep are not mentioned in the invoice of the year. Number of carriages worth over fifty dollars, 17.

Stephen Kendrick, Wareham Morse, Timothy Kenrick and Calvin Benton were the merchants at the Center; Josiah Barnes at East Lebanon and the Lymans across the river from West Lebanon.

The tavern-keepers were Moses Greenough at the old Lafayette, where the Whipple block now stands, who had for a sign only a large O painted green; Moses Abbott, son of Beriah Abbott at the head of School Street, now the Stickney place; Josiah Barnes and Col. Luther Delano at East Lebanon; Daniel Freeman where Joel Baker now lives; Silas Leach on Mount Support; Ephraim Wood on the Ben Wood place on the Meriden road; Capt. Joseph Wood, and Ira A. Brown on the river road. All the merchants and all the "taverners" were licensed to retail spirits; the people of that day, almost without exception, were their customers.

Clark Aldrich, near Chandler's mills; Eliel Peck at Scytheville, Uriah and Joel Amsden at the Center, Jesse Cook at East Lebanon, Joseph Wood and White River Falls Co. at West Lebanon, Orren Hubbard, near Hubbard bridge, had sawmills.

Paul Buswell had his tannery where the key shop of Kendrick & Davis is located; Osgood True also had a tannery where Ebenezer Cole lives, and was also licensed to sell spirits. The machine shop of Cole & Son was occupied by Stephen Kendrick as an oil mill. The Mechanics Cotton and Woolen factory occupied the site of the lower shops of Mead, Mason & Co., now Riverside. The Lebanon cotton factory was in operation at East Lebanon. Andrew Post had his hat factory near the Gustin shop by the iron bridge in the center village, and there was another factory on the opposite side of the street soon after. Daniel Hinkley was a clothier in the southwest part of the town on True brook.

Frederick Lull, whose shop was a little west of the store of Brown Bros. and Alexander Grimes, whose shop stood on the ground of the high school building near the blacksmiths of the center. Haynes Jewett had a shop a little south of the bridge in Butmanville, a Mr. Gates at East Lebanon. John Winneck was a saddler and storekeeper at East Lebanon; Simon Peter Slapp was a tailor at East Lebanon. Samuel and Ammi B. Young and Azel Peck and Joseph Mason were the builders of the time. Alpheus Baker, Philo Sprague and Ahirah Griswold were the brick masons.

The doctors were Phineas Parkhurst, Benjamin Gallup in the Center, and Caleb Plaistridge at East Lebanon.

The lawyers were Aaron and James Hutchinson and Samuel Selden.

Mr. Potter was dead and the Congregationalists were without a pastor till November 1823, when Calvin Cutler was settled. John Foord was preaching to the Second Congregational church, the Universalists had no settled minister and the Methodists had only occasional meetings. The only place of worship was the present town hall, standing on the park about 200 feet south of its present location.

The means of transportation were by the Fourth New Hampshire Turnpike, four, six and eight-horse teams carrying the produce of the farms to market and returning with groceries and dry goods for the merchants. Many of the farmers carried their pork, butter and cheese to Boston and Portsmouth, bringing back supplies for their own families and others, having, generally, good times on the road and at the taverns. The trip usually occupied from two to three weeks. Among the well-known teamsters of the period was Amasa Hurlburt, who died in this town in 1870, aged 84 years.

The Connecticut River was the means of communication between Hartford, Conn., and the towns of New Hampshire and Vermont, large boats being used which floated down with the current, and were forced back by poles and oars, sometimes assisted by sails when the wind blew up stream. The Lymans, at what is called the Point, on the Vermont side, were extensive dealers in the merchandise of the day, and large numbers of these flatboats could generally be seen at the mouth of White River discharging or taking on their cargoes.

AMI B. YOUNG.

DR. BENJAMIN GALLUP.

DR. CALEB PLASTRIDGE.

A little later an attempt was made to employ steamboats as carriers in this trade. "A diminutive steamer, the *John Ledyard,* under the command of Captain Nutt, who died a few years ago at White River Junction, came puffing up the river about 1830, and was received at various places with speeches and such other demonstrations as were deemed appropriate to the opening of steam navigation on the upper Connecticut. Captain Nutt went up as far as Wells River, near which place he found obstructions which he was unable to surmount.

"Two or three hundred Scotchmen who lived in the vicinity and were anxious to have the steamer go farther, undertook to pull her over the bar by the aid of ropes, but after raising her so far from a horizontal position that an explosion of the boiler became imminent, they were asked by the captain to desist and it took thirty or forty of them to pull her back into deep water. The next season another steamer, the *Adam Duncan,* was built at Wells River, under the superintendence of Captain Nutt. Other steamers had been put upon the river at various points below the previous season, and the *Adam Duncan* was designed to ply between Wells River and Olcott's Locks, but after a single season of practice in backing off the sandbars between the two places, was attached for debt, her works were taken out and sold and the remainder of the hull for many years lay a few rods above the falls."—Address of William H. Duncan, Esq.

William S. Ela, then a young man just commencing life for himself, assisted in building some of these steamers. He worked upon the *Adam Duncan* at Wells River. The smokestack was hinged, so as to be let down when passing bridges. When the steamer was put into the water in the spring the river was high and it was found that she could not pass under the bridge at Haverhill, even when the smokestack was laid down on deck, and there was nothing to be done but to wait till the water fell. The river was persistent and the workmen finally came home by the stage. Mr. Ela relates that the people of the towns on the banks of the Connecticut contributed freely to the building of these steamers, expecting great things from them, to be soon disappointed. He added that the first money, to any amount, which he received was for work upon these steamers, with which he purchased some shares in the old Bank of Lebanon, which he still holds.

Among the matters which especially interested the people of this town about this period was the Dartmouth College controversy. Eleazer Wheelock, the founder of the college, was well known to most of the early settlers of the town, coming as they did from the same neighborhood in Connecticut. Naturally they took a deep interest in his novel and daring enterprise of planting a college in the wilderness. They contributed generously of their possessions, gave him aid in many ways, encouraged him by their sympathy and gave him their sons to educate, and could only end by being deeply concerned in the welfare of that institution, when its very existence was threatened.

This controversy was long and bitter, involving both church and state, but was finally settled by decrees of United States courts.

FROM 1820 TO 1830.

The Federalist party disappears in 1820, both in town and state, and Samuel Bell, Republican, is elected governor until 1823 without opposition. He was personally popular with all parties and an able and upright man. In 1823 there were two Republican candidates, Samuel Dinsmore and Levi Woodbury. In the town Dinsmore had 168 votes and Woodbury 45, but by the votes of the state Woodbury was elected. In 1824 there was a change in the names of the parties, they being called after the names of their leaders, Jackson and Adams. But there was little change in the principles of the parties and none in the bitterness between them, but rather an increase. In 1824 David Morrill, Adams, had 143 votes for governor and Levi Woodbury had 88. Neither had a majority in the state, but Morrill was chosen by the legislature. In 1825 Morrill was chosen governor, with little opposition through the state, there being only 563 scattering votes in the whole state.

About this time there began to be used the party term "amalgamation," concerning which it has been aptly said, "the most learned could not define it, but which the most ignorant daily used." It designated the union of Federalists and Republicans to bring about the election of John Quincy Adams to the presidency.

In 1826 David Morrill, Adams, had in the town 129 votes; Benjamin Pierce, Jackson, had 104. Morrill was elected.

In 1827 Benjamin Pierce, Jackson, had for governor in the town, 191 votes, while Morrill, Adams, had only five votes. A surprising change in one year. And there was a like change in the state, Morrill having only 2,529, while Pierce had 23,695.

In 1828 there was another overturning. John Bell, Adams, had in the town 238 votes, and Pierce, Jackson, had 116. Bell was elected governor.

In 1829 John Bell, Adams, had in the town 207 votes. Benjamin Pierce, Jackson, had 119. Pierce was elected by the votes of the state, having about 3,000 majority.

The above record shows great disturbance and uncertainty in political affairs as well as bitterness in the strife.

In 1791 the legislature established four post routes, "to ride in and through the interior parts of this state." The second route was to be as follows: From Concord to Boscawen, Salisbury, Andover, New Chester, Plymouth, Haverhill, Piermont, Orford, Lyme, Hanover, Lebanon, Enfield, Canaan, Grafton, Alexandria, Salisbury. The post rider was required to go over his route once a fortnight, and at stated times they were to reverse the routes, that is, they were to take the towns in the reverse order from that given above.

The postage on all private single letters to be six pence for every forty miles and four pence for every number of miles less than forty an other letters and packetts according to their weight and bulk, which shall be the exclusive perquisites of the post-riders.

John Lathrop of Lebanon was appointed post rider on this route. At this time there were few postmasters in the state. The nearest to Lebanon was at Hanover. The post rider delivered letters and packages at the houses of the people.

THE TOLERATION ACT.

In the early settlements the towns built meeting-houses, called, settled and supported ministers in their civic capacities. The people were taxed for these purposes in the same way as for any other purpose. The plan was a good one, for it provided religious privileges and instruction long before the churches were able to maintain public worship. But as the population increased, the people were no longer of the same sentiments and belief, and those who dissented from the "Standing Order," which was the Congregationalists, began to think it a hardship to be taxed for the support of a form of worship with which they did not sympathize; to build meeting-houses in which they never worshipped, to pay for preaching which they never heard gladly, or not at all. There began to be complaints against this system. The "Standing Order," who were in the majority, opposed any change, but about 1819 a law was passed doing away with this method of supporting public worship, casting all the denominations on their own resources. The churches more especially concerned were greatly discouraged, but finding themselves *then* able to do what they could not have done at first, they soon came to regard it as a good and wholesome law, inasmuch as it gave them that independence which all churches ought to have and maintain. The system had served a good purpose for a time, but in the increase of dissent from the forms and faith of the order which it most benefitted it was best to lay it aside.

The following items embrace the action of the town respecting purely local matters.

In 1820 they began to agitate the building of Stony Brook road and chose a "committee to go and view the route and report at the next annual meeting Diarca Allen Esq, Mr. Stephen Billings and Col. Thomas Waterman were chosen. At the annual meeting, 1821, voted to accept the report of the Committee but took no farther action. 1822, Voted that the Selectmen be directed (if they think proper) to lay out the road to the line of Enfield, keeping as near stony brook as circumstances will admit."

Attention is called to the words in parentheses in this vote, "if they [the selectmen] think proper." Heretofore the town in such cases has referred the matter to the discretion of the selectmen, or has absolutely directed them to build or not to build proposed highways. The careful wording of the vote seems to indicate some doubt as to the authority of the town in reference to highways. The decisions of the courts before that time, and abundantly since, imply that a town has no legal right to instruct or require by vote their selectmen to build a proposed highway. The matter is entirely in the power of the selectmen.

The laying of this road along the Stony Brook was in place of an old road which led over the hills and was a great improvement.

At the annual meeting, 1824, was the first movement for an organized fire department, for they voted to adopt the second section of an act entitled an act to regulate the proceedings for extinguishing fires that may accidentally or otherwise be kindled, passed April 6, 1781, and also an act passed June 27, 1818. Chose Stephen Kendrick, Esq., Samuel Selden, Esq., and Calvin Benton, fire wards.

The preamble of the act of 1781 is as follows:

Whereas it frequently happens when buildings contiguous take fire, that the people assembled to extinguish it proceed without order or regularity, whereby the end in view is often defeated. An as goods at such a time are inevitably exposed to plunder, some hardy evil minded persons take advantage of the calamity and steal such goods, whereby the loss of such sufferers is increased; and the laws of this state respecting the proceedings to extinguish fires, &c, being found ineffectual for the purposes for which they were made, Therefore, &c.

The second section, which was adopted, reads as follows:

SECT. 2. *And be it enacted by the authority aforesaid* That the freeholders and other inhabitants of Portsmouth in the County of Rockingham, and state aforesaid being qualified voters, may at their annual or other legal town meeting choose and appoint any suitable number of freeholders, being persons of approved ability and fidelity, who shall be denominated firewards, and have for a distinguishing badge of their office, a staff five feet long, painted red, and headed with a bright brass spire six inches long. And the firewards afore mentioned are hereby required, upon notice of the breaking out of fire in said town, to take with them the badges of their office, and immediately repair to the place where such fire may be, and vigorously exert themselves, and require and demand assistance of any inhabitants of said town to extinguish and prevent the spreading of such fire, and to remove goods and effects out of any houses or places endangered thereby; and the firewards may appoint necessary guards to secure and take care of such goods and effects

The section gives the firewards authority to require and demand assistance, to pull down, blow up or remove any buildings thought necessary by a majority of them, to suppress with force, if necessary, all tumults and disorders, and to direct and order the labor of all persons. Any persons refusing to obey the orders of the firewards were liable to a fine not exceeding ten pounds.

Though this act was framed for Portsmouth, yet any other city or town might adopt its provisions.

The act of 1818 gives to the firewards the entire control and direction of all fire engines, fire-hooks, hoses and other implements used for extinguishing or preventing the spread of fire. They were given also control of engine companies, axe companies, or any other associations whose special duty it may be to help in extinguishing fires. These companies were exempt from militia and jury duty.

At the meeting in November, 1824, the town voted to procure a hearse for the use of the town.

The meeting-house by this time required repairs and painting; accordingly at this same meeting:

Voted to choose a committee to paint and repair the meeting house, and that the same be done as soon as may be next spring. Capt. Samuel Young, Timothy Herrick, Ziba Alden, Capt Joel Amsden and Edward Bosworth were chosen said committee.

Remarkably prompt and harmonious action where a meeting-house was concerned. This was in November, so that the people had time to think the matter over and discuss it, and when they came together in their annual meeting in March, 1825, they were of a different mind, for under Article XIX of the warrant, "To see what sum or sums of money the town will vote to raise to repair the meeting-house in said town," they "voted to postpone acting on this article indefinitely."

At the annual meeting in 1826 the town voted to direct the selectmen to repair the *outside* of the meeting-house. This word, the "*outside*," sheds a ray of light on the action of the town.

At a meeting held April 29, 1826:

Voted to authorize the Selectmen to sell the pews belonging to the town excepting the pews where the stoves stand at public auction, or private sale as they may think best.

On the first day of January, 1827:

Voted that the meeting-house *may* be divided among the several denominations in the town in proportion as they own property in the House

Voted that the town recommend to each Religious society to meet other Societies by their Committee on Monday next at Mr Benton's tavern at one o'clock in the afternoon, for the purpose of arranging and dividing the Meeting-house.

When in 1824 the town voted so promptly to repair and paint the meeting-house, they did not think of the condition of things. At first the meeting-house was built by the town as a place for public worship for the people of the town, to which every voter contributed his portion, and the town, as such, maintained public worship by a tax assessed as other taxes were.

By the Toleration Act the towns were released from that obligation. In the meantime the town had sold its right and property in the pews to individuals and so, in a certain sense, owned only the "outside" of the meeting-house, hence the vote directing the selectmen to repair the *outside*, intending that those who owned the inside should take care of *that*.

Since the meeting-house was built the population had increased to about 1,700, and with this increase there was an increase of denominations, and it became an important question who should occupy the place of worship, since all had a right to have their own preaching. The town could think of no better way of settling this question than to proportion the occupancy according to the pew ownership. Of course, pews, under that rule, were much sought after and the town took advantage of the demand to sell the pews which it had retained in its own possession. There were at the time two Congregational societies, the First Society having been divided; a Universalist society had been formed, a number of Methodist, as yet without a distinct organization, as well as some Baptists. The allotment was as follows: First Society, 14 Sabbaths; Second Society, 22; Universalist Society, 12; Baptists, 4. This proportion was changed from time to time as circumstances demanded.

It was a bad arrangement for all the societies, productive of jealousies, bitterness of feelings, each society having only fragmentary services.

The First Congregational Society was the first to see the disadvantages of the arrangement, and built, by great self-denial, a house of their own. The Second Society became extinct, leaving the control of the house to the Universalist Society.

For the first time (1825) the town chose two representatives to the general court. The two chosen were William Benton and Samuel Young.

In 1826, at the annual meeting, voted that the selectmen build a tomb in the burying ground in as cheap a manner as will answer the use intended. But at a meeting held April 29, 1826, they voted to reconsider this vote, and the town remained without a tomb until that at Glenwood Cemetery was built in 1872.

At a special meeting held April 29, 1826, the town by vote gave leave to erect a clock in the belfry of the meeting-house at individual expense. People were not so liberal in their contributions as it was hoped they would be, for at their annual meeting, 1827, the town voted to pay thirty-five dollars towards a clock to be placed on the meeting-house. This was the first clock placed upon the meeting-house.

At this meeting liberty was given to Edward Howe "to erect a pair of Hay scales at the East end of the horse-sheds." This location was a little west of the present location of the town hall.

About this time there was much talk about what should be done with the poor of the town. Hitherto they had been placed in families which would receive them for a small compensation in addition to the services which they might render. They were discussing more or less the plan of a farm where they might be taken care of together.

The records of 1828 indicate that some time in August or early in September there was a great freshet, doing much damage, for September 22 they held a special meeting at which it was voted to raise one thousand dollars for the necessary expense of the town in repairing bridges, roads, etc. At the annual meeting of the year they had voted the same sum for the care of highways. We may infer that the damage was severe to require double the usual amount.

FROM 1830 TO 1840.

POLITICAL AFFAIRS.

In the town, 1830, Timothy Upham (Adams) had 209 votes; Matthew Harvey (Jackson) had 128, but in the state the Jackson men prevailed, Harvey being elected by a majority of about 3,000 votes.

In 1831 Ichabod Bartlett, Adams, had 208 votes; Samuel Dinsmoor, Jackson, had 142. In the state Dinsmoor had a majority of 4,822, indicating an increase of the Jackson men.

But the next year there was a change, the candidates being the same. In the town Bartlett received 163 votes, Dinsmoor 143, a large falling off of the Adams vote in the town. But in the state Bartlett received a small majority.

In 1833 there was a great overturning of parties. Arthur Livermore, Adams, received in the town but one vote, while Dinsmoor, Jackson, received 163. In the state there was similar falling off in the Adams vote, Livermore having in the state 3,959, while Dinsmoor had 28,277.

About this time the different parties began to be known by different names; they became Whigs and Democrats. In 1834 the vote in the town was for governor, William Badger, Democrat, 117, while there was but one vote for any other candidate. And the same was true in the whole state, Badger having 28,542 votes, with 1,631 scattering. It seems that they were not as yet organized or else generally voted with the Democrats.

In 1835 the vote for governor was as follows: For Joseph Healey, Whig, 148; Badger, Democrat, 128 votes. In the state, Healey had 14,825, Badger, 25,767, with about 300 scattering.

In 1836 the vote for governor in the town was for Isaac Hill, Democrat, 129; scattering, 2. In the state Isaac Hill had 24,904, while other candidates and scattering had 6,021.

In 1837 the vote for governor in the town was 116 votes for Isaac Hill; scattering, 3. In the state Joseph Healey, Whig, had 557; Isaac Hill, Democrat, had 22,361; scattering, 1,614.

In 1838 the vote for governor in town was: James Wilson, Whig, 230 votes; for Isaac Hill, Democrat, 129 votes. In the state Wilson had 25,675; Isaac Hill, 28,697; scattering, 198. The increase in the Whig vote is very noticeable, showing that the people were taking sides with decision.

In 1839 James Wilson, Whig, had 210 votes; John Page, Democrat, had 141 votes. In the state Wilson had 23,928; Page had 30,518. The Whigs lose and the Democrats gain.

MEETING HOUSE.

While the people were questioning whose duty it might be to repair the meeting-house, the house itself fared badly. In the warrant for the annual meeting for 1832 appears this article: "To see if you will vote to repair the windows in the meeting-house;" also, "To see if you will direct the selectmen or some other person to prosecute for any damage done to the meeting-house."

The matter of repairing the windows, they coming within the former vote to repair the "outside," was referred to the selectmen, and they were also directed to prosecute for any damage done to the house. Whether the offenders were discovered and prosecuted does not appear. Probably not, for the small boy has great facility for being somewhere else when mischief is done.

In 1835 a new movement was made concerning the meeting-house. At the annual meeting the following article appears in the warrant:

To see if the Town will consent to a proposed alteration of the Old Meeting-house by the Committee of the First Universalist Society, by laying a floor even with the gallery and removing the body pews below, or act hereon.

The following is the action taken on this article:

Resolved that the Committee mentioned in the Article 17th in the warrant have leave to make the proposed alteration in the Old Meeting House; to be made under the direction of the Selectmen, and that the said Selectmen see that it is left in proper situation for town use

The Congregationalists had already built their own house, the Methodists had done the same a few years previous, so that there could be no objection to this plan. It was duly carried out, the upper part making a place of worship and the lower part arranged for town meetings.

POOR FARM.

At the annual meeting in 1832 the town took further action relative to the purchase of a farm for the support of the poor, and they voted to choose a committee of three to investigate the matter. Daniel Hardy, Isaac Doty and Joseph Wood composed the committee. At a meeting held April 17, 1832, they voted to postpone the matter indefinitely and the poor were committed to the care of the selectmen.

In 1835 at the annual meeting the subject came up again, when the town "voted to authorize the selectmen to buy a farm if they deem it expedient."

At the next annual meeting they passed another vote, "that the selectmen be authorized to purchase a farm." This vote is different from the preceding, in that it does not leave the subject to the discretion of the selectmen. But the question was not settled by this vote, for at the annual meeting held March 14, 1837, another plan was brought forward, for they then passed the following vote: "That a committee of three be appointed to confer with similar committees from the towns of Hanover, Lyme and Orford, concerning purchasing a farm for the support of the poor in said towns, and report their doings at some future meeting of the town." This plan failed, for at the annual meeting in 1838 the following action was taken: "Voted to choose a committee to purchase a farm for the support of the poor of the town of Lebanon and that a sum, not exceeding forty-five hundred dollars of the public deposits, be appropriated for that purpose." James Willis, David Hough and George H. Lathrop were the committee chosen. It is to be noted that this is the first time any appropriation is made for this purpose. This action was final. The farm now owned by G. W. Worthen in the south part of the town was purchased for that purpose. Capt. Ephraim Wood was appointed superintendent and the town authorized him to spend a thousand dollars to purchase stock-farming tools and provisions for the use of the farm.

NEW ROADS.

For some time a new road was in contemplation westerly from what was then the Ira Gates farm, now Baumhaure's, through Poverty Lane to Plainfield line. The only road to that misnamed territory was that from Hubbard Bridge—a "long way around." At the annual meeting the town voted "that the selectmen of the Town meet the Selectmen of Plainfield, or such Committee as may be appointed by said town of Plainfield, and consult on the contemplated (or any other) route for a road to Plainfield, and if the public good required it, to lay out the road in the most suitable place." The road was finally built.

There had been for a long time a plan for a road from Packard's (Chandler's) mills to East Lebanon on the north side of the Mascoma River. At the same meeting, "Voted to choose a Committee of five to meet the Committee appointed by the proprietors of 4th Newhampshire Turnpike road on the subject of the contemplated route from near Packards bridge, Eastward, and to report at the next Town meeting." George H. Lathrop, John Lowe, David Hough, Uriah Amsden and Richard Kimball were appointed the committee.

At a meeting held on the 17th of April, 1832, the committee reported, when another committee of three was chosen to confer with the Fourth New Hampshire Corporation at their next annual meeting respecting an alteration of the road from Stony Brook to Josiah Barnes', and that said committee have power to make such proposition to said corporation as they may deem most advantageous to this town, and obtain such propositions from said corporation as they see fit to make, and report to the annual town meeting next March. The selectmen were chosen said committee, viz.: Roswell Sartwell, Alpheus Baker and Halsey R. Stevens.

When the Fourth New Hampshire Turnpike was located, it passed over the hill by B. F. Fellows' house, the Cleaveland place, then turning southward came onto Mascoma Lake near the Abner Packard place. The location proved inconvenient and difficult and it was proposed by the turnpike corporation to change the road to the southerly bank of the Mascoma River, from Stony Brook to East Lebanon near the outlet of the lake. The town desired to take advantage of the new part and the conference with the turnpike corporation was to secure this privilege. Finally the parties agreed that upon a contribution of seven hundred and fifty dollars towards the expense of the construction of the road, they should have the right to use it. The town appropriated first six hundred dollars and afterward one hundred and fifty more, the final vote being at the annual meeting in 1834.

How great an improvement this was may be easily seen, when it is known that the only road to East Lebanon was either by this road past the Fellows place on the south side of the river, or on the north side over Mount Tug.

In 1834, what is now called the Pine Plain road at West Lebanon, was laid out by a court committee, as a substitute for the old river road. This old road turned to the right, just south of the dwelling of Jeremiah Wood and ran along the river bank, coming out northerly of True bridge.

SUPPORT OF PRIMARY SCHOOLS.

At the annual meeting, 1834, the following record was made: "Resolved *unanimously* that our Representatives be requested to use their best exertions to repeal a law approved July 5, 1833, entitled an act in amendment of primary schools passed July 6, 1827."

The act to which the town was "unanimously" opposed was the following:

Be it enacted That it shall be the duty of the Selectmen of the Several Towns in this State to assign to each School District, in their respective towns and places, a proportion of the money assessed in each year for the support of schools, according to the valuation thereof for that year, unless the said towns and places, shall, at a meeting holden for that purpose, direct it to be divided according to the number of scholars in each district.

Upon a comparison of this act with that for which it was a substitute, no great difference is to be found. Section 2 of that act provides that the money raised for the support of schools shall be paid to the districts in proportion to the "valuation thereof for that year, or in such other manner as the several towns at their annual meeting shall direct."

The only difference in the two acts seems to be this: That under one law the town at its annual meeting can decide *how* the school money shall be divided, but in the amended act the towns could decide between two methods only, wholly by the valuation, or wholly by the number of scholars. They could not combine the two, as was often done, part by the scholars, part by the valuation. Division of the school money was always, and still is, a vexed question. The historian finds from the records that in a great majority of cases the division was "Same as last year."

RAILINGS ON BRIDGES.

At a special meeting held September 6, 1834, "Voted that the selectmen put railings on all Town Bridges they think necessary." This action was undoubtedly prompted by the fact that there had been accidents on the bridges from want of sufficient protection, for this article is found in the warrant for the annual meeting of 1834: "To see if the Town will pay Andrew Post for loss of his horse and damage of his Waggon in consequence of falling from the Bridge near Eliel Pecks Mills."

A RAILROAD IN PROSPECT.

From a vote passed at the annual meeting in 1836 the subject of a railroad through the town was before the people. The vote was as follows: "Voted that the Selectmen pay the expense of the survey of the contemplated Rail Road route through this Town." The vote, passed more than ten years before the road was in operation, shows that the people discerned their true interests.

Strange as it may seem to the present generation, there was at first intense and bitter opposition to railroads. The farmers opposed them because they did not want their farms divided and encumbered by the track, because their cattle were likely to be killed or mutilated. They said it would spoil the market for their horses, as there would be no call for them on stages and the big teams which carried their produce to market, and brought back groceries, dry goods *and* old Medford rum. What should they do with their oats?

Besides there was at the time bitter hatred to all corporations in New Hampshire. So strong was this opposition, and so difficult was it to obtain any charter for a railroad from the legislature of the state, that the threat to pass *around* New Hampshire was openly made. This would have been disastrous to the state in all its interests and retarded its development in manufactures and in all its highest interests. Fortunately there were those who had discernment to see the advantage of railroads and charters were granted to them.

PUBLIC MONEY FROM U. S. SURPLUS REVENUE.

This surplus came from the sale of public lands. In congress there were long and heated discussions as to its disposition. Finally it decided to distribute it among the states in proportion to their population, but under certain conditions, chief among which was that it must be repaid whenever the United States

ROBERT BYRON KIMBALL.

ROBERT KIMBALL.

should demand it. Under a like condition it was to be distributed to the towns. This condition occasioned no little reluctance on the part of the towns as to receiving, as it might place them in a difficult position, if it should be demanded again after they had spent it.

TOWN CLERK'S RECORDING DEEDS.

At the annual meeting in 1838 the town voted on this question: "Is it expedient for the Legislature to enact a law authorizing Town Clerks to record deeds?" The vote was, yeas 107, nays 5. This measure was probably suggested by the practice of Vermont. This was actually done when the town was in union with that state; there is among the town papers a book in which a large number of deeds are recorded. While this town favored the measure, the state was against it. It has its advantages and also its disadvantages and the latter are in excess.

At this same meeting came up this question of disannexing the town from Grafton County and annexing it to Sullivan County, but the town took no action on the question, but the fact that the measure came up shows that there was even then dissatisfaction among the people concerning their disadvantages as to attendance upon courts.

Also they voted to "become responsible to the state for the Rifles now used by the Rifle Company and also for any other arms that may be furnished by the State for the use of Soldiers of Lebanon."

Further they voted, "That the Selectmen purchase of Robert Kimball Esq. the piece of land to enlarge the burying ground if, in their opinion, it can be had at a fair price." This was the portion of the village cemetery in the rear of the high school building and the Methodist Church.

THE MEETING HOUSE UNEASY.

At the annual meeting, 1839, the following vote was passed: "Voted that the town give to Colbee C. Benton and others liberty to remove the Meeting House from where it now stands [on the common] to land back of the Common owned by Edward A Howe or Rev John Moore, provided they satisfy the Selectmen that it can be safely removed without danger of losing the Common, and provided they give to the Town a deed of the land to which they remove it, and also provided they give to the town a bond, with ample security, that they will remove it without any expence to the town, and leave it in as good repair as it now is, and place it as high as it now stands, and leave the ground around it in as good situation as it now is, and that a space of two rods be left on all sides of it and included in the deed.''

This enterprise was inaugurated by the Universalist Society, which had become the sole occupant of the house as a place of worship.

The Common was given to the town by Robert Colburn as a place for a meeting-house, with the provision that it should only be held for a site for a house of worship and a parade ground. There was danger that the ground would be lost to the town unless some arrangements should be made with his heirs.

Notwithstanding this vote, the meeting-house remained on its first location for years after.

FROM 1840 TO 1850.

POLITICAL AFFAIRS.

In the vote for governor in the town in 1840 Enos Stevens, Whig, had 206 votes; John Page, Democrat, 111, but in the state Page had a large majority.

In the vote for governor, 1841, in the town, Enos Stevens, W., had 201; John Page, D., had 150 votes, a large gain for the Democrats in the town. John Page was elected by a reduced majority. A new element appears among the old parties, that is, the Free Soil. Though Daniel Hoit, the candidate of that party, received no vote in the town, yet he received in the state 1,273 votes.

In 1842 the vote for governor was for Stevens, W., 128 votes; Henry Hubbard, D., 147; John H. White, I. D., 52. In the state there was a great variety of votes. Daniel Hoit, F. S., had 2,812; John H. White, I. D., 5,869; Enos Stevens, W., 12,234, a great loss; Henry Hubbard, 26,831, a loss also. An Independent Democrat was a Democrat opposed to the *extension* of slavery; a Free Soiler was opposed to slavery everywhere.

In 1843 the vote for governor was: Anthony Colby, W., 176; Henry Hubbard, D., 145; John H. White, I. D., 18. In the

STATE AND TOWN OFFICERS, ETC.

state Daniel Hoit, F. S., had 3,402, John H. White had 5,497, Anthony Colby 12,551, Henry Hubbard 23,050.

In 1844 the vote for governor was, for Anthony Colby, W., 168; John H. Steele, D., 113; John H. White, I. D., 20; Daniel Hoit, F. S., 19. This is the first time that Free Soil votes appear in the town.

In the state the vote was, for Daniel Hoit, F. S., 5,767; John H. White, I. D., 1,988; Anthony Colby, W., 14,750; John H. Steele, D., 25,986. This indicates a decrease in the Independent Democrat, an increase in the Free Soil, Whig and Democrat vote. From this time the Independent vote disappears, most of them joining the Free Soilers.

In 1845 the vote for governor was, for Anthony Colby, W., 160; for John Steele, D., 95; Daniel Hoit, F. S., 34. The Democrats lose, the Free Soilers gain.

In the state, Daniel Hoit, 5,786, a slight gain; Anthony Colby, 15,579, a gain; John H. Steele, 23,406, a loss.

In 1846, for governor, Anthony Colby, W., had 151 votes; Jared W. Williams, D., 117; Nathaniel S. Berry, F. S., 45, a gain. In the state, Anthony Colby had 17,707; Jared W. Williams, 26,740; N. S. Berry, 10,379. In this year there was a larger vote for all parties, the Free Soilers nearly doubling their vote. But there was no election by the people. Anthony Colby was elected by the legislature.

In 1847 the vote for governor was, Anthony Colby, W., 180; Jared W. Williams, D., 167; Nathaniel Berry, F. S., 45. In the state the vote for N. S. Berry, 8,531; Anthony Colby, 21,109; Jared W. Williams, 30,806. Williams elected.

In 1848 the vote for governor was, for N. S. Berry, F. S., 202; Jared W. Williams, D., 153. In the state N. S. Berry had 28,829; Jared W. Williams, 32,245. In both town and state the Whigs were not represented in the vote of the year; the majority of the Whigs probably voted for Berry.

In 1849 the vote for governor was, Nathaniel S. Berry, F. S., 27; Levi Chamberlain, W., 182; Samuel Dinsmore, Jr., D., 146. In the state, N. S. Berry, 7,045; Levi Chamberlain, 18,764; Samuel Dinsmore, Jr., 30,107.

The remarkable decrease in the Free Soil vote indicates very plainly that the Whigs voted with them in 1848.

The period from 1840 to 1850 was one of great division of opinion and intense excitement of feeling throughout the land. The people were discussing many things pertaining to their welfare, upon which they could not, or did not agree. Among these questions the continuance of an United States bank; the Seminole war; disputed boundaries on the northeast and the northwest of the territory of the United States; the rise and persecution of the Mormons; the Log Cabin and Hard Cider campaign; a rebellion in Canada and in Rhode Island; the expeditions of Fremont to the coast of the Pacific; the seizure of California, in which he was a prominent actor; the Mexican war; the distribution of the surplus revenue to the states.

But the most potent factor in these disturbances was the subject of slavery. The Abolitionists, standing upon the broad assertions of the Declaration of Independence, bitterly denounced slavery itself, and would have no compromises with it of any kind. They would accept nothing but immediate emancipation. Others, while they disliked slavery with more or less feeling, did not quite see their way clear to immediate extinction of that system, but *were* determined that it should have no more territory to occupy, by which to strengthen itself. Then another large and powerful party held negro slavery to be a good institution in itself, and having the divine approval, and this party was not confined to the territory where slavery existed, but had sympathy and advocates all through the people. To threaten this institution was to threaten their temporal prosperity and all their interests. Naturally enough they resented any interference with this cherished institution with bitterness and direful threats.

Circumstances kept alive these feelings and passions and kindled them to hotter activity. In 1839 the schooner *L'Amistad*, bound from Havana to Port Principe, with fifty-four blacks on board, while lying near the coast of Connecticut, is seized by Lieutenant Gedney of the United States brig *Washington* and taken into New London in August. The blacks proved to be slaves, purchased at Havana, who had risen in mutiny and killed the captain and three of the crew. Cingues, son of an African chief, a leader in the mutiny, with thirty-eight others, were held for trial. The acting Spanish minister demanded from our government the surrender of the vessel, her cargo and the slaves to the Spanish authorities. Before the United States Circuit Court in Hartford, Conn., the counsel for Spain demanded the release of the blacks. Judge Thompson promptly refused the demand. Then ensued a long controversy as to the jurisdiction of the courts. The claim of the officers and crew of the *Washington* complicated matters still farther. Finally, in January, 1840, Judge Judson of the District Court decides in favor of the jurisdiction of the courts, in favor of the claim of the crew to salvage, but refused the demand of the authorities of Spain for restoration, and finally adds this curious judgment that the actual *murderers being blacks*, must be set free; had they been whites they would have been tried and executed as pirates. That they must be delivered to the president of the United States to be returned to Africa.

It is difficult to understand the ground of this decision, unless we take the word blacks as synonymous with slaves who had the natural right to gain their freedom *by any means*. An appeal was taken to the District Court and to the United States Supreme Court, where all the previous points were affirmed, except as to sending the blacks back to Africa; they were given their absolute freedom. The next year the brig *Creole* leaves Richmond, Vt., for New Orleans with one hundred and thirty-five slaves. The slaves mutiny, kill one of the owners and injure the crew, and take the vessel to Nassau, New Providence. Nineteen of the slaves are imprisoned for mutiny and murder. The demand of the United States consul for their surrender to be sent to the United States was denied.

Later the secretary of state, Mr. Webster, instructs the minister to England to present the case to the British government. It is discussed in parliament and ended with a refusal to surrender the fugitives, or the mutineers, and they were all ordered to be released.

All these things were discussed abundantly by the newspapers and the people with great earnestness and much excitement.

In 1842 John Quincy Adams presented in the senate a petition from citizens of Haverhill, Mass., asking that measures might be taken for the peaceable dissolution of the Union. Mr. Adams had no sympathy with the object of this petition, for in presenting it he moved its reference to a select committee, with instructions to report the reasons why the petition should not be granted. The presentation of such a petition produced intense excitement. Resolutions of censure upon Mr. Adams were offered by one senator for presenting such a petition. Another offered a substitute declaring Mr. Adams' action the deepest indignity to the senate and people. Violent debates followed and ended in the senate's refusing to receive the petition. Never was Mr. Adams greater than when he advocated the sacred right of petition, guaranteed by the constitution, in the face of a hostile senate, and that, too, in a prayer with which he had no sympathy.

This action kindled anew the fires of discord and awakened intense indignation in the minds of hundreds of thousands who had no sympathy with the objects of that petition, but did believe in the sacred right then denied.

Abolition riots occur in various parts of the country, involving loss of life and property.

In the meantime Texas had gained her independence from Mexico, and established a republic, and soon sought admission to the Union. All parties saw at once the meaning of this movement. The South advocated the admission of Texas because it would enlarge slave territory, make a market for their slaves, and give them predominance in national affairs, for though their slaves could not vote, yet they were *counted* to make up the number requisite for a representative to congress. The North was alarmed. While for the most part they were not disposed to meddle with slavery where it was already established, they earnestly objected to the extension of its territory. Certain action taken in the New Hampshire Legislature indicates clearly and forcibly the sentiments and feelings which the annexation of Texas produced.

Whereas the government of the United States, by the annexation of a foreign nation [Texas was a part of Mexico] and the admission of the State of Texas into the Union with a constitution which, in effect, makes slavery perpetual therein have placed us before the world in the false attitude of supporters and defenders of a system of oppression, odious to every friend of liberty, and abhorrent to every principle of humanity and religion; and

Whereas the constant, progressive and increasing encroachments of the slave power have become so formidable and imperious that forbearance ceases to be a virtue and to be silent is to be false to the great interests of liberty; Therefore,

Resolved by the Senate and House of Representatives, in General Court convened, That Newhampshire solemnly and deliberately announces and reiterates her abiding and unchanging adherence to the great principle of the declaration of our Revolutionary fathers, that "all men are created equal," reasserted in the first article of the Bill of Rights of our own Constitution; that she declares her firm determination, that in the great contest now being waged between slavery and freedom, her voice shall be heard on the side of the oppressed; that she pledges her cordial sympathy, and within the limits of constitutional action, her coöperation with the friends of civil liberty throughout the land, in very just and well directed effort for the suppression and extermination of that terrible scourge of our race, human slavery.

Approved July 10, 1846.

The following resolution was passed at the same time:

Resolved by the Senate and House of Representatives in General Court convened: That the Senators and Representatives from this State in the Congress of the United States be respectively requested to urge in that body the passage of measures providing for the extinction of slavery in the District of Columbia; for its exclusion from Oregon, and other territories that now or any time hereafter may belong to the United States; for all constitutional measures for the suppression of the domestic slave trade and to resist the admission of any new state into the Union, while tolerating slavery.

Resolved that his excellency the Governor be requested to furnish copies of the foregoing Resolve to the Legislatures of the several states, and to our Senators and Representatives in Congress.

Plainly the "irrepressible Conflict" waxed stronger and fiercer, producing endless discussions everywhere. Families were disrupted, father against son, brother against brother, and even the bark of Cupid was wrecked on these shoals. The present generation knows little about this division among the people, the strength of feeling, the bitterness of hostility evoked by these issues now so plainly and boldly made. In this we may discern the meaning of those strange changes in the voting of the people, the gathering and falling away of parties. In these conflicts we may discern the gathering of that cloud which later, surcharged with lightning and tempests, burst upon the devoted land.

DIVIDING GRAFTON COUNTY.

In 1840 the following article was inserted in the warrant for the annual meeting: "To take the sense of the town (agreeable to a Resolution passed the N. H. Legislature, June Session 1839) upon the following Question: Is it expedient to divide the County of Grafton?"

This indicates that some of the people were still discontented with their position in county affairs and desiring better accommodations.

The vote of the town was, yeas 49, nays 52; and so the matter rested for a time.

SURPLUS REVENUE.

At this same meeting the town voted that "the sum of three hundred of the Surplus Revenue deposited with the Town be paid to the Overseer of the Poor for the use of the Town Farm, and all the residue of said surplus be appropriated for town purposes."

At the annual meeting in 1845, the town voted "that it is expedient to receive the portion of the Surplus Revenue due this State from the United States." This was in addition to a sum already received. In 1849, "Voted to appropriate the Surplus Revenue to Town purposes." At a subsequent meeting in August the vote was renewed.

4TH N. H. TURNPIKE.

For some time the Fourth New Hampshire Turnpike had been unprofitable to the corporation, and a movement was made to have it declared a free road. In view of this the town at its annual meeting, 1840, "Chose Col. Abel Baker agent for the Town with regard to the Fourth New Hampshire Turnpike being made a free road."

At a meeting held on the second day of November, 1840:

Voted that the Selectmen be and they hereby are authorized, and directed to borrow on the credit of the town the sum of sixteen hundred dollars for the purpose of paying to the Proprietors of the Fourth N. H. Turnpike Corporation the damages as assessed by the Court's Committee in December last. The Selectmen are also directed to take charge of the road and put it in good condition.

At the annual meeting in 1841 the town:

Voted that the Selectmen be authorized to expend three Hundred dollars of the Town's money to repair the old Turnpike in addition to what may be necessary to repair the bridges &c.

Thus passed away one of the noted institutions of this region and of the state. It was one of the paths from the interior to the seaside, over which there was an immense traffic. In one direction went the product of the farms of Vermont and New Hampshire, beef, pork, mutton, butter and cheese, eggs and poultry, potatoes and grain. In the reverse direction were carried groceries, dry goods, all manner of supplies for the family, many casks of New England rum, farming implements, iron and steel for blacksmiths, tools for the mechanic, toys for the children, medicine for the sick, and almost everything needed in the affairs of life.

It required many horses, many drivers, many wagons, many harnesses, many blacksmiths along the route. There were eight-horse teams, six-horse teams, four-horse teams and two-horse teams. These last were called "Pod teams." Besides these regular teams, farmers, especially in the winter, "went to market" with their own teams, neighborhoods joining together for the sake of company and mutual assistance. Ceaselessly these teams went to and fro, often in long procession.

In addition to these freight teams were the stages, carrying passengers and the mails passing over this great highway.

Fortunate in those days was the man, usually a farmer, who lived at the top of a long and hard hill, for these teams were loaded to the last pound and required assistance up the hills, and the man had a span of horses or yoke of oxen ready to render that assistance—for a consideration. It was helpful to the teamster because by this occasional assistance he could transport a heavier load; it was more profitable to the farmer than many of his most fertile acres. But sometimes the farmer missed his fee, for neighbors or friends traveled in company, and when a difficult hill was reached one of the wagons was left at the bottom and the horses attached to the other and it was drawn to the top of the hill, and then the horses were returned to the wagon at the foot of the hill and that was drawn up. This was called doubling up.

In these days the country taverns flourished mightily. They were to be found every two or three miles along the route. There were seven or eight in this town alone. At night there were from twenty-five to sixty horses to be housed and fed, with their drivers. These teamsters were acquaintances and had good times in the evening when the toils and hardships of the day were over. Experiences were compared, the condition of the highway criticised, stories were exchanged, religious doctrines were discussed, for in those days these subjects had a strong hold upon the minds of the people. They were pondered more than they are today, and the discussion of them and the thinking of them naturally developed a strong intellectual grasp—not so common today. Politics had a large place in their discussions, and they grew warm and heated over these matters, for in those days differences of opinion were not accompanied with any spark of courtesy or amiability.

In the winter, gathered around an open fire of well seasoned logs, they had their lively frolics, helped on by visits to the bar, then openly and unblushingly kept. Those were the days when liquors were pure and indulgence in them only added exhilaration to their spirits without making them quarrelsome. Many were the practical jokes they played upon each other. One found his boots full of ice, a companion having filled them with water and set them outdoors. But that debt was repaid soon after when the roguish companion found an obstruction in his boots as he sought to pull them on one morning in the shape of a young kitten, whose claws and teeth resented the introduction of the unwary foot.

This sketch of the ancient turnpike would be incomplete without the mention of the stage drivers. These were a class of men above the teamsters, the aristocrats of the road, gentlemen, well dressed, much trusted, proud of their occupation, the envy of all the boys who made their manners by the roadside as the gaudy Concord coach rolled swiftly by, whose ambition was to be a stage driver when old enough. They were skillful men, knowing every rod of their routes,—just where all the bad spots in the road were in the darkest night. It would pay a stranger to go a mile or two to see one of these four or six-horse teams come up to the tavern door at full speed in a cloud of dust or

JOHN W. PECK.

J. W. PECK HOMESTEAD. BUILT 1780.

snow, pulling up exactly at the landing place, to leave the mail bags and passengers, while a crowd of loungers admired or criticised the skill of the driver.

These drivers had an annual ball in Concord, than which none was more select; an invitation to attend their ball was an honor greatly coveted by the highest in the land.

When the railroads were built this valuable class of men disappeared from these pathways, and most of this generation have never seen a genuine stage driver and cannot find them without going hundreds of miles. Some of them, however, found employment as conductors on the railroads in their early days.

THE MEETING-HOUSE.

The meeting-house, still standing on the common, grew more dilapidated and forlorn, and it became evident that something must be done to prevent danger from accidents. So, at the annual meeting, 1840, it was "Voted that the sum of twenty-five dollars be appropriated to be expended, if necessary, under the direction of the Selectmen in repairing the bell deck of the old Meeting-house." Note that it has come to be the "old meeting-house."

At the annual meeting in 1841, "Voted that the Selectmen fit up the Town House, so as to make it convenient for Town purposes—not to exceed one hundred dollars in expense." This was the lower part of the house, the Universalists occupying the upper part.

In December 25, 1841, at a special meeting the town "voted to appropriate the sum of two hundred dollars to repair and improve the town house so that it will be more convenient for public meetings and doing town business. Voted to appoint Watson K. Eldridge, Alpheus Baker, and John W. Peck committee for the above purpose. Voted that said committee procure two suitable stoves and funnel for the town house, not to exceed in the amount the sum of fifty dollars."

At the annual meeting, 1842, a new duty was imposed upon the town clerk, as follows: "Voted that the Town Clerk take charge of the Town House and see that the same be kept in proper repair, and generally open the same for the use of any portion of the Inhabitants of the town upon all proper occasions

& to any Gentlemen for scientific purposes, and if at any time said Clerk shall doubt as to the expediency of opening the Hall, he shall consult with the Selectmen, and the board shall settle the right." The town clerk to whom this important duty fell was Timothy Kenrick. It may be safely presumed that the town clerk "faithfully and impartially discharged and performed" his duty in this matter, for neither meeting-house nor town house appear upon the records again until 1845, when this vote was passed at the annual meeting: "Voted that the Selectmen paint in a good and substantial manner the lower part of the outside of the town house up to the top of the lower windows, and one half of the steeple or belfry above the roof of the house, provided the Universalist society, will, in like manner, paint the other part of the outside of said house and steeple or belfry."

It does not appear that the selectmen ever did the work assigned to them.

At a special meeting held July 2, 1849:

Voted that the Selectmen be directed to purchase the reserved rights of the heirs of Robert Colburn to the Meeting House common, provided that the whole can be obtained for a sum not exceeding two hundred and the necessary expense not exceeding twenty-five dollars

Voted that the Town consent that the town-house be removed, provided a good deed of a strip of land 72 feet wide from the common and one hundred feet back towards E. A. Howe's house be given to the Town & provided said house be raised a suitable height above the land of the common when graded & to be set not more than one hundred feet from said common & provided E. Blaisdell G. S. Kendrick, C. C. Benton & H. R. Stevens give bonds to the town to remove said House and put in as good repair as it now is, without expense to the town, this to be done under the supervision of the Selectmen.

SALE OF SPIRITUOUS LIQUOR.

At a special meeting held December 23, 1843, the following resolution was adopted:

Resolved: That we consider the sale and use of spirituous liquor in all its forms, except for medical purposes, and then under the direction of medical men, as immoral and unbecoming in a Christian community; as decidedly injurious to health, as destructive to sound happiness, as a great incitement to crime, as one of the greatest and most alarming causes of increasing pauperism and as the source from which comes more of moral and political evil than any other single vice to which man is addicted.

HARVEY MURCH.

ELISHA P. LISCOMB.

Therefore voted that the Selectmen of this town be directed not to grant any license for the sale of spirituous liquors or wines of any kind for any other than medical purposes, and that under such restrictions as they may judge proper for the promotion of a strictly temperance community.

The vote was eighty-six to four in favor of the resolution.

They also voted to postpone indefinitely the question of granting a license to tavern-keepers and retailers.

At a meeting held February 1, 1848, the town voted not to grant a license to any person for the sale of spirituous liquors or wines except for medicinal or mechanical purposes. The vote was 139 to 88 in favor.

At the annual meeting in 1849 the town reaffirmed the preceding vote.

Railroads.

At the annual meeting in 1844 the following preamble and resolutions were adopted:

Whereas we believe Railroads to be one of the greatest improvements of the present age, and above all others best calculated, not only to facilitate and cheapen travel and transportation over our hills and along our vallies, but to bring together and harmonize the various feelings and interests of our common Country and thereby strengthen and perpetuate that union and harmony without which human society can scarcely be called a blessing, and

Whereas it is contemplated by many individuals to petition the next Legislature for a charter from Concord to the valley of the Connecticut river, and

Whereas there are some who believe the Legislature is prohibited from granting a charter for Rail Roads with the right of way, and others who believe the right of way may be obtained by purchase of the individuals over whose lands such Rail Road may pass, without the grant of such right of way by the Legislature, and Whereas we believe the Legislature of this State have by the Constitution full power to grant the right of way for Rail roads as well as for other great public roads and ways for public use and convenience, and

Whereas from full examination recently made, we are satisfied that no such right of way can be obtained without an act of the Legislature authorizing such Corporation to take the land of individuals for such way,

Therefore Resolved that our Representatives this day elected [E. P. Liscomb, G. H. Lathrop, be instructed, and we do hereby especially instruct them, by all fair and honorable legislation to promote the ease and convenience of the inhabitants of the State by voting for charters for Rail Roads in all proper and necessary places, with right of way under such restrictions, and with such reasonable provisions as shall insure to land-owners, full and ample compensation for any lands they may be required to surrender for such right of way, and at the same time with such liberal priviledges, as shall enable the Corporation to carry forward this great enterprise through and not around New Hampshire

The Preamble passed on division of the house 194 yeas to 14 nays. The Resolution passed on division of the house 190 yeas to 18 nays.

The town clerk was directed to publish the above action in some newspaper.

At the annual meeting, 1845, the following action was taken:

Resolved that by the making of the contemplated Rail Road through this town its inhabitants would be relieved for ever from the cost and expense of great and important alterations in its present leading roads, as also of much of the expense of keeping them in repair for the heavy teams which are now continually passing over them; and whereas individuals have already expended large sums for surveys for said Rail Road; and whereas further sums are necessary to procure its location, and, as we believe its ultimate success, which would be of great advantage to the town in relieving its inhabitants from the burden aforesaid

Therefore voted that the Selectmen pay over to the Rail Road Committee a sum not exceeding two hundred dollars of any money belonging to the town to be by said Committee expended in procuring the location of said Rail Roads, and to take a receipt of the chairman of said Committee, that the sum be refunded to the town, with interest, upon the completion of said railroad, and not otherwise

By a subsequent vote the selectmen were directed to pay to T. J. Carter the sum of one hundred dollars toward expense of the survey.

OPENING OF THE NORTHERN RAILROAD TO LEBANON.

On Wednesday, the 17th of November, 1847, the Northern Railroad was farther opened to Lebanon, in New Hampshire. This event was celebrated by a large number of persons who came from Boston for that purpose, and by a great concourse from the neighboring region. The train made a halt at South Franklin for the purpose of taking in Hon. Daniel Webster, then on a visit to his farm in that place. A collation had been prepared for the company at Lebanon. At this entertainment, a toast in honor of Mr. Webster was proposed by Charles T. Russell, Esq., of Boston, chairman of the committee of arrangements, to which Mr. Webster responded as follows:

I wish, Sir, that the gentleman who has done me the honor to propose the toast just given had called upon some other person than myself to address the meeting and had left me in the position of a listener merely; but I could not properly refrain from expressing my sincere thanks for the manner in which my name has been announced by the president and received by the assembly. Thus called upon to speak, I cannot disregard the summons. Undoubtedly the present is a moment of great interest, and I now have to perform the pleasing duty of congratulating the directors and stockholders of this road upon the successful completion of their enterprise; and also the citizens residing in this part of the country, upon the result which has been witnessed today, the entire accomplishment of this most important work. It is an undertaking not only important in itself but also very important when regarded as a link in the great chain of railroads which is to connect the West with the seacoast.

For myself, in considering the progress of railroad structures throughout the country, I have been, doubtless many other individuals have been, generally contented with admiring the enterprise manifested, the ingenuity displayed, the industry shown in carrying them forward to completion. But here, on this occasion, there is to me a matter of peculiar interest. Perhaps, and very possibly, this is because the road whose completion is now to be hailed runs not only through New Hampshire, my native state, but also through that part of New Hampshire in which I have a considerable personal interest. This is but natural, for the road passes through my own farm, my own New Hampshire home.

This Northern Railroad is destined to be connected with two other roads of vast importance, each having Montreal for its end. The one will traverse Vermont, passing Montpelier, and proceeding along the valley of the Winooski to Lake Champlain, while the other will extend itself up the valley of the Passumpsic. Each, for the present, has its terminus at Montreal, so that the traveler from the Atlantic coast, arriving at Lebanon, might have a choice to make between the routes. This choice, perhaps, may occasionally be perplexing. The passenger from the coast to the St. Lawrence may now know on which line travel is best, or which is most convenient for his purposes. It may not improbably so happen that the traveler will compromise the matter, deciding to go on by the one route, and return by the other. So far as I am concerned, both lines have my best wishes for their entire success.

My friend, the presiding officer, has spoken of Burlington and Montreal as the termini of this road; but in point of fact, this is a mere link, a part of a line of land navigation, by steam, from Boston to Ogdensburg, and thence, by land and water, to the Great West. I do not exactly remember whether it was Mr. Gouveneur Morris or Mr. Clinton who said, with regard to the Erie Canal, that the object and aim of that undertaking were to "tap Lake Erie and draw down its waters to New York harbor." One or the other of these two great men it was, and the design has been carried out. It may not, perhaps, be proper for me to say, that the design of this road, with its extensions, is to tap the St. Lawrence, but it can be asserted, and with truth, that it was to relieve that noble river of a large portion of its great, rich, overwhelming burdens, and deliver its freight, or at least a great part of its freight, at the Atlantic shore by a more safe, speedy and cheap conveyance than any before available. That, I imagine, must be clear to all.

Again, no one can fail to perceive how greatly instrumental this road, with its extension, will prove in bringing Ogdensburg near to Boston,—as near, indeed, as Buffalo now is to Albany. This connection between Ogdensburg and the capital of New England would open at once a new thoroughfare for the products of the West, an outlet hitherto untried, through which the commodities of Lake Superior and the other upper lakes may seek and reach the Atlantic by the way of Massachusetts Bay and its chief port. I will not undertake to compare the little city of Boston with the great city of New York, preëminent as New York is among the cities of America, for her extended commerce and her facilities for its increase. The great city of our neighboring state towers above all rivals in respect to every advantage of commercial position. Let her enjoy all the benefits she can, let her claim all the credit she can from this circumstance. Neither envy nor malice, on my part, shall contribute to rob her of one of her well deserved laurels; but without any very great arrogance, or any very undue exhibition of local pride, we may say that Boston, with her adjacent towns, throughout all the neighboring shore from Hingham to Marblehead—which extent of country, in effect, is but one seaport, certainly one so far as commercial and manufacturing industry is concerned—is entitled to command some degree of respect from the whole confederation of our states. Standing, indeed, upon the summit of Bunker Hill, one can look around upon a territory and a population equal to that of New York and her immediate suburbs. In fact, from Boston to Newburyport it is all one city; and by the development of her own enterprise, Boston, with her environs, has made herself a rival not lightly to be contemned by any city of the country. I will for one not undertake to estimate the increased extent of her commerce when all the links in her chain of railroad communication shall be completed.

There is another consideration which will commend itself to those who would contemplate the immediate future. It is this, that there will soon be an entire railroad line from New York, through New Haven, Hartford and Springfield, not only to Boston, but up the valleys of the Connecticut and Passumpsic, to Montreal. It is the impression of many, that land in New England is poor; and doubtless such is the fact with regard to a great portion of it. But throughout the whole United States I do not know of a richer or more beautiful valley, as a whole, than that of the Connecticut River. Parts of it are worth two hundred and fifty dollars an acre for the purpose of cultivation, and there is no land in the West worth half so much. I cannot say so much for the land of the Merrimack Valley for cultivation, but that portion of the country is rich in water-power, rich in manufacturing industry, and rich in human energy and enterprise. These are its elements of wealth: and these elements will soon be developed, in a great measure by the means of railroad communication, to a surprising extent. The whole region of country along this line of road, a distance say of about one hundred and twenty miles, will, before our children have ceased to be active among the sons of men, be one of the richest portions of the whole world. Such, I really believe, is the destiny of the Merrimack valley. Rich, not in the fertility of the soil on its banks, but in its almost illimitable water-power, the energy and industry of its people, and the application of these elements to the improvement and extension of productive machinery. It may soon be said of this beautiful river, with even more truth than applied to the poet's glorious lines upon the Thames,—

"Though with those streams it no resemblance hold,
Whose foam is amber and whose gravel gold,
Its greater, but less guilty, wealth explore,
Search not its bottom, but survey its shore."

And now what is the particular cause of all the prosperity and wealth which I foresee in this valley? What is it that has chiseled down these Grafton rocks and made this road which brings my own house so near to the home of my most distant New Hampshire hearer? It is popular industry; it is free labor. Probably there never was an undertaking which was more the result of popular feeling than this. I am told there are fifteen hundred stockholders in the enterprise, the capital being two millions and a half. That single fact would serve to show the generally diffused interest felt by the people in its success. It is but three or four years since, when, having occasion to visit my farm at Franklin, I observed a line of shingles stretching across my fields. Asking my farmer what was the meaning of all this, I was answered, "It is the line of our railroad." Our railroad!! That is the way the people talked about it. I laughed at the idea at first; and, in conversation with a neighbor, inquired what in the world they wanted of a railroad there. "Why," was the reply," the people want a ride behind the iron horse, and that ride they will have." This day they have had it. The result has proved, not that my friend was too sanguine, but that I was too incredulous.

It is the spirit and influence of free labor, it is the indomitable industry of a free people, that has done all this. There is manifested in its accomplishment that without which the most fertile field by nature must remain forever barren. Human sagacity, skill and industry, the zealous determination to improve and profit by labor, have done it all. That determination has nowhere been more conspicuously displayed than here. New Hampshire, it is true, is no classic ground. She has no Virgil and no Eclogues. She has a stern climate and a stern soil. But her climate is fitted to invigorate men and her soil is covered with the evidences of the comforts of individual and social life. As the traveler pursues his way along her roads, he sees all this. He sees those monuments of civilization and refinement, churches; he sees those marks of human progress, schoolhouses, with children clustering around their doors as thick as bees. And they are bees, except in one respect. The distinction is, that whereas the insect day after day returns to its home laden with the spoils of the field, the human creature is admitted to the hive but once. His mind is furnished with the stores of learning, he is allowed to drink his fill at the fountains of knowledge, his energies are trained in the paths of industry, and he is then sent out into the world, to acquire his own subsistence and help to promote the welfare of his kind.

It is an extraordinary era in which we live. It is altogether new. The world has seen nothing like it before. I will not pretend, no one can pretend, to discern the end; but everybody knows that the age is remarkable for scientific research into the heavens, the earth, and what is beneath the earth; and perhaps more remarkable still for the application of this scientific research to the pursuits of life. The ancients saw nothing like it. The moderns have seen nothing like it till the present generation. Shakespeare's fairy said he would

"Put a girdle round about the earth
In forty minutes."

Professor Morse has done more than that; his girdle requires far less time for its traverse. In fact, if one were to send a dispatch from Boston by the telegraph at twelve o'clock, it would reach St. Louis at a quarter before twelve. This is what may be called doing a thing in less than no time. We see the ocean navigated and the solid land traversed by steam power, and intelligence communicated by electricity. Truly this is almost a miraculous era. What is before us no one can say, what is upon us no one can hardly realize. The progress of the age has almost outstripped human belief; the future is known only to Omniscience.

In conclusion, permit me to say that all these benefits and advantages conferred upon us by Providence should only strengthen our resolves to turn them to the best account, not merely in material progress, but in the moral improvement of our minds and hearts. Whatsoever else we may see of the wonders of science and art, our eyes should not be closed to that great truth, that, after all, "the fear of the Lord is the beginning of wisdom."—The Works of Daniel Webster, Volume II.

Historical Miscellany.

CAPITAL PUNISHMENT.

At the November meeting, 1844, the following article appeared in the warrant:

To take the sense of the votes upon the question, Shall capital punishment be abolished?

Votes in favor of the abolition, 70.

Votes against the abolition, 159.

EXTINGUISHMENT OF FIRES.

At the annual meeting in 1845 the town voted to choose a committee of three to take into consideration the whole subject of the extinguishment of fires and the adoption of certain laws relating thereto. Timothy Kenrick, Watson K. Eldridge and Elisha P. Liscomb were named as that committee.

At an adjourned meeting held April 1, 1845, voted to adopt certain sections of Chapter III of the Revised Statutes. These sections define the duties of firewards in towns, give them authority over all fire apparatus and firemen, the precautions against fires and measures for extinguishing them.

One of the sections provides as follows: "Every house or building with fireplaces or stoves shall have thereon a good secure ladder or ladders, reaching from the ground to the ridgepole, and shall be provided with one leathern bucket of such size and form as the firewards may prescribe for every two fireplaces or stoves in such houses; and if the owner shall not provide and keep in repair such buckets and ladders he shall be liable to a penalty of six dollars for every three months' neglect."

By a vote of the town all persons living two hundred and fifty rods from the town house were exempt from the duties prescribed by this section.

Other acts or parts of them relating to the same subject were adopted from time to time, when at a special meeting held May

29, 1848, the town voted to appropriate the sum of five hundred dollars towards purchasing a fire engine and all necessary apparatus, on condition that the same sum be raised by subscription or otherwise and the said engine and apparatus be to the satisfaction of the selectmen. This was the engine now known as No. 2, and proved to be of excellent quality. Before this the town had used a small engine made by Stephen Kendrick, upon which W. S. Ela says he worked. It was of little power, had no hose and remained for years as a curiosity, and finally succumbed to the depredations of the small or large boys.

VOTE OF THANKS TO GEORGE H. LATHROP.

At the close of an adjournment of the annual meeting of 1845 the following vote was passed: "Voted that the thanks of this meeting be rendered to George H. Lathrop Eq. for the Courteous, able, and impartial manner with which he has presided over the deliberations of this meeting."

This was an unusual proceeding and indicates that the meeting had been a stormy one. Mr. Lathrop was an excellent presiding officer, having all the qualities ascribed to him in the vote.

TEACHERS' INSTITUTE.

The legislature in its June session, 1846, passed an act authorizing towns to raise, "in addition to the amount by law required to be raised therein for the support of common schools, a sum not exceeding five per cent of such amount, to be applied to the support of a Teachers' Institute within the limits of the county in which said town is situated."

At the annual meeting in 1849 the following resolution was adopted:

Resolved that we approve of the plan of establishing a 'Teachers' Institute' in the Western Judicial District of the County of Grafton, and that the Selectmen be directed to pay out of any of the towns money not otherwise appropriated our proportion of such expense as may be necessary for the same, not exceeding twenty-eight dollars ($28), when they shall be satisfied that the same is established and in operation, and that our jurymen and other Gentlemen attending Court at Haverhill, in April next, be requested to attend any meeting that may be held there for the organization of a "Teachers Institute' and act therein in behalf of the town

This prompt action of the town in behalf of an institution which has been of great service to the common schools of the state shows a commendable interest in education.

At this same meeting the town provided for the printing of the reports of town officers thereafter. In 1890 the town clerk succeeded in finding a copy of the reports for each year and had them bound together in one volume, greatly to the convenience of the town officers and the public.

NEW BURYING GROUND.

At the annual meeting, 1845: "Voted that the Selectmen immediately lay out the new Burying Ground into suitable lanes, alleys and suitable lots, putting up monuments to designate or marking the same, and make a plan of the same and lodge the same with the Town Clerk of said town; that they designate one half of said lots as for sale, at a price not exceeding five dollars for any one lot, and so in proportion to their situation, and that the other lots be free for the use of any of the inhabitants of said town without any pay, and that any person desiring any lot appraised by said Selectmen, may have the same by paying the price so set by said Selectmen to said lot, and having his name written in said lot in the plan in the Town Clerk's office, and that the price for which any lot or lots may be sold be laid out in putting up permanent monuments to said lots and in other ways of improving and ornamenting said Burying ground & that it be the duty of the Selectmen and all others concerned, to see that the lanes and alleys be not infringed upon, and that these regulations be strictly adhered to, and that it be the duty of the Town Clerk to enter the name of any inhabitant on any of the free lots, when the same may be used by any of the inhabitant's family as a burying lot."

These instructions refer to that part of the village cemetery lying in the rear of the Methodist Church. There was some difference of opinion as to the way of disposing of the lots, for in the November meeting of the same year, when the question came up, "To see what course the Town will take with regard to selling the lots in the Burying ground," it was voted to postpone the Article indefinitely. But at the annual meeting in 1846 the town reaffirmed the former instruction to the selectmen.

HON. A. H. CRAGIN.

TOMB.

In 1843 the town again directed the selectmen to erect a tomb in the village cemetery, and also gave liberty to individuals and families to do so, but nothing was done.

After the close of the annual meeting in March, 1849, it was discovered that the meeting was illegal. Application was made to Timothy Kenrick, a justice of the peace, to call another meeting, who states that "the meeting appears to him not to have been held according to law," but does not state the ground for his belief. The curiosity of the historian was excited, a careful scrutiny of the warrant was made; no defect was apparent. It seemed to be properly signed, sealed and duly certified as to posting. The posting seemed to be according to law, viz., "A true and attested copy" at the place of meeting, and a like copy at the tavern of Harlow S. Nash. The time it remained posted, not counting the day of posting or the day of meeting, seemed to be according to law—fourteen days. The question was submitted to others; they were no wiser. It finally occurred to the historian to examine the law as to the time of posting, and he found that law *then* required *fifteen days* and not fourteen. Of course the town lost its vote for all state and county officers, but was represented in the legislature. At the first meeting A. H. Cragin was chosen town clerk, in place of Timothy Kenrick, but at the second meeting Kenrick secured the office.

1850 TO 1860.

POLITICAL AFFAIRS.

In 1850 the vote for governor was as follows: Nathaniel S. Berry, F. S., 36; Samuel Dinsmore, I. D., 146; Levi Chamberlain, W., 186.

In the state Nathaniel S. Berry, F. S., 6,472; Samuel Dinsmore, I. D., 30,750; Levi Chamberlain, W., 18,512.

In 1851 the vote for governor was as follows: John Atwood, F. S., a new candidate, 55; Thomas E. Sawyer, W., 134; Samuel Dinsmore, D., 134.

In the state, John Atwood, F. S., 12,049; Thomas E. Sawyer, W., 18,458; Samuel Dinsmore, D., 27,425.

The Free Soil vote increased 5,577; in the Whig vote there was a slight loss; the Democratic vote decreased 3,326. There was no election by the people and Samuel Dinsmore was chosen by the legislature.

In 1852 the vote for governor was as follows: John Atwood, F. S., 27; Thomas E. Sawyer, W., 210; Noah Martin, D., 145. A loss for the Free Soilers and a large gain for the Whigs.

In the state, John Atwood, F. S., 9,497; Thomas E. Sawyer, 19,857; Noah Martin, D., 30,800. The Free Soil vote decreased while that of the Whigs and Democrats increased.

In 1853 the vote for governor was as follows: John H. White, F. S., 37; James Bell, W., 159; Noah Martin, D., 134.

In the state, John H. White, 7,995; James Bell, 17,590; Noah Martin, 30,934. Both the Whig and Free Soil vote decreased, a slight gain to the Democratic vote.

In 1854 the vote for governor was as follows: Jared Perkins, F. S., 52; James Bell, W., 181; Nathaniel B. Baker, 134, showing an increase in the Free Soil and Whig vote.

In the state, Jared Perkins, 11,080; James Bell, 16,941; Nathaniel B. Baker, 29,788. The Free Soil vote increased, Whig and Democratic votes decreased.

In 1855 a new factor in political affairs suddenly developed itself—the Know Nothing or American party. This was a secret organization, whose action was mainly directed against Catholicism. In the town the vote was as follows: Asa Fowler, F. S., 9; James Bell, W., 33; Nathaniel B. Baker, D., 101; Ralph Metcalf, 282.

In the state, Asa Fowler, 1,237; James Bell, 3,436; Nathaniel B. Baker, 27,055; Ralph Metcalf, 32,769.

An analysis of the vote in town and state shows that the American party drew its support from the Whigs and Free Soilers.

In 1856 the vote for governor was as follows: Ichabod Goodwin, W., 29; John S. Wells, D., 137; Ralph Metcalf, American, 304.

In the state, Ichabod Goodwin, 2,360; John S. Wells, 32,031; Ralph Metcalf, 32,119. It will be noticed that the Free Soil vote disappears in both town and state. Metcalf not having a majority, was chosen by the legislature.

During 1856 this uncertainty in the minds of the people came to an end. Purposes and aims became fixed, issues were framed and the people took their positions on the great questions of the time and held them until these questions were decided once for all coming times.

The Free Soil, the Whig and the American parties disappeared and became the Republican party, while the Democratic party continued on its way.

In 1857 the vote for governor was as follows: John S. Wells, D., 154; William Haile, R., 292.

In the state, John S. Wells, 31,214; William Haile, 34,216, who was the first Republican governor.

In 1858 the vote for governor was as follows: Asa P. Cate, D., 149; William Haile, R., 311.

In the state, Asa P. Cate, 31,679; William Haile, 36,212, an increased majority.

In 1859, the vote for governor was as follows: Asa P. Cate, D., 165; Ichabod Goodwin, R., 329.

In the state, Asa P. Cate, 32,802; Ichabod Goodwin, 36,326.

TEACHERS' INSTITUTE.

At the annual meeting in 1850 the town appropriated twenty-five dollars for the support of a Teachers' Institute. In 1851 the same vote was passed.

TOWN HOUSE.

At the annual meeting in 1851 the following Resolution was adopted:

Resolved that the sum of five hundred dollars, heretofore voted by the town for the purchasing of an engine, with an addition of two hundred dollars be appropriated by the town to purchase land on which to remove the Town House, if within six months a subscription of responsible individuals for a sum in the opinion of the Selectmen, sufficient to remove and underpin the same be lodged with them. And Abner Allen, Roswell Sartwell and Ephraim Wood are hereby appointed a Committee to buy for the Town and take a deed of such piece of land as they may judge best, and direct where the house shall be set; and those who subscribe shall begin the work of moving and setting, and carry it on under the direction of the Selectmen to completion, and to their final acceptance—the Universalist Society being allowed and secured the same privileges they now enjoy for occupying the upper story, and the Village Precinct be allowed to fit up and use one half of the basement for an Engine House and for fire apparatus And the vote heretofore passed by the town, appropriating five hundred dollars towards an Engine is hereby rescinded and annulled.

To this action of the town there was much opposition, as the following indicates:

July 20, 1850, at a special meeting:

> Voted that the vote passed at the annual meeting in March last appropriating a sum not exceeding seven Hundred dollars for the purchase of land on which to set the Old Meeting house be confirmed; provided that a good and sufficient bond be given to the town to the acceptance of the Selectmen; that said house be removed without damage, and well fitted up to the satisfaction of the Selectmen, before the work of moving it is commenced

Another vote passed at the same meeting may explain the withdrawal of five hundred dollars which had been appropriated to the purchase of a fire engine.

> Whereas the town at a meeting in May 1848 voted to appropriate the sum of five hundred dollars toward the purchase of a Fire Engine upon the condition mentioned in said vote and Whereas the Engine has been purchased by the Precinct without the money, voted therefore to rescind said vote and that the Selectmen never pay out the money or any part thereof.

At the annual meeting in 1851 the following resolution was adopted:

> Resolved that the Selectmen employ some suitable person to take charge of the Town House and suffer it to be opened for the use of the Inhabitants of this Town on all proper occasions, and for all free Lectures and discussions, which are in no way connected with shows or exhibitions for money; but on no occasion to open the house for the exhibition of shows of any kind, nor for lectures which are not free for all the Inhabitants of this town

In 1849 the town house was moved from the Common where it stood about sixty-seven years, to its present position, all the conditions having been complied with. At a special meeting held October 8, 1850, the town voted to indefinitely postpone the following article: "To see if the town will vote to direct the Selectmen to put up the spire and lightning rod on the town-house, and send the bell and get it recast and put it up again."

Nevertheless, without further action on the part of the town, the work was done by the selectmen in 1851, as the following bill indicates, taken from the report of the selectmen of 1852:

Repairing town house amounting to $103.10

Paid P. A. Alden bill, iron work for vane spire arms &c	$6.25
" J. L. Drew 12 books gold leaf	4.75
L. Smith 6 3-4 days work self Chadwick and Morse	12.00
M. Partridge & Co. bill painting and gilding	4.75
J. Gustin 146 feet tinning on spire and dome	24.34
J. Gustin repairing dome	6.25
Wm. S. Ela 10 days work 862 ft boards and 16 lbs nails	22.42
Simons & Darcent bill Material and labor on vane letters &c	22.34
	$103.10

Of these persons only one is now living in the town, William S. Ela.

The bell on the town house had been cracked and after many attempts to repair it, by sawing and filing out the cracks, it was resolved to have a new bell. There is no record of any formal action of the town on the matter, but the old bell was to be recast with additional metal procured by subscription. The bell is dated 1853 and is the one now in use.

HORSE SHEDS.

At the annual meeting, 1854, the town authorized the selectmen to receive proposals from the persons wishing to build sheds in the rear of the town house, stating what quantity of land they wished for and the terms and rent for the same, and report at the next town meeting. This matter does not appear again till the annual meeting in 1855, when it was "Voted that a Committee of three be appointed to examine the land asked for sheds, appraise the value or rent of the same, and report to the town The committee named H. Hatch Jas Murch, E. Wood."

At a special meeting held September 4, 1855, this committee reported as follows: "Your committee having attended to their duty, make the following report: That the petitioners John Peck and others, and their assigns have the lease of a piece of land at the Northwest corner of the Town House lot sixty feet North and South, and eleven and one half feet East and West to be used for sheds, so long as the Room over the Town Hall is used for public worship, and that they pay a rent of fifty cents into the town treasury annually,—South corner post to be three feet from corner, and said sheds to be kept in good repair and kept white-washed."

These sheds were on the east side of the Thompson building. The rent is not very clearly expressed, it not appearing whether the fifty cents is for the whole ground, or for each shed; probably the latter.

THE COMMON.

At a special meeting held October 8, 1850:

Voted that the town consent that the inhabitants of the village may grade fence, and otherwise ornament the Common in this Village in such a manner as a committee may designate and determine, provided that no fence, trees or any other obstruction be built, set or placed within five rods of the outside of the Common

The committee appointed, Abner Allen, Abel Lowe, Jr., and Seth Blodgett.

There was much opposition to this plan, inasmuch as there were roads through the Common, one going east and west through the center, another from the southeast corner to the northwest corner. If fenced in, then all vehicles must go around, which was considered a hardship.

While it was decided to fence the Common there was great diversity of opinion as to the form which should be given to the enclosure. Many advocated right angular enclosure, because then the sides would correspond to the lines of the buildings surrounding the Common. Others objected to this form of the enclosure as too stiff and formal, the fact that the buildings were on angular lines requiring *different* lines in the enclosure for the purpose of variety—and they suggested an elliptical enclosure as more pleasing. Others still preferred a diamond form. Jonathan Adams, the chief engineer of the Northern road, laid out such a form, but it did not meet with general acceptance. The angular advocates prevailed finally. The castings for the fence were made in Lebanon. The granite posts were from Lebanon. The work was done under the supervision of George Post, noted for his extreme accuracy in work of all kinds. The expense was met by subscription.

It is a curious indication of the change which time creates in the preferences of a community that while a fence, and a high, substantial one, was then thought highly appropriate, now the wish that it was taken away is not infrequently uttered.

THE HUMPHREY WOOD BRIDGE.

The bridge and abutments over Great Brook near the Ancel Kinne place had been rebuilt in 1850 and became the subject of earnest discussion. Complaint was freely made that the expense was too great, even extravagant. The town at its annual meeting in 1851 took action in the matter as follows: "Voted that the whole subject-matter relating to the Bridge, wall, and road near Humphrey Wood be referred to a Committee to investigate the whole subject, with power to send for persons and papers and make a report to the town at the next town-meeting." Abner Allen, John Wood and William Cole were the committee.

At a special meeting November 29, 1851, the committee made their report, but it does not appear what it was; but at a meeting March 9, 1852, there was the following vote: "That if the Contractors or persons who built the abutments, wall and road at the bridge near Humphrey Wood's, will pay or refund to the town the sum of eighty-seven dollars and fifty cents the town will relinquish any further claim upon them," indicating a compromise. No further reference to this matter appears upon the records, but it was discussed a long time afterwards.

FIREMEN'S PAY.

At the annual meeting, 1851, the town voted to pay the members of the engine company the same sum annually that is allowed by law to soldiers doing military duty, which was one dollar annually.

In 1852 the town voted the sum of fifty dollars to Engine Company No. 2, provided they discharge the duties of enginemen and keep the engine in good repair and in condition to be used, to the satisfaction of the selectmen. The same sum was appropriated to the fire department in 1853. In 1857 voted to pay the members of the fire company three dollars a year—the number of members not to exceed forty.

RAILROAD TAX.

At the annual meeting, 1852, the town "Voted that hereafter the sum of three hundred dollars of the money received by the town of the Rail Road tax be annually appropriated for the use of schools, to be equally divided among the several districts."

CEMETERY AT WEST LEBANON.

1852 Voted to appropriate a sum not exceeding three hundred dollars for the purchase of a suitable lot for a burying ground at West Lebanon to be laid out by the Selectmen

This is the present cemetery at West Lebanon.

At the same meeting the following vote was passed:

That, whereas the Connecticut Valley Agricultural Society has voted to hold their Next annual Fair in this town Therefore Resolved that the use of such part of the Common and Town Hall, as they may need, be granted to the Committee of Arrangements of said Society for the purpose of their exhibition.

This was the first agricultural fair ever held in the town. In 1853 a similar vote was passed.

SCHOOL DISTRICTS.

For years the matter of the bounds of the different school districts was a matter of great perplexity. Almost every year there were petitions of individuals to be set off from one district to another. Sometimes the change was sanctioned, as often denied.

In 1852 they appointed a committee "to divide the town anew into school districts or to make such changes in the old Districts as they may judge convenient and best calculated to promote the cause of Education, to define and establish the limits of all the School Districts, to number the Districts anew, and to make report of their doings to the town as soon as may be." The committee were W. G. Perley, Horace Hatch and Fitch Loomer. This committee made their report to a special meeting September 17, 1853.

The report was laid upon the table and the selectmen directed to procure the printing of four hundred copies for distribution, to insert an article in the warrant for the next annual meeting to place the subject before the town.

WILLIAM G. PERLEY.

DANIEL RICHARDSON.

At that meeting the report was recommitted to the selectmen for the purpose of reporting a plan of districting the town, disturbing the small districts as little as possible, not reducing the number of districts below twelve and describing the bounds and dimensions according to law and report as soon as may be.

At the annual meeting, 1855, "Voted to choose a committee of three to divide the town into school districts and fix the boundaries thereof according to law."

Elijah Blaisdell, Daniel Richardson and Richard S. Howe were the committee. At this meeting there were several applications for changes in district relations. On the 7th day of July this committee made its report. The report was recommitted to the committee and the "Selectmen directed to procure the printing of the report as it now stands, and the Committee directed to obtain such other statistical information in regard to the number of the scholars in each of the proposed School Districts * * * of use to the inhabitants of the town and make such alterations as they may think necessary.

On the 4th of September the report of the committee was accepted, and their divisions of the town into School Districts entered upon the records.

All this perplexity about school districts resulted from the fact that families decreased in number of children, leaving, perhaps, a dozen in a district where there used to be fifty or sixty, while the number of farms occupied was the same. The increase of population in the villages of Lebanon and West Lebanon added to the difficulty.

FENCE AROUND THE VILLAGE BURYING GROUND.

In 1854 the selectmen were directed to build a new and suitable fence around the burying ground in the Center village, with suitable entrances, gates and locks. The expense was $283.97. The expense for painting the fence of the West Lebanon "Burying Ground" the same year was $122.10.

In 1857 the selectmen were directed to fence the burying ground at East Lebanon.

INSTRUCTION TO COLLECTOR OF TAXES.

In the annual meeting of 1853 the town passed the following vote: "That the Selectmen be instructed that when they make a contract for collecting the Taxes that it be distinctly understood and agreed, that if the Collector does not collect and pay over to said Selectmen the whole amount of taxes on his bill for collection (except so much as they may abate) on or before the 20th day of February next, said Selectmen are forthwith to issue an extent against said Collector for all that may be due from said Collector."

This certainly means business. Looking for the occasion of so stringent a requirement it is found that the collector for 1851 was behind at the close of the financial year $660.90, for 1852, $518.35. Was the requirement efficacious? In the report for 1853-'54 no deficiency of the collector is noted. An "extent" is a fearful legal implement, being a "writ of execution against the body lands or goods."

GROCERIES.

At the annual meeting in 1854 the following resolution was adopted:

Resolved that the groceries in this town for the sale of strong Beer and Cider, as carried on for the last year are great nuisances, and that they ought to be discountenanced by all good citizens as not only corrupting our youth but as bringing disgrace on our whole community.

At the same meeting the following resolution was adopted:

Whereas the progress of Temperance has been essentially sustained and promoted by stringent enactments in other States therefore:
Resolved that our Representatives be instructed to coöperate with other members of the Legislature in procuring the passage of a law whereby the traffic in intoxicating liquors may most effectually be prevented and further resolved that our Gentlemen Representatives be a Committee in behalf of this town to wait on the Hon. Senator from Dist. No 11, requesting him to use all due efforts in the cause of eradicating traffic

The "Gentlemen Representatives" were A. H. Cragin and William S. Ela. The "Hon. Senator from Dist. No. 11," was Jonathan E. Sargent, afterward Chief Justice of the state.

RAILROAD BRIDGES AND CROSSING.

At first small engines and low cars were used on railroads. After a time larger engines and taller cars came into use, so that higher bridges were needed, involving changes in the grades when crossing highways, subjecting towns to inconvenience and expense, hence the following vote:

That the Selectmen be instructed to object to the raising of the Railroad bridge near Mrs. Hutchins and the bridge at East Lebanon and see that the rights of the public are fully sustained in regard to the damages and grading.

The first bridge is that on Hanover Street.

Formerly the railroad passed over the highway near Solon Peck's on grade, but in 1857 a change was made so that the highway should pass under the railroad, and the town instructed the selectmen to supervise the work and lay out the highway accordingly, and petition the court for leave to discontinue the old highway which was a part of the Fourth New Hampshire.

About this time a large maple tree, which for more than fifty years had been a landmark in this locality, being one of the bounds of the Fourth New Hampshire Turnpike, was taken down on account of old age.

HEARSE FOR WEST LEBANON.

At the annual meeting, 1857, the town instructed the selectmen to procure a hearse and build a suitable house for the same for the accommodation of the inhabitants of West Lebanon.

POLICE OFFICERS.

In 1859 the town adopted Chapter 114 of the Revised Statutes. This chapter provides for the appointment of police officers, not to exceed seven in number, whose term of office should terminate on the last day of March. They were to be constables and conservators of the peace, to make regulations for the stand of hacks, etc., the height and position of awnings and shades on or near any buildings, respecting any obstruction of streets, lanes and alleys, the smoking of any pipe or cigar therein, or in any stable or other outbuildings. These regulations could only be in force upon the approbation of the selectmen, and being recorded by the town clerk and published a reasonable time in one or more newspapers.

Nothing seems to have been done under this act, beyond its adoption.

1860 TO 1870.

POLITICAL AFFAIRS.

Political parties, before so numerous, and so uncertain in their action, had by this time become consolidated into two great parties, each having definite principles and aims—the Republicans and the Democrats. Matters came to a crisis in 1860 by the election of Abraham Lincoln as president.

At the annual meeting in 1860 the vote was as follows for governor: Ichabod Goodwin, R., had 328; Asa P. Cate, D., had 187 votes. In the state Goodwin had 38,037; Cate, 33,544.

In 1861 Nathaniel Berry, R., had 316; George Stark, D., 159. In the state Berry had 35,467; Stark, 3,141.

In 1862 Berry, R., had 292; Stark, D., 150. In the state Berry had 31,150; Stark, 28,566.

In 1863 Walter Harriman, I. D., had 28 votes; Ira A. Eastman, D., 168; Joseph A. Gilmore, R., 328. In the state, 363 scattering. Walter Harriman, 4,372; Gilmore, 29,035; Eastman, 22,833. There was no choice by the people, but Gilmore was elected by the legislature. Harriman had always been a Democrat, but parted with his party on the issues of the war. He was among those who were known as War Democrats.

In 1864 Joseph A. Gilmore, R., had 379 votes; Edward W. Harrington, D., had 173. In the state Harrington had 31,340, Gilmore had 37,006.

At the annual meeting in 1865, Frederick Smyth, R., for governor, had 330 votes; Edward W. Harrington, D., had 132. In the state Harrington had 28,017, Smyth had 34,145.

In 1866, at the annual meeting, for governor, Frederick Smyth, R., had 334 votes; John G. Sinclair, D., had 144. In the state Sinclair had 30,484 votes, Smyth had 35,136.

In 1867, at the annual meeting, Walter Harriman, now become a Republican, for governor, had 335 votes; John G. Sinclair, D., had 167 votes. In the state Sinclair had 32,663 votes, Harriman had 35,809.

In 1868 Walter Harriman, R., had, for governor, 469 votes; John G. Sinclair, D., had 208. A large vote, the largest ever cast up to this date in the town and the largest in the state.

In the state Sinclair had 37,260, Harriman, 39,778, making with the addition of 30 scattering, 77,068.

For the first time *three* representatives to the legislature were chosen this year.

In 1869 at the annual meeting the vote for governor was, for

Onslow Stearns, R., 350 votes; for John Bedel, D., 200. In the state Bedel had 32,057; Stearns had 35,772.

In this period only the ordinary town matters will be noted. The centennial celebration and the war history will be given in separate articles.

It was not often that the people of the town had any great contests in their choice of officers, but one of the most remarkable struggles happened in 1860. The first representative was chosen at the first ballot, when the town proceeded to ballot for the second representative, with the following result:

Daniel Richardson had 181 votes.
Jewett D. Hosley had 174 votes.
Harlow S. Nash had 32 votes.
Asa M. Moore had 14 votes.
Watson K. Eldridge had 6 votes.
James H. Kendrick had 5 votes.
Charles B. Haddock had 4 votes.
James Hubbard had 1 vote.
James Murch had 1 vote.
Philander Hall had 1 vote.
John Clough had 1 vote.
Emory Whitaker had 1 vote.
John W. Bean had 1 vote.
Farris Cummings had 1 vote.
Rodney Lund had 1 vote.

There was no choice. There was none on the second ballot, but the candidates were not quite so numerous. In the third ballot a new candidate appears in the contest, Frances A. Cushman, who was chosen by a majority of two votes. The historian remembers the day as full of excitement, the friends of the different candidates shouting the names of their preference with all their might. Yet there was no violence. But of all those voted for that day not more than two are living today, Frances A. Cushman and Rodney Lund.

COUNTY FARM.

At the annual meeting, 1860, the town gave an expression of opinion on the question whether it was expedient to establish a county farm by a vote of 150 in favor and 10 against it.

BURYING GROUNDS.

In 1860 the selectmen were authorized to improve the burying ground at Lebanon Center at an expense not exceeding two hundred dollars. This cemetery had become so fully occupied that more ground was needed, and in 1863 the selectmen were directed to "examine and report on location and grounds for a new burying ground for the town." In 1864 these instructions were renewed.

In 1867 the selectmen were instructed to "purchase such additions and make such repairs as they shall deem proper to the old Burying Ground near General Luther Aldens, sufficient to make it a Cemetery for the Town, and that the Moderator appoint a Committee of three to cooperate and advise with the Selectmen." The committee were Daniel Richardson, Adoniram Smalley and Nathan B. Stearns. All this shows that there was a great variety of opinion as to the proper place for so sacred a purpose. The location mentioned above was the first ground devoted to this purpose.

In 1868 the matter was still undecided, for then this vote was passed: "That the Selectmen be authorized and directed to purchase land for a Burying Ground near the centre of the town."

In June of the same year the question came up again and a committee of three consisting of Nathan B. Stearns, Colby C. Benton and J. C. Sturtevant, was appointed to act with the selectmen and report at an adjourned meeting. In the meantime several different locations were examined, one of which was on land now owned by Horace Hatch, but it did not meet the minds of all the people, so the whole subject was referred to the same committee in a meeting held on August 8, to report at the next town meeting.

In 1869 the selectmen were instructed to select and purchase a lot for burial purposes before the next annual meeting, but the period closed without any final action, so difficult it was to suit all the people or even a majority of them.

In 1870 the committee purchased a tract of land for a cemetery, lying north of C. M. Messenger's dwelling-house, since known as the Trotting Park. But this did not satisfy the people, so at the annual meeting, 1871, the selectmen were directed

JESSE C. STURTEVANT.

to sell the land "for the most they could get," and that a committee of three should be chosen to select new ground for a cemetery, and the committee to select a spot and ascertain the cost of erecting a receiving tomb and report to a future meeting called for that purpose.

F. A. Cushman, Orrin Bugbee, L. C. Pattee, committee. This committee made their report to the annual meeting in 1872, when the following resolution was adopted:

Resolved that the Town of Lebanon has not and does not possess a suitable or convenient spot of ground for a Cemetery for the use of the centre and East part of the town, and with a view of the great and pressing necessity for immediate action, that a committee of three be chosen, who shall be and are hereby authorized to purchase and establish a Cemetery, fence and lay out the same into lots to be deeded to persons purchasing the same, by the Selectmen, and to erect a public tomb on the same, and to make such other improvements as they shall deem necessary, and that the sum of three thousand dollars be appropriated for this purpose.

The same committee was continued to carry out the terms of the resolution.

The committee purchased of J. C. Sturtevant the tract now known as Glenwood Cemetery. The tomb which had been so often voted to be built was constructed by P. H. Freeto & Sons. The ground was laid out into lots by C. A. Downs & Sons. The total cost of the cemetery, including the land, was about $4,000.

Thus the long difference of opinion as to the location of the cemetery was ended, though not to the satisfaction of everybody. But as time passes away the wisdom of the location becomes apparent. It is secluded, yet within a few minutes' walk from the village. It has a varied surface, affording advantages for great beauty of form. Constant improvement is now annually made, making it an attractive place for the final rest.

It has been noted as an interesting coincidence that the first occupant of both the village cemetery and of Glenwood bore the same family name—that of Hough.

SHADE TREES.

The following resolution indicates that the people were awakening to higher ideas as to their dwelling-place. They began to wish it to be beautiful and attractive as well as convenient. At the annual meeting, 1861, they resolved, "that the inhabitants of the town be allowed to set out shade trees and make sidewalks on the sides of the streets, not to exceed eight feet in width, where the width of the street will admit of it." Not a little of the beauty of our village is owing to the work then begun and encouraged. Benjamin Gallup, now of Chicago, then a young man, deserves recognition for the trees he planted on School Street.

ENGINE CO. NO. 2.

In 1862 the town voted "to pay each member of Engine Company No. 2 the sum of three dollars per annum" from the date of their organization, which amounted to $158.50.

In 1864 the town voted to pay the members of the company five dollars a year.

HEARSE.

At a special meeting held November 28, 1863, the selectmen were instructed to purchase a hearse for the town, to be kept at the hearse house in the village.

TO PROVIDE A PLACE FOR THE POOR.

On March, 1864, the house on the poor farm was destroyed by fire, leaving the inmates without a home. April 7 a meeting of the town was held to consider the matter of rebuilding the house, at which they declined to raise money for that purpose, but authorized the selectmen "to buy or hire a house and land for the convenience of the town in the support of the town's poor, or otherwise provide as they shall deem best for the interests of the town."

The selectmen "deemed it best" to distribute the poor among different families in the town. The house was never rebuilt, nor any other bought or built. So far as the town poor are concerned the practice continues to the present time.

In 1865 the town authorized the selectmen to deed the town farm to G. W. Worthen. Price, $3,300.

SEXTONS FOR CEMETERIES.

In 1866, at the annual meeting, the selectmen were instructed "to appoint for each of the public burying grounds, a suitable person to take charge of the hearse and take care of the grounds, and answer the calls of those desiring his services, by their paying him for such service."

ENCOURAGEMENT OF MANUFACTURES.

At the annual meeting, 1866, the following resolution was adopted unanimously:

> Resolved that we, the legal voters of the Town of Lebanon, do cordially extend a hearty invitation to Manufacturing capital to come among us, and that we will vote at the earliest opportunity to give our assent to the act entitled an act to encourage manufacturing, passed July 3, 1860.

On the 14th of April, 1866, the town adopted this law.

This was the first public encouragement given to manufacturing by the town, which, continued from time to time, has been so effective in increasing its population and wealth.

PARK ON HANOVER STREET.

As early as 1866 there were plans to fence in a triangular piece of land at the junction of Hanover and High streets, for a park, for then Enoch F. Hough, Dan Storrs and others petitioned the town for liberty to build a fence there. The petition was referred to the selectmen.

On the 14th of April, 1866, upon the recommendation of the selectmen, leave was granted to Enoch F. Hough, Dan Storrs and others "to fence ten feet of the road Leading past Ziba Durkee's garden for the purpose of a Park and for no other purpose Provided that said E. F. Hough shall also give his heater piece lying between the three roads for the same purpose." Nearly thirty years passed before the plan was realized. It is a good use of the piece of land.

Much credit should be given to Miss Mary Lyman Storrs for her patience and perseverance in procuring the realization of a plan of so many years ago. In September, 1894, Frank G. Hough, son of E. F. Hough, presented the town with a deed of the "Heater piece."

ROADS DISCONTINUED ACROSS THE COMMON.

At the annual meeting in 1866, the town instructed the selectmen to petition the supreme court for leave to discontinue all highways leading through the Common. In due time leave was granted.

TOWN HOUSE.

The lower part of the town house had remained substantially in the same condition in which it was when removed from the Common, a very inconvenient and unsightly room. Little had been done to the outside, notwithstanding all the votes which had been passed directing the painting and repairing. Meantime the town had increased in population and wealth and desired a better place in which to transact its business and hold its gatherings for various purposes. They considered it,—and justly, too,—unworthy of a town such as Lebanon had then become, the most prominent in northern New Hampshire. It was not only inconvenient and uninviting to the people themselves, but likely to repel strangers who might wish to find a home in a town having, in many respects, great advantages and attractions. The people began to talk and to plan about a new or better town hall with the following results:

At the annual meeting in 1868 the following resolution was adopted:

Resolved that a Committee of five be appointed by the Moderator to ascertain at what price the pewholders of the Universalist Society will dispose of their interest in the Town House Building, and that said Committee be authorized to procure plans and estimates of the proposed alterations, and to make all necessary arrangements for the purchase of the interest of the Universalist Society, and report at a special meeting of the town, to be called for that purpose at the earliest practicable time.

The committee were A. W. Baker, I. C. Sturtevant, F. A. Cushman, J. W. Gerrish and Martin Buck.

On April 25, 1868, the committee made the following report:

We, the Committeee appointed at the last annual town meeting to ascertain at what price the pewholders of the Universalist Society will dispose of its interest in the town house building, and to procure plans and estimates of the proposed alterations, and to make all necessary arrangements for the purchase of the interests of said Universalist Society, and to report at a special meeting of the town called for that

COL. FRANK C. CHURCHILL.

WILLIAM H. COTTON.

JOSEPH W. GERRISH.

ALPHEUS W. BAKER.

purpose, having performed the duties assigned us, respectfully submit the following report:

The Universalist Society, as a society, having by vote of the town gained permission to occupy the upper part of the house as a house of worship in 1835, and having now reserved to them in the deed of 1850 of the land on which the house now stands, all the right, title and interest which was granted to them by the vote of the town in 1835, have voted, at a meeting duly called, to exchange their interests in the upper part of the house, in case the town should vote to repair the house, for town purposes, for the same privileges in the lower part of the house they now have, in the upper part, or to abide the decision of disinterested appraisers.

At a meeting of the pew-holders it was voted to sell the pews to the town, the same to be appraised by a Committee of three disinterested persons. The Committee further report that they have procured plans and made estimates of the proposed alterations and that the plans by them procured are substantially as follows: To take out the whole interior of the house, to raise the building six feet; put on to the north end an addition of thirty feet; at the South end to build out 13 feet even with the tower; having the entrance through the bell tower; basement story $9\frac{1}{2}$ feet high. Upon the first floor it is proposed to have the entrance from the front with double doors, an entry on either side of which are to be stairs leading to the gallery. Directly opposite the outer doors are the doors opening into the main room, designated the audience floor. At the North end of the house is the platform $3\frac{1}{2}$ feet high, 15 feet wide and 26 feet long, on either side of which are ante-rooms 12 feet square, opening to the platform. The gallery itself is to be built around the south side of the house and upon the East and West sides, extending as far as the scond window from the North end of the house. The bell deck to be remodeled and repaired, to correspond in outward appearance and symetry to the house. All to be clapboarded and painted.

Your Committee further report that a house constructed on this plan will be well adapted to town purposes and business, and for public use; comfortable at all times, sufficiently large and commodious, and so well arranged as to be adapted, not only to meet the wants and requirements of the town at the present time, but sufficient also to meet the demands and requirements of the future growth and increased population of the town, for town purposes and uses on public occasions.

Your Committee also report that they have made liberal and careful estimates of the cost of remodeling and repairing the house, agreeably to the proposed plan, calculating the cost of every separate item by itself necessary to alter and repair the same in a good plain and workmanlike manner, and estimate that the cost will not exceed $6487.

Signed

A. W. Baker, F. A. Cushman, J. C. Sturtevant, J. W. Gerrish, Martin Buck.

After reading the report the following resolution was adopted:

Resolved that the town do alter and repair the old Meeting-House for town purposes, agreeably to the plan reported by the Committee, and that a Committee of three be appointed by the Moderator to superintend and conduct said alterations and repairs, and that the work be commenced and carried on to completion as economically and expeditiously as may be, and make report of their doings at the first town meeting thereafter.

Resolved that the pews and interests of the Universalist Society in the Town Hall be appraised; that the Selectmen be instructed to appoint a Committee of three disinterested persons, one of whom shall be chosen by themselves, one of whom shall be nominated by the pewholders, and one by the society, the same to constitute a Committee to appraise the pews and the interests of said Society, and to pay to said pewholders and Society, the full value of their respective interests, as determined by such appraisal, upon demand.

It is to be noted that a distinction is made between pew-holders and the society; this was necessary because some of the pew-holders were not connected with the society, some of the people never having parted with their interest in pews bought originally of the town.

Resolved that the Selectmen be authorized to raise by loan, and give town notes, a sum of money sufficient to make such alterations and repairs of the Town House as have been voted, and to purchase the interests of the pew-holders and the Society, at their appraised value—the sum so raised not to exceed eight thousand dollars.

The committee appointed by the moderator to superintend the alterations and repairs was Jesse E. Sturtevant, Lewis C. Pattee and Horace Hatch.

At a meeting held November 3, 1868, the following vote was passed: "That the Selectmen be authorized to appoint some suitable person, whose duty it shall be to take charge of the Town House, and to have the entire charge of the same, subject to said Selectmen, and that they be further authorized and instructed to fix the rules, regulations and prices for the use of the [Hall] for all purposes, and that all persons using or renting said hall or house shall be subject to and governed by said rules and regulations." William H. Richardson was the first agent for the town hall.

At the same meeting the following resolution was adopted:

Resolved that E. J. Durant, A. M. Shaw, J. C. Sturtevant, Lewis Pattee, J. W. Gerrish, and such others as may be associated with them,

EDWARD J. DURANT.

ALBERT M. SHAW.

be allowed, at their own expense, to put into the Town Hall building suitable gas fixtures for lighting the same, and that the free use of the Town Hall be given to them for the purpose of holding seven concerts or other public gatherings to raise money to compensate them for the money so advanced; said fixtures to be the property of the town.

At the annual meeting, 1869, P. E. Davis, O. W. Burnap and George Blood were appointed a committee to investigate the accounts of the Town Hall Building Committee and report to the selectmen.

At the annual meeting in 1870 the town "voted to pay L. C. Pattee & others for labor and material expended on the Town Hall basement; to assume the indebtedness of the Gas Association for the gas fixtures in the Town Hall; that the Selectmen be instructed to finish up the basement story and tower of Town Hall, and the painting of the building as they think proper, either by contract or otherwise."

The cost of these alterations and repairs, as found in the report of committees in accordance with the foregoing instructions, was as follows:

Total expenditures less amount received for material sold	$11,746.57
Amount paid to pew-holders and Universalist Soc	1,500.00
Cost of Lower Town Hall	1,621.00
	$14,867.57
To this should be added cost of gas fixtures, &c., which is not easy to ascertain exactly, say	1,000.00
	$15,867.57

This practically finishes the strange history of the meeting-house to date, resulting in a town house equal in all respects to any then existing in the state.

PURCHASE OF HOSE.

At the annual meeting in 1868, the town voted to raise $500 to purchase hose for Engine No. 2, to be expended under the direction of the selectmen.

COMMON—REGULATIONS.

At a special meeting June 9, 1868, the town voted to establish certain regulations for the protection and preservation of its park or Common. The regulations established at this meeting were subsequently changed and the following adopted, August 8, 1868:

1 No person shall play at any game of ball or other games without permission of the Committee.

2 No person shall pass or cross the same except upon the gravelled walks.

Resolved that the Committee chosen to enforce such regulations be authorized to place upon the park or common notices of said regulations, and have the care of the common

A penalty of five dollars was established for every violation of these regulations, to be recovered "in an action of Debt. by the Committee, and the fines to be used for the improvement of the Common. Joseph W. Gerrish. E. J. Durant and E. A. Kendrick. Committee."

TOWN POUND.

At a special meeting May 21, 1869, the town voted to instruct the selectmen to sell the interest of the town in the town pound, near Solon A. Peck's. at auction or by private sale.

1870 TO 1880.

POLITICAL AFFAIRS.

At the annual meeting. 1870. the following was the vote for governor:

Lorenzo D. Barrows, T., 4 votes; Samuel Flint, Asst. D., 43; John Bedell, D., 159; Onslow Stearns. R.. 484.

In the state, Barrows. 1,135; Flint. 7,369; Bedell. 25,058; Stearns, 34,847.

For the first time a distinctly temperance ticket appears in town and state. An Assistant Democrat was a Labor Reformer.

In 1871 the vote in the town for governor was: James A. Weston. D., 203; James Pike, R.. 489. No temperance vote appears in the town.

In the state. scattering. 24; Horton D. Walker, 17; Albert G. Comings, T., 314; Lemuel P. Cooper, Asst., 782; James Pike, R., 33,892; James A. Weston. D.. 34,700.

In 1872 the vote in the town for governor: James A. Weston. D.. had 281 votes; Ezekiel A. Straw, R., 570.

In the state, scattering, 14; John Blackmer, T., 436; Lemuel

P. Cooper, Asst. D., 446; James A. Weston, 36,584; Ezekiel A. Straw, 38,752.

In 1873 the vote of the town for governor was: John Blackmer, T., 1; Samuel K. Mason, Asst. D., 1; James A. Weston, D., 244; Ezekiel A. Straw, 482. In the state: Mason, 687; Blackmer, 1098; Weston, 32,016; Straw, 34,023.

In 1874 the vote of the town for governor was: John Blackmer, T., 2; James A. Weston, 290; Luther McCutchins, R., 487. In the state: Scattering, 40; Luther McCutchins, 34,143; James A. Weston, 35,608; John Blackmer, 2,100.

In 1875 the vote of the town for governor was: Person C. Cheney, R., 597; Hiram R. Roberts, D., 322. In the state: Scattering, 19; Nathaniel White, 773; Roberts, 39,121; Cheney, 39,293.

In 1876 the vote of the town for governor was: Person C. Cheney, R., 640; Daniel Marcy, D., 289. In the state: Scattering, 14; Asa T. Kendall, T., 411; Marcy, 38,133; Cheney, 41,761. The total vote in the state was 80,319, the largest vote ever given up to that time for governor and not reached for many years after.

At the annual meeting, 1877, the vote for governor was: Daniel Marcy, D, 261; Benjamin F. Prescott, R., 601. In the state: Asa S. Kendall, T., 338; Marcy, 36,721; Prescott, 40,755.

At the annual meeting, 1878, the vote for governor was: Frank A. McKean, D., 255; Benjamin F. Prescott, R., 555. In the state: Samuel Flint, 269; Asa S. Kendall, T., 205; Frank A. McKean, 37,860; Benjamin F. Prescott, 39,372.

At this time a law making elections for all officers, except those for a town, biennial was passed and another election was held November 8 of the same year, at which the vote of the town for governor was: Warren G. Brown, Greenback, 30; Frank A. McKean, D., 259; Natt Head, R., 526. In the state: Kendall, T., had 91; Brown, 6,407; McKean, 31,135; Natt Head, 38,075. The most noticeable feature of this period in political matters is the nearly equal division of the two leading parties.

Town Bonds.

For some years the town had declined to fund its debt, but at the annual meeting in 1871 the following resolution was adopted:

Resolved that the sum of forty-thousand dollars of the indebtedness of the town of Lebanon be bonded in conformity with the provisions of chapter nineteenth of the laws of 1870, and that bonds to that amount are hereby authorized to be issued, payable as follows: Ten Thousand Dollars Jan 1st 1877; Ten Thousand Dollars January 1st 1882; Ten Thousand Dollars January 1st 1887; Ten Thousand Dollars January 1st 1892. Said Bonds shall interest Coupons attached to them, which interest shall be at the rate of six per cent per annum, payable Semiannually in Gold at the Bank of Lebanon; and that three persons shall be appointed by the Selectmen, who, together with said Selectmen, and the Treasurer of the Town, shall constitute a Committee of seven, who shall determine the denomination of said Bonds procure the same, and dispose of them as they may deem to be for the interest of the town

Only $30,000 of the amount authorized was bonded, bringing a premium of $300. The bonds were redeemed from time to time as they matured; they were occasioned by the "war debt" of the town.

Hay Scales.

In 1871 H. B. Benton received permission to erect hay scales at the west end of the common.

Hanover Street Bridge.

A bridge had been erected across the river on Hanover Street, a wooden and covered bridge. Objections were made to it as unsightly, as cutting off the views of some, and likely to cause collisions of teams entering from opposite ends. Upon application of ten or more legal voters a special meeting of the town was called by the selectmen, August 19, 1871, when the following resolution was adopted:

Resolved that the Selectmen be and hereby are instructed to procure and erect an Iron Bridge with suitable side-walks, in place of the bridge now standing in the line of Hanover street, and that any funds in the treasury of the town, not otherwise appropriated, be placed at their disposal. The Selectmen complied with the instructions given, and erected the iron bridge which now spans the river. The wooden bridge was removed and afterward placed over the road leading to Glenwood Cemetery.

The cost of the iron bridge, as reported by the selectmen in 1872, was $2,181.44.

Encouraging Manufacture.

At a meeting held November 5, 1872, the town voted to adopt an act exempting manufacturing establishments for the time of ten years and also the following resolution:

Whereas the town of Lebanon does possess great natural facilities and inducements for manufacturing by the large water power on the Connecticut and Mascoma rivers, now lying idle and unoccupied, and whereas being anxious to offer every inducement possible to draw enterprise and capital into said town.

Be it Resolved that all manufacturing establishments now erected, but not in operation, or that may be hereafter erected, together with the capital employed in the same within the next three years, from the adoption of this resolution and the law passed at the June Session of the Legislature of New Hampshire, 1871, as set forth in chapter 25 Pamphlet Laws, shall be exempt from taxes for the term of ten years from the completion of said manufactories if kept in actual operation where the capital employed shall not be less than five thousand dollars.

At a special meeting of the town, January 7, 1873, the following preamble and resolution were adopted:

In order to encourage the increase of business and capital in the Town of Lebanon be it

Resolved that for purposes of taxation the Invoice valuation for 1872 of the Manufacturing establishment of J. C. Sturtevant & Co. and of the Capital Stock used in operating it shall remain the same as now, notwithstanding any increase of business or capital or change of ownership—that is, that said establishment and the capital used in operating it, shall be exempt from taxation, beyond the amount of their present invoice valuation, said exemption to be for the benefit of whosoever may own or operate said establishment and to continue for the term of ten years.

At the annual meeting, 1875, the following resolutions were adopted:

Resolved that the Selectmen be authorized and are hereby empowered to make a binding contract on the part of the town, with any parties who will put in operation, within two years, three or more sets of woolen machinery, to exempt the capital, Real Estate and machinery employed for this purpose, from taxation for the term of ten years, and that such contract shall be recorded on the record books of the town.

Resolved that the real estate of the Granite Agricultural Works, and the capital used in operating the same, be exempt from taxation for a period of ten years from this date

Resolved that the Selectmen be instructed to arrange with any parties from abroad, who may within one year from the first of April next invest in any legitimate manufacturing at the Lebanon Slate Mill, at East Lebanon, a sum not less than $3000, an exemption for the term of ten years.

This policy of favoring manufacturing, thus begun in Lebanon, has been pursued steadily and with ultimate benefit to the town.

Hearse for West Lebanon.

At the anual meeting, 1873, the selectmen were instructed to purchase a new hearse for the use of the town, to be kept at the West Lebanon cemetery ground.

Survey of Streets.

At the same meeting the following resolution was adopted:

Resolved that the Selectmen are hereby instructed to cause an accurate survey of the streets, both in this village and the village at West Lebanon, to be made and stone bounds set at the corners and angles of the same and to have a plan of both villages made, of suitable size, to keep in the selectmen's office, and that new streets hereafter layed out be similarly bounded, and entered upon the plans kept by the selectmen—also that the Selectmen cause suitable names to be applied to each street and posted by suitable signs on the corners of the same.

This was done by C. A. Downs & Sons, and a plan made for both villages, now remaining in the office of the selectmen.

First Board of Health.

At the annual meeting, 1874, the following resolution was adopted:

Resolved that we now proceed to elect by nomination a Board of Health Commissioners, consisting of five, on which Board at least two Physicians shall be placed, to act and perform the duties devolving on such commission, according to the laws of the State for the ensuing year.

William Duncan, E. A. Knight, M. D., C. W. Manchester, M. D., Pliny E. Davis, James A. Davis, M. D., constituted the board.

SOLON A. PECK.

Fire Precinct Extended.

At the annual meeting, 1875, the following resolution was adopted:

Whereas the present Fire Precinct comprises more than one half of the taxable property of said town and have already expended expended large sums for the purpose of supplying suitable apparatus for the extinguishment of fires, which is virtually for the benefit of the town; and whereas, under existing regulations, the present fire department have no jurisdiction or authority to act outside of the limits of the present Fire Precinct therefore

Resolved That the Selectmen be instructed to so extend the limits of the Fire Precinct as to include the whole town

At the Same meeting voted That all the members of the Fire Department, recognized as such by the fire wardens be paid the sum of five dollars each, annually, for their services.

Lyman's Bridge.

For some years there had been a desire to have Lyman's Bridge a free bridge, as most of the bridges connecting New Hampshire and Vermont had become. An article in the warrant for the annual meeting, 1875, was as follows: "To see if the Town will buy Lyman's Bridge, so called?" Upon this article the following resolution:

Resolved that the Selectmen be a committee of three to examine Lymans Bridge and Ascertain the terms upon which it can be purchased, and to investigate all matters relating to the purchase of it by the town, and report to the town as soon as practicable.

The selectmen were Solon A. Peck, William S. Ela and Thomas P. Waterman. At a special meeting, held June 9, 1875, this committee made a verbal report, and upon that report the following resolution was adopted:

Resolved that Lewis C. Pattee, Daniel Hinkley and F. L. Owen be agents on the part of the town to investigate and examine into all matters, questions and controversies, relating to the title, interest or claim which the Town has in, to or unto said Bridge and that they are hereby authorized to take such necessary action, as in their discretion and judgment may seem proper, and as soon as possible, in the name of the town, in order most expeditiously to protect, secure, settle and perfect the right, title, and interest of the town, to, in or unto said bridge or under the charter thereof.

At the annual meeting this committee made a report, which was ordered on file.

The charter of Lyman's Bridge was granted in 1836 by the New Hampshire legislature, by which it had the exclusive right and privilege to build or purchase and forever have and maintain a bridge over and across the Connecticut River between the town of Lebanon and the town of Hartford, at any place between the lower bar in White River Falls (Olcott Falls) and the south line of Lebanon. It was enacted that a toll be granted and established for the sole benefit of the corporation, the subjects and rates to be determined and settled by the justice of the Superior Court; the net proceeds not to exceed ten per cent. per annum on costs and expenditures. It was further provided that the corporations by their directors should, at the next term of the court in Grafton County, and once in five years thereafter, cause an exhibit, under oath, to be made of the costs and expenses incurred by said corporation for said bridge, and an account of all tolls received therefrom down to the time of making such exhibit; and upon the omission or neglect to make such exhibit all the rights and privileges granted by said act should be subject to forfeiture. By the act it was also provided that the capital stock should consist of 200 shares, which were transferable. Asa and Oscar Barron had purchased, in 1866, all the stock, and so composed the corporation.

Upon inquiry and examination it was found that the provisions of the charter had not been complied with; that a return had been made in 1837, and another in 1842, but none after that time. Information in the nature of a *quo warranto* was brought to the Superior Court in 1876. Judge Smith in his decision takes the following ground:

> The neglect of the defendants for more than thirty years, to make the returns required by their charter, presents a very strong reason for decreeing a forfeiture of their franchise By the terms of the act itself such neglect renders their Charter subject to forfeiture. But, inasmuch as the defendants pray to be admitted to make such returns I think such permission should be given. Upon an examination thereof, and a hearing, the Court can determine whether "in equity and good conscience a decree of forfeiture should be made"

The cause was committed to a referee, who reported substantially as follows:

> That the provisions of the defendant's charter, in respect to making returns of the tolls received and of the costs and expenses incurred

on account of their bridge have not been performed; and found that in equity and good conscience a decree of forfeiture should not be made, for the following reasons: Because the neglect of the defendants to make returns was not wilful; because there has not been and is not any bridge across Connecticut river, and no public way by which the river can be crossed—except on the Northern Railroad bridge—for a distance of five miles above and twelve miles below the defendants bridge; because the defendants have always kept their bridge in good repair and suitable for the public travel; and because it has been so managed as to accommodate the Public travel

Upon the report of the referee the following is in substance the decision of Judge Smith:

The question tried before the referee was, whether equity and good conscience required the forfeiture of the defendants charter, and as bearing on this question evidence of the receipts, expenses and cost of the bridge since the last return made in 1842, and evidence as to the way in which the bridge has been managed how far it had accommodated the public wants, how far it was necessary to meet the future wants of the public, and how much the proprietors had received and expended, was pertinent and properly received. In this view, the fact that the statements presented by the defendants to the referee did not contain all the information required by their charter presented no legal reason for their exclusion.

Although the corporation has been guilty of gross neglect in not making the returns required by its charter, yet the facts laid before us do not, we think, furnish sufficient reasons why a forfeiture of the charter should be decreed upon the first application therefor. * *

The neglect of the corporation to hold its annual meetings does not operate to dissolve the corporation. Provision is made by Gen. st c. 133 ss 15, 16 whereby the organization may be continued

Case discharged

58. N H 370-371

At the annual meeting 1877, the following article was upon the warrant:

13th To see if the town will instruct the Selectmen to lay a road over Lymans bridge, or unite with the Selectmen of the town Hartford, Vt. in the purchase of said Bridge, in accordance with Pamphlet Laws of 1870, entitled "an act in relation to the construction and support of Highways and Bridges over the Connecticut river or act thereon"

When this article came before the meeting for action they "voted to pass over article 13."

A petition had been presented to the selectmen to lay a highway over Lyman's Bridge to the Vermont line. In 1878 the selectmen could not act in the matter and the petition was filed in the Supreme Court, and referred to the county commissioners. A highway was laid out by them to the supposed line of Vermont. They awarded to the Barrons as damages $3,000, which the Barrons accepted under protest and appealed to the court for increased damages. The court appointed referees, who awarded the farther sum, including costs, of $3,404.52, making the total cost of the bridge $6,404.52.

So far as New Hampshire territory was concerned, Lyman's Bridge was free, but its freedom was greatly obstructed by the fact that some twenty-three feet of the western end of the bridge was on Vermont soil, and that some rods between the end of the bridge and the toll bar was the private property of the bridge owners, no highway having ever been laid over it; so the Barrons mantained the toll bar and had a right to demand toll of all who sought to pass over the bridge. This fact produced a great commotion on both sides of the river. Excitement was intense and resulted in the following action of the town at a special meeting, October 4, 1879, when William S. Ela offered the folowing preamble and resolution:

Whereas the citizens of Lebanon are aggrieved and impeded in their rights of travel upon a public highway known as the Lymans Bridge in West Lebanon by the wilful, unreasonable and unjustifiable conduct of Asa T. Barron, and whereas the town of Lebanon has by their course and Courts of Justice been decreed the right to enjoy a free and uninterrupted travel on said highway of which they are deprived by said Barron and his agents without right

Be it resolved, therefore, that a Committee of three be chosen to investigate the legal aspects of the case as between Asa T. Barron and said town of Lebanon, and to determine what measures legal or otherwise should be taken to secure to the citizens of Lebanon an open, free and unobstructed right of way to and from the State of Vermont.

2d Resolved that said Committee be instructed to report to this meeting on Nov 1st 1879.

3d That when the meeting adjourns it do adjourn to Nov. 1st 1879.

4th That Hiram Orcott, Hon. L. C. Pattee and Wm B. Weeks constitute the Committee on behalf of said Town

The foregoing preamble and Resolution were read and William B. Weeks moved their adoption which motion was seconded by Hiram Orcut, and after the subject was fully ventilated by Mr. Orcut in a lengthy speech, giving a full description of the subject before the meeting But before a vote was called, in consideration that the

Resolutions included the subject of the 3d & 4th Articles in the Warrant, the Motion Wm B. Weeks was amended so as to include the action of both Articles in the Warrant.

The motion was adopted with only two opposing votes L. C. Pattee being one of the members of said Committee asked to be excused from serving on account of other business which would occupy his whole time, and on motion he was excused and J. D. Hosley was elected to take the place of L. C. Pattee on said Committee.

Meeting adjourned to November 1 at two o'clock.

At the adjourned meeting the committee rendered a verbal report. Hiram Orcutt saying he had looked into the matter and according to the best of his opinion Asa T. Barron had no right whatever in said bridge, or any right to any land on the west bank of the Connecticut River which would authorize him to take toll.

William B. Weeks, another member of said committee, made quite a lengthy detailed verbal report, giving an account of the affairs, quoting the law relative to the western boundary of the state of New Hampshire as established by the courts of said state, establishing the line between the states of Vermont and New Hampshire to be at high water mark on the western bank of the Connecticut River. He also stated that said Barron had no right whatever to collect toll for passing from Lebanon to Hartford over said bridge and recommended the adoption of the following resolution:

Be it resolved that we as a town, so far as in our power We are authorized by the laws of the State of New Hampshire, do hereby instruct the present Committee to institute such proceedings as may be necessary, either by a bill in equity and injunction, or otherwise as they shall see fit, in our name or others, against Asa T. Barron to restrain and enjoin him, his agents, and all others from obstructin by bars or gates the public highway in Hartford Vermont, leading from the westerly line of Lyman's Bridge, as laid out by the Commissioners of the County of Grafton in N. H. as a free public highway through the Town of Hartford; as also from taking tolls or money for the passing and repassing thereon

Mr. Jonas Scott moved the adoption of the Resolution which was duly seconded. The voters being seated, and all those in favor of the adoption of the resolution, were requested to rise, and A. W. Baker was requested to count those standing and announced 19 in favor; those against the adoption were requested in like manner to arise and 21 being the number voting against the adoption of the Resolution, and the said resolution was declared not adopted

There is evidently some mistake or else great obscurity in this record. Mention is made in the resolution "of obstructing by bars and gates the public highway in Hartford, Vermont, leading from the westerly line of Lyman's Bridge as laid out by the Commissioners of the County of Grafton as a free public highway through the town of Hartford." The language seems to imply that the commissioners of Grafton County had laid out a "free public highway through the town of Hartford," which, of course, they had no authority to do.

The real condition of the affairs was as follows: The commissioners of Grafton County had laid out a highway over Lyman's Bridge to the Vermont line, which they assumed to be medium water; the court confirmed their doings; Lyman's Bridge became free to this line, but no farther. One could drive across to this line, turn around and go back without being liable to pay any toll. But this point did not extend quite through the bridge, leaving the western abutment on Vermont soil. In addition there was land between the bridge and the toll bar which had never been made a public highway by any of the means by which land becomes a highway.

About the time the Fourth New Hampshire Turnpike was chartered, there was also chartered a turnpike on the Vermont side, known as the White River Turnpike Co. The design of both of these roads was to furnish a road for passengers and merchandise to and from the seaside to certain portions of New Hampshire and Vermont, so that they should furnish a continuous route, and the same parties, to a great extent, were interested in both turnpikes.

The White River Turnpike is described as commencing at a point on the west bank of the Connecticut River, and upon this point there were learned and earnest discussions, when it was settled that the bank of a river was where the soil and water met. Such a point would vary greatly with the low water or floods, and would be very uncertain; but it was at once assumed that the bridge connected the New Hampshire and Vermont turnpikes, and inasmuch as the Vermont Turnpike had been years before made free, the bridge was free. But this was hasty reasoning, for the record of the laying out of the White River Turnpike fixed definitely the point where it commenced, which was

"S.45°E. 9 rods 13 links from the South East Corner of Lyman's store." Upon a survey made with care, the beginning of the turnpike was proved to be at the point where the toll bar had been located for years, leaving a space between that and the bridge over which there had never been a public highway but was the property of the bridge company. This was the finding of a court's commission of Vermont. Upon the ownership of this strip of land and a portion of the bridge rested the right of Barron to take toll of those who passed over them. The authorities of Hartford therefore laid out a highway over this intervening strip of land and when all the necessary formalities were completed, the whole became legally free. The court's commission awarded Barron $1,000 for his interest in the west end of the bridge and the intervening land, making the total cost of freeing the bridge about $7,404. It might have been done in the beginning for $3,000.

During this controversy there was great excitement on both sides of the river. So sure were some of the persons interested in the controversy in their own opinions of their rights that they ran the toll bar. The bar itself had no certain dwelling place, being frequently found floating down the Connecticut River. The result of running the gate, in some instances, proved that it would have been economical to have paid toll.

A reader of the files of the *Free Press* of the period would be surprised to find how many things there asserted and proved were not true, except in the opinions of the writers. He would find instances of a physical paradox, that there may be intense heat without much light.

BEQUESTS TO THE TOWN.

At the annual meeting, 1875, the town voted to accept a bequest of $200, left by Col. Ezra Alden, for building a receiving tomb, but as the terms of the will confined the location of the tomb to the village cemetery, the bequest was never used.

At the annual meeting, 1876, the town voted to accept the bequest of the late Jacob S. Prescott of $1,000, the interest of which was to be paid annually. Mr. Prescott was a native of Springfield, and came to Lebanon when twenty-one years of age, working on the farm of Deacon Porter, and after his death for the Stearns, father and sons; afterwards for Samuel Craft and some others. He never received over $125 per year, beside his board, yet he accumulated several thousand dollars. The bequest to the town has proved of great value, yearly furnishing some of the comforts of life to those who would otherwise be without them.

Centennial Fourth of July.

In the year 1876, the centennial year, there was much talk of an "old fashion Celebration of the Fourth of July," and preparations were made for such a celebration. There was a feeling among the people that the town itself ought to take some action in the matter and give assistance. Accordingly, upon a petition to the selectmen, a meeting was called and held upon the 28th day of June, at which meeting it was "voted to appropriate a sum not exceeding six hundred dollars from money not otherwise appropriated to be expended in the proper observance of the coming Centenial Fourth of July." The celebration of the great natal day of the country was held, the full account of which is elsewhere given.

Town Pump.

Need of a watering place on the common for persons and animals had been felt, and the citizens of the village had taken up the matter and constructed a well on the north side of the common. The expense had been larger than expected, when the town came to the rescue, voting at a meeting held on the 7th day of November, 1876, "to pay the expense incurred in constructin the well on the Common."

This was the first and only town pump, located near the elm on the north side of the common. It served a good purpose, giving grateful refreshment to many thirsty men and beasts, and an unfailing source of pleasure to the small boys until it was superseded by the fountain on the west side of the common. At this same meeting the town took action for the organization of a police court, appropriating the sum of $100 as a salary to the justice.

The late James G. Ticknor received the first appointment as justice of the court from the governor and continued to hold the office until 18—, when he became disqualified by age. C. A. Downs followed as justice of the court, holding the office a little over three years, when he became disqualified by age. He was succeeded by Jesse E. Dewey, appointed July 12, 1893; resigned August 12, 1895.

Sale of Cider and Sewage.

At a special meeting held on the 8th day of September, 1877, the town adopted an act passed by the legislature in the preceding June, forbidding the sale of cider in less quantities than ten gallons, and also the act passed in 1870, relating to sewage.

At a meeting held on the 12th day of October, 1878, the town again voted to adopt an act regulating the sale of both cider and lager beer, the previous act having been somewhat amended.

Hog Reeves.

At the annual meeting in 1878, the town voted for the last time for these "ancient and honorable officers." An elaborate printed ticket was used containing the names of ten candidates, each having a title of amazing dignity and daring significance. Whoever has the curiosity to know with what brilliancy this fat office expired may consult page 477 of Vol. 6, where the whole ticket is entered in full with the high offices of each candidate.

This office seems to have never been taken seriously in this town. The election of the candidates was always the signal for fun and frolic. Squeals and grunts of pigs and hogs were heard in every direction. The first election to this office was at the annual meeting, 1774, when Charles Hill, Huckin Storrs and Lt. John Griswold were chosen. At the annual meeting in 1775 Joseph Wood, James Jones, Samuel Bailey, Abel Wright and Charles Hill were chosen.

The office was not filled again till the annual meeting, 1788, the people having their minds occupied by the serious and absorbing affairs of the Revolution, when Lemuel Hough, Elisha Tilden, Elihu Hyde, Esq., and Abel Wright were chosen hog reeves.

At the next annual meeting the following record was made: "Voted that swine shall not run at large from the 1st of May till the middle of October—Voted that Maj John Griswold Capt. David Hough, Capt. Nathl Hall Mr Robert Colburn, Col. Elisha

Payne Aaron Hutchinson Esq. and Col Edmund Freeman be Hog Reeves for the year ensuing."

These were the most eminent citizens of the town; captains, majors, colonels, lawyers. David Hough was afterwards a member of Congress; John Griswold and Nathaniel Hall were officers in the Revolution; Aaron Hutchinson was the first lawyer in town; Col. Elisha Payne was lieutenant governor and chief justice of Vermont, and one of the most prominent men of the day; Col. Edmund Freeman, the famous "First Settler of Hanover," was an officer in the Revolution. Robert Colburn was the donor of the park which bears his name, as a location of the meetinghouse.

In this fact the fun of the whole proceeding consisted, the contrast in the standing of the men and the office. Sometimes the people paid dearly for their fun, for occasionally a man took the office seriously, and according to his oath of office, proceeded "to faithfully and impartially discharge and perform his duties, to the best of his ability, agreeably to the rules and Regulations of the Constitution and laws of the State." Hogs and pigs were unaccountably missing, to be found later at the town pound, with fees to pay for their release; or perhaps they received notice to "ring" and "yoke" their swine, as the law required, with other charges to pay. All this was not as funny after all.

About the beginning of the present century this custom of choosing the eminent citizens to this office was abandoned, and newly married men became the favorites of the people, and so continued to be until the year 1874, when it was filled for the last time, as before narrated.

It may be of interest to the present generation to learn what other officers there were in ancient times but now unknown. Among these were deer reeves, inspectors of fish, sealers of leather, the names of the officers indicating their duties. Another was culler of staves.

In early times there was much timber in town, of which articles useful and profitable might be manufactured, and among these were staves for barrels, tierces and hogsheads, and other casks. All these were required by law to be of certain dimensions and qualities before they could be put upon the market for domestic use or export. It was the duty of the culler to inspect these staves, selecting the poor from the good and finally putting his official seal upon the bundles, receiving a prescribed fee. When the material of which staves could be made failed, the office became a nominal one; there was nothing for the officer to do. Tradition tells of a certain waggish shoemaker who thought to have some fun with the officer of the year. His shop-tub fell to pieces and he gravely summoned the culler to perform the duties of his office. He came and gave his whole attention to the duty before him, laid the good and the poor in separate piles and then demanded and secured his legal fee. It was not so funny as the son of St. Chrispien thought it might be.

Another officer well known, and not well loved, was the tything-man. The early laws concerning the observance of the Lord's day were very strict. Some of the provisions of the law of 1799 are the following: All labor except works of necessity and mercy, all games, play and recreation are forbidden; all travel on the Lord's day, between sun-rising and sun-setting, unless from necessity or to attend public worship, visit the sick, or do some office of charity, is prohibited. If any person, on the Lord's day, within the walls of any house of public worship, or about such house, whether in the time of public service or between the forenoon and afternoon services of said day, or any part thereof, did behave rudely or indecently he or she must pay a fine, not exceeding six dollars nor less than fifty cents. There was a provision in the law to this effect: "That it shall and may be lawful for any justice of the peace, on application, to grant a license for any person to travel, or do any secular business on that day, which shall appear to him to be a work of necessity or mercy."

At the close of the act it was "recommended to the ministers of the Gospel to read this act publickly in their congregations, annually on the Lord's day next after the choice of town officers."

After some experience it was found "that Justices of the Peace, under a misapprehension of the law, gave permission to travel on the Lord's day, contrary to the true spirit of the act."

Accordingly, it was amended to this effect: "That licenses should not be granted to any person in the stile and capacity of a teamster or carrier, with any team or carriage of burthen, to any person or persons found travelling on said day, in the stile and capacity of a drover with any horses, cattle or other beasts, and that all licenses granted to such persons shall be utterly null and void, any law, usage or custom to the contrary notwithstanding.''

Of course the provisions of the law gave rise to much discussion concerning their application. What exactly is a work of "necessity"? Some things would appear necessary to be done to one, and not to another. What exactly is a "work of mercy"? Many acts would be clearly works of mercy, right and reasonable, while many acts might appear merciful without being truly so. The courts were often required to give a ruling on such matters. Again, not to put too fine a point upon it, could "courting," of which there was an abundance, come under the forbidden recreation?

Now the tything-men were especially charged with the enforcement of this law, and inasmuch as they were required to be "men of good substance and sober life," they were not likely to be favorites with many of the people, especially the young. The time when and the place where the tything-man was most in evidence was in the meetinghouse galleries, during public worship, it being his duty to keep the young folks awake, but not too lively, and of good behavior in all respects. They often carried a little rod, and when a boy or girl became unruly they were brought to order by a tap from the rod. Sometimes they had their ears pulled, and not gently.

Tradition tells of a couple seated side by side one Sabbath in the gallery, greatly enjoying each other and a bag of beech nuts, which in ancient days held the place of the modern peanut. The watchful eye of the tything-man caught this innocent couple in their offending conduct. Now this tything-man was of good substance physically, large and stout. He takes a seat between the couple, most effectually separating them and bringing them to order. It would be a strange sight in our Sunday congregations today to find several men moving about among the worshippers to keep them in order. Were the young people then better in their behavior than now, more sedate and orderly, as we are so often told they were?

The last incumbents of the office in this town were John Gustin, Josiah Bowen, Humphrey Wood and John W. Peck, chosen at the annual meeting in 1845. About that time the law requiring the election of these officers was repealed.

COASTING.

At the annual meeting in 1877 the following resolution was adopted:

Resolved that all persons shall hereafter be prohibited to coast within the limits of any public highway in the town, and that any person so doing, unless permission shall be granted by the Selectmen shall forfeit as a penalty the sum of one dollar for each offence to enure to the use of the town.

In all cases there is conflict between law and its subjects. Never was there a law passed, or regulation made, to which implicit obedience was rendered. From the beginning of society of every kind there has been an irrepressible conflict between the young and the old. Their tastes are different; their ways of looking at things are different. Young folks think old folks are fools, old folks know young folks to be such. Boys and girls like games and sports. If they are forbidden, or under any restraint or limitation, a new zest attaches to them. Old people of short memory of their own youth frown upon such things. Boys and girls from time immemorial have loved to slide down hill, coasting, and have always preferred public places in which to indulge their taste. The elder people thought it was dangerous and so passed a resolution forbidding it; but it did not stop it. They gathered as aforetime at their favorite localities. Sometimes an officer would appear to stop them. Of course, they would stop then, at that place, only to gather in another. So the conflict, always good-natured, went on year after year. The resolution passed was only a town regulation, not a statute by the legislature under the solemn "Be it enacted by the Senate and House of Representatives in General Court convened"; but in 1883 the General Court set up its authority and made a law absolutely prohibiting coasting "in a highway or public street in a village or thickly settled portion of a town or city, to the danger of travelers." A source of weakness in the resolution of the town is eliminated. There is no provision, "unless permission shall be granted by the selectmen." Still, every year the attempt at coasting begins; sometimes promptly stopped, more generally tolerated, until some irate citizen is run down, or escapes the threatened danger by unwonted agility, when complaint is made and the sport stops intermittingly.

At special meetings held September 8, 1877, and October 12, 1878, the town adopted the acts regulating the sale of cider and lager beer, keeping up with temperance legislation.

1880 TO 1890.

At the annual meeting, 1880, the town instructed the sealer of weights and measures to procure a stamp containing the letters L. S., to be used in the performance of his duty. This was done to comply with the provisions of the law.

SOLDIERS' MONUMENT.

For some time the matter of a monument to the soldiers who had given their lives in behalf of their country had been talked of and planned for by individuals, but it first came up before the town at the annual meeting in 1880, at which time the town voted to appropriate $750 for a soldiers' monument, upon condition that $800 more would be raised by subscription, and a committee was appointed to carry out the provisions of the resolution. The history of this movement in honor of the fallen soldiers of the town will be given in a separate chapter.

C. C. BENTON'S BEQUEST.

At a meeting of the town November 2, 1880, the following action was taken in respect to a bequest of Mr. Benton for moving the tomb from its present location to some place in or near the old cemetery in the village, and for the purpose of ornamenting the old cemetery in the center of the village by setting out elms, evergreens and other trees. Voted to defer action on the subject until the next annual meeting. At the annual meeting, 1881, the town declined to move the receiving tomb, but accepted the bequest of "the late Colbee C. Benton of $300 for the purpose of ornamenting the old cemetery in the Center Village by setting out trees and appointed F. L. Owen to superintend the business." It is to this bequest that the village is indebted for the beautiful evergreens which truly ornament the cemetery.

Stocking Streams with Trout.

At the annual meeting in 1881 the following resolution was adopted:

Resolved that a sum of money not to exceed fifteen dollars be and the same is hereby appropriated for the purpose of stocking the streams and waters within the town of Lebanon with brook trout, and that all person be and are hereby prohibited from taking from any waters so stocked any brook trout for the term of three years from the time such waters shall have been so stocked as provided in Section 9 Chapter 176 General Laws, except as otherwise provided in said chapter

In early times the streams of Lebanon abounded in the beautiful and toothsome salmo fontinalis. The stories told of the number and weight of trout captured in those days were very wonderful and quite as true as those told today; but persistent fishing, in season and out, by fair and foul methods, had about exhausted the streams. It is only owing to this early action of the town and annual stocking that any fish remain in our streams at present; yet, with this system of replenishing these waters, and honest observance of the provisions of the law by all parties, these fine fish inhabitants might continue in abundance. In few matters is greed more destructive than in the violation of the provisions of the wise fish and game laws.

Heating and Lighting the Town Hall.

From the earliest days the heating and lighting of the town hall had never been satisfactory to everybody. The methods did not suit the people in the year 1881, and they began to devise improvement by voting "that the Selectmen be and hereby are authorized to make such changes in the method of heating the Town Hall as in their judgment may be deemed necessary." The selectmen to whom this important business was entrusted were Solon A. Peck, John S. Freeman and Charles M. Drake. There is no reasonable doubt but that this board of selectmen did what seemed to them wise and best, but their efforts did not satisfy the people any more than the efforts of many predecessors, and it began to seem as if selectmen were not adequate to this work, for at the annual meeting in 1884, only three years later, the town adopted the following resolution:

Resolved that the Selectmen be and hereby are instructed and empowered to make such further provisions for lighting and heating the Town Hall and to make such additions and repairs to said Hall as in their judgment may be necessary for the safety convenience and comfort of all who resort thereto, and that the expense of such provisions and repairs be paid out of any monies of the town not otherwise appropriated.

The former board of selectmen, we gather from the resolution, had done something but not enough. The selectmen to whom the matter was again committed were Solon A. Peck, Charles A. Downs and John K. Butman. Under these instructions an addition was built at the rear of the hall, providing for ante-rooms at the rear of the stage, and room for storage above and below. Two furnaces had been employed to heat the hall, which were sufficient in moderate weather, but failed in the coldest times. A third furnace was placed in the northwest corner of the lower hall, to be used in emergencies. These furnaces, used with good judgment, gave sufficient heat, and continue to the present time.

When the interior of the town hall was changed in 1868, gas pipes were introduced to afford means of lighting better than kerosene lamps. Gasoline began to be employed for lighting purposes. This substance gave good light when all conditions were just right, but seems to be endowed with an unusual amount of the perversity said to inhere in all material things. It was quick to resent any want of care, or lack of nice adjustment of the machinery by which it was operated. Its lights would flicker, die down to the merest spark and suddenly flash into intense brilliancy, causing the people to wonder what it would do next. Sometimes the light went out entirely at unseemly times and in exasperating ways. Matters went on much in the same way till 1880, when the town decided to light the town hall by electricity. This illuminating agent has its eccentricities as well as the others before employed, but is far better than any other for lighting purposes, and infinitely better so far as comfort and health are concerned.

STREET LIGHTS.

At the annual meeting in 1882 the first steps were taken to introduce street lights by instructing the selectmen "to make such provisions for lighting the main streets of Lebanon Center and West Lebanon as they deemed proper.'' The streets were lighted first by whale oil in lamps suspended from posts; then by kerosene, for which new and improved burners were adopted, without ever reaching satisfactory results, when electricity in 1891 took the place of everything else.

Manufacturers' Exemption from Taxation.

At a special town meeting held April 30, 1881, the following preamble and resolution were adopted:

Whereas In the town of Lebanon we have the largest amount of unoccupied water-power of any other town in the state; and whereas it is of no value in its present normal condition, but if occupied our town would soon contain a manufacturing population and wealth only second to the city of Manchester, and whereas it has become almost universal for towns and cities with manufacturing facilities to offer to capital seeking opportunity for investment in this and other New England states, such inducements as the legislature has seen fit to grant, with the good wishes of their inhabitants and we, seeing the importance of similar action for the interests of our community

Resolved that we, the legal voters of the town of Lebanon do cordially extend a hearty invitation to manufacturing capital, and that we will vote at the earliest opportunity to exempt all new Capital employed in manufacturing when five thousand dollars or more shall be invested for the term of ten years from the time when such manufacturing shall commence and that the clerk be requested to forward a copy of this Resolution to the Crocker Co Holyoke Mass

From this time to the present the town passed many votes exempting manufacturing plants from taxation. Probably the amount exempted would be in the neighborhood of a million dollars. In some cases the period of exemption has already expired and in other cases the limit is not distant.

Spring at West Lebanon.

At the annual meeting in 1882 the town voted to instruct the selectmen to lease to the Congregational Society at West Lebanon the spring situated in the cemetery ground. Little was thought at that time of the necessity of guarding carefully the sources of palatable water.

Town Clocks.

The clock which for many years had been a faithful sentinel in the tower of the town hall, marking the passage of time and regulating the life of the inhabitants in many ways, had become worn and more or less disabled in its functions, so at the annual meeting in 1881 the following resolution was adopted: "That the selectmen are hereby authorized to procure a new clock for the Town Hall and put the same in running order at an expence not exceeding four hundred and fifty dollars."

The selectmen employed F. B. Kendrick, then a jeweller and watchmaker, to procure the clock and place it in the tower. Expense, $447.59. The people of West Lebanon desired to have their time measured out to them in a reliable manner and in 1882 made application to the town at the November meeting for a town clock. Action upon the article in the warrant was postponed to the annual meeting in 1883. At that meeting the town voted to adopt the following resolution: "That the selectmen be authorized and instructed to purchase a suitable town Clock to be placed in the village of West Lebanon whenever a suitable and proper place shall be prepared and furnished without expence to the town, to the satisfaction of the Selectmen." The "suitable and proper place" was not prepared and furnished until the erection of the West Lebanon High School building in 1892. The clock was purchased by C. A. Richardson, watchmaker, at a cost of $400.

Balance of the Dog Tax.

The law required the money received by tax on dogs, and later from license, to be used first in paying for damage done by dogs and any balance to be appropriated to the support of schools. How this balance was to be divided became a vexed question in town meetings. At the November meeting, 1882, the vote was "to divide the remaining dog tax money equally among the school districts." In 1885 the vote was renewed, and again in 1886. The following resolution was also adopted: "That the Selectmen are hereby instructed to enforce Section 9 of Chapter 115 of the General Laws of New Hampshire, respecting the licensing of dogs and repealing the by-law passed in 1880." For many years towns were given the right "to make by-laws for licensing, regulating or restraining dogs as they deemed expedient"; but the towns generally took no action toward licensing dogs. An addition to the law was passed, in case the towns failed to pass by-laws for licensing dogs, requiring the selectmen to prepare such by-laws and affix penalties for the violation thereof.

In the meantime a statute had been enacted, 1863, directing the selectmen to levy a tax of one dollar on all male dogs and two dollars for female dogs; this was outside of a license fee. Finally, in 1891, the present law concerning the licensing of dogs was enacted, requiring two dollars to be paid for each male and five dollars for females. The framers of the law neglected to repeal the law as to taxation, so that the people for about two years had to pay three and seven dollars for keeping a dog, according to sex. The tax was afterwards repealed. The town did make one by-law as to dogs in 1880 requiring a fee of five cents, but it was illegal and repealed.

In 1886, at a special meeting held on the 31st day of March, the following action was taken on the following resolution:

Resolved that the penalty for a failure or neglect to license a dog or dogs owned by any person or harbored by them be and is hereby fixed at fifty cents. The resolution was adopted by a vote of 102 for and 78 against, but was never inforced

This question was finally settled by law, requiring the balance of dog money to be treated as any other school money. Dogs are by many considered as useless animals, but they have a place in the affairs of society and their uses. It has been said that no people could emerge from barbarism to civilization without the aid of the dog. He does not go to school himself but he helps others to an education by contributing to the school fund, after paying for the damage some of the inconsiderate members of his race have done to sheep. The amount of the balance of the dog money to be added to the school money for 1896 is $351.90, which would require an invoice of about $18,000. The valuation of the sheep for 1895 was $2,492, so that the dogs contributed more than eight times as much for the support of schools as the sheep—a result surprising to those who have not considered the matter.

COLBURN PARK.

The Center Village was known for many years as the meeting house. Then the people of the village spoke of the enclosure as the "Common." At the annual meeting in 1884 the town voted "that the Common be hereafter known as Colburn Park in honor of the donor." How this land came to be given to the town has already been narrated in the history of the meeting-house.

POSTMASTERS OF LEBANON.

The names of postmasters, with the dates of their appointment, are as follows:

James Ralston, January 1, 1801.
Thomas Hough, October 1, 1805.
Andrew Post, October 1, 1811.
William Benton, July 1, 1814.
Calvin Benton.
Nathan B. Felton.
Elijah Blaisdell, January 1, 1835.
George S. Kendrick, May 19, 1841.
Calvin Benton, January 14, 1845.
Edward J. Durant, August 3, 1861.
Elisha P. Liscomb, January 22, 1866.
Alpheus W. Baker, January 19, 1881.
William M. Kimball, January 25, 1886.
Charles H. Clough (died in office), December 21, 1889.
William A. Churchill, January 15, 1891.
Albion T. Clark, January 15, 1895.

GEORGE S. KENDRICK,
May, 1841.

EDWARD J. DURANT,
August 5, 1861.

ELISHA P. LISCOMB,
June 22, 1866.

ALPHEUS W. BAKER,
January 19, 1881.

WILLIAM M. KIMBALL,
January 25, 1886.

CHARLES H. CLOUGH,
December 21, 1889.

WILLIAM A. CHURCHILL,
January 15, 1891.

ALBION T. CLARK,
January 15, 1895.

POSTMASTERS OF LEBANON.

The Town in the Rebellion.

The war of the rebel gun turned against Fort Sumter penetrated to these peaceful valleys. The people were at once aroused and excited, and Lebanon began to have a War History. At the first call for volunteers, men here sprung to arms. In the month of April, 1861, ten men answered to the call of the president for seventy-five thousand volunteers. Their names are Joseph Harris, E. D. Cumming, William Hall, B. Clifford, Charles C. Seavey, Henry C. Norton, Heman Maynard, Corliss C. Wheeler, Joseph Sennett, Daniel Dacy. Subsequent calls were met, until Lebanon had representatives in every regiment and military organization of the state.

In compiling the war history of the town, I propose to give first the formal action of the town as found upon the records; second, an alphabetical list of the soldiers who represented Lebanon, with the branch of service in which they were employed, together with a brief notice of each so far as can be ascertained; third, expenses incurred; fourth, events and incidents.

I.

Town Meetings.

At a legal town meeting held on the 18th day of May, 1861, voted to adopt the following resolutions:

Resolved that the town of Lebanon appropriate a sum not exceeding one thousand dollars, out of the treasury of the town not otherwise appropriated, for the benefit of citizens of said town, who have volunteered and entered the service of the United States, and such as may hereafter may volunteer for such service and b accepted, and for the benefit of their families

Resolved: That the Selectmen of Lebanon are authorised and instructed to pay to each citizen of Lebanon who has recently entered the service of his country, and all who may hereafter volunteer and be accepted the sum of *ten* dollars, and faithfully provide for and support such of the families of said volunteers as may require or need assistance

At a legal town meeting held on the 9th day of Nov. 1861:

Voted to instruct the Selectmen to borrow, on the credit of the town, a sum of money not exceeding fifteen hundred dollars to carry out the provisions of Chap. 2480 of the Pamphlet Laws

This was an act authorizing cities and towns to aid the families of volunteers and for other purposes.

Voted that the Selectmen be committee to disburse this money in accordance with the provisions of said Chap 2480.

Voted to accept the following Resolution: viz.

Resolved that the Selectmen be authorized and directed to pay to each inhabitant of the town of Lebanon, who has been accepted and mustered into the service of the United States, or may hereafter be mustered into said Service in the state of New Hampshire or elsewhere, provided he enlisted into some company raised in the State of New Hampshire, the sum of ten dollars out of money in the treasury not otherwise appropriated; provided that those who have already received a bounty of ten dollars heretofore voted by the town, are not to receive any farther bounty, unless they have been, or shall be, after being honorably discharged, re-enlisted and accepted mustered into said service.

At a legal town meeting held on the ninth day of Aug., 1862:

Voted to adopt the following resolutions

Resolved: that the town of Lebanon will pay a bounty of fifty dollars to any inhabitant thereof who has enlisted since the first day of August 1862, or may hereafter enlist and be mustered into the Volunteer service of the United States from this State; provided such soldiers are non-commissioned officers and privates.

Resolved that a like bounty of fifty dollars be paid to any person, who has not been enrolled in any town in this State, and is not liable to do military duty in this State, and who may enlist in this town and be mustered into the Volunteer service of the United States from this State; provided such bounty shall not be paid to such persons after the number necessary to complete the quota of the men or soldiers shall have been furnished.

At a legal town meeting held on the 30th day of Aug., 1862:

Voted to pay fifty dollars to each inhabitant of Lebanon who has enlisted since the first day of July last, or who may hereafter enlist and be mustered into the Volunteer Service of the United States, in addition to the sum heretofore (Aug 1st 1882) voted.

Voted to pay the sum of two hundred dollars to any inhabitant of this town, who may volunteer and be mustered into the service of the United States for the term of nine months, to answer the call for the three hundred thousand men, to be drafted from the militia.

Voted to adopt the following Resolution viz:

Resolved that the selectmen of the town of Lebanon be authorized and directed to pay to the families of the nine months volunteers from this town, who may be accepted and serve instead of drafted militia for the State of New Hampshire, under the call of the Prest. of the United States dated May 4th 1862, for 300,000 drafted malitia the same sums per month as are now authorized by law to be paid to families of Volunteers for three years or during the war; subject to the same conditions and limitations in every respect; provided provisions are not made by the State, for paying said families the same as volunteers are now paid. And the select-men are hereby authorized to borrow money, on the credit of the town, for the purpose of carrying out the [provisions] of this Resolution, and the votes heretofore passed.

At a legal town meeting held on the 15th of August, 1863, voted to adopt the following resolutions, viz.:

Resolved: That the town of Lebanon hereby votes to raise and appropriate, and the Selectmen are hereby authorized and directed to pay as a bounty the sum of three hundred dollars to each of the members of the enrolled militia of the said town who may be drafted or conscripted for the present prospective draft, under the laws of the United States to serve in the army of the United States during the existing rebellion, or to the substitutes for such conscripts, who shall actually enter the service of the United States as aforesaid provided that such bounty shall not be paid to any such conscript or substitute, or his order, until thirty days after he shall have been duly mustered into the service of the United States.

Resolved: That the Selectmen of the town of Lebanon are hereby authorized and directed, to any volunteer from this town, or to any volunteer from any other town, or place, who has already been in the service of the United States for a term not less than nine months, and who can count on the quota required from this town the sum of two hundred dollars, in addition to the bounties and pay offered, or which may hereafter be offered by the United States, the money to be paid after such volunteer has been duly mustered into the service of the United States.

Resolved: That the Selectmen of the town of Lebanon are hereby authorized and directed to pay [to] every volunteer from this town, or to any volunteer from any other town or place, who has not heretofore been in the service of the U. S. and who can count on the quota required from this town the sum of $300.00 as a bounty, payment to be made after such volunteer has been duly mustered into the service of the U. S.

At a legal town meeting held on the 28th of November, 1863, voted to adopt the following resolution, viz.:

Resolved, that the town of Lebanon approve the action of the selectmen in procuring thirty-three volunteers for said town, that being the quota of the town under the last call of the President of the United States; and that said selectmen be authorized to borrow and appropriate, the sum of $147.15, for the purpose of paying for said volunteers, according to the arrangement already made by said Selectmen.

At a legal town meeting held on the 8th of March, 1864:

Voted that the town pay to re-enlisted men $200.00, and to all new men $100.00 as a bounty; and continue to pay this for all men who can count on the quotas of this town till the rebellion is put down. And when the government bounty ceases to new recruits, then the town pay $300.00 for all new recruits, to privates and non-commissioned officers only.

At a legal town meeting held April 7, 1864:

Voted that the town authorize the selectmen to pay a bounty of $200.00 to re-enlisted veteran volunteers; and to all new recruits a bounty of $100.00 and continue to pay this to citizens of Lebanon who can hereafter be accredited to the town, the number not to exceed 22 men, after filling the quota of the last call of two hundred thousand men; and when the government bounties cease, to pay to new recruits the sum of $200.00. The above bounties to be paid to privates and non-commissioned officers only.

At a legal town meeting held August 9, 1864:

Voted that the Selectmen be authorized and directed to pay the highest bounty authorized by law to volunteers substitutes and representative recruits, drafted men or their assigns, who may be mustered into the service of the United States, and be credited to the town of Lebanon, and raise money for that purpose.

Voted that the Selectmen be requested to use their utmost endeavors to fill the quota of this town, in the most speedy manner and on the best terms, and that they be authorized to employ one or more agents, and pay all necessary expenses for that purpose.

Adjourned to the 13th day of August instant.

Met according to adjournment Aug. 13th 1864. Voted that the Selected men be authorized and instructed to fill the quota of this for the present call of the President of the United States, for men; and to raise sufficient money therefor.

Voted to adjourn until Saturday next.

COL. JAMES G. BENTON.

THE TOWN IN THE REBELLION.

Met according to adjournment and Voted to instruct the Selectmen to canvass the town for recruits.

At a legal town meeting held August 30, 1864:

Voted that the Selectmen of the town of Lebanon be authorized to pay to any person, who may for three months previous have been an inhabitant of the town, and shall enlist on the quota of this town and be actually mustered into military, navy, or marine service of the United States, for one years service the sum of six hundred dollars; for two years service the sum of eight hundred dollars, and for three years service the sum of ten hundred dollars, and they are hereby authorized to raise money and appropriate the same for that purpose

Voted that the thanks of this town be presented to Daniel Richardson 71 years of age, and Benjamin Smith 2d 73 years of age for pulling in representative recruits which are credited to this town.

SELECTMEN DURING THE WAR.

1861.
Wm. S. Ela, Solon A. Peck, O. L. Stearns.

1862.
Solon A. Peck, O. L. Stearns, Ebenezer Cole.

1863.
Solon A. Peck, O. L. Stearns, Ebenezer Cole.

1864.
Wm. S. Ela, Ebenezer Cole, Solon A. Peck.

1865.
Solon A. Peck, Ebenezer Cole, J. Warren Cleaveland.

Robert Ash, Fifth Regiment, Company E; mustered October 19, 1861; died of disease in Fairfax County, Va., January 16, 1862, after eight weeks' sickness. He had first typhoid fever, then measles, mumps, another fever, ending with camp dysentery. The following tribute was paid to his memory by one of his comrades: "He was one of our best boys and a true soldier; he was highly esteemed by all his comrades, and his soldier-like bearing had won for him the confidence of his officers. He placed his confidence in Him who rules the universe, and was willing to die in his country's cause and be laid where the weary are at rest." Colonel Cross, in announcing his death, thus speaks of him. "As I sat by the bedside of that dying boy and saw the tide of life slowly ebbing away, and beheld with what bravery and Christian fortitude he awaited death, I thought then how, in his humble life and death he had set us a glorious example, not only as a soldier, but as a man. The heroism of a soldier's life and death is not confined to the battlefield. It requires more courage to suffer a lingering illness and 'die in hospital' than to meet death amid the din of arms."

Zenas P. Alden, enlisted Seventh Regiment, Company C; mustered November 15, 1861; promoted to corporal November 28, 1863; mustered out December 22, 1864.

John Adams, s., Sixth Regiment, Company G; mustered November 21, 1863, three years; deserted at Camp Nelson, Ky., January 1, 1864.

John H. Ansel, Company I, First Cavalry; mustered one year, April 5, 1865; mustered out May 6, 1865.

Albert Aspinwall, Lebanon, mustered September 23, 1864, three years; musician, Second Brigade Band, Tenth Army Corps; mustered out July 4, 1865.

Lawrence Albach, Lebanon, Third Regiment, Company K; mustered November 24, 1863; wounded May 18, 1864; sick July 20, 1865.

Charles G. Balch, enlisted in Seventh Regiment, Company C; mustered November 15, 1861; drowned at Beaufort, July 26, 1862.

Capt. Daniel C. Buswell, enlisted in the First Regiment, Minnesota. This, we believe, was the first regiment tendered to the government, and Captain Buswell's name the second on the roll of his company. He was in the first battle of Bull Run and at the siege of Yorktown. He was seized by camp dysentery and only saved by the care of E. P. Liscomb, Esq., to whom many a soldier is indebted for kindness shown when most needed. He returned to Lebanon, his birthplace, to recruit his health. While here he was transferred to the Ninth New Hampshire Regiment, with a captain's commission in Company E, which he enlisted at Lebanon. No finer company left the state than this. He was in the battles of South Mountain and Antietam, under Burnside in

Kentucky, at Vicksburg and in the campaign for Richmond. On the 22d of July, 1864, while on picket duty before Petersburg, Va., he was mortally wounded. Died in hospital August 8, 1864. His remains were brought to Lebanon and committed to their last resting place with abundant honors.

Joseph Bean, s., Lebanon, Second Regiment, Company H; mustered November 11, 1863, three years; died of wounds received in action June 3, 1864.

Michael Bow, Third Regiment, Company B; mustered December 7, 1864, three years; mustered out July 20, 1865.

William Banch, Lebanon, s., Third Regiment, Company H; mustered November 24, 1863, three years; wounded June 16, 1864; died of wounds July 5, 1864, at Point of Rocks, Va.

George Borley, Lebanon, Third Regiment, Company K; mustered November 12, 1863, three years; supposed to have deserted en route to regiment.

George F. Biathrow, First Cavalry, Company L; mustered March 31, 1865, one year; mustered out May 6, 1865.

Joshua M. Balch, Heavy Artillery, Company H; mustered September 7, 1864, one year; mustered out June 15, 1865.

Moses T. Brown, Lebanon, Seventh Regiment, Company C; mustered November 25, 1861; discharged for disability at Hilton Head, S. C., August 25, 1864.

William A. Bowen, Lebanon, Second Regiment, United States Sharpshooters, Company F; mustered November 26, 1861, musician; mustered out November 26, 1864.

Bierney Corlis, s., Lebanon, Ninth Regiment, Company E; mustered August 8, 1862, three years; deserted at Concord August 23, 1862.

Bourgoi Joseph, s., Lebanon, Ninth Regiment, Company E; mustered August 8, 1862, three years; deserted at Concord August 23, 1862.

John Boyd, s., Lebanon, Sixth Regiment, Company G; mustered November 21, 1863, three years; deserted at Camp Nelson, Ky., January 1, 1864.

John Beaer, s., Lebanon, Fourth Regiment, Company I; mustered November 21, 1863, three years.

John Blair, s., Lebanon, Fourth Regiment, Company G; mustered November 21, 1863, three years; transferred to U. S. Navy April 27, 1864.

John Bawn, s., Sixth Regiment, Company F; mustered June 11, 1864; absent sick since October 1, 1866.

Charles Bashaw, Heavy Artillery, Company H; mustered September 3, 1864, one year; discharged for disability at Fort Bayard, D. C., March 25, 1865.

Thelesphor Bernard, Lebanon, Heavy Artillery, Company M; mustered February 16, 1865, one year; mustered out June 9, 1865.

Joseph Bernard, Heavy Artillery, Company M; mustered February 16, 1865, one year; mustered out June 9, 1865.

Charles Brown, insurgent states; mustered August 6, 1864, U. S. Sharpshooters, Company F, three years.

Elbridge Brown, insurgent states; mustered August 30, 1864, three years.

William Blufilah, insurgent states; mustered August 19, 1864.

W. J. Barron, Navy; mustered September 21, 1864.

——— — ———, Navy; mustered September 21, 1864, three years.

Henry Barns, mustered October 27, 1863, three years.

William Bennett, mustered November 4, 1863, three years.

John Bergeron, mustered August 10, 1864, three years.

Henry Banks, mustered August 10, 1864, three years.

Thomas Brown, Lebanon, Fifteenth Regiment, Company H; mustered October 16, 1862; mustered out August 13, 1863.

Luman F. Brooks, Lebanon, Sixteenth Regiment, Company A; mustered October 16, 1862; first sergeant; mustered out August 20, 1863; commissioned chaplain in the Third Regiment of Infantry, Corps d'Afrique, September 20, 1863; stationed in Louisiana; promoted major October 5, 1864; discharged November 25, 1864.

Hobart E. Bliss, Lebanon, Sixth Vermont Regiment, Company D; mustered October 2, 1861; severely wounded through the body May 5, 1863, at Fredericksburg, Va.; transferred to Veteran Reserve Corps, Sixth Regiment, Company A; sergeant; discharged Oct. 25, 1864.

Harvey A. Bean, Lebanon, Fifth Regiment, Company C; mustered October 12, 1861; wounded at Fair Oaks June 3, 1864, and

HARRY H. HOSLEY, U. S. N.

at Cold Harbor, Va.; mustered out October 29, 1864; died at Lebanon June 16, 1875, the eve of the one hundredth anniversary of the battle of Bunker Hill.

Orville Barker, Lebanon, Sixteenth Regiment, Company A; mustered October 16, 1862; mustered out August 20, 1863.

John Benois or Beniro, Fourth Regiment, Company I; mustered November 21, 1863.

William Bennett, unknown.

Henry Burns, unknown.

John Barron, Lebanon, Sixth Regiment, Company B; mustered January 10, 1864.

Herman Bigman, s., Third Regiment, Company K, Lebanon; mustered November 24, 1863; captured August 17, 1864; paroled October 7, 1864; deserted.

Robert Barrell, Lebanon, Fourth Regiment, Company E; mustered October 6, 1863; transferred to Navy April 27, 1864.

Simon Baslow, s., Fourth Regiment, Company B; date of muster unknown; died of disease February 17, 1864, at Morris Island, S. C.

Edward D. Comings, Lebanon, First Regiment, Company K; mustered May 7, 1861, three months; mustered out August 9, 1861; re-enlisted in Sixteenth Regiment, Company E; mustered October 16, 1862; mustered out August 20, 1863.

Blanchard Clifford, First Regiment, Company K; mustered May 7, 1861, three months; mustered out August 20, 1861.

Norman D. Corser, Lebanon, Fifth Regiment, Company C; mustered October 12, 1861; re-enlisted March 29, 1864; promoted sergeant; wounded June 3, 1864; mustered out June 28, 1865.

Thomas W. Cross, Lebanon, Fifth Regiment, Company C; mustered October 12, 1861; discharged for disability November 14, 1862; re-enlisted.

Dennis W. Cross, Lebanon, Fifteenth Regiment, Company H; mustered October 16, 1862; mustered out August 13, 1863.

Harvey H. Carter, Lebanon, Sixteenth Regiment, Company F; mustered October 16, 1862; mustered out August 20, 1863.

Edwin Chandler, Lebanon, corporal, Sixteenth Regiment, Company A; mustered October 16, 1862, nine months; mustered out August 20, 1863.

James Cornell, Fourth Regiment, Company C, s.; mustered November 14, 1863; deserted at White House, Va., June 3, 1864.

George Chapman, s. d., Lebanon, Third Regiment, Company C; mustered October 12, 1863; captured at Laurel Hill, Va., October 7, 1864; died at Salisbury, N. C., November 29, 1864.

Charles Cooper, s. d., Seventh Regiment, Company A; mustered October 31, 1863; deserted to the enemy June 1, 1864.

Charles Campbell, s. d., Seventh Regiment, Company C; mustered October 19, 1863; deserted to the enemy at Bermuda Hundred, Va., August 25, 1864.

Edward A. Cotting, corporal, Lebanon, Heavy Artillery, Company B; mustered August 31, 1863; mustered out September 11, 1865.

William Coffee, Norwich, Vt., Third Regiment, Company A; mustered August 22, 1861; promoted corporal July 20, 1862; sergeant, January 21, 1864; reënlisted February 14, 1864; reduced to ranks November 20; promoted to sergeant March 1, 1865; mustered out July 20, 1865.

Clarendon A. Cochran, Lebanon, Eighteenth Regiment, Company B; mustered September 13, 1864; wounded April 2, 1865; mustered out June 8, 1865.

Henry N. Colston, Fourth Regiment, Company F; March 29, 1862; discharged for disability May 9, 1863.

Byron C. Cheney, First Cavalry, Troop A; mustered March 26, 1864; promoted sergeant May 1, 1864; mustered out July 15, 1865.

Peter Carpenter, First Cavalry, Troop C; mustered April 9, 1864; discharged for disability August 5, 1865.

Eugene T. Chase, First Cavalry, Troop G; mustered March 28, 1865; mustered out July 15, 1865.

Charles Cross, First Cavalry, Troop L; mustered March 23, 1865, one year; mustered out July 15, 1865.

Reuben T. Cross, First Cavalry, Troop L; mustered March 24, 1865, one year; mustered out July 15, 1865.

Morris Catrick, Fifth Regiment, Company A; mustered November 24, 1863; transferred to U. S. Navy April 26, 1864.

Ethan A. Dickenson, Lebanon, Fifth Regiment, Company C; mustered October 12, 1861; he was wounded at Fair Oaks, Va., June 1, 1862; died September 5, 1862.

Ferdinand Davis, Lebanon, Seventh Regiment, Company D; commissioned first lieutenant October 27, 1863; severely wounded February 20, 1864; mustered out December 22, 1864.

Peter Demas, Third Regiment, Company B; mustered November 25, 1863, three years; mustered out July 20, 1865.

Daniel C. Dacy, First Regiment, Company K; mustered May 7, 1861; mustered out August 9, 1861; reënlisted October 16, 1862, Sixteenth Regiment, Company A; corporal; volunteered form storming party at Port Hudson; mustered out August 20, 1863.

Mahlon E. Davis, Lebanon, Seventh Regiment, Company C; mustered November 15, 1861; promoted captain First S. C. Volunteers, June 5, 1863.

Joseph Demosh, Fifth Regiment, Company E; mustered October 19, 1861; discharged December 3, 1862, for disability.

Jason A. Daniels, Lebanon, Ninth Regiment, Company E; mustered August 6, 1862; mustered out June 10, 1865.

Jeremiah Driscoll, First Cavalry; mustered April 4, 1865, three years; mustered out May 6, 1865.

Morris Digo, insurgent states, U. S. Sharpshooters, August 7, 1864.

David Durgin, s., unknown; mustered August 10, 1864, three years.

Solon M. Davis, Lebanon, Second United States Sharpshooters; date of muster unknown; transferred to Fifth Regiment January 30, 1865.

John W. Dewey, Sixteenth Regiment, Company F, Iowa Volunteers; instantly killed near Atlanta, Ga., July 7, 1864; he was quartermaster sergeant and had many warm friends in the regiment.

Charles H. Emerson, Lebanon, Sixteenth Regiment, Company A; mustered October 16, 1862; mustered out August 20, 1863.

George H. Emerson, Lebanon, Sixteenth Regiment, Company wagoner; mustered October 16, 1862; mustered out August 20, 1863.

James Emerson, Fourth Regiment; mustered October 19, 1863; deserted at White House, Va., June 1, 1864.

George W. Emmons, Lebanon, Company G, Third Regiment;

commissioned first lieutenant August 22, 1861; promoted captain Company G, April 2, 1862; resigned September 18, 1863.

John Evans, s. d., Fourth Regiment, Company H; mustered October 17, 1863; mustered out August 3, 1865.

George Edmonds, s. d., Seventh Regiment, Company C; mustered October 30, 1863, three years; supposed to have deserted.

Charles Elmer, Lebanon, Eighteenth Regiment, Company B; mustered September 13, 1864; died of disease at Washington, D. C., April 5, 1865; interred in National Cemetery, Arlington, Va.

Amos Elms.

Daniel Eldredge, Third Regiment, Company K; mustered August 24, 1861; promoted corporal May 3, 1863; sergeant, July 1, 1863; commissioned second lieutenant January 7, 1864; first lieutenant, July 7, 1864; wounded severely August 16, 1864; declined captain January 20, 1865; honorably discharged June 22, 1865, to accept appointment V. R. C.

Alonzo S. Elkins, Lebanon, Fourth Regiment, Company F; date of muster April 7, 1862; died of disease at Folly Island, S. C., July 6, 1863.

Henry Ellis, Thirty-third Regiment, Massachusetts Volunteers; sergeant; he was with Sherman in his famous march to the sea; wounded at Bentonville March 21, 1865, and died in hospital April 13, 1865.

John S. Flanders, Lebanon, Fifth Regiment, Company C; mustered October 12, 1861; reënlisted January 1, 1864; wounded June 3, 1864; promoted to sergeant January 14, 1864; mustered out June 28, 1865.

Albert W. Fogg, Lebanon, Ninth Regiment, Company E; mustered August 13, 1862; transferred to Veteran Reserve Corps, October 30, 1863.

Elisha H. Ford, Third Regiment, Company H; mustered September 9, 1862, three years; mustered out June 22, 1865.

John Farrell, s., Third Regiment, Company C; mustered November 20, 1863; wounded August 16, 1864; mustered out July 20, 1865.

Thomas Flynn, Eighth Regiment, Company C; mustered December 31, 1861; promoted corporal December 1, 1862; reënlisted, First Cavalry, Company I; mustered April 4, 1865; died at Lebanon April 12, 1871. He was every inch a brave and true soldier, participating in all the marches and battles of the Eighth, one of the best regiments of the state. He lived to partake of the fruits of his toil.

Julian Fox, s. d., Fifth Regiment, Company K; mustered October 5, 1863; discharged for disability February 18, 1864.

Frank P. Flynn enlisted Company E, First Vermont Cavalry, October 11, 1861; credited to Pomfret, Vt.; after being captured and paroled, re-enlisted December 28, 1863, Company K, First New Hampshire Volunteer Cavalry; mustered out July 15, 1865, as first lieutenant and breveted captain.

William F. Gould, Lebanon, Second United States Sharpshooters, Company F; mustered November 26, 1861; reënlisted December 21, 1863; transferred to Fifth Regiment January 30, 1865; mustered out June 28, 1865.

Lucian Gilatt, Lebanon, Fifth Regiment, Company G; mustered October 12, 1861; mustered out October 29, 1864.

Horace P. Griswold, Fourth Regiment, Company H; mustered September 18, 1861; promoted to corporal; discharged for disability July 14, 1863; wounded.

Ira H. Gates, Fifth Regiment, Company C; mustered October 12, 1861; wagoner; mustered out October 21, 1864.

George H. Greeley, Lebanon, Fifth Regiment, Company C; mustered October 12, 1861; promoted sergeant; wounded at Fredericksburg, Va., December 18, 1862; was last seen in the city. His grave is unknown.

Alexander Griffith, Lebanon, Fourth Regiment, Company E; mustered August 13, 1862; wounded December 13, 1862; deserted February, 1863.

Story H. Gates, Lebanon, Sixteenth Regiment, Company A; mustered October 16, 1862; mustered out August 20, 1863; reënlisted, First Regiment Cavalry; mustered March 10, 1864; promoted to sergeant May 1, 1864; mustered out July 15, 1865.

Truman N. Gray, Sixteenth Regiment, Company A; mustered October 16, 1862; discharged at New York City.

Roswell P. Griffin, Sixteenth Regiment, Company A; mustered October 16, 1862; mustered out August 20, 1863.

Henry Gray, s. d., Fourth Regiment, Company E; mustered October 19, 1863; wounded and captured in action May 16,

1864; died at Andersonville, Ga., August 22, 1864; grave No. 6,516.

Grant Harrison, December 9, 1861, Company B, Sixth Regiment; deserted on march, April 16, 1863.

William Hall, First Regiment, Company K; mustered May 7, 1861; mustered out August 9, 1861; reënlisted in Seventeenth United States Infantry, January 16, 1862; mustered out January 17, 1865.

Joseph H. Harris, First Regiment, Company K; mustered May 7, 1861; mustered out August 9, 1861. Reënlisted Fifth Regiment, Company C, September 17, 1862; discharged for disability June 8, 1863.

William Henry Hoffman, Lebanon, Fifth Regiment, Company C; mustered October 12, 1861; badly wounded in the shoulder at Fair Oaks, June 1, 1862; died in the hospital at Philadelphia, Pa., June 25, 1862; strongly attached to his comrades and a good soldier.

John C. Hoffman, Lebanon, Second United States Sharpshooters, Company F; mustered November 26, 1861; deserted December 2, 1861.

James H. Hildreth, Lebanon, Second United States Sharpshooters, Company F; commissioned first lieutenant September 19, 1861; resigned August, 1863.

Charles A. Hale, Lebanon, Fifth Regiment, Company C; mustered October 12, 1861; corporal; promoted sergeant-major, February 8, 1863; promoted second lieutenant, Company H, March 1, 1863; promoted first lieutenant, Company B, July 2, 1863; captain, Company F, January 3, 1865; mustered out June 28, 1865.

George P. Hoyt, Seventh Regiment, Company C; mustered November 29, 1861; died of disease at Laurel Hill, Va., December 2, 1864.

John L. Hazetine, Lebanon, Third Regiment, Company K; mustered August 24, 1861; among the first to come to the defence of his country, bearing a good reputation as a soldier; died December 9, 1861, at Hilton Head.

Willis B. Hough, Sixth Regiment, Company B, Vermont Volunteers; enlisted October, 1861; died of disease at Newport News, Va., where his remains rest.

Jerome B. House, Seventh Regiment, Company C; commissioned first lieutenant November 6, 1861; promoted to captain April 29, 1862; mortally wounded in an assault on Fort Wayne, July 18, 1863. The wound was in the thigh joint and the bullet could not be extracted. He was brought home and after severe suffering, borne with a soldier's fortitude and a Christian's resignation, he departed for a better country October 7, 1863. A brave and faithful officer, an upright man.

William Hannegan, Fifth Regiment, Company C; mustered October 12, 1861; discharged for disability March 27, 1863.

Elias F. Holt, Lebanon, First Battalion Cavalry; mustered December 17, 1861; saddler; promoted regimental saddler sergeant, September 1, 1862; not officially accounted for.

Charles M. Holt, s., Third Regiment, Company B; mustered November 20, 1863; deserted at Staten Island, N. Y., November 8, 1864.

Moses T. Hale, Eighteenth Regiment, Company B; mustered September 13, 1864; mustered out June 10, 1865.

Leonard Hadley, First Regiment Cavalry, Troop A; mustered March 23, 1864; appointed wagoner; mustered out July 15, 1865.

Thomas Hynes, s., Heavy Artillery; mustered December 22, 1864; deserted en route to regiment.

Thomas Harrington, s., Heavy Artillery, Company M; mustered December 22, 1864.

Abiel C. Hurlburt, United States Navy; mustered September 7, 1864.

Albert Hemmingway, s.; mustered August 10, 1864; branch of service unknown.

Joseph D. Hawkins, First Cavalry, Troop C; mustered April 5, 1864; discharged for disability at Concord, N. H., October 18, 1864.

George M. Harris, First Regiment Cavalry, Troop C; mustered April 20, 1864; transferred to Troop M, April 20; died of disease at City Point, Va., August 6, 1864.

Edward D. Howe, Lebanon, Fifth Regiment, Company C; mustered October 12, 1861; corporal; mortally wounded at White Oak Swamp, Va., June 27, 1862. Corporal Howe though young was a good soldier, ever ready to do his duty without complaint. Modest, quiet, he was beloved by both officers and comrades. The company was lying on the ground in front of the enemy when a cannon ball struck Corporal Howe in the right thigh, nearly severing the limb from the body. Rising again, it took off his left hand. Strict orders had been given that no one should leave the ranks to remove the wounded. Captain Randlett, seeing his peril, buckled a strap around the limb, hoping to stop the flow of blood. He was finally carried to a field hospital where everything was done to save his life. The army falling back, the wounded fell into the hands of the enemy. Nothing more is known of his fate. His remains rest in an unknown grave, but his memory is kept alive.

John S. Hebbard, Lebanon, Fifth Regiment, Company E; mustered October 19, 1861; sergeant; discharged for disability at Fortress Monroe, January 17, 1863.

Charles Hill, s., Fourth Regiment, Company C; mustered November 14, 1863; died of disease August 16, 1864.

Patrick Hogan, s., Third Regiment, Company D, mustered November 17, 1863; discharged by order July 12, 1865.

Henry P. Hyde, Lebanon, enlisted in Company B, First Vermont Volunteers, for three months; reënlisted in Company C, Seventeenth United States Infantry; stationed at West Lebanon as recruiting sergeant; afterwards at Fort Preble, Me.; took the field and was killed in action at Spottsylvania, Va., May 9, 1864. He was the first man to enlist from Lebanon. In every position he was found faithful and efficient. He had been promoted to be second lieutenant when he died.

William H. Ingalls, Eighteenth Regiment, Company G; mustered December 28, 1864; promoted to corporal May 29, 1865; reduced to ranks June 19, 1865; mustered out July 29, 1865.

Calvin Johnson, Fifth Regiment, Company C; mustered November 21, 1863; supposed to have deserted en route to regiment.

Edward Jones, s., Third Regiment, Company I; mustered November 24, 1863; wounded severely May 18, 1865; absent sick July 20, 1865.

Lewis Jordan, Lebanon, Seventh Regiment, Company C; mustered Nov. 15, 1861; reënlisted February 27, 1864.

Marcellus Jenks, First Cavalry, Troop K; mustered March 22, 1865, three years; mustered out July 15, 1865.

Beb. Javaw, Third Regiment, Company G; mustered November 20, 1863; deserted at New York, January 20, 1865.

George W. Jackson, Third Regiment, Company K; mustered October 10, 1863; deserted Staten Island, N. Y., November 8, 1864.

George B. Kempton, Lebanon, enlisted July 14, 1862, Ninth Regiment, Company E; died of disease, Falmouth, Va., February 7, 1863.

Alonzo Kellam, Third Regiment, Company H; mustered September 6, 1862; killed at Drury's Bluff, Va., May 16, 1864.

George W. Kelley, Lebanon; mustered October 16, 1862; Company A, Sixteenth Regiment; mustered out August 20, 1863.

Harvey B. Kimball, Lebanon, Sixteenth Regiment, Company A; mustered October 16, 1862; corporal; mustered out August 20, 1863.

Rufus Knapp, s., Fourth Regiment, Company H; mustered November 23, 1863; taken prisoner May 16, 1864; exchanged August 16, 1864.

Lewis Kerriger, s., Eighth Regiment, Company D; mustered November 5, 1863; killed at Sabine Cross Roads, La., February, 1864.

John Kelley, s., Fifth Regiment; mustered October 22, 1863; deserted at Point Lookout, Md., November 17, 1863.

William Krafts, Third Regiment, Company K; mustered December 12, 1864; sick at Wilmington July 20, 1865; no discharge.

Lewis Kershett; not traced.

Henry T. Latham, Lebanon, Fifth Regiment, Company G; mustered October 12, 1861; musician; discharged September 6, 1862, for disability; reënlisted September 7, 1863.

Charles F. Liscomb, Lebanon, Fifth Regiment, Company C; mustered October 12, 1861; corporal; promoted to sergeant-major September 10, 1862; promoted second lieutenant October 1, 1862; promoted first lieutenant December 19, 1862, Company A. Lieutenant Liscomb was the first man to enlist in Company C. He was slightly wounded at Antietam. His promotion to first lieutenant was for bravery at Fredericksburg, Va. He was in all the battles of the "Fighting Fifth," except that of Chancellorsville. He never shrank from any duty, however arduous; always brave and encouraging others by his coolness in danger.

At the battle of Gettysburg, Lieutenant Liscomb commanded Company A. They went into action with twenty-three men; at the roll-call after the battle, three men only answered to their names. He was the first to discover and report the retreat of the rebel army. Being on picket duty at night after the last day's fight, the absence of any noise in the enemy's picket lines awakened suspicion that they might have retreated. To make sure of the fact, the lieutenant cautiously crawled through the underbrush, armed only with a stout stick, to the rifle-pits of the enemy; searching right and left, he found them deserted and at once reported the retreat. He died at Point Lookout, Md., January 6, 1864.

Charles E. Lane, Lebanon, Seventh Regiment, Company C; mustered November 15, 1861; discharged for disability June 26, 1862; died May 10, 1863.

Andrew J. Lane, Lebanon, Seventh Regiment, Company C; mustered November 15, 1861; promoted sergeant; promoted to second lieutenant April 29, 1862; killed at Fort Wagner, July 18, 1863. Brave, faithful, prompt to every duty, somewhere he fills the grave of a Christian soldier.

Levi A. Leighton, Lebanon, Fifth Regiment, Company C; mustered October 12, 1861; sergeant; killed in action at Fair Oaks, Va., June 1, 1862. A good soldier.

Isaac Loungeverns, Lebanon, Fifth Regiment, Company C; mustered October 12, 1861; died.

Homer Lawton entered the navy as a seaman in November, 1861. He served in the ships *Lodona* and *De Soto*. On the 2d of September, 1863, he volunteered with others to storm Fort Sumter, where he received a slight wound. The entire party were captured and sent to Andersonville prison, where he died.

Tennaus Lagacys, Third Regiment, Company E; mustered November 12, 1863; killed at Drury's Bluff, May 13, 1864.

John Lovett, s., Fourth Regiment, Company E; mustered October 19, 1863; wounded August 16, 1864; deserted while on furlough November, 1864.

John Lennox, s. d., Seventh Regiment, Company D; mustered October 26, 1863; wounded slightly February 20, 1864; deserted at Jacksonville, Fla., April 14, 1864.

John Leonard, s., Sixth Regiment, Company D; mustered June 2, 1864; reported deserter.

Niles Ladegard, s., Third Regiment, Company E; mustered December 13, 1864; mustered out June 15, 1865.

John Lamonette, First Cavalry, Troop A; mustered March 10, 1864; mustered out July 15, 1865.

Maj. Solon A. Lathrop, a native of Lebanon, though not a resident here at the time of the war, enlisted in the regular army about the time of Lincoln's inauguration; was immediately promoted to captain; was variously employed on guard and staff duty; died at Victoria, Texas, October 7, 1867. An intelligent and trustworthy soldier. His remains rest at Buffalo, N. Y.

Henry Miller, Lebanon, Sixteenth Regiment, Company A; mustered October 16, 1862; mustered out August 20, 1863; died Northwood May 19, 1886.

Webster I. Martin, Lebanon, Sixteenth Regiment, Company A; mustered October 16, 1862; mustered out August 20, 1863.

Albert Miller, Lebanon, Tenth Regiment; mustered October 16, 1862; mustered out August 20, 1863.

William S. Moses, Lebanon, Sixteenth Regiment, Company A; mustered October 16, 1862; musician; mustered out August 20, 1863.

Albert Meyer, s., Second Regiment, Company K; mustered November 11, 1863; promoted to corporal May 1, 1865; mustered out December 19, 1865.

John McKay, s., Third Regiment, Company B; mustered September 29, 1863; deserted at Jacksonville, Fla., April, 1864.

Frank Mercelle, Third Regiment, Company F; mustered November 20, 1863; wounded slightly May 18, 1864; absent since June 17, 1864; no discharge furnished.

Victor Manuel, s., Fifth Regiment, Company K; mustered November 24, 1863; transferred to United States Navy, April 26, 1864.

J. Martin McAvoy, s., Fourth Regiment, Company C; mustered October 19, 1863; discharged for disability at Beaufort, S. C., February 20, 1864.

Jackson Murray, Eighteenth Regiment, Company G; mustered December 10, 1864; mustered out July 29, 1865.

Thomas J. McGinniss, Eighteenth Regiment, Company G; mustered out July 29, 1865.

David M. Moody, Lebanon, Fourth Regiment, Company D; date of muster April 4, 1862; discharged for disability July 15, 1863, at Folly Island, S. C.

Robert Miller, Seventh Regiment, Company C; mustered December 25, 1861; reënlisted February 27, 1864; died at Lebanon July 24, 1871. A good and faithful soldier.

H. D. Moore, Lebanon, United States Sharpshooters, Company F; mustered November 26, 1861; transferred to Veteran Reserve Corps.

Thomas Manchester, Sixteenth Regiment, Company A; mustered October 16, 1862; mustered out August 20, 1863.

Heman L. Maynard, Lebanon, First Regiment, Company K; mustered May 7, 1861; mustered out August 9, 1861; reënlisted, Seventh Regiment, Company C; mustered November 15, 1861; wounded February 20, 1864; discharged at St. Joseph's Hospital, New York, September 17, 1864; died March 14, 1872, at Soldiers' Home, Hampton, Va.

William Miller, Fifth Regiment, Company C; mustered October 12, 1861; died May 3, 1862, at Ship Point, Va.

Harrison G. Mann, Lebanon, Seventh Regiment, Company C; mustered November 15, 1861; promoted corporal; wounded and captured June 16, 1864, after which no more was heard of him.

Carlos H. Miller, Sixteenth Regiment, Company A; Heavy Artillery, Company M; mustered February 16, 1865; mustered out June 9, 1865.

Henry Moody, insurgent states; mustered August 6, 1864, three years; service unknown.

John McKay, s., Third Regiment, Company K; mustered November 12, 1863; mustered out July 20, 1865.

Patrick Martin, s. d.; mustered October 27, 1863; branch of service unknown.

Henry C. Norton, First Regiment, Company K; mustered May 2, 1861; mustered out August 9, 1861.

Albert B. Nye, Fifteenth Regiment, Company H; mustered October 16, 1862; sergeant; mustered out August 13, 1863.

Franklin Norton, Sixteenth Regiment, Company A; mustered October 16, 1862. After going through the campaign with his regiment in Louisiana, died on his way home, at Mound City, Ill., August 18, 1863.

Alfred Neugerman, s., Fourth Regiment, Company I; mustered November 21, 1863; mustered out August 23, 1865.

Patrick O'Connell, Tenth Regiment, Company F; mustered September 1, 1862; discharged for disability.

Thomas O'Shaughnessy, s., Fourth Regiment, Company F; mustered November 14, 1863; discharged for disability at Fortress Monroe, Va., July 19, 1864.

George E. Percival, Lebanon, Fifth Regiment, Company C; mustered October 12, 1861. The same shot which wounded Corporal Howe at White Oak Swamp, Va., June 30, 1862, took off the right arm of Percival. He fell into the hands of the enemy and was heard of no more.

Joseph Peepot, s., Second Regiment, Company K; mustered November 11, 1863; absent sick since October 1, 1864; no discharge furnished.

Nelson S. Preston, Sixth Regiment, Company D; mustered August 30, 1862; promoted to corporal; mustered out June 3, 1865.

Joseph Peterson, s., Sixth Regiment, Company B; mustered November 21, 1863; deserted at Camp Nelson, Ky., December 23, 1863.

Lewis Phillips, s., Sixth Regiment, Company G; mustered June 10, 1864; supposed to have deserted en route to regiment.

Hiram B. Philbrick, Fifteenth Regiment, Company H; mustered December 11, 1862; sergeant; promoted first sergeant; mustered out August 13, 1863.

Frank Parent, First Cavalry, Troop A; mustered March 10, 1864; taken prisoner November 12, 1864, in the Shenandoah Valley; confined at Andersonville, where he died of destitution. A brave and faithful soldier.

Marcellus Parker, First Cavalry, Troop L; mustered April 7, 1865; mustered out May 6, 1865.

George C. Perkins, Lebanon; mustered in Vermont; musician, Post Band, Tenth Army Corps, Hilton Head, February 13, 1863; mustered out July 4, 1865.

James B. Perry, Fifth Regiment, Company C; commissioned captain, October 12, 1861. While rallying his company before

Fredericksburg, December 13, 1862, with the colors in his hand, the color-bearer having been killed, he received a minie ball in his shoulder, which penetrated towards the heart. The wound was immediately mortal. Captain Perry was an upright man, temperate, and a genial companion. He was one of the first to see the necessity of and persistently advocated the justice of emancipation.

Nathan H. Randlett, Fifth Regiment, Company C; commissioned first lieutenant, October 12, 1861; promoted to captain, September 8, 1862; severely wounded at the battle of Antietam, September 17, 1862; discharged May 3, 1863; entered Veteran Reserve Corps, 1863, captain; Texas Bureau, Abandoned Land, Refugees and Freedmen; discharged December 31, 1868.

James Richardson, Sixteenth Regiment, Company A; mustered October 16, 1862; mustered out August 20, 1863; reënlisted, Eighteenth Regiment, Company B, September 13, 1864; sergeant; mustered out June 10, 1865.

Silas J. Richardson, Lebanon, Eighteenth Regiment, Company B; mustered September 13, 1864; detailed drummer; mustered out June 10, 1865.

Edward Redding, insurgent states, United States Sharpshooters, Company F; mustered August 6, 1864.

James M. Sisco, First Cavalry, Company K; mustered March 22, 1865; mustered out July 15, 1865.

William H. Sampson, corporal, Heavy Artillery, Company H; mustered September 13, 1864; reduced to ranks December 19, 1864; mustered out June 15, 1865.

Charles C. Seavey, Lebanon, First Regiment, Company K; mustered May 7, 1861; mustered out August 9, 1861; reënlisted, Sixteenth Regiment, Company A; sergeant; mustered October 16, 1862; mustered out August 20, 1863.

Thomas J. Scribner, Lebanon, Seventh Regiment, Company C; mustered November 15, 1861; discharged for disability August 15, 1862.

William H. Sanborn, Eighteenth Regiment, Company B; mustered September 13, 1864; discharged June, 1865.

Justus Sargent, enlisted in the band of the Fourth Vermont Regiment, September, 1861.

William A. Seavey, Lebanon, Sixth Regiment, Company A;

MAJ. N. H. RANDLETT.

mustered November 27, 1861; discharged at Newport News, Va., March 7, 1863.

Ezekiel Seynor, s., mustered August 20, 1864; branch of service unknown.

Alexander Sanborn, s., mustered August 22, 1864; branch of service unknown.

John Smathenes, s., United States Sharpshooters, Company F; mustered August 8, 1864.

Alfred Spencer, s.; mustered August 16, 1864; branch of service unknown.

William F. Strickland, United States Sharpshooters, Company F; mustered December 25, 1863; transferred to Fifth Regiment, January 30, 1865; mustered out June 28, 1865.

Joseph Sennott, Lebanon, First Regiment, Company K; mustered May 7, 1861; mustered out August 9, 1861.

Henry H. Smith, Lebanon, Fifth Regiment, Company E; mustered October 19, 1861; promoted sergeant; mustered out October 29, 1864.

William W. Scott, Lebanon, United States Sharpshooters, Company F; mustered November 26, 1861; musician; promoted sergeant; reënlisted December 22, 1863; discharged June 29, 1865; died at Lebanon, July 24, 1871. A good soldier.

Albert B. Stearns, Lebanon, Ninth Regiment, Company E; mustered August 8, 1862; wounded May 26, 1864; mustered out May, 1865.

John S. Short, Lebanon, Fifth Regiment, Company C; mustered October 12, 1861; reënlisted December 31, 1863; wounded June 3, 1864; mustered out June 28, 1865.

Thomas J. Sweat, Lebanon, Ninth Regiment, Company E; mustered August 8, 1862; died at Paris, Ky., October 2, 1863.

Orlando Sargent, Lebanon, Sixteenth Regiment, Company A; mustered October 16, 1862; mustered out August 20, 1863; reënlisted, Heavy Artillery, Company M, February 15, 1865; mustered out June 9, 1865.

Elias F. Smith, Lebanon, Sixteenth Regiment, Company A; commissioned November 4, 1862, captain; mustered out August 20, 1863; commissioned captain, Eighteenth Regiment, Company B, September 20, 1864; mustered out June 10, 1865.

Joseph Sherman, s., Third Regiment, Company G; mustered

November 19, 1863; wounded August 16, 1864; absent sick July 20, 1865; no discharge furnished.

Charles Smith, Seventh Regiment, Company C; mustered December 2, 1864; sick at Hampton Roads since January, 1865; no discharge furnished.

John Smith, s., Third Regiment, Company C; mustered November 12, 1863; deserted at Jacksonville, Fla., April, 1864.

James Schneider, s., Third Regiment, Company D; mustered October 14, 1863; killed at Drury's Bluff, Va., May 13, 1864.

James C. Salisbury, s., Fourth Regiment, Company K; mustered October 16, 1863; captured; died at Andersonville, Ga., August 12, 1864; grave No. 5,438.

Peter Shehan, s., Fourth Regiment, Company F; mustered October 19, 1863; mustered out August 23, 1865.

Alonzo Steele, s., Fourth Regiment, Company E; mustered October 19, 1863; wounded May 16, 1864; deserted at White House, Va.

Rheinhold Schom, s., Seventh Regiment, Company K; mustered October 30, 1863; promoted to corporal, June 30, 1864; mustered out June 30, 1865.

Henry Spaulding, s. d.; unknown.

Paul Steward, s., Second Regiment, Company I; mustered December 6, 1864; deserted at White House, Va., March 24, 1865.

John M. Thompson, Lebanon; enlisted Nov. 7, 1861, as private, Company E, Seventh Regiment; assigned to First Regiment, S. C. Volunteers, Nov. 28, 1862; transferred to Thirty-eighth Infantry, U. S. A., as second lieutenant, July, 1866, and to Twenty-fourth U. S. Infantry in 1869; retired as brigadier-general, 1904.

Edward L. Tascar, Lebanon, Seventh Regiment, Company C; mustered November 23, 1861; died of disease August 10, 1862, at Hilton Head.

Hiram H. Thomas, Lebanon, Cavalry, Company I; mustered December 17, 1861; blacksmith; reënlisted January 5, 1864; blacksmith; mustered out July 15, 1865.

George B. Tracy, Lebanon, Ninth Regiment, Company E; mustered August 8, 1862; corporal; promoted to sergeant. Sergeant Tracey's enlistment was from the highest principle after anxious and prayerful consideration. To the altar of his country he brought the highest social virtues and brightened all by the virtues of the true soldier. Modest, sincere, trustworthy, kind-hearted, he won an honorable name in his company and regiment. In a charge May 12, 1864, he was wounded. Left on the field for a time, he was rescued by his companions after forty hours of suffering, without care. He died at Washington June 6, 1864.

Kendall H. Thomas, Company A, Lebanon, Sixteenth Regiment; mustered October 16, 1862; mustered out August 20, 1863; reënlisted, First Cavalry; mustered March 26, 1864.

Peter Thompson, s. d., Fourth Regiment, Company E; mustered October 19, 1863; transferred to United States Navy, April 27, 1864.

Samuel Trevitt, s. d., Seventh Regiment, Company H; mustered October 26, 1863; died of accidental wounds, January 21, 1864.

Robert Thompson, s. d.; unknown.

Enos Thompson, s., Second Regiment, Company G; mustered December 3, 1864; mustered out December 19, 1865.

Frank Thomas, Lebanon, First Cavalry, Company L; mustered January 31, 1865; mustered out May 6, 1865.

James V. Toomy, s., Heavy Artillery, Company B; mustered December 3, 1864; mustered out September 11, 1865.

Nathaniel Taylor, Heavy Artillery, Company M; mustered December 2, 1864; deserted en route to regiment.

Melvin A. Tenny, Lebanon, First Battalion, New Hampshire Cavalry, Company I; mustered December 17, 1861; wagoner; discharged by order, October 8, 1863.

John Wilson, s., Third Regiment, Company C; mustered November 20, 1863; wounded May 10, 1864, and October 27, 1864; absent sick; no discharge furnished.

George Winters, s., Fifth Regiment, Company G; mustered November 19, 1863; deserted at Point Lookout, December 22, 1863.

James Wilson, s., Fourth Regiment, Company K; mustered October 15, 1863; promoted to corporal, transferred to United States Navy 27th, 1864.

Henry Williams, s. d., Fourth Regiment, Company H; mustered October 17, 1863; wounded May 15, 1864.

Augustus F. Wright, s. d., Seventh Regiment, Company I; mustered October 27, 1863; promoted corporal; wounded February 20, 1864, at Olustee and captured.

James Wood, s. d., Fourth Regiment, Company F; mustered October 17, 1863; transferred to United States Navy, April 27, 1864.

Corliss C. Wheeler, Company K, First Regiment, May 7, 1861; reënlisted August 9, 1863, Company B, Fifth Regiment; discharged for disability December 19, 1863.

Samuel G. West, s. d., Eighth Regiment, Company G; mustered November 3, 1863; deserted at New Orleans, La., August 27, 1864.

George White, s. d., Eighth Regiment, Company C; mustered November 4, 1863; deserted at New Orleans, La., March 2, 1864.

George Wood, Heavy Artillery, Company M; mustered December 5, 1864.

William S. Wood, Lebanon, United States Sharpshooters, Company F; mustered February 5, 1864; wounded May 6, 1864; transferred to Fifth Regiment, January 30, 1865; mustered out June 28, 1865.

Lewis Young, First Cavalry, Troop A; mustered March 10, 1864; sick since August 12, 1864; no discharge furnished.

Lewis Victor, s. d., Eighth Regiment, Company I; mustered November 9, 1863; deserted at Carrollton, La., July 10, 1864.

William H. H. Wilson, s.; mustered August 27, 1864; branch of service unknown.

Corliss C. Wheeler, Lebanon, First Regiment, Company K; mustered May 7, 1861; mustered out August 9, 1861; reënlisted Fifth Regiment, Company B, August 19, 1863; discharged for disability December 19, 1863.

Simeon Ward, Jr., Lebanon, Eighteenth Regiment, Company B; mustered September 13, 1864; mustered out June 10, 1865.

Richard W. Ward, Lebanon, Eighteenth Regiment, Company B; mustered September 13, 1864; mustered out June 10, 1865.

Lucius Welch, Lebanon, Eighth Regiment, Company H; mustered December 27, 1861; died at Camp Parapet, La., August 29, 1862.

Read J. Walker, Lebanon, United States Sharpshooters, Com-

CALL FOR TROOPS, SPANISH WAR.

pany F; mustered November 26, 1861; discharged for disability October 14, 1862.

John Williams, insurgent states, United States Sharpshooters, Company F; mustered August 6, 1864.

John H. White, Lebanon, Sixteenth Regiment, Company A; mustered October 16, 1862; died on his way home at Mound City, Illinois, August 12, 1863.

Edwin C. Whittaker, Sixteenth Regiment, Company A; mustered October 16, 1862; died of disease at New Orleans, 1863.

William Williams, s., Second Regiment, Company H; mustered November 11, 1863; promoted to corporal February 15, 1864; promoted to sergeant July 1, 1864; promoted sergeant-major May 22, 1865.

Thomas Williams, s., Third Regiment, Company E; mustered November 25, 1863; wounded slightly May 13, 1864; mustered out July 20, 1865.

STATE AID, &C.

Paid to families of Soldiers according to a law of this State for the year Ending March

1862	Paid	$609 32
1863		2651 33
1864		2188 70
1865		1830 60
1866		773 00
		———$8052 95

Expences incured in Enrolling Militia &c by order of the Governor.	$27 75
Expences incured in procuring Soldiers &c.	$843 29
	8923 99
Brought forward	62715 00
	$71638 99
	7750
Total	$79388 99

REIMBURSEMENT.

RECEIPTS.

1862	Received of State on a/c of aid to Soldiers families	1327 88
1863	" " " " " " " " " "	2526 14
"	" " " " for Bounties Refunded	3300 00

1864	"	" U. S. " "		. .	. 2046 00
"	"	" State on a/c of aid to families		. .	. 1915 75
"	"	" " for Bounties refunded		. .	. 3465 75
1865	"	" " " " "		. .	. 2028 33
"	"	" " " aid to Soldiers families		. .	. 1858 20
1866	"	" U. S. Bounties refunded		. .	. 1940 00
"	"	" State on aid to families		. .	. 340 00
1867	"	" U. S. Bounties refunded		. .	. 646 00
1868	"	" " " " "		. .	. 1200 00
1870	"	" " " " "		. .	. 672 00
1872	"	" Reimbursement of war Expenses		. .	. 15416 67
1873	"	" " " " "		. .	. 109 00
"	"	" U. S. Bounties Refunded		. .	. 143 20
1874	"	" " " "		. .	. 128 00

                                                                   39063 12

CENTENNIAL AND PATRIOTIC CELEBRATION.

(As published by the committee in 1861.)

July 4, 1861, the town of Lebanon was one hundred years old. Invitations had been sent to those who had gone from the town to return and unite with the people of the town in celebrating the day. A large number, considering the state of the country, accepted the invitation, and came once more to the place of their birth, renewing old acquaintances and reviving many pleasant memories of the past.

If we had been permitted to make our selection from all the fair days of the calendar, we could scarcely have suited ourselves better. The day was cloudless; abundant rains had insured us against dust. Perhaps we should have inserted a few whiffs from the North Pole to cool the air a little, but, then, we remembered that the heat was good for the corn, and it served to remind us of the endurance of our soldiers at the South and stir our sympathy for them.

The day was ushered in by a salute by thirteen guns, fired by a squad of nine cadets from Norwich University, under the command of Capt. A. B. Hutchinson.

These cadets did good service during the day, displayed high skill as artillerists, and won respect by their gentlemanly conduct.

The parade of the Horribles was a pleasant feature of the day.

The procession was formed at half-past nine, under the direction of Capt. E. A. Howe, chief marshal, and his assistants, Messrs. Shaw, Noyes and Randlett. Headed by the Lebanon Cornet Band and escorted by the Mascoma Engine Company, No. 2, and the Franklin Lodge of Masons, they marched around the Common to the stand for speaking.

Exercises on the Stand.

G. H. Lathrop, Esq., President of the Day.

The exercises were opened by a fervent prayer by Rev. George Storrs, from New York, a native of the town and a descendant of one of the early settlers.

2. Singing by a choir under the direction of Mr. J. M. Perkins, who during the day furnished excellent music.

3. Historical address by Rev. D. H. Allen, D. D., of Lane Seminary, Ohio, a native of the town.

4. A poem by Rev. C. H. Fay of Providence, R. I., also a native of the town.

5. Reading of the Declaration of Independence by Hon. A. H. Cragin.

6. Oration by Prof. J. W. Patterson of Dartmouth College.

At the close of the exercises on the stand, the procession re-formed and marched to the tent, prepared for the collation. When the head of the column reached the place, a slight *contre temps* occurred. The people were ready, but the dinner was not. Time, however, soon remedied this. Nearly four hundred and fifty took their seats at the tables. Rev. Dr. Lord implored the divine blessing. Of this part we have only to say that the good old dietetic rule was observed, "to leave off hungry."

Toasts and Speeches.

Rev. G. W. Bailey acted as toastmaster.

1. "Our Centennial Birthday—with all its pleasant and interesting associations."

2. "The Fourth of July, 1761—Lebanon a houseless wilderness; 1776—her noble sons rush to Lexington and Bunker Hill

to defend her rights; 1861—the wilderness has budded and blossomed."

The third toast was introduced by reading a letter from Barrett Potter, Esq., a son of the first minister of the town, Rev. Isaiah Potter. Mr. Potter is now in his 85th year. He gave at the close of his letter the following toast:

3. "The Early Settlers of Lebanon—Silas Waterman, William Dana, Charles Hill, William Downer, Levi Hyde, and Nathaniel Porter, the pioneers and first settlers in the town of Lebanon, who, with subsequent settlers in 1768, gathered and established the first church therein, and 1772 settled Rev. Isaiah Potter, the first ordained minister in said town."

Responded to by Rev. George Storrs, who said: "We have come to our native town once more, many of us from a distance. We find great changes. We find an improved country, forests are cleared away, new homes have sprung up. We find new modes of travel, the lightning-like speed of the railroads. It was not so with our fathers; they came by forest paths, upon ox-sleds, by boats on the river, where civilized foot had never before trod. They were superior men. I delight to recall their memory. Let the memory of our fathers be blessed; let it dwell in our minds. They came not only to plant colonies, not only to better their fortunes, but to plant temperance and religion and establish churches with their blessed influences. We should be deeply grateful to them. We should be deeply grateful to the first minister of the town, for his labors and influence. I shall never forget a single sentence that fell from his lips. All is held fast in my memory. When on one occasion he used the words, 'O Ephraim, how shall I give thee up,' they seemed to come to me and say, 'O George, how shall I give thee up.' They were blessed and fruitful words in me. Honor and success followed him. Let his mantle fall upon his successors."

4. "The Sons of Lebanon, at Home and Abroad." Responded to by Rev. C. H. Fay, who said:

"I am to speak of the sons absent and present. It is not a poetical theme. You will not expect me to speak in rhyme. If it had been the daughters of Lebanon, I could not have avoided rhyme, so inspiring is such a subject. I have but a slight knowledge of the absent sons. I have met them occasionally. They all seem to be doing well, to bring credit to the place that gave them birth. You have a good specimen of them in the orator of the day. Of those at home, what shall I say? The scene before me reminds me of the progress we have made in one cardinal virtue—Temperance. O those old Fourths of July! With their wine and spirits, and women banished from the tables, because they were not fit places and scenes for them. But now we find wine banished and women admitted. They are far more inspiring than wine.

"Let me tell you a story, related to me by one of the fathers, showing the advance temperance has made in the town, and how they managed in the old times. It was the custom for a neighborhood to select one of their number to take their produce to market,—their butter, cheese, beef, pork, etc. He went 'below' (that is to Boston) for the rest. If successful, he was gone about a fortnight. He was always commissioned to bring back a cask of rum or brandy. On one occasion a number of neighbors were assembled in an orchard. It was in the Jefferson campaign— they were talking politics. Of course the word 'federalist' occurred frequently. One said to another, when he had attempted to use the word, 'What do you say fetherlist for,—why don't you say feth-fetherlist?' 'Oh, you can't say it yourself. I can say fetherlist as well as you. Others tried the word with about the same success. After testing themselves by this novel shibboleth, they concluded that they were not quite sober. And now I trust that you, their sons, will always be able to say 'federalist,'—that none of you will ever be in a condition to say 'fetherlist.'

"Of the sons at home, I conceive that they are much like the man's nigh ox. He had a yoke to sell. He praised the off one highly, and at great length. Finally the purchaser said, 'Why don't you say something of the nigh ox?' 'O, he can speak for himself.'"

5. "To those who, not having the good fortune to be born in town, have endeavored to retrieve their fortunes by taking a

wife who was." Responded to by Rev. Dr. Swain of Providence, R. I., who said:

"I am one of the unfortunates not born in Lebanon. I plead guilty to the misfortune, to the crime, if it is a crime, of not having the wisdom to be born here. But with my folly, I have mingled wisdom, for I have taken a wife that 'was.' The 'was' is emphatic, 'who was born here.' But I have some pleas to offer in extenuation of my misfortune, of my crime, if it was a crime. The privileges of a son-in-law are often found to be greater than those of a son. My misfortune might have been greater, for if I did not have the good fortune to be born in Lebanon, I have 'retrieved my fortune by taking a wife who was.' I might have had the double misfortune of not being born here, or finding 'a wife who was.' So I have mingled good with evil, wisdom with folly. In these days of secession, let me say: The daughters of Lebanon, 'the cedars of Lebanon,' let not wife, nor mother, nor daughter of them all, ever be found a *se-cedar!* Let them love and defend our institutions to the last generation. May their posterity equal and surpass their ancestry."

6. "The Clergymen of Lebanon." Responded to by Rev. Mr. Case of West Lebanon, who said:

"This at least merits large notice. The subject is an extensive one, for the clergymen were many; it is at least a lofty subject, for the first three ministers of the town taken together measured some inches over eighteen feet. They were high priests. I mention it as a significant fact, that the clergymen of Lebanon were ever devoted to temperance. Considering the customs of former times, it is wonderful that no more ministers fell into intemperance. The records of another town show that in a population of six hundred and forty, forty barrels of rum were used in a year, besides other liquors. Every man in old times would think himself wanting in hospitality if he did not place a bottle before the minister when he called. Considering their temptations, they escaped wonderfully. Of the ministers of Lebanon, it may be said of them, that they have ever been loyal. The first of them all set a good example to the rest. For when the country was struggling for independence, he went out to encourage and comfort her troops as a chaplain. He was a strong man. A little story will show this. Passing through the camp one day, he saw two men trying to lift a cannon. Taking hold of it alone, he easily lifted it to its place. One of the men, in his astonishment, let slip an oath, when the other silenced him by telling that he was a chaplain, when he hastened after him and begged pardon for his profanity.

"It is a significant fact that in the first records of the town we trace their anxiety for a ministry among them. It shows the love of our fathers for these institutions which have so much to do with our prosperity. Lebanon ranks high in the number and quality of the ministers she has raised up. About thirty have gone forth from her. Among them have been doctors of divinity who have made their mark in the world. Others have found and filled worthy places in colleges and theological seminaries. One is buried in a foreign land, who went forth as a missionary to the heathen. Let the next one hundred years equal the past."

7. "The Lawyers of Lebanon." Lebanon has not been very fruitful in this class, and none were found to respond.

8. "Dr. Phineas Parkhurst and the Physicians of Lebanon." Responded to by Dr. Dixi Crosby, who said:

"Dr. Parkhurst was born in Plainfield, Conn. Early in life he removed to Royalton. Like other young men he went a-courting, and stayed on one occasion to breakfast. During the meal he saw Indians approaching. He immediately went out and caught the Narragansett mare, and helping his lady-love and her mother to mount, got up behind them and set out for the Connecticut River. The Indians followed and fired upon them, wounding Parkhurst, the ball passing through from behind and lodging in the skin before. He seized it in his fingers and held it till he arrived in West Lebanon, when it was extracted by Dr. Hall. This incident first turned the thoughts of Parkhurst to the practice of medicine. He became an apprentice of Dr. Hall, for so they termed students in those days. In due time he began to practise, his first case being in a department in which he was afterwards very successful—obstetrics. More than three thousand received their introduction into the world by him. In due time he married—for money it is supposed—the portion of his wife consisting of one cow, three cups and three knives. He first lived in West Lebanon and knew what it was to be poor—often with but two shirts, and one white cravat, to which he was very partial, which was washed over night. But success and prosperity came in due season.

"As a physician Dr. Parkhurst was not learned, but skillful by experience. After listening on one occasion to the learned talk of some of his brethren, he said: 'I am much gratified with all I have heard; I can't talk, but, by Judas, I can practise with the best of you!' As a physician he was skillful, prompt, self-denying, always ready at call, night or day, in cold or heat. He was noted for his unbounded hospitality; the string was ever hanging out at his door. He was the father of a large family—two sons and nine daughters. He exemplified the great precept of religion—beneficence towards his fellow-men. Those who have succeeded him have been worthy and skillful members of his profession."

9. "Dartmouth College became the Alma Mater of fifty-four sons of Lebanon." Responded to by President Lord of Dartmouth College, who said:

"A respectable clergyman of Hanover was asked to give a short extempore address. He replied that it was impossible; 'I must write everything. Why, if I should find that I had forgotten to write "Amen" at the close of my sermon, I should faint away.' I am very much like him. Absurd and ridiculous as it may appear (pulling out his manuscript), I must resort to my notes.

"Mr. President, I acknowledge the great courtesy which gives me this occasion to commemorate a remarkable fact in the history of Lebanon, viz.: That there have been raised up fifty-four sturdy men, each of whom was born of two mothers. I am still more glad to say that these two prolific mothers are yet in their bloom, and their offspring is likely to be indefinitely increased, till I know not but they will be sufficient to found a nation; particularly as these remarkable children are all sons who are very apt to marry in the family. At least the sisters find Swains without going abroad to visit.

"But, Mr. President, I better like your courtesy, because it proves that Lebanon is not disposed to appropriate all the honor of sending out into the world such a noble company of educated men. The natural mother divides credit with the foster mother. This is well, and speaks well—so let it be. What Lebanon has brought forth Dartmouth has nourished, to become an ornament to both and a blessing to the world.

"Mr. President, I cannot speak from the book, but I think that your good town of Lebanon must have produced a larger number of educated men than any other town of our educating state. I will not even except the larger commercial, political and manufacturing towns. But, however, it must have exceeded other towns of the same age and population. She deserves to bear the banner, and I trust the banner will be flung here to the breeze, at your next centennial, July 4, 1961—in a time of peace and glory, inscribed to learning, wisdom and virtue—the guide and safety of the state. Sir, I am aware that every man who happens to be born in Lebanon and educated at Dartmouth does not thereby necessarily gain for himself, his town, or college, a true honor.

"I cannot deem that Lebanon or Dartmouth, or any other town or college would choose, in all cases, to recognize the parental relation. I remember what happened at a time when I was a boy. A young man from a neighboring town was sent to Harvard. No matter what his name—let us call him Simplon. He proved to be what students frequently make a subject of their good-natured, but sometimes extravagant sport. His father's house was on the line of Kittery and York, and that line bisected it. It was a problem at college in which end of the house Simplon was born, and hence some lively classmate gave out the following epigram:

> "Kittery and York, 'tis said,
> For Simplon's birth contest;
> The strife is sharp, and Kittery wins.
> But York comes off the best."

"Now it is not my opinion that Lebanon or Dartmouth has ever given occasion for quite such pleasantry as this. Or, if it were so, I should not choose to speak of it in such a company. I have to say what is to better purpose, viz: That your list of graduates is one of which any town or college may be proud. It were impossible to speak of them now in detail. But they would bear the criticism of the world; from those old schoolmen, dead, the Woods and Harrises, who have left a shining mark in the history of their times, down to the Mediaeval period of her Young, and the living men so well represented by the honored and beloved orator of the day. Had Lebanon and Dartmouth done no more than to send out such a company, that alone would make them worthy of record among the true benefactors of mankind.

Mr. President, we joyfully this day cement the fellowship and friendship of Lebanon and Dartmouth. I speak for Dartmouth. Send us still your young men and we will nourish them. That kind of patronage is not all we want, but it tells most upon the world. It is better even than wild lands—though possibly not better than would be the confidence and rational patronage of the state. But let what will betide, Dartmouth will be for the state, and the whole of it; not for sect or party, but mankind."

10. "The Farmers and Mechanics of Lebanon—none better." Responded to, in behalf of the farmers, by Daniel Richardson, Esq., who said:

"Now you will see the difference between knowledge and ignorance"—alluding to the learned gentleman who preceded him. "I have been a farmer all my life, and have not had the advantages of education. I cannot make a speech. I may say in behalf of the farmers, that we are under great obligations to them. They have cleared away the forests, subdued the wild soil, and brought it into the service of man—made room for these many pleasant homes. It is the ambition of farmers to raise the largest ox, the best horse, the fattest hog, or largest crop. In old times they took pride in one other thing—in raising up the largest and best families. Let their posterity imitate them."

For the mechanics, Mr. L. F. Brooks—one of them—briefly responded with a handsome tribute to their skill.

11. "The President of the United States." In response to this toast, Hon. A. H. Cragin spoke as follows:

"The President of the United States is the legal and constitutional head of the government. He is the agent of the people

—the executive of the Constitution and laws, and as such, is entitled to respect. The present Chief Magistrate was elected by a constitutional vote, in due form of law, and is therefore as justly entitled to administer the government as ever was Washington or Jackson. He has his commission from the same authority, and is alike responsible. He is clothed with all the powers conferred by the Constitution, and is under the most solemn oath to preserve, protect and defend that Constitution. It is manifestly the duty of those whose agent he is, at all times to aid the President in the discharge of his proper duties, and to strengthen and uphold his hands in support of the government which he is called upon to administer.

"The present occupant of the presidential chair entered upon the discharge of his duties under the most extraordinary and trying circumstances. Dissatisfied with the result of the late presidential election, a portion of the people in the Southern States, regardless of their constitutional obligations, defied the will of the majority, and were conspiring to destroy the government. They had boldly raised the flag of rebellion and resistance. Men were in arms against the government that had so long afforded them protection. Treason was doing its work. Forts had been captured, arsenals had been plundered of arms and munitions of war; national ships had been seized and employed by the insurgents; treasuries and mints with vast sums of money had been embezzled and appropriated for the support of rebellion; the national flag had been insulted, and the Union pronounced a curse. Such was the state of things, and worse than this, when Abraham Lincoln was inaugurated President of the United States.

"He appealed to the reason and patriotism of the misguided people, and by the memories of the past, the hopes of the future, and the graves of the patriotic dead, called upon all true citizens to rally in support of the Union and the laws of the land. His patriotic and paternal appeal was derided by the traitors. The government paused, while the work of destroying the Union went on. The gallant little band in Fort Sumter, hemmed in by a wall of iron batteries, were on the point of starvation. The government at the last moment resolved to supply the fort with provisions. When this purpose became known, ten thousand rebels opened deadly fire upon less than one hundred starving defenders of the Union. The fort surrendered, but instantly the country was aroused. The war for the Union began. The President called for 75,000 volunteers, and forthwith they were ready. More were called for, and today 300,000 men are under arms for the defence of the Union. The spectacle of the uprising of the people is truly magnificent. The North is nearly a unit in their patriotic efforts to support the President in his determination to preserve the Union. Party lines are obliterated and all classes vie with each other in their zeal to maintain the government. There is but one voice heard, and that is, that the Union 'must and shall be preserved.'

"This government was formed after great sacrifice, and at a very great cost. We have been accustomed to applaud its founders, as wise and patriotic men, and to cherish the inheritance which they left us, as of priceless value. It has already performed a great mission, but its work is only begun. To the union of these States, the nation owes its unprecedented increase in population, its surprising development of material resources, its rapid augmentation of wealth, its happiness at home and its honor abroad. The light of our example has illumined the whole earth, and today the hopes of the world for the preservation of liberty and free government center in the preservation of this Union. God helping us, we will preserve it.

"If this Union perish now, it will be the most stupendous failure that the world ever saw; and it must be inferred that our national sins have become so great in the eyes of heaven, that God can no longer withhold his vengeance.

"Trusting that the same wise Providence which sanctioned the work of our fathers in the Revolution, has much to accomplish for his own glory and the benefit of mankind through the instrumentality of this government, I believe the Union will be preserved.

"I am inclined to believe that the purposes of God are visible in this causeless rebellion. There is no accounting for it from the usual motives for human actions. 'Whom the gods destroy they first make mad,' is a familiar adage. I accept the fact as the manifest work of Providence, and fully believe it portends no ultimate evil to our country, or the inalienable rights of man."

COL. HENRY L. KENDRICK.

12. "The Stars and Stripes." "They have floated over our cradles—let it be our prayer and our endeavor that they shall float over our graves." Song by Messrs. Ingalls and Alden, Mrs. Davis and Miss Porter—"Star Spangled Banner."

13. "The staple products of New England:

> Land—hard to till, and piled with granite gray,
> Men—hard to kill, harder to drive away."

VOLUNTEER TOASTS.

By Robert Kimball, Esq. "The memory of Stephen A. Douglas."

> "Brief and eventful was his bold career,
> An iron will, a soul devoid of fear;
> Wrong—he perchance has been in time now past;
> Right—minds like his will surely prove at last."

"Lebanon and Hartford chartered the same day; settled by liberty-loving pioneers from the same town in Connecticut, situated side by side in the same charming valley; may their united devotion to the great interests of religion and constitutional freedom be as constant as the flow of the noble river which beautifies their banks." Responded to by D. B. Dudley of Hartford, Vt.

Letters were received from many gentlemen, natives of the town, expressing their interest in the celebration, and regretting their inability to share in the occasion. From Rev. E. L. Magoon, of Albany; from Maj. Henry L. Kendrick of West Point, offering the following sentiment: "My native town. Her children rise up to do her honor and reverence." From John Potter, Esq., of Augusta, Me., with the sentiment: "The land where our venerated forefathers sleep, and the cherished birthplace of their descendants. Let liberty and union be forever inscribed upon her annals, and preserved as a precious inheritance to the latest generation by her sons." From Mr. J. A. Durkee, Esq., of New York: "The Star-Spangled Banner and the next Centennial Anniversary. May the rays of the sun which rises on the next centennial anniversary, shine upon that banner with its stripes unsullied and stars undimmed; waving over a happy people, bound by no chain but the silken cord of brotherly affection, and no bond but peace, no creed but love to God and goodwill to men." Also letters from H. R. Stevens, Esq., and William D. Ticknor, of Boston, and Capt. James Benton of the U. S. Army. At a late hour the company broke up after singing "Old Hundred."

Committee of arrangements: E. P. Liscomb, C. C. Benton, John Clough, Rufus Case; Samuel Wood, 2d, William S. Ela, Solon A. Peck, selectmen; Oliver L. Stearns; Charles A. Downs, George W. Bailey, Secretaries.

MEMORIAL BUILDING.

The men and women of Lebanon never faltered in times of war, and the records of both state and nation give evidence that in no place have the people shown greater patriotism.

When the great struggle for the maintenance of the Union was ended, there was early discussion as to what form a fitting memorial to the town's heroes should take, it being admitted that some lasting monument to the memory of heroic deeds must be provided. During the period immediately following the war for the Union, memorials took the form of granite or marble shafts, as a general rule, and monuments of this type were erected by towns and cities throughout the country, and such a monument to be erected on the Common (Colburn Park) was talked of, and by many considered the most appropriate.

The first tangible movement towards the erection of a monument of any particular kind, was started by Elisha P. Liscomb, then postmaster at the center village. Mr. Liscomb had served as commissioner to look after the welfare of the soldiers in the field, and had himself lost a gallant son at the front, and being moreover an ardent patriot, he was aggressive in having public sentiment aroused to the point that needed funds would be forthcoming. He proposed a metallic or zinc shaft on the common, and secured contributions of one dollar each from about one hundred persons, which sum was afterwards turned over to the Memorial Building Fund. It will be observed that the amount mentioned was small, which is accounted for from the fact that the people generally believed some other memorial would be more suitable. While discussion of the subject was carried on inter-

LAYING CORNER STONE MEMORIAL BUILDING.

SERGT. JESSE E. DEWEY.

mittently for some years following Mr. Liscomb's efforts, the matter was not forgotten, and finally crystallized into a well-defined plan, suggested by Capt. Nathan H. Randlett and Sergt. Jesse E. Dewey, both of whom were literally men of '61 and in actual service at the very beginning of the war. These gentlemen presented their proposal to have a Memorial Building, to a group of their comrades, who had casually met at the postoffice in August, 1881. The plan met with the universal endorsement of those present, and the following agreement was then and there signed:

Lebanon, N. H., August 25, 1881.

We, the undersigned, veterans of the late war, earnestly desiring the erection of some suitable memorial to perpetuate the memory of voluntary sacrifices, by our Citizen Soldiery, to the grand idea, that governments are made for the people, and which may be of benefit not only to ourselves, but to our posterity, do hereby agree to give the sum set opposite our names, for the erection of a memorial building, within the village of Lebanon, which shall include a Memorial Hall, where may be gathered, such relics of the late war, as may be voluntarily contributed, and tablets which shall contain the names of those of our comrades who participated with honor in achieving a final victory for the Union, and in which shall be a suitable library free to all, under such restrictions, as the town of Lebanon or its duly authorized agents may from time to time deem it expedient to make. Provided a sum sufficient for the erection and completion of said building shall be raised, either by subscription or vote of the town.

N. H. Randlett	$20.00
Ferdinand Davis	20.00
Alpheus W. Baker	20.00
Jesse E. Dewey	20.00
O. W. Baldwin	20.00
O. J. Muchmore	20.00
A. W. Shapleigh	20.00
W. S. Carter	20.00

The signers of this agreement were all influential citizens, and the Memorial Building idea was at once accepted as the solution of the long-deferred problem. Young and old at once set out to provide ways and means to carry out the project, and it was not long before the people were aroused to the needs of the hour, albeit there were some who found excuse for declining to help on the ground that a monument on the common would cost less to maintain; then it was that the influence and labors of those interested in having a public library made their efforts felt, and it was clearly shown that something besides a memorial to the soldiers was to be realized by the plans of its projectors.

A Building Association was organized with the following officers: President, Rev. Charles A. Downs; Vice-President, J. D. Hosley; Treasurer, J. E. Dewey; Secretary, A. W. Baker; Board of Trustees, A. M. Shaw, D. W. Marston, O. W. Baldwin, C. B. Plastridge, Frank C. Churchill and Ferdinand Davis, and later a building committee consisting of Frank C. Churchill, Alpheus W. Baker and Ferdinand Davis was chosen. Ferdinand Davis was selected as architect, and he presented several plans, the most desirable one being reluctantly rejected by the trustees for want of funds to carry the same into effect.

During the early struggles to erect the building no one dared hope with the then prevailing sentiment outside the village, that the town would appropriate funds towards the building, but this was, however, brought about later, and the town voted in all the sum of $3,580. The Tenney house and lot on the north side of the common was bought for $3,200, and the buildings thereon and a part of the land was sold by the trustees for $1,400, so the real cost of the lot used for the building was $1,800.

Were it possible to do so, probably it is not altogether best that a full list of donors be published at this time. Many contributed liberally in cash, numerous persons giving one hundred dollars each, while others gave but little in money, but by their energy and helpful suggestions aided greatly, as did others who gave freely of their time and their skill; all these things being needed, it may be said that each did his part. As showing something of the spirit of the times it is worthy of record that the very first *cash* contribution came from a fair held by the two grandchildren of Mrs. Joseph W. Gerrish, viz: Joseph W. Gerrish, 2d, and his sister, Helen M. Gerrish, neither of whom could have been over five or six years old, but their fair raised the sum of one dollar which went towards the building. Other young people also gave the proceeds of entertainments, one being the Appollo Club, which gave $6.20; Granite Hook and Ladder Co. gave $25, and the Acrasian Skating Club gave $55.05, with a stipulation that it could be "used for Memorial Building only." The ladies gifted in music—and Lebanon has always had many—gave a grand concert in Lebanon and another at the College Church in Hanover, from which they secured $270.05, following which the men, not wishing to be wholly outdone, also gave a concert and realized $126.82. These concerts were in 1884 and the entire receipts given in aid of the building, the men gracefully acknowledging that the ladies had outdone them after all. The largest contribution came from the profits of a grand fair held for several days in the town hall, in the winter of 1884, from which $944.15 was raised, and it may be said that almost everybody in town contributed something to this fair, either directly or indirectly, as the attendance was large.

In the spring of 1886 a sufficient sum of money had been pledged to warrant the building committee to begin operations, and by vote of the trustees the Grand Lodge of Free and Accepted Masons were invited to lay the corner-stone, which was graciously accepted, and the ceremonies took place on May 30 of that year in the presence of thousands of interested spectators. The superstructure was completed during that year, when for want of funds the work ceased. At last there was a decided change in sentiment, and the town voted the necessary money, already referred to, to complete the building. In the summer of 1890 the officers of the New Hampshire Department, Grand Army of the Republic, kindly consented to perform the dedicatory service of that fraternity, by invitation of the trustees, and the occasion was celebrated July 4, 1890, when the whole town took part in making the event a success. In addition to the ceremonies of the G. A. R. ritual, appropriate exercises were conducted in the town hall, where Capt. J. E. Dewey presided and Rev. C. A. Downs delivered an oration. A dinner was served and numerous distinguished guests were present. As a part of the dedication program, Hon. Frank C. Churchill, chairman, and in behalf of the building committee, addressed the chairman of the board of selectmen in the following language:

"Mr. Chairman of the Board of Selectmen: In April, 1882, the first steps were taken looking to the erection of the memorial structure which we have today assembled to dedicate. The Memorial Building Association was at once formed and subscriptions solicited for the purpose. After a sufficient sum had been pledged to warrant it, a building committee was elected consisting of Lieuts. Ferdinand Davis, Alpheus Baker, and myself. It is needless to recite the many obstacles that confronted the committee. They were indeed many, and at times discouraging. We will simply say that after the town had appropriated $3,000 our citizens took hold of the work of raising the necessary additional funds with a zeal and determination worthy of the town in which we live.

"The corner-stone was laid by the Grand Lodge F. and A. Masons of the State of New Hampshire on Memorial Day, 1886. Hon. A. M. Shaw was president of the day and Rev. Charles A. Downs delivered an oration, and I may say the whole town took part in the exercises. After a struggle of five years the building was completed. It is a substantial edifice, well calculated to last for a long period of years, and suited, we believe, to the purposes for which it was designed. About two-thirds of the money used has been raised by subscription. The town made a second appropriation in 1889, amounting to $580. Its total cost, including land, has been $9,239.26, and every dollar expended is supported by itemized vouchers, which at the proper time we desire to turn over to the trustees of the building elected at the annual town meeting held in March, 1890, and we respectfully ask an audit of our account. The building was designed by one of our associates, Ferdinand Davis. The foundations were laid by W. W. Thompson and M. A. Northrop. The timber was furnished by L. E. Hilliard and the framing was superintended by Nathan W. Morse. The roof is probably the strongest of any building of its size in New Hampshire. The bricks were made by Jason Densmore and laid under the superintendence of Sylvester Austin. The slating was done by J. H. Orcutt of Northfield, Vt. The inside finish was put in by Muchmore & Whipple and Miner & Bucklin under the direction of Carlos Dyer. This work and the stair work, done by Harlan P. Goodrich, are models of their kind. The painting was done by W. H. Morris. The furnace was bought at a reduced price of C. M. Baxter. The Memorial windows were presented by friends of distinguished Lebanon soldiers. Nearly all materials and labor have been furnished by artisans and merchants of our own town. In employing workmen veteran soldiers have invariably been given the preference. I believe, sir, that the long wait since the close of the war before erecting a monumental structure has come more from a profound desire to have an appropriate memorial than from feelings of indifference or neglect of duty on the part of the generous and patriotic citizens of Lebanon. And now, Mr. Chairman, having to the best of our ability performed the duties assigned us, nothing remains for the committee but to ask your acceptance of our work and to place in your hands the keys to the building." (Delivering the keys.)

The building lot was purchased by the Building Association, and the title held by that organization up to July 29, 1891, when it was deeded to the town with the following limitations and conditions: "That the above described premises shall be forever preserved for a Soldiers' Memorial, for a Free Public Library and for a place for meeting for veteran soldiers and sons of veterans, and for only such purposes as shall preserve the memory of patriots and teach coming generations loyalty and devotion to their country."

The Lebanon Soldiers' Memorial Building was the first to be erected in New Hampshire.

The *Granite State Free Press*, in its issue of July 11, 1890, gave a very full account of the dedication of the Memorial Building.

The Village Fire Precinct and Great Fire of 1887.

State of New Hampshire.

To the Inhabitants of the town of Lebanon in the County of Grafton in said State qualified to vote in town affairs and resident in the territory hereinafter described viz: Commencing at the South East corner of Uriah Amsden's (H B. Bentons) home farm, thence running easterly to the 4th N H Turnpike (so called); thence by the south side of said road to the North East corner of W. K. Eldridge's Benton lot; thence Westerly by said Eldridge's land to the road leading from Lebanon Center Village to Dartmouth College; thence Westerly to the North East corner of J. W. Pecks; thence Westerly to the North West corner of said Peck's farm; thence South Westerly to the Staple Bridge (so called and Mascoma River; thence up said river on the South side of O. W. Websters land (now F B. Kendricks); thence Southerly to the South West corner of said Webster's land thence Easterly to the South East corner of Mrs Fanny White's land   thence Easterly to the place of beginning.

You are hereby notified to meet at the Town House in said town on Tuesday the 25th instant at 2 o'clock p. m. to act on the following subjects

1st to choose a Moderator

2d To see if the Inhabitants living within the bounds of the above described territory will adopt an Act for making farther provisions for the extinguishment of fires approved July 6 1849

Given under our hands and seal this eighth day of September A. D. 1849

William Cole } Selectmen
Samuel Wood 2d } of
Abel Low Jr } Lebanon

A True copy   Geo. S. Kendrick Clerk

At a legal meeting duly notified and holden at the Town House in Lebanon, County of Grafton on the 25th day of September A. D. 1849, the legal voters, residents within the territory described by the Selectmen of said Lebanon in their warrant dated September 8th 1849, by major vote

1st chose Abram Pushee Moderator, who being present took the oath of office by law prescribed

2 Chose George S. Kendrick Clerk

3. Voted to adopt the Act entitled "An act making further provisions for the extinguishing of fires"

4 Voted to adjourn this meeting, to meet at the same place (The Town House in Lebanon) Saturday, October 6th 1849, at 7 o'clock P. M.

George S. Kendrick, Clerk.

1849 Oct. 6. Met agreeably to adjournment, and 1st Geo. S. Kendrick being present took the oath of office by law prescribed

2 Voted to hear the report of a Committee upon the expence of a fire engine and apparatus

3 Voted to accept the report

4 Voted to raise the sum of $700. for the purpose of purchasing an engine and all suitable apparatus.

5. Voted that this meeting be dissolved

Geo. S. Kendrick.

This was the beginning of a separate organization for the extinguishment of fires. Its powers were somewhat limited and not well defined. The meetings were called by the selectmen for some time after the organization.

At a meeting held December 3, 1849, the precinct again voted to raise the sum of $700, to purchase a fire engine, hose and other necessary apparatus, and building a house for the same for the use of the precinct. Hiram A. Simons, E. J. Durant and John Burnham were appointed a committee to carry out the wishes of the precinct.

At a meeting held December 25, 1849, "Voted to raise $300 in addition to the $700, to purchase an Engine and apparatus."

The time of the annual meeting was voted to be on the first Wednesday after the second Tuesday of March.

At a meeting held on the 9th day of November 1854 the Precinct voted to refer the question of an Engine House and land, additional Hose and repairs, to a Committee to report at an adjourned meeting W. N. Baker, E. J. Darant and Lorin Smith to be the Committee

Nov. 16 1854, heard the report of the Committee and voted to raise the sum of six hundred dollars for the purchase of additional Hose, procuring by lease or by building an Engine House.

J. H. Kendrick, Lorin Smith, and J. C. Sturtevant appointed a Committee to carry out these votes. Meeting adjourned to Dec 7 1854

From this time onward to about 1869 little can be learned from the records. An engine was purchased with hose, and an engine house built upon the ground now occupied by the present house, and various other provisions made or projected to increase protection against fires.

Meetings of the precinct were called by the selectmen, and the same authority appointed the fire wards.

In 1868 the precinct was incorporated under the provisions of what is known as the Keene Act. The precinct was organized under this act at a meeting called by the selectmen for August 24, 1869. F. A. Cushman chosen moderator. The fire wards were J. C. Sturtevant, Solomon Cole, P. E. Davis, W. S. Moses, M. P. Durkee, W. N. Baker, C. C. Benton.

Something of the conditions of the precinct property may be gathered from the following report:

Engine House 18x30 one story high in good condition except the under pinning which is a very poor condition and the grading in front needs repairing. One Hose Cart One Fire Engine in good condition. 200 feet of new hose in good condition 50 feet lengths 300 feet of old, as good as could be expected. 50 feet, old, 25 ft Lengths one hose cart in good condition. One stove, two lanterns O C.

Signed N. B. Marston Foreman

Also two ladders, one of which was out of repair; two hooks, one in bad condition.

A committee, called a water committee, began a report which continued for several meetings. The purpose of this committee was to find or make a supply of water to use for extinguishing fires. In the course of their investigations they asked and receeived one hundred dollars to enable them "to employ a practical engineer to make surveys, give distances, etc."

At a meeting held October 18, 1869, the precinct voted to purchase a force pump, forty-five rods of suitable iron pipe to lay from the river to the park, and hydrants to be attached to the same; to purchase 500 feet of hose, with the necessary couplings and nozzles; to purchase five ladders, three roof ladders, 100 feet 1½-inch rope, necessary hooks and pikes; to provide a place to keep the same; to defray the necessary expense to ditch and lay said pipe, and put said pump in good running order, all to be done in two months from the date of the meeting.

They also voted to raise three thousand dollars to carry to completion all these projects.

C. C. Benton and P. E. Davis and Solomon Cole were appointed the agents of the precinct to superintend the work.

This committee was authorized to hire the three thousand dollars for twelve months upon precinct notes. L. C. Pattee and J. W. Gerrish offered in the meeting to loan the money at six per cent interest, payable in gold, and principal in currency, which offer was gladly accepted.

After several adjournments, January 10, 1870, the above committee made a report of their work, from which it appears that the expense of the pump, iron pipe, ditching, etc., was $1,549.83.

We learn also that cement was used in the joints of the pipe, which upon trial proved insufficient, when the pump was disconnected from the pipe and 650 feet of hose attached with which several trials were made as to the power of the pump, which proved satisfactory in part only. It was found that the pump was lacking in power. It appears that the work was done at great disadvantage from the lateness of the season. The hose was not purchased by the committee.

At the annual meeting held 1870, a petition from the members of Mascoma Fire Engine Co., No. 2, asking for the building of a new engine house and hall suitable for the company to meet in for the transaction of general business was presented. Upon this petition a committee of investigation was appointed—P. E. Davis and W. N. Baker—and the meeting adjourned for two weeks. The records are silent as to this meeting.

The next meeting was called, upon petition, by the selectmen, to be held August 13, 1870. For some reason which does not appear the preceding meeting was illegal. New officers were chosen. The committee which had reported the January preceding, made an additional report, from which it appears that the iron pipe had been relaid. Upon trial of the pump the system proved entirely satisfactory, throwing on the common two streams equal to two fire engines.

It was also voted to authorize the selectmen to levy and collect a tax in the precinct amounting to eighteen hundred dollars.

A resolution offered by E. H. Cheney inaugurating the attempt to find a full and reliable supply of water for the precinct. The provision of the resolution was as follows:

A Committee to be elected by ballot whose duty should be to secure the services of a competent and disinterested Engineer not a resident of the town to make surveys of several proposed routes and plans for supplying the Precinct with water including Stony Brook and Enfield Pond; the practibility of supplying water by hydraulic rams force pumps to a reservoir on the hill East of the Village, to make careful estimates of each plan, report of the whole to be submitted to an adjourned meeting.

The sum of three hundred dollars to be appropriated to pay the expense

The committee elected were William Duncan, P. E. Davis and L. C. Pattee.

At the same meeting the fire wards were authorized to buy 500 feet of hose, and give the precinct's note for the amount expended.

The force pump was located in Hall's mill, now W. F. Shaw's.

At an adjourned meeting September 3, 1870, the committee reported progress and the meeting adjourned for four weeks. Adjournments continued to October 24, 1870, when P. B. Sawyer of Manchester, the engineer employed, read his report, which the precinct accepted and ordered a vote of thanks. Some difficulties about the location of the force pump and the use of a wheel to operate it having arisen, a committee was appointed to confer with Mr. Hall.

Also voted that the committee be instructed to report upon the probable expense of building reservoirs in all parts of the precinct, and supplying them with water for fire purposes.

At an adjourned meeting held November 5, 1870, Mr. Duncan reported that ten cisterns would be necessary for use of the precinct at a cost of forty dollars each. It was voted that the pump system be adopted; that is, that the cisterns should be filled by pumping water from the river.

It was further voted that the sum of fifteen thousand dollars be raised to carry into effect this and other votes of the meeting, including the construction of ten iron cisterns, but at a subsequent meeting the whole action was annulled. The committee reported their action with Mr. Hall, and the precinct voted to pay him one hundred and fifty dollars.

The affairs of the precinct seem to have fallen into confusion at this time, approaching disorganization. No meetings were held until the 26th of September, 1871, when a meeting was called by the selectmen, upon petition, to choose all necessary officers and for other purposes, especially to consider the financial condition of the precinct.

The officers were duly chosen, the finances discussed, and adjournment followed to September 29, 1871. The clerk was directed to make such arrangements with holders of notes against the precinct as he could best do, either by extension of the notes or borrowing money to pay them.

A resolution was also adopted to introduce running water to be stored in a reservoir on the hill east of the village.

A meeting was called October 17, 1871, to act upon the following articles:

1. To adopt the Act of 1868, to enable the precinct to establish water-works.

2. To choose a committee of five to carry out the provisions of the resolutions adopted at the previous meeting.

3. To authorize the board of fire wards to erect a hose tower.

The first article received a negative vote. The second and third were passed, and the meeting adjourned without day.

At a meeting held November 2, 1871, voted by a small majority to adopt the Act of 1868, establishing water-works in Lebanon.

At an adjournment of this meeting it was voted that a committee of five be raised to put the force pump in working order in some suitable place, and to purchase a chemical engine.

The committee consisted of J. W. Gerrish, P. E. Davis, Wm. Duncan, Solomon Cole, and E. J. Durant.

At a meeting held June, 1872, the fire wards were authorized and instructed to procure and place ready for use proper and sufficient pipes and hydrants to connect with the force pumps of J. C. Sturtevant & Co., and extend the same so as to furnish the best practical protection to the property in that vicinity, and also to connect with and supply the hydrants near the common, and also to locate and put in proper cisterns or reservoirs, not to exceed six in number, provided that an agreement satisfactory to the fire wards can be obtained of said Sturtevant & Co., relative to the use of said pumps.

The fire wards were directed to borrow, upon the credit of the precinct, such sum of money as may be required to carry out the action of this meeting, not to exceed four thousand dollars.

A contract carrying out these instructions was made with the J. C. Sturtevant Co.

The chemical engine was purchased on trial and found to be satisfactory, and has continued to prove one of the best investments the precinct ever made.

At a meeting held September 19, 1872, the precinct voted to purchase a new fire engine, and appointed Orimel T. Muchmore, A. W. Baker and P. E. Davis a committee to purchase it; $2,500 appropriated for the purchase.

At a meeting held February 8, 1873, the following action was taken:

Resolved that the Selectmen of the Town of Lebanon be and are hereby requested to enlarge the boundaries of the Center Village Fire Precinct of said town of Lebanon to the boundaries of the town, and that said Selectmen be requested to appraise the property of the Precinct and when the Precinct shall be enlarged they shall assume the debt of the present Precinct, to the amount of said appraisment, and the present Precinct shall pay the balance of indebtedness up to the date the same shall be enlarged

The meaning of the above resolution is somewhat vague, but when "the property of the precinct" which was to be appraised is limited to fire engines, hose and other apparatus, the meaning is clearer. The enlarged precinct was to assume whatever indebtedness there might be upon that kind of property, but for whatever debts there might be for construction of iron pipes buried, etc., the original precinct was to be held responsible.

The action of the town on this extension of the boundaries of the precinct was as follows:

At the annual meeting held in 1875, the following resolution was adopted:

Whereas the present Fire Precinct of Lebanon comprises more than one half of the taxable property of said town and have already expended large sums for the purpose of supplying suitable apparatus for the extinguishment of fires which is virtually for the benefit of the town

And whereas, under existing regulations, the present fire department have no jurisdiction or authority to act outside of the limits of the present Fire Precinct. Therefore;

Resolved that the Selectmen be instructed to so extend the limits of the Fire Precinct as to include the whole town

It will be noted that this action of the town was two years after that of the precinct.

The following is the record of a meeting of the fire wards held March 26, 1873: "The meeting was called to order by W. N. Baker, who stated that the meeting was called for the purpose of receiving the new Fire Engine from the hands of the Committee appointed by the Precinct to purchase the same. The Committee submitted a report of their doings and formally delivered the new Fire Engine, the Athletic No. 3, into the hands of the Fire Wards."

The engine was left in the charge of the foreman of Mascoma No. 2 until other arrangements could be made. A company was formed to take charge of the Athletic, to serve without pay. At the same time C. M. Hoffman was requested to form a company for the extinguisher.

At a meeting held June 4, 1873, the precinct voted to purchase a hook and ladder outfit at a cost not exceeding $700; also to purchase a uniform for the Athletic No. 3 company at a cost not exceeding $480.

At this time the affairs of the precinct were in great uncertainty and confusion. Many doubted the legality of their votes and action.

In 1873 the Legislature passed an act recognizing the Lebanon Center Village Fire Precinct, as duly organized under the laws of the state, with all the powers and privileges incident to such organizations.

By section 2 the precinct could, at any meeting duly notified and holden, ratify and confirm any votes heretofore passed by the precinct, and any action heretofore taken by the precinct, and any acts of the officers and agents of said precinct heretofore done and performed in pursuance of any vote or action of said precinct, and all such votes, actions and acts when so ratified and confirmed shall be valid, legal and binding upon said precinct and the inhabitants and property thereof.

At a meeting held August 2, 1873, to consider this act, the precinct found it difficult to decide what votes and action to ratify.

One resolution offered was "to ratify and confirm the acts and doings of all former meetings of the precinct, excepting four resolutions." What these resolutions were does not appear. The resolution was withdrawn and the meeting adjourned to August 16.

At this meeting a motion was made, "to commence with the records of the precinct and ratify such resolutions and motions as may be required." The motion was carried. A motion to "appoint a Committee of three to examine the records and report what portion was necessary to be ratified" was lost.

Another motion was made, "to appoint a Committee of three to examine the records of the Precinct and make a report in two weeks of all it was necessary to ratify." This motion prevailed. A part of the committee appointed by the chair declined to serve. While there was delay in securing this committee another motion was made, "to ratify and confirm all the Precinct's acts and doings at former meetings with the boundaries as they now stand recorded, together with all the acts which the officers and agents have heretofore done." The motion prevailed.

A short time after this wholesale ratification of *all* acts relieved the precinct from a serious difficulty. In obedience to the instructions of the precinct, the chief engineer had purchased uniforms for Athletic No. 3. This instruction was given June 4, 1873. The action was considered illegal, as being outside of the powers of the precinct. Nevertheless the creditors were pressing for their pay and it was held to be hard to hold the chief engineer personally responsible for the payment of the bills. Some one in examining the records discovered that the instruction given to the chief engineer was just previous to the passage of the act of the Legislature, and was one of the doings which had been ratified. Accordingly the precinct ordered the bills to be paid.

In 1875 a petition was presented to the selectmen requesting that the boundaries of the precinct might be extended to those of the town. The town at its annual meeting the same year had voted to instruct the selectmen to make the change in the boundaries. When the matter came before the selectmen in a formal manner there was no other course open to them but to grant the request of the petitioners. And this was their decision and a proper record of it made upon the books of the precinct. From the record it does not appear that there was any opposition made to this change.

The precinct had adjourned the choice of its officers until the decision of the selectmen was made known, so that the rest of the town could take part in the election.

At the meeting of the precinct it was decided to elect eleven fire wards, one at East Lebanon, two at West Lebanon, one at large and seven at the Center.

These fire wards were Charles B. Plastridge at East Lebanon, Jewett D. Hosley and A. S. Eaton at West Lebanon, John T. Breck at large, J. C. Sturtevant, H. P. Goodrich, A. W. Baker, Moses P. Durkee, C. P. Mahan, D. B. Emerson at the Center Village.

This union, although sought by both parties, did not prove to be a happy one. It subsisted but a single year, during which a precinct tax was assessed upon the whole town. No record exists of the dissolution of the union, but the historian learns after much and patient inquiry that it was dissolved by petition to the selectmen by those outside of the original bounds of the precinct. No opposition was made by the precinct.

The precinct continued in its work of providing means for extinguishing fires by laying pipes, providing hydrants. The J. C. Sturtevant Co. had placed force pumps in their building for their own protection, and the precinct connected their pipes with this pump by consent of parties. It was voted to purchase 800 feet of new hose to connect with hydrants to enlarge the territory to which protection could be given. This was a compromise between five hundred and a thousand feet.

The annual meetings had been held at various dates, but was fixed in 1876 to the first Tuesday in April, and so continued to the present time.

The property of the Sturtevant Company had passed in 1877 into the hands of Mead, Mason & Co. The Sturtevant Company had claims against the precinct for the use of the force pump and its apparatus. At a meeting held February 27, 1877, a committee was appointed to take all these matters into consideration and report upon them.

Their report at the annual meeting in substance was as follows: That it was inexpedient then to make any arrangement with the Mead, Mason & Co., for the use of their steam pump. They recommend the attachment of the Holley pump owned by the precinct to some water-wheel then in use, which attachment was estimated to cost not more than $200.

They report it inexpedient at that time to purchase of W. S. Moses the hose carriage uniforms, which had been used before in working the hydrants.

After hearing the report it was voted to instruct the fire wards to attach the Holley pump to any water-wheel of sufficient power, expense not to exceed $200, for the next year.

The precinct continued to extend its pipes, erect hydrants and provide reservoirs for the years 1878-'79.

On the third day of March, 1881, the precinct, acting through their chief engineer, Lyman Whipple, made a contract with the Mead, Mason & Co. to the following effect:

For and in consideration of the sum of one hundred dollars paid to them annually by the Lebanon Center Village Fire Precinct Mead Mason & Co. will put their pump or engine at the Upper Shop (so called) in good order, and will keep up steam and furnish power sufficient to run said force Pump to its fullest capacity in case of fire, said steam to be kept up at hours both day and night during the time the Precinct may contract for. It being expressly understood that said Precinct are to have full control of the Force Pump, and to keep the same in repair after receiving it; and in case the said Upper Shop should be destroyed by fire, Mead Mason & Co. reserve to themselves the right to annul their obligations, and in that case the Precinct are only to pay pro rata up to the date of such destruction; this agreement to continue for the term of one year, and after the expiration of said year either party can discontinue this arrangement by giving the opposite party one year's written notice to that effect; and said agreement to continue in full effect one year from and after the date of said notice; this agreement, when entered into, to commence from January 1st 1881.

At the annual meeting in 1883, the number of fire wards was reduced to three instead of seven, to be known as chief engineer, first assistant and second assistant. Lyman Whipple was chosen chief; H. P. Goodrich, first assistant; George C. Perkins, second assistant.

At the annual meeting in 1884, the following resolution was adopted, on motion of J. L. Spring:

> Resolved that a Committee of 7 be chosen to investigate the subject of introducing running water, procure full information and estimates and report to an adjourned meeting.

The committee was Charles A. Downs, Edward J. Durant, G. S. Joslyn, Charles M. Baxter, A. M. Shaw, John L. Spring and L. C. Pattee.

This meeting for some reason which does not appear found great difficulty in adjourning.

The first motion was that when the meeting adjourn it shall be to one week from today. An amendment was offered substituting one month for one week. The amendment was not accepted by the mover of the first motion, but the meeting voted to adjourn to one month from date at 7.30 p. m., May 1.

On motion it was voted to reconsider the vote, and it was moved that when the meeting adjourn, it adjourn to the first Tuesday in May. As the *hour of the day* was not mentioned the motion was amended so as to read that when the meeting adjourns, it adjourns until the first Tuesday in May at 7.30 p. m., which was satisfactory and the meeting adjourned. The historian offers this criticism, that in none of the motions was the *place to which* the meeting was to adjourn mentioned.

At the adjourned meeting the committee made a verbal report which was accepted with thanks, and the article under which the committee acted was laid upon the table. After the transaction of some other business it was voted to take the committee's report from the table, whereupon the meeting adjourned, a step towards the fatal catastrophe!

The annual meeting of the precinct, 1885, was chiefly remarkable for the difficulty of securing a board of fire wards. After having elected a moderator and a clerk, the meeting adjourned until Saturday evening.

At the adjourned meeting Lyman Whipple was elected first fire ward, Harlan P. Goodrich was elected second fire ward. Mr.

Goodrich saying that he had served fifteen years as a fire ward, asked to be excused. Upon vote he was excused.

Upon a second ballot for a second fire ward, George C. Perkins was chosen, who declined to serve and asked to be excused. His request was granted.

Two more ballots were taken, resulting in no choice. At the next balloting William A. Churchill was elected.

Proceeded to ballot for third fire ward, when there was no choice. At the second ballot Frank Sayre was chosen, having eight competitors.

The precinct voted that the fire wards be instructed to construct a reservoir near the southeast corner of land of John L. T. Brown on Hanover Street, which was done.

At a special meeting held September 1, 1886, A. M. Shaw, in behalf of the Village Improvement Society, presented a detailed report as to the cost of introducing water from Mascoma River, to be pumped into a reservoir on the hill east of the village.

Upon motion of J. L. Spring, an informal vote was taken upon the question, Shall the precinct introduce water for the purposes specified? Upon a division 97 voted in the affirmative and 34 in the negative.

Upon motion of C. A. Dole, the following resolution was adopted:

That a Committee of three be appointed by the Moderator to ascertain how many of the owners of water powers on Mascoma River below the Chandler Power (so called) will gratuitously sign a quit claim to the Precinct to draw from said River at or near the Chandler power, all the water the Precinct may desire for protection against fire, and for supplying the Precinct generally with water and report at an adjourned meeting.

The moderator appointed C. A. Dole, J. L. Spring and R. W. Cragin. Dole and Cragin declined and were excused. A. W. Baker and C. D. Smith were appointed. Mr. Baker declined and was excused, whereupon E. F. Emerson was appointed.

Upon motion of C. A. Dole, the following resolution was adopted:

Resolved that a Committee of three be appointed by the Moderator to ascertain at what amount the land damages can be adjusted for laying and maintaining from some point on the Mascoma River near the Chandler Power, so called to the contemplated Reservoir and thence to Shaw street, and also, at what price the land needed for said Reservoir can be obtained

The moderator appointed the same committee as before.

At the adjourned meeting held September 8, 1886, the committee reported as to land damage. W. M. Kendall agreed to accept $25 for the right to lay and maintain an aqueduct pipe, and upon payment thereof to execute proper release and conveyances. Upon payment of $50 C. W. Gerrish agreed to do the same, with the proviso not to conflict with any right heretofore given.

W. M. Kendall further agreed to convey the right to build and maintain a reservoir on the northerly side of his farm, with needed right of way, and stone to be taken from his farm for the sum of $50. At this meeting a resolution was adopted which was reconsidered and withdrawn at an adjourned meeting held September 18, 1886, at 2 o'clock in the afternoon, and the following adopted in its stead:

Resolved that a Committee consisting of Charles A. Dole, Solon A. Peck, Carlos D. Smith, Lyman Whipple and Harlan P. Goodrich be authorized by the Precinct and they are hereby authorized to procure necessary surveys, and specifications for putting in water works for the protection of the Precinct against loss by fire, and for supplying the Precinct with water, to be taken from Mascoma Lake or River, to call for proposals for putting in the works, and to contract for the same, provided it can be done at an expense not exceeding forty thousand dollars

And said Committee are hereby farther authorized if bonds of the Precinct may be legally issued, or whenever they may be legally issued, to prepare, execute, and dispose of the bonds of the Precinct, sufficient to pay for said water works not exceeding the sum of forty thousand dollars; the rate of interest upon said bonds not to exceed five per cent; said bonds to be made payable in twenty years from their date; the interest to be payable annually or semi-annually and at such place as the Committee may determine; and if such bonds are ever issued the Committee are to use the avails therof to pay for said works

This being a special meeting, the law required that a ballot be taken upon the resolution and that the checklist be used. Such a list had been prepared and was used for the first and last time in precinct meetings. By vote the polls were to close at 8 o'clock in the evening. A few moments before 8 o'clock it was voted that the polls close at 8 o'clock and 30 minutes.

Upon sorting and counting the ballots the following was the result:

Whole number of tickets given in was,	303
In favor of Mascoma Lake,	2
In favor of the resolution,	295
	297
Against the resolution,	6
Majority in favor,	291

It being ascertained that one-half the number of voters in the precinct whose names were on the checklist at the annual meeting in 1886 was 277, the resolution was declared adopted.

This was a movement in the right direction, but none heard, none saw the fearful calamity swiftly coming.

The annual meeting was held April 5, 1887, at which only routine business was transacted. In four weeks from the adjournment of this meeting the calamity came.

By the courtesy of the proprietors of the *Granite State Free Press* the following account of the one great fire of Lebanon is given from their files just as it was prepared at the time, dated May 13, 1887:

AT LAST.

LEBANON'S GREAT CALAMITY HAS COME—80 BUILDINGS BURNED—600 MEN THROWN OUT OF EMPLOYMENT—40 FAMILIES HOMELESS.

When Monday's sun set peacefully in the west the busy hum of industry in twenty or more manufacturing establishments, large and small, on five dams, on both sides of the Mascoma River in the center village of this town, had just ceased for the day, and the 600 employés therein wended their way to their homes for the night's rest preparatory to another day's toil. When Tuesday's sun rose every one of those shops and mills was a heap of smouldering ruins, after a desperate fight of five hours to save them, and the devastation was being stayed for want of anything on

AFTER THE FIRE, 1887.

which to feed down the river, and the interposition of brick walls and piles of green logs, as well as by the arrival of timely help, in other directions.

At about 12.45 o'clock Watchman Berry at the Governor Hale woolen mill, recently purchased by Carter & Rogers, was awakened by a light flashing through his window. Rising quickly he could see two fires apparently at the south end of Mead, Mason & Co.'s lower shop. He dressed quickly and hastened out to give the alarm. About the same time or a minute later, and just as Berry came out of the mill, Watchman Bullock at Kendrick and Davis' key factory saw the light and rung the key factory bell, and almost simultaneously Watchman Webster at the shop where the fire was discovered it. He pressed the electric key connecting with the fire gong at the upper shop, and then rung the lower shop bell. Watchman Duplisse at the upper shop was on his round when the electric alarm sounded, and a minute was lost in getting to the gong, and another minute by pulling the wire so violently as to break it, necessitating the hunting up of a wrench. In those minutes the fire made rapid strides, as it was among shavings under the shop, and everything in the vicinity was especially combustible. The whole room above was a mass of flame in less than no time as it seemed, and when the first help arrived it was apparent that the whole lower shop was doomed. It was still hoped to save the immense three-story warehouse on the opposite side of Water Street, and connected by a covered overhead bridge, containing probably an acre of floor, and packed full of manufactured furniture and house finish, much of it elegantly upholstered. This bridge, however, proved a flue through which first an immense volume of smoke and then a sheet of flame poured into the warehouse, which also contained the counting room and the safes, and in fifteen minutes this, too, was enveloped in flames. Very little of the contents were removed, and these largely were afterwards burned. The stock of manufactured goods was unusually large, being held back on account of the interstate commerce law, in hope to get a living rate for freights. There is probably not another such tinder box in the state of New Hampshire. The flames shot up 200 feet into the air, affording a sight appalling and sublime. The heat was intense, rendering near approach by

25

the firemen impossible. The firemen rallied promptly to the dismal alarm which sounded out on the stillness of the awful night, but one of the hydrants refused to open, even by the aid of the stoutest wrench, and the line of hose laid from it had to be abandoned and allowed to burn on account of the intense heat. The streams from the force pumps did not seem to come with wonted power for some reason, while that from Athletic Engine Co. No. 3, Eagle Extinguisher No. 1, seemed to have little more effect than common boys' squirt guns. Our fire department, 120 men, with the appliances they had, were never intended to cope with such a fire, and were powerless before it.

Alas! Alas! As we have twenty times expressed a fear, prophesying what has now occurred as only a question of time—the water-works, though put under contract and to be completed by September, have come one year too late. How we have plead for them through all these years. They would have saved at least eight times their cost. But, alas, three months too late, and the burden increased upon the taxable property left in the precinct by the wiping out of one-fifth or one-sixth of it. O Folly, thy name is Humanity, and thou art everywhere. But enough of this.

The heat was awfully intense. It did not need the cinders which went hundreds of feet into the air and then fell on all sides in that awful stillness upon roofs almost blistered with the heat of the previous day—it did not need this to inflame the buildings on all sides; the heat was enough. The fire leaped simultaneously to the tenement house of Mead, Mason & Co. at the corner of Mascoma and Water streets on the east; to the key factory on the south; across the river to the Hale factory and Cole & Son's foundry on the west; and across Mascoma Street to the dwelling and livery stable of Dan Scott on the north. The department could scarcely hold the flames in check in one direction—what could they do with all these fires? Almost absolutely nothing.

About 2 o'clock the telephone operator succeeded in arousing Enfield, and Protector Engine Co., Capt. Cross, was here by 3 o'clock, a locomotive being detached from a freight train to bring it and a large corps of fresh and hardy men. Never were men more heartily greeted or did better service.

There was harder luck with Hanover. The telephone would not work, and a messenger was despatched. The Hanover company, Capt. ———, responded and arrived in time to be of service. Concord could not be reached by telegraph; the line would not work for some reason. The telephone line to Concord would not work. She was finally reached by way of Bellows Falls by telephone, thence by telegraph, and assistance asked for. It was an hour of intense agony. The flames licked up as if a dainty morsel the tenement house known as the Lawton house, standing near in the lower shop yards, and G. A. Elliott's carriage shop close to the lower or Mascoma Street bridge; burned this bridge, but without waiting for that to burn leaped over it to the B. T. Tilden building on the opposite side of Mascoma Street, occupied by Muchmore & Whipple, house builders, N. B. Marston, rake manufacturer, and Ira Bucklin, carpenter and builder. This building also went like tinder. The precinct pump was in the basement. The operator stood by it until the falling timbers made life insecure, and he left it running. A minute later escape would have been impossible save by jumping into the river, and two minutes later by any method. The wheel is running still, but to make a wreck of the pump was the work of only a few minutes and it ceased to work, and being left open, operated as an open valve to deprive the steam pump of the Mead, Mason & Co.'s upper shop of its power.

There was nothing now but hand engines to fight the largest fire New Hampshire ever saw—two or three hand engines and a little extinguisher. Meantime the flames had worked up Mascoma Street toward the park, destroying a two-tenement house belonging to Mrs. Ellis, and two tenement houses belonging to Mrs. P. E. Davis, occupied by Charles Woodward, Miss E. M. Camp, dressmaker, and two other families. The fire was successfully resisted in this direction by a desperate and successful fight to save the house owned by Mrs. Davis and occupied by Mr. Hoisington. The flames pressed up the stream, destroyed the Northern Railroad bridge, and attacked the splendid flour and grist mill, one of the best in the state, of William F. Shaw, occupied by Shaw & Wright, also by A. W. Rix, machinist, and the Shaw Rifles' armory. This seemed reluctant to burn, as the sheet-iron covering at the south end protected it for awhile, but it was impossible to get a stream of water to the ridge pole, and it succumbed at last. The *Free Press* building came next, owned by Patrick Jordan, occupied by the *Free Press*, Freeman & Richardson, job printers, and the families of Patrick Coogan and John Bushway, two tenements being empty. Here it seemed highly probable the fire would be cut off, and having removed books, files and valuable papers, and got some other things ready to go in a hurry if necessary, we were indulging in the hope of going immediately to work to get out an extra. Fifteen minutes later the extra got us out on the double quick. A quarter-inch stream of water for ten minutes would have saved us, as it would many a more valuable building, but it could not be had. It was now towards daylight, and a stream was turned on the blacksmith shop of P. Jordan, next north of us, and the tenement in the rear occupied by Mr. Townsend, which was half consumed, and here the fire was stayed in this direction.

Meantime it had crept up the south side of Mascoma Street to the park, destroying Mead, Mason & Co.'s lumber shed, the old Lafayette Hotel building, owned by S. S. Houghton of Boston, and occupied by L. W. Smith, carriages and sleighs, and by three families; also the building occupied by Billings' marble works, second and third stories empty, and the large livery stable connecting. It crept up the east side of Mill Street, taking a business block owned by O. T. Purmort and occupied as a storehouse by different parties; also the gristmill sheds, the old house in front of our office, owned by C. O. Hurlbutt and occupied by two families, the corner house, occupied by Mr. Rose, and the billiard room and restaurant of P. S. Lemay.

From the Lafayette the fire communicated to the engine house and to W. P. McFee's house on Hanover Street, which being brick lined made quite a stubborn resistance, but in vain, thence to the adjoining harness shop of Mr. McFee and shoe shop of A. Rock, second story occupied by Frank Morgan and mother as a residence. Next came Baldwin's wooden block, lower story occupied by J. E. Lincoln, dry goods, and C. E. Marston, undertaker's goods, and C. E. Colburn, groceries and crockery; upper story by C. N. Walker, sewing machines, organs and pianos, rooms and residence, and H. P. Granger, tenement and photograph rooms. The next was a block owned and occupied by

C. E. Pulsifer, grocer, second story by Athletic Club rooms. All these blocks were destroyed, their contents being largely removed in a damaged condition. This brings us to the new and elegant brick block of G. C. Whipple, where a most desperate and finally successful fight was made, thanks to the timely arrival of the Enfield company. All of the occupants of this building removed their goods, the heat being so intense. On the lower floor G. C. Whipple, dry goods; P. M. Kenyon, tailor; F. Walton & Co., boots and shoes; I. N. Perley, druggist.

The west side of Hanover Street—Hildreth's block, Whipple's old block, and Worthen's block were in the greatest danger, the first named being on fire several times. The slightest breeze in that direction would have doomed them, and with them the whole of North Park Street, including the town hall. The fight was made mainly on Hildreth's block, and it was admirably made, too, by means of pails of water and small force pumps. A. C. Richardson, foreman of the squirt gun company, says that the chimney was so hot he could not bear his hand on it. Down the river from the point of starting, the flames swept till there was nothing further for them to devour. The key factory, C. M. Baxter's machine shop, the old saw mill, and Mead, Mason & Co.'s lumber yard are a heap of ashes.

A scene of awful destruction was meantime being enacted on the west side of the river. The flames leaped the river at the point of first start to Cole & Son's pattern house and foundry. They leaped again both across the river from the Muchmore & Whipple building and across Mascoma Street from the foundry to Cole & Son's machine shop. They leaped again from Shaw's mill across the river to Mead, Mason & Co.'s upper shop, the river side of which was covered with wood dust from the blower, and it went like tinder. Nothing could oppose it, and nothing tried to oppose it. Not a stream of water was put on, not a line of hose was laid on the west side until everything was flat. There was water enough in the river, but no hose. The shop, the dry house, and boiler house, containing the company's powerful steam force pump and the precinct fire steam gong, went like a flash. There was great terror and dread of an explosion. The gong valve opened and sent its deep, dismal, half-suppressed groan through minutes that seemed hours. It seemed like a howl from the infernal regions.

The large three-story storehouse, full of furniture in the white, and immense piles of hardwood lumber between it and the boiler, made a terrible fire. T. D. Marston's sawmill came next up the river. It was nothing to lick that up. But the pile of green logs above it afforded a chance to fight the fire fiend to some advantage and the chance was improved, stopping it just short of Franklin Tucker's house. It took a plucky fight with blankets and buckets and force pumps to save the houses along High Street, opposite the upper shop. The extinguisher, relieved from other duty, finally came to the rescue and helped to save them. A dozen dwellings must have gone, if a fire too big for buckets had once started here—probably more. Long before this the fire from Cole & Son's foundry had communicated to their counting house, thence to F. C. Churchill's tenement house on the east side of High Street, occupied by Charles Dow and E. A. Cotting, which was burned.

Turning back now to the early morning hour, it will be remembered that the fire at the starting point leaped the river, setting fire to Cole & Son's foundry. It communicated thence to their counting room building; thence to a house on the corner of Mascoma and Mechanic streets owned by Mrs. Lynch and occupied by Mrs. Balduc; next came a house owned and occupied by Mrs. Lynch, Mascoma Hotel, owned and occupied by S. D. Jones, house owned by M. B. Foss and occupied by P. Duplisse and Charles Burdette, and one owned by Mrs. P. E. Davis, with two tenants. The fire was stopped at the next house, that of Henry Benton, by a desperate effort, aided by the timely arrival of a lot of fresh men by train from West Lebanon and White River Junction. Had the immense stock barn of Justus Sargent, next to this, caught fire there is no knowing where the end would have been in this direction. It was about half-past two o'clock when the fire was checked here, and in common with multitudes of people on the east side, we did not know that there was any fire on the west side till about 4 o'clock, so busy had we been in fighting on our side. In the rear of these houses and on the nameless street leading to the woolen mill, were four cottage houses belonging to Thomas Fahey and Dan Driscoll, and occupied by themselves and several tenants.

This ends the record of buildings destroyed, which, not counting sheds and small outbuildings, number 80, as shown by the insurance map of the village. The last serious fight was on High Street about 5 o'clock, and it was indeed a most desperate one. Blankets and carpets kept constantly wet did the business, aided finally by the Extinguisher Co. The fight at O. W. Burnap's house was important as a long row of houses close together on West Street were in the rear of it, with the West Street schoolhouse. North of West Street no serious damage was done.

Just as this last fight had been successfully made, and it became reasonably sure that the last house was burning, the steam engine Governor Hill and Kearsarge hose carriage arrived from Concord, about 5.45 o'clock, having made the trip of 65 miles in 85 minutes with two stops, one of which was four minutes. This is the quickest time ever made on the road except possibly that in competition for the Canadian mails about thirty years ago, when an engine made the trip from White River Junction to Concord, 70 miles, in 90 minutes. The train contained two platform and one passenger car, drawn by the locomotive Greenfield, Nelson Braley, engineer, and was in charge of Conductor Dan. Lary. Chief Engineer Dan. Newhall personally had charge of the Concord apparatus. There was still need of a great deal of water to be thrown, and the Governor Hill was welcomed with great joy and afforded a feeling of relief to our tired firemen and citizens. It was stationed on the Hanover Street iron bridge.

Colburn Park presented a strange scene. There was not a spot ten feet square but what was piled with store or household goods, machinery, and property of almost every conceivable kind. Every dooryard deemed far enough away to be safe, on both sides of the river, was similarly occupied. Many goods were moved several times. A great many goods were burned after being gotten out. It was impossible to get one team where ten were needed. To add to the mishaps of the day, over which some infernal spirit seemed to preside, the steamer Governor Hill became disabled after playing an hour or two and was rendered unserviceable. The ring of the Athletic's bell was heard every few minutes all the day and evening, calling for men to man the brakes, to keep the glowing embers within due bounds and prevent a second fire. It was an awful fire. No New Hampshire town ever saw its equal. God grant that none other may ever have a like experience.

People came by hundreds all day to witness the disaster.

Many families spent all day guarding their little piles of goods, while the head of the family hunted for quarters. Happily the number of houseless families was not so large—we reckon it 43—but that all could find shelter of some kind. The smaller losses, below $100 in the list which we give elsewhere, are mostly losses to poor houseless families by goods burned or damaged in removal. Not one in ten of them was insured. Nearly all the buildings, except some of Mead, Mason & Co.'s, were insured.

The insurance companies might well stand appalled in face of so great a calamity, but their agents were promptly on hand and were as busy all day Wednesday and Thursday as were the reporters on Tuesday. A large portion of the insurance is already satisfactorily adjusted.

We cannot express in too warm words the gratitude of the people of Lebanon to the stalwart men from Concord, Enfield, Hanover, West Lebanon and White River Junction, who came to our aid in the hour of our distress. We have not room to say more now.

There is great reason for gratitude that no lives were lost. David Perkins became overheated and had to be carried home, and it was reported that he was dead, but he finally came out all right. No serious casualty has been reported to us.

The following list of losses is the result of personal interviews with nearly all the losers, and the estimates by friends as to such as we were unable to find. We judge the estimates to be reasonably fair, and that under-estimates and the absence of some that we failed to get will balance any possible over-estimates. We have accepted the press estimate of $100,000 for Mead, Mason & Co. as a fair one in our own judgment. They do not like to give one of themselves, but we feel that it is due to our readers that the best estimate we can get be given.

AFTER THE FIRE, 1887.

LIST OF LOSSES.

Mead, Mason & Co.	$100,000
S. Cole & Son	50,000
Kendrick & Davis	30,000
W. F. Shaw	20,000
Carter & Rogers	20,000
C. M. Baxter	16,000
J. E. Lincoln	10,000
C. E. Pulsifer	8,000
Shaw & Wright	7,000
Charles Dow	400
L. W. Smith	700
C. E. Colburn	1,800
P. M. Kenyon	1,000
Ira Bucklin	900
A. Rock	250
W. H. Stickney	60
Albert Blish	50
Peter Russell	50
Noble Webster	100
Nelson Sargent	50
I. N. Perley (settled)	100
A. W. Rix	5,000
T. B. Marston	3,500
F. Walton & Co.	1,500
F. C. Churchill	3,200
G. C. Whipple	3,000
Muchmore & Whipple	1,500
B. T. Tilden	3,500
Misses Brown	50
H. P. Granger	1,000
John Bushway	50
C. D. Scott	5,000
J. E. Dewey	2,000
Mrs. P. E. Davis	5,100
W. H. Morris	30
S. S. Houghton	9,000
Mrs. Lynch	2,500
Richard Lindsay	400

D. H. Currie	$400
Mrs. James Griffin	200
P. Garland	100
David Deforge	125
Shaw Rifles	100
Lebanon Fire Precinct	2,000
P. Jordan	3,000
John Townsend	50
P. Coogan	50
Lowell Richardson	50
G. A. Elliott	1,200
O. T. Purmort	2,000
B. & L. Railroad, bridge	7,000
Town of Lebanon, bridge	1,500
Four freight cars	2,000
Mrs. Buck	300
J. L. Spring	50
S. D. Jones	4,000
Mrs. Baldue	25
Thomas Fahey	3,000
Dan Driscol	2,500
M. B. Foss	2,000
——— Duplisse	300
Charles Bodette	300
O. R. Rose	250
Henry Benton	3,500
James Lawrence	25
W. M. Kendall	300
Miss M. E. Camp	75
Charles Woodward	75
H. G. Billings	4,500
C. N. Walker	1,500
I. Titus & Co., Brattleboro	1,500
C. E. Marston	2,500
O. W. Baldwin	6,500
E. H. Cheney, *Free Press*	1,200
Freeman & Richardson	3,000
O. W. Burnap	50
Jo. Demosh	300

Joseph Plomondon	$50
W. P. McFee	4,000
E. A. Cotting	50
Extinguisher Co.	250
Athletic Co.	400
Frank Morgan	500
N. B. Marston	2,500
Total	$374,565

INSURANCE.

The following shows the amount of insurance so far as is known at present. There may be some few policies in outside companies, but if any the amount is small:

C. E. Pulsifer, Pulsifer block,	
Capital	$1,500.00
Capital Association	1,000.00
Baldwin's block,	
Granite State	1,000.00
Guaranty	500.00
Sullivan	1,000.00
Cheshire	2,000.00
F. C. Churchill, house,	
Fitchburg	1,000.00
Merchants & Farmers	800.00
T. B. Marston, sawmill, etc.,	
Granite State	500.00
New Hampshire	500.00
People's	500.00
B. T. Tilden's building,	
Granite State	500.00
Guaranty	500.00
Capital	500.00
People's	500.00
Ira Bucklin, stock,	
Manufacturers & Merchants	350.00
Muchmore & Whipple, stock,	
Amoskeag	500.00

N. B. Marston, stock,
    Mascoma $500.00
    Phœnix Mutual 400.00
    Indian Head 400.00
G. A. Elliott, building,
    New Hampshire 500.00
Chas. E. Colburn, stock,
    Underwriters 500.00
    Amoskeag 1,000.00
C. E. Marston, stock,
    Mascoma 500.00
    Capital Association 500.00
    Granite State 500.00
J. E. Lincoln, stock,
    Mascoma 1,000.00
    Guaranty 1,000.00
    Manufacturers & Merchants 2,000.00
    Concord 1,000.00
    Mt. Holly 1,000.00
    People's 1,000.00
    New England 2,000.00
W. P. McFee, stock,
    New Hampshire 1,000.00
W. P. McFee, house,
    Capital 850.00
    Granite State 850.00
Peter Lemay, houses and shop,
    Guaranty 1,800.00
C. D. Scott, stock,
    Mascoma 400.00
Pat. Jordan's block,
E. H. Cheney, stock,
    Mascoma 300.00
    Granite State 650.00
Freeman & Richardson, stock,
    Granite State 500.00
    New Hampshire 1,000.00
    Cheshire 1,000.00

Shaw's grist mill,
- Mascoma $2,000.00
- Underwriters 1,500.00
- Capital Association 1,000.00
- Amoskeag 1,250.00
- People's 1,250.00

A. W. Rix, stock,
- Capital 1,000.00
- People's 1,000.00

Shaw & Wright, stock,
- Guaranty 1,000.00
- New Hampshire 1,000.00
- Mascoma 1,500.00

C. D. Scott, houses,
- Capital Association 1,087.50
- Granite State 800.00
- Capital 1,087.50

Lafayette Hotel, S. S. Houghton,
- People's 1,000.00

Charles Goss & Co., storehouse and stock,
- Granite State 1,000.00

L. W. Smith, stock,
- New England 750.00

Thos. Fahey, house,
- Capital Association 1,100.00
- Springfield 700.00

Mascoma House,
- New Hampshire 1,600.00

Mrs. Lynch's houses,
- Springfield 850.00
- Phenix 800.00

C. Cole & Son, office and storehouse,
- Granite State 1,000.00
- Manufacturers and Merchants . . . 1,000.00
- New Hampshire 500.00
- People's 1,000.00
- New England 750.00

S. Cole & Son, machine shop and contents,
- Underwriters 750.00
- Amoskeag 1,000.00

Guarantee	$1,000.00
Manufacturers and Merchants	750.00
People's	1,000.00
Other insurance	1,000.00
Cheshire	2,750.00
Mead, Mason & Co., upper shop,	
Underwriters	500.00
Guaranty	500.00
Amoskeag	500.00
Manufacturers and Merchants	500.00
Capital	500.00
Dover	500.00
Other insurance	4,700.00
Mead, Mason & Co., stock, lower shop,	
Underwriters	1,000.00
Manufacturers and Merchants	1,000.00
Kendrick & Davis, shop and stock,	
Mascoma	1,500.00
Underwriters	1,000.00
Capital Association	1,000.00
Granite State	1,500.00
Amoskeag	1,000.00
Guarantee	1,000.00
Manufacturers and Merchants	300.00
Capital	1,000.00
Indian Head	1,000.00
Concord	1,500.00
People's	1,500.00
C. M. Baxter, shop,	
New Hampshire	2,000.00
People's	1,000.00
Lebanon Woolen Mill,	
Mascoma	1,000.00
Underwriters	1,000.00
Guaranty	1,000.00
Manufacturers and Merchants	1,000.00
New Hampshire	1,250.00
Capital	1,000.00
People's	1,250.00

Daniel Driscoll, houses,
  Phenix $1,700.00
Mary Houghton's livery barn,
  Concord 500.00
H. G. Billings' livery stock,
  Underwriters 750.00
  People's 750.00
H. G. Billings' marble stock,
  Guarantee 500.00
Mrs. P. E. Davis, house,
  New Hampshire 1,000.00
J. E. Dewey, house,
  Merchants and Farmers 1,600.00

The burned area presents a scene of awful desolation viewed from any point of approach. It extends 100 rods or more up and down the river with varying width, and is variously estimated at from 8 to 12 acres. The extent of water fall can be taken in at a glance now, and no man can look at it and believe that it is to lie idle. It is impossible. Our people are full of courage. Some men are going to need temporary help, but nobody is going to fail, and every real estate owner is able to rebuild. It is believed that most of them will do so, and so build as to enable them to do business to better advantage.

"RESURGAM"

is written all over Lebanon, and she can be depended upon to redeem her pledge, her faith be realized. We shall yet behold Beauty for Ashes, the Oil of Joy for Mourning, and the Garment of Praise for the Spirit of Heaviness.

NOTES ABOUT THE FIRE.

We still live.

Nil desperandum.

The sound of the axe and the hammer is already heard.

A town meeting is called to see if the town will exempt manufacturing establishments rebuilt on the burned district. Of course there can be but one opinion about it. There is just one thing to do, and the heartier the unanimity the sooner we will recover from this shock.

The material saved from our office was scattered all over the village, and during Tuesday our office was "all along the shore." It was about like saving one hind wheel and one forward wheel, a whiffletree, and the seat cushion of a wagon, with a dead horse for motive power. The loss that will bother us most is that of our newspaper press. We are under obligations to the Hanover *Gazette,* the *Landmark* and Royal Cummings at White River Junction, *The Reporter* at Canaan, the *Monitor* at Concord, the *Journal* at Franklin Falls, the *Mirror* at Manchester, and the *Journal* at Windsor, Vt., for kind offers of assistance. We decided to get out only a two-page sheet this week and found it most convenient to accept the offer of Bro. Barney at Canaan, who knows what it is to be burned out himself. It is an easy job to replace type, but a press does not come so easy, and we shall be compelled to get our paper printed out of town for a few weeks.

The light was seen at Claremont, and it is reported at Laconia.

It will take piles of brick and lumber to supply this market for awhile.

Now, Mr. Densmore, push that brickyard for all it is worth, night and day.

The Mascoma Falls can now be seen somewhat as the Indian saw them.

It is thought the insurance as finally adjusted will amount to about $110,000.

Good-bye, old Lafayette. The glorious Frenchman once rested, we believe, under its roof.

T. B. Marston is already at work rebuilding his sawmill. He will put in a saw as soon as he can get in a foundation and cover it while running.

General Bridge Master Haseltine of the B. & L. and Division Bridge Master Spaulding were promptly on hand Tuesday to put in a trestle in place of the burned bridge. Work was begun at 6 o'clock Tuesday evening and trains passed over it before 2 o'clock the next day.

Too much praise cannot be awarded to the ladies of Lebanon who organized a relief corps very early Tuesday morning, were everywhere present among the exhausted firemen, with coffee, lemonade and water, and served a bountiful early breakfast in the town hall.

Some cinders from the fire were picked up a mile and a half from town.

Schools did not keep Tuesday on account of the excitement caused by the fire.

Rebuilding has already commenced. Baldwin and Pulsifer are to build one block.

The safes of the losers by the fire came out successfully, only the outside being injured.

The call for our fire company from Lebanon, Tuesday morning, was received here by telephone a few minutes before two o'clock. Ten minutes later E. B. Huse had his span of big horses attached to the engine and started, but on reaching the depot word was received that a train then at Canaan would be right along and take it, so it was loaded on a flat car, but it was nearly three-quarters of an hour before the engine came—it seemed much longer—but in eight minutes after, the Protector No. 2 was unloading in Lebanon, and in a very few minutes more was at the iron bridge and had a stream on the fire. We will let our Lebanon neighbors, who were exhausted and almost dismayed by two hours' hard combat with the flames, say how they felt to receive assistance just at that time. Our boys were fresh, and were only too glad to be able to help when help was most needed.

The origin of the fire is a mystery. The watchman's clock was opened Thursday afternoon in our presence, and in that of other gentlemen, and shows beyond all cavil that he made his proper rounds, once an hour, from 7 to 12 o'clock. There is no possibility of mistake about it. The watchman's name is Noble A. Webster. He lived in one of the burned houses and lost everything, including the money with which he was paid off

Monday. It was mostly paper. Some of the silver was found in the ruins.

RELIEF WORK.

On Monday afternoon at 2 o'clock a fair number of ladies and gentlemen gathered at the town hall to consider ways and means of relieving any suffering there might be among us as a result of the late fire. The meeting was called to order by Judge Ticknor. C. C. Rogers was elected chairman and Rev. E. T. Farrill secretary. The selectmen were elected a committee to receive any aid that might be volunteered. A committee of nine was elected to investigate cases of need and to distribute aid, consisting of the following persons: Mrs. Lyman Whipple, Miss Mary Kimball, W. H. Morris, Mrs. Mary Daniels, Miss Mary Sargent, T. D. Simmons, Mrs. T. D. Simmons, Peter Lemay, Mrs. C. C. Rogers. The meeting was adjourned to next Saturday evening, at the town hall, 7 o'clock, to consider the general business interests of the village in view of the recent disaster.

While the people have responded nobly with their assistance in our emergency, the old truth has had several very practical and emphatic illustrations that the real needy are best reached and provided for, not by promiscuous giving, but by systematic investigation and distribution.

The appeal for aid has been most generously met, and much relief has been afforded by the contributions of clothing, furniture, etc.

The benevolent association of ladies connected with the Congregational Church appointed a relief committee to take prompt action in relieving distress among those turned out of home. Tuesday p. m. the chapel reminded one of some of the scenes of war times when the ladies met to sew for the soldiers.

WHO WILL REBUILD.

A large force of men are already at work rebuilding Kendrick & Davis' watch key factory. The building will be 35 x 100, two stories high, of wood.

G. A. Elliot is putting in the foundation of his carriage shop on the old spot, near the Mascoma Street bridge.

Hon. A. M. Shaw will rebuild his flour and grist mill, and work has already commenced.

T. B. Marston has the honor of having the first enclosure on the burned ground—a small board shanty on one corner of his sawmill lot, to be used as counting room and tool house. He is pushing his sawmill and will be sawing in a few days, probably by Monday or Tuesday next. He has purchased one of Lane's latest improved sawmills.

Cole & Son announce by handbill that they are "cast down but not destroyed," and will immediately rebuild, on the south side of the street.

C. E. Pulsifer has the foundation of his new block next G. C. Whipple's brick block, well advanced. He builds a wood shell, to be encased in permanent brick walls as soon as brick can be had.

O. W. Baldwin is putting in the foundation to rebuild his block.

Workmen are repairing the railroad spur entering the lower shop yards, and are rebuilding the trestle work for the track which was used by the grist mill and upper shop. These tracks are going to be used, too.

The building in which the fire originated, used for the manufacture of sash, blinds, furniture and house finishing, was said to be the oldest in the country; that is, it continued the longest time without burning. No one can read the preceding graphic account without feeling that there was a fatality in the event. It had been threatened before, several times had a narrow escape from destruction, but now everything worked adversely. First, the watchman in the upper shop on his round hears an alarm and in natural excitement pulls a wire connecting with an alarm too violently, breaking the wire, necessitating the hunting up of a wrench; there was delay. Seconds then counted towards destruction. A hydrant could not be opened even by the aid of the stoutest wrench, and the hose stretched to it had to be abandoned. After some delay Enfield was reached and Protector Engine Co. was summoned and reached Lebanon about 3 o'clock, by the help of a freight engine. "Never were men more heartily greeted or did better service." But the fire had a start of two hours and fifteen minutes.

The telephone would not work to summon Hanover and a messenger was despatched, which added two hours more to the liberty of the devouring flames. Concord could be reached neither by telegraph nor telephone directly; a telephone message was sent to Bellows Falls and from there a despatch sent to Concord summoning assistance. About 5.45 the steam fire engine Governor Hill arrived and gave welcome and needed assistance to weary firemen and citizens. But the steamer, brought at such speed from a distant city, capable of doing such good service, such a relief to tired firemen, was after an hour or two disabled. But to crown the whole series of disasters, the precinct pumps became useless. Hydrants had to be hastily abandoned from the intense heat and left open, valves that should have been closed were left open, and the water sent out by the pumps went back into the river or wasted on the ground. The system which had been adopted was a good one, essentially the same now in use in large cities, but it failed in the hour of supreme need, as any system will fail if proper care and management fail. Fate was supreme that terrible night.

Many suffered loss in the terrible conflagration, but the sufferers did not lose courage. The fire was still smouldering when arrangements were made for rebuilding, temporarily at first, but more solidly than ever before. The manufacturing district of Lebanon today is better, far better, than it was on the eve of May 9, 1879.

The origin of the fire was a mystery at the time; it is not less so after more than nine years have gone by. Today, as at the time, the probabilities point to an incendiary origin.

Churches of the Town.

BY JOHN E. WHITLEY.

THE LEBANON CONGREGATIONAL CHURCH.

In accordance with the Act of Incorporation of the town of Lebanon, the first town meeting was held May 15, 1765. At that meeting it was voted to have a minister preach during the summer, and that Aaron Storrs should take around a subscription paper, and the selectmen should seek quarters for the minister and provide for his accommodation. This action on the part of the early settlers indicates the value they put upon church privileges. According to votes taken at different times ministers were called to labor here for a stated period, sometimes for a summer, sometimes for one or two years. In the town records mention is made of Rev. Mr. Treadway, Rev. Mr. Niles and Rev. Mr. Wales. In those days taxes were raised to support the minister, because he was a town officer, and thus all the affairs pertaining to his ministry were brought before the town meeting. The town, which had at that time about twenty families, called and dismissed the pastors.

The next step taken was the organization of a church. It is recorded that the six men who are charter members were Azariah Bliss, Jonathan Dana, Joseph Dana, Zacheus Downer, John Slapp, and John Wheatley. Azariah Bliss was from Connecticut and became useful in town affairs. Jonathan and Joseph Dana were from Ashford, Connecticut. Joseph was one of the original proprietors. Zacheus Downer was a public-spirited man and a brave soldier in the Revolution. John Slapp was from Connecticut, an officer in the French and Indian War, in which he acquired the title of major. He was also in the War of the Revolution. Because of his military knowledge and experience, he was of great service to the early settlers of Lebanon. John Wheatley was the son of an Irish surgeon in the British navy. Coming to this country he fell into the hands of a kind citizen of Norwich, Connecticut. With a small party of emigrants he came up the Connecticut Valley and settled here. By his native ability and education he developed qualities of leadership. He became justice of the peace under the royal commission, and for years was the legal adviser in this town. Rev. Phineas Cooke, in a Thanksgiving sermon preached in the present Congregational Church, November 25, 1830, says of John Wheatley: "He presided at the town meeting held September 12, 1765. Were I to single out an individual to whom this town in its early days was especially indebted for his exertions in its behalf, I would name John Wheatley, Esquire. He was the first town clerk and for nearly twenty years the first civil magistrate; the first schoolmaster and the first representative under the present Constitution of New Hampshire. To all his acknowledged qualifications for civil life was added piety, and such religious gifts as made him a suitable person to lead in the meetings of the church in the absence of the minister. He was the first man who fixed his habitation amidst the lofty pines of this plain."

It was such a company of men that took upon themselves the organization of the first church in the town of Lebanon. An old log schoolhouse which stood east of Capt. Joseph Wood's residence was used for the religious services. In passing it is worthy of note to say that the first school and the first church in Lebanon were organized the same year, 1768. Our forefathers believed that the schoolhouse and the church, representing education and religion, are the foundation stones of an enduring community. Two historic spots in Lebanon are worthy of recording because of their unusual interest. One spot is the Eastman place, now owned by N. S. Johnson, on South Main Street, West Lebanon. As far as historical knowledge and tradition can aid us, it was on this lot of land, on the east bank of the Connecticut River, where the first congregation in Lebanon assembled for Christian worship. Here also was solemnized the first public wedding in town. Here also, August 25, 1772, Rev. Isaiah Potter, the first settled pastor, was ordained to the gospel ministry. In the open air, under a large, spreading elm tree, a temporary platform was built and the impressive service of ordination was conducted. The visiting clergymen were Rev. Bulkley Olcott of Charlestown and Rev. James Wellman of Cornish, and in addition to these President Wheelock, Dartmouth's first

CHARLES H. DANA.

president, and appointed delegates from Hanover were present. What Plymouth Rock is to all New England, in a restricted and yet as important a sense, that spot on the east bank of the Connecticut River should be to all the inhabitants of Lebanon. The original proprietors and early settlers assembled there to acknowledge and to worship God before permanent homes were built, and before the permanent schoolhouse and church appeared. The other spot of unusual interest is a portion of the field west of the Luther Alden place. It was here that the first meeting-house was erected in 1772. In this first meeting-house, which stood for twenty years, the early settlers met Sunday after Sunday, in a simple form of worship, with Ziba Huntington as chorister, Charles Dana as deacon, and with that earnest and faithful pastor known as Priest Potter, who, like Moses, was the leader of his flock forty years in this wilderness.

The Congregational Church was organized September 27, 1768. Meetings were held in the log schoolhouse and private residences for four years.

The year 1772 stands out conspicuous in the church history of the town. It was in this year when the town, numbering about 300 souls, was ready to take definite steps and organized efforts in several matters. June 24, 1772, saw the small church adopting as its own articles of agreement, a confession of faith and a covenant. One of the articles reads—"the constitution of the church is to be what is commonly called Congregational." On July 6, 1772, the church extended a call to Isaiah Potter to settle here in work of the gospel ministry. The ordination services already referred to took place August 25, 1772. The next enterprise was the building of a church. Upon the location for it the people could not agree. But the earnest remonstrance of the young pastor brought about harmony. It was finally decided by the strenuous thud of a walking stick owned by the pastor, and by that spot the church was built. The spot has already been referred to, in the field west of the Luther Alden place, near the old burying ground. At a church meeting legally warned October 29, 1772, Mr. Joseph Dana was made choice of for deacon and the first sacrament of the Lord's Supper and doubtless in this newly built meeting-house, was on November 15, 1772. Thus if Thanksgiving was observed it must have been a joyous one. From 1762, when four men passed their first winter here, to 1772, when the town had a population of about 300 souls, there were many causes for thanksgiving. The town meeting was formed, an organized church was in working order, a settled pastor had come, a schoolhouse was built, and a house for public worship was erected, a deacon and officers were chosen and the Lord's supper administered.

The meeting-house was an old-fashioned building, 48 feet in length, 34 feet in breadth, while the posts which supported the room were 12 feet high. In the reading of the records during Mr. Potter's ministry, one soon perceives that the church paid scrupulous attention to particular cases of discipline which resulted in some instances in excommunicating the persons charged with the breaking of a commandment or with the breach of the covenant. July 24, 1777, was observed as a public fast day, on account of the distress of the war and the near approach of the enemy after Ticonderoga was given up. The covenant of the church was solemnly renewed. Several years pass by and the church votes that the Psalms should be sung in public worship without reading, but hymns, for want of books, should be sung line by line. The first chorister mentioned is Enoch Reddington, who was chosen to lead the singing. Ziba Huntington was the second chorister to serve the congregation. He was appointed March 7, 1782. At the same meeting a Mr. Waters was asked to build a communion table. On the Lord's Day, April 28, 1782, fifty-two persons united on confession of faith, doubtless the fruit of a revival led by Mr. Potter, who was regarded as one of the successful revivalists in the state. One may judge of the sentiment held by the good people of the town in those early days from an item under date March 3, 1784, which reads as follows: "Voted that the church view it unbecoming the profession of godliness for young people, professors, to practise frolicking and vain mirth, likewise for elderly persons to indulge in idleness, in foolish talking and jesting. Voted that they should set a watch about themselves and in the future refrain." But, alas, how often was this rule broken! There are many today who can heartily sympathize with Molly Estabrook, Polly Waterman and Otis Freeman who were earnestly admonished by the pastor before the congregation one Sunday morning.

After twenty years' standing the old meeting-house was partially destroyed one night, and some of the timber removed near by the dwelling-house of Henry Farnam. The record of May 18, 1792, informs us that the church voted to suspend those members for the present who were active in pulling down the meeting-house. This necessitated new quarters for the religious exercises of the town. (I have been unable to find any definite information about the rebuilding of the church near by Elihu Hyde's place, or as now owned by Farnam. The timbers have been shown me, but tradition alone, without any particular records, is not always a safe guide. It may be that the church was temporarily rebuilt on the hill to accommodate the increased population, but the records, where are they? My belief is that for the short period from spring to early winter in 1792, worship was conducted in private dwelling-houses and occasionally in the old meeting-house that was only partially destroyed.)

A new meeting-house for the benefit of all in the town was erected on the common in 1792. The records, however, imply that in 1793 meetings were held in the old as well as in the new meeting-house.

During Mr. Potter's ministry 372 names were inscribed upon the roll. Out of this number 12 were ministers of the gospel, among whom were Rev. Samuel Wood, D. D., of Boscawen, Rev. Walter Harris, D. D., of Dunbarton, Rev. Benjamin Wood of Upton, Mass., Rev. John Griswold, Rev. Experience Porter, Rev. Reuben Mason and Rev. Luther Wood. Mr. Potter was endowed with a splendid physique and possessed unusual strength. For awhile he was chaplain of one of the New Hampshire regiments in the Revolution. In mental power and grasp he was above the average. His ministry was crowned with success. Through his untiring efforts the church grew in numbers and in religious fervor, and had great influence in the county and state. After a long and useful life he died July 2, 1817, aged 71, having been connected with this church as supply and settled pastor about forty-five years. His death occurred in what is called the Breck farm, now owned by G. A. Miller. When he was ordained there were about forty families in town and shortly after his death the population was 1,710.

THE DECADE 1817 TO 1827.

From 1817 to 1827 church matters were in an unsettled condition. During this period there was one meeting-house for the whole town. One of the members writes: The pulpit was supplied by the labors of several ministers for a few Sabbaths each and under a joint committee of the church and people, whose object was to procure a great popular preacher to suit all denominations, so that all would help support the minister and the minister's tax be light. The church was soon made to feel how small her influence was when merged in the population of the town.

A condition of indifference set in. On August 18, 1818, the church withdrew from the town meeting-house, being virtually excluded from it, and remained out for at least two years and had no stated meetings. Occasionally, however, religious services were held at the dwelling-house of Ira Gates and again at the schoolhouse near Eliel Peck's, and again at the schoolhouse near Mr. Abbot's. Thus from 1818 to 1823, a period of five years, this church had no abiding place. In February, 1823, the town assumed the right of controlling the occupancy of the meeting-house on the common, and portioned out the use of it among all the denominations in town. The Congregationalists were given fourteen Sabbaths in the year, the Independent church, whose pastor was Rev. John Foord, twenty-two Sabbaths, the Universalists twelve and the Baptists four. By a new arrangement in 1827 the Congregationalists were given twenty Sabbaths in the year.

The church during this period extended a call to Rev. John Foord of Piermont. He was a thorough scholar, as judged from part of his library, now in the possession of Mr. Goodrich in this town. He was a liberal in his theological views, far ahead of the average minister of his day. With all his faults he possessed some excellent traits of character and doubtless set the orthodox party thinking. After serving the church for a brief period it was voted not to engage him longer to minister to this people or to administer the sacraments. The date of this action was October 14, 1819. On June 5, 1821, a communication was received when 32 members withdrew fellowship to unite with the Independent church under charge of Rev. John Foord.

March 23, 1823, the church takes action on the low state of religion in the community. A committee of eight was appointed to go two by two from house to house to pray with and converse with the people in the interests of religion. In the spring of 1823 Rev. Calvin Cutler is the preacher. To him a call was extended August 11, 1823, and he accepted. The council for ordination was October 5, 1823. It is an interesting day. The council met at the dwelling-house of Stephen Kendrick; the examination of the candidate was held at the schoolhouse which stood on the corner of Prospect Street by the Catholic Church, and the ordination service was held in the town meeting-house on the common. President Tyler of Dartmouth preached the sermon and the address to the people was given by Rev. Samuel Wood, D. D., of Boscawen.

The first Sabbath school in Lebanon was organized at the house of Ira Gates on April 11, 1825. Abner Allen united with the church October 19, 1826. In that same year there was a flourishing singing school in town. A church fast was declared December 7, 1826. Rev. Calvin Cutler ended his ministry in this town September 13, 1827. Mr. Cutler was an able, faithful and laborious minister, and his labors were attended with divine blessing. There were 49 persons received into fellowship from the close of Mr. Potter's ministry in 1817 to the dismission of Mr. Cutler September 13, 1827.

From Lebanon, his first pastorate, he went to be the religious leader of the Presbyterian Church at Windham, of this state. He remained there as pastor till his death in 1844. His son, Rev. Charles Cutler of Talmadge, Ohio, born in Lebanon 80 years ago, recently bore the expense of a memorial tablet of Italian marble in memory of his father. The tablet is placed upon the front wall near the pulpit of the Presbyterian Church at Windham.

With the coming of 1828 a new lease of life was experienced. It is a conspicuous year in the church history of Lebanon. A number of brethren had already met together to take council concerning their future course of action. It was decided that a separate church building should be erected and one which should be entirely under the control of the members. For this new enterprise subscriptions poured in and encouraged the brethren to go forward. Sufficient money being on hand the foundation was laid and the building started. The frame was built April 24, 1828, and the house dedicated August 13, 1828. The cost of the church building and the lot of land amounted to $3,162. A dwelling-house and some land adjoining were generously donated by Deacon Nathaniel Porter, to be used as a parsonage. In addition to all this material prosperity, the church raised a fund of $1,000, the annual interest of which was to be devoted to the support of the gospel. Thus with a place of worship of their own, with a parsonage under their control and a fund already on hand, the church began to seek for a pastor. Before the year closed they were ready to call Principal Newell of Meriden Academy, but the call was not extended to him until January 23, 1829, when Mr. Newell saw fit to decline. February 7, 1829, Rev. Phineas Cooke of Acworth was invited to preach to the congregation, and the result was a call extended to him to become the settled pastor. He accepted the call and on May 18, 1829, he was installed. On June 4, 1829, Rev. Phineas Cooke, Stephen Kendrick, Nathaniel Porter, Sr., and Nathaniel Porter, Jr., and Deacon Isaac Allen were appointed a committee to examine the records of the church and to report what alterations and improvements in their judgment they may deem expedient for their day. September 23, 1829, the committee reported and the result was a unanimous vote of the recommendations. This meant the adoption of a revised confession of faith and articles of agreement and covenant. Now the people and pastor were happily united for Christian service in a new environment and under new conditions. The church prospered year by year.

January 17, 1833, this resolution was adopted: "No person shall be admitted as a member who will not engage to abstain from making, selling or using ardent spirits as an article of drink or luxury. In 1835 sixty-seven persons united and 39 at one communion. In 1841 appears the first manual giving the confession of faith and covenant and a catalogue of pastors, dea-

REV. PHINEHAS COOKE.

cons and members from its organization in 1768. Mr. Cooke ended his ministry here May 13, 1848. The records give full evidence that he was a successful pastor; 233 persons were received into membership during his time. He was tall and of a commanding figure, possessing remarkable social qualities. He was a judicious and faithful pastor and an able minister.

Near the close of the ministry of Mr. Cooke, there arose a difference of opinion with reference to the continuation of his services. To some extent matters were adjusted temporarily. The separation that immediately followed seemed inevitable. Rev. Charles A. Downs was the supply during the rest of the year 1848. However on the records the first mention of Mr. Downs is January 11, 1849. It is with the view of having him settle in Lebanon. The call was extended July 9, 1849, and the church voted on September 8 to give Mr. Downs $450 as an annual salary, with the use of the parsonage.

The records inform us that a communication signed by 37 members was read. The purpose was to organize a new church at West Lebanon. Letters of dismissal were asked for and the requests were granted. The mother and daughter have lived in harmony. The church at West Lebanon was organized by council convened for that purpose November 8, 1849, and the pastor-elect, Mr. Downs, and Deacon Abner Allen were appointed to represent the mother church.

November 21, 1849, Mr. Downs was ordained and installed as pastor of this church. At this council the candidate was privileged by having present as moderator and also speaker chosen to give the charge to the pastor his maternal uncle, Rev. Nathaniel Bouton, D. D., of Concord. Dr. Richards of Hanover preached the sermon. The daughter church was represented by the acting pastor, Rev. Charles B. Haddock, and Mr. Joseph Wood as delegate.

Thus auspiciously began the second longest pastorate in the history of the church. As supply and settled pastor for a quarter of a century, Mr. Downs was closely identified with the life of this church. Work prospered under his care and leadership. The financial condition of the church was excellent. The society never failed but once in 25 years to pay the pastor his salary on the day it was due. For benevolent causes a systematic plan was adopted and in 1854 $210 was raised for benevolence.

During the civil war some of the best sermons and public addresses of the pastor were brought out. In 1869 forty-four persons united. In 1873 at his own request Mr. Downs resigned the pastoral office. He was a faithful leader, a choice peacemaker and a Christian comforter. The influence of his personality extended far beyond the limits of the parish. His studious turn and ready wit, his preaching ability, his public spirit and patriotism, and his advocacy of the cause of freedom and union when it cost something to stand squarely for honest convictions, and in addition to this his skill in mathematics and natural taste for language and historical research—all tended to launch him out into the open and make of him a leader in town, county and state matters. He served in several important public offices very creditably and "his works do follow him." Just before his death, September 20, 1906, he was the oldest living member of the church, uniting at the same time along with his wife January 4, 1850. During his ministry here 226 persons were received into membership and some of these are the faithful and loyal supporters of the church today. For many years Mr. Downs was collecting data for this history of Lebanon.

During the fall of 1873 and the spring of 1874 the pulpit was supplied by several ministers. At the preparatory lecture, May 1, Rev. Walter H. Ayers was voted in to be received as a member by letter. During the intervals between the pastorates in 1772, 1828, 1848, the church called special meetings to consider the advisability of making improvements and changes if deemed necessary. So now in 1874 improvements were made. Several articles were added to the rules of government of the church. The first recorded annual meeting was started. The second manual appears. An effort was made to do away with the afternoon services, and about this the Methodists and Baptists were consulted. It was the purpose now to get along with two services instead of three. After such clearing up the church was again ready to search for a pastor. A call was extended to Rev. Walter H. Ayers, June 18, 1874. Within ten days it was accepted. Mr. Ayers was born in Canterbury, N. H., April 26, 1847. He graduated at Dartmouth, 1868, and at Andover Theological Seminary in 1872. He was ordained at the Congregational Church, Winooski, Vt., July 16, 1872, and from there he came to take up the work in Lebanon. The installation service was held July 7, 1874, and thus began the shortest pastorate in the history of this church. As the months went by 13 persons were admitted into fellowship by letter. As a surprise the letter of resignation was read September 12, 1875. A council met and assented to the action of the pastor and church. Mr. Ayers was a diligent student, a faithful preacher and a devoted pastor.

The church voted February 14, 1876, to extend a call to Rev. John Mason Dutton, who was at that time a senior in Yale Divinity School. April 1 the call was duly extended through an appointed committee. The salary was stated at $1,400. Under date April 10 the acceptance of the call appears. Mr. Dutton was ordained June 20, 1876. As the months and years went by pastor and people were happily united. This pleasant harmony shows in results. All the work progressed under such healthful religious conditions. The Sunday school reached an enrollment of 200. The benevolent offerings steadily increased. In 1878 thirty-one persons united and some of these are faithful workers today. In 1879 the state association met with the church. His resignation was a surprise to all. During his pastorate of nine years, which ended May 20, 1885, a debt of $4,000 was paid, the church edifice was repaired and 118 persons were received into membership. The resolutions that were passed at the dismissal council voiced unanimously the sentiment of the parish. The spirit of unity and harmony that prevailed resulted in the prosperity and growth of the church and society in every respect. Mr. Dutton never forgot the people of his first charge and according to his wish he rests from his labors in the cemetery close by the church he served so well. Three of the pastors lie buried in Lebanon cemeteries.

Mr. Dutton was born in Craftsbury, Vermont, April 14, 1847. He attended Craftsbury and Johnson schools; graduated at Kimball Union Academy in 1869. His college was Dartmouth, where he finished the course in 1873. He graduated at Yale Divinity School, 1876. His first regular pastorate was Lebanon, where he served nine years, his second regular pastorate was Somersworth, N. H., where he served for eight years, his third regular pastorate was at Newtonville, Mass., where he served for seven years. His last pastorate was at Newport, Vermont. His persistency and energy and abounding vitality contributed much to the building of the handsome church edifice at Newtonville, Mass. For several years he was superintendent of schools at Somersworth, N. H., and a trustee of Kimball Union Academy. In his short pastorate at Newport, Vermont, he won a position of influence in the whole community. After a brief illness he died June 17, 1900, aged 53 years. The funeral was conducted by Rev. E. M. Chapman assisted by Rev. C. H. Merrill, D. D., and Rev. C. R. Flanders. The memory of such a religious leader in this town is part of the rich spiritual legacy of this church.

During the summer of 1885 two prospective candidates for the vacant pastorate were considered, but no definite plan was consummated. The men were Rev. Gulick and Rev. W. A. Bartlett of Hanover. In September and October a call was extended to Rev. Edgar T. Farrill of Hopkinton, salary $1,650. Mr. Farrill accepted and the new relations began on the first Sunday in November, 1885. Installation services were held December 17, 1885. The sermon was preached by Rev. Franklin D. Ayer, D. D. of Concord. Scripture was read by Rev. N. F. Tilden of the Baptist Church, Lebanon, and the invocation by Rev. Calvin Stebbins of the Unitarian Church, Lebanon. The address to the people was given by the preceding pastor, Rev. John M. Dutton. Thus auspiciously began the ministry of the seventh pastor and fourth in length of service. In 1887 Grafton County Conference held its fifty-ninth anniversary with one church. The benevolence as reported for the same year was $800. In 1893 the 125th anniversary of the church was appropriately observed. Special services were held during the anniversary week. Year by year new additions to membership came, so that during Mr. Farrill's ministry from 1885 to 1902, a period of 17 years, 125 persons were enrolled as members. Rev. Edgar T. Farrill resigned and the resignation went into effect October 31, 1902.

Mr. Farrill was born in Providence, R. I., August 21, 1854. After receiving his early training in private and public and military schools he entered Brown University, from which he graduated in 1879. He graduated from Andover Theological Seminary in 1882, and he was ordained to the gospel ministry September 27 of that same year. His first pastorate of three years was at Hopkinton, N. H., from which charge he was called to labor in Lebanon. From Lebanon he was called to his third pastorate, where he now labors, Kenosha, Wisconsin. Mr. Farrill has been an active worker for the temperance cause and the Sunday school and Christian Endeavor. He has already served as trustee of Kimball Union Academy and on the Lebanon school board.

The present pastorate began September 1, 1903. To the end of 1906 thirty-five persons have united with the church. Benevolence for the same year, 1906, $800. Confession of faith, covenant and rules of government revised and the third manual has appeared.

The church has had eight pastors, 14 clerks, 26 deacons and 1,161 members.

THE WEST CONGREGATIONAL CHURCH.

In the year 1848 the west part of the town, embracing the Connecticut valley from Hanover to Plainfield, having become quite thickly settled and the selection of this point as the terminus of the Northern Railroad having settled the question of the future village, whose population were four miles from church privileges, a meeting was held at the house of Oliver Stearns on May 22, at which ten members of the church at the Centre were present, viz.: Richard Kimball, Ebenezer Kimball, Henry G. Wood, John Wood, Thomas Wood, Oliver Stearns, Daniel Richardson, Elias H. Richardson and Aruna Hall. The meeting was duly organized and it was "voted to appoint a committee to select a site for a meeting-house somewhere in West Lebanon, to be improved at a suitable time." The committee chosen made choice of the location where the present house of worship and parsonage now stand. In the autumn of 1849 the house was ready to be dedicated. On November 8 a council called by 37 members dismissed from the Centre and seven others assembled. The church was organized and the house dedicated. On December 27 three deacons were chosen, Samuel Wood, David Richardson and Nathan B. Stearns, the last named still holding that office. The pulpit was supplied by the professors of Dartmouth College till the summer of 1851. On June 26, Rev. Rufus Case was installed as pastor and continued in that office till March 12, 1862. On February 3, 1863, Mr. John H. Edwards was ordained and installed pastor. He served the church faithfully for nearly eight years and was dismissed in 1871, January 12. Rev. A. B. Rich, D. D., was installed pastor May 17, 1871, and continued in service till May 18, 1880. Rev. T. C. Pease was called to the pastorate and served the church from September, 1880, to December 2, 1884. Rev. C. E. Havens was the next pastor. His term of service was from October 20, 1885, to October 25, 1893. The present pastor, Rev. C. Fremont Roper, was inducted into office April 17, 1894. The deacons who have served the church are Samuel Wood, 2d, chosen December 27, 1849; David Richardson, chosen December 27, 1849; Nathan B. Stearns, elected December 27, 1849; Charles H. Dana, January 3, 1868; Horace French, July 6, 1878; Leonard A. Estabrook, July 6, 1878. The four last named are now in active service. Since the church's organization 478 have been received to its membership, of whom 170 are now members. During the history of nearly half a century the church has had six pastors, all unanimously called and dismissed in peace.

Thus the church has had a degree of harmony, peace and fruitfulness such as is enjoyed by few throughout their history.

(Rev.) C. Fremont Roper.

West Lebanon, N. H., August 1, 1895.

The Baptist Church.

Men and women connected with Baptist churches, near and remote, were not wanting in Lebanon during the first half of the 19th century. They appear to have gradually increased in numbers. The nearest Baptist churches were at Hanover Mill Village (now Etna) and at East Plainfield, the latter becoming extinct or merging with the Meriden church near the middle of the century. There was a Free Will Baptist Church on Methodist Hill, in Enfield, but near where Enfield, Plainfield and Lebanon corner, together owning a union meeting-house, with the Methodists. This house, long in disuse, was only removed in 1906. That at East Plainfield disappeared in the 60's. The families which maintained both nearly all moved away, some to

BAPTIST CHURCH.

Lebanon. Churches, like schools, drifted to the business centers, and the advent of railroads changed business centers. The sixth decade found Baptists numerous and increasing in the village. Nearly all were men and women of deep and earnest piety. They allied themselves in Christian work and worship with the Congregational and Methodist churches, and were helpful in the religious, Sunday school, and social work of those congregations. They greatly endeared themselves by godly lives to the membership of those churches and became greatly attached to them in turn. It was natural that the members of those churches were loathe to part with so helpful an element and slow to recognize the necessity for a separate interest. Baptists in those days more than now, by their views as to baptism and the Lord's supper, so called, were self-deprived of privileges which they greatly desired. They occasionally absented themselves from their accustomed place of worship, and went singly, by twos or threes, and sometimes a two-horse load, to Meriden or Mill Village on Communion Day. Naturally their hearts burned within them all the way with a desire for a church to their liking. They believed they could be more useful therewith. They at length began to think that the prospective growth of the center village warranted the establishment of another church. These were conscientious, devout, earnest, practical, large-hearted Christian men and women. Every light that can be turned on their lives attests it. Every trip to a neighboring church intensified the feeling.

Into this circle of believers, in the autumn of 1860, came one who was to prove the magnet to draw them together, the center around which they could rally, a leader who was to impart to them his own abiding, unquestioning faith, his indomitable courage and his exalted ideas of the duty of generous giving for the cause of Christ. That leader and magnet was Rev. Sumner Hale. He had the very best of helpers in his wife, Hannah T. Hale. He was a graduate of Waterville College and of Newton Theological School. A chronic throat trouble hindered his usefulness as a preacher, and regarding it as providential, he turned to his trade, that of a scythe finisher, at which he was very skillful, devoting most of his savings to religious purposes. He was following his trade at Fitchburg, Mass., when the firm of Emerson and Cummings, scythe-makers, heard of him and sent one of the firm, Mr. Joseph Cummings, a Baptist, to induce him to enter its service. It was not until he had made careful inquiry into the religious conditions in Lebanon, and saw that here was a coveted opportunity, that he was induced to change his residence. In a few weeks he had made the personal acquaintance of every person of known Baptist proclivities in town, and had them assembled for prayer, praise and consultation. The first meeting was held at the house of Joseph Cummings, in December, 1860. Present, Rev. Sumner Hale, Mrs. Hannah T. Hale, Joseph Cummings, Mrs. Chloe H. Cummings, Charles V. Cobb, Mrs. Betsey A. Cobb, Asa Chase and Gilman C. Whipple. Meetings were held Tuesday evenings during the winter, with steadily increased interest. The following spring a paper was drawn up binding the signers to certain duties, with reference to a prospective formation of a church. It was signed by 24 persons, some of whom left town before the project matured, while others came and signed it. No public meetings were held for want of a suitable place. All continued helpful in the other churches. This broad-minded spirit yielded rich fruit afterward in the cordial feeling of the other churches. The civil war hindered for awhile. Early in 1862 it was decided to erect a chapel, and a society was organized under the statutes. A committee was appointed consisting of Thomas E. Hough, Joseph Cummings and Charles V. Cobb, to purchase a lot, raise funds and receive proposals. A lot was purchased on Green Street. It was the lot on one-half of which the house of William B. Cole now stands, the other half still open as a lawn. The house next west (the Foster house) was used as a parsonage till 1874. The first five pastors lived there. The sixth owned a house when called, and the parsonage was disposed of.

It was never owned by the society, but was held by the owner, Mr. J. H. Purmort, at the disposition of the society as long as wanted. Mrs. Purmort was an original member, and he came early into the church, from the Free Will Baptist Church on Methodist Hill. He was the heaviest contributor to the cost of the house of worship, and the largest payer towards ordinary expenses. Quite a proportion of the members had indeed been Free Will Baptists.

The contract was given to Mead, Mason & Co., and by August

ELIAS H. CHENEY.

GILMAN C. WHIPPLE.

the building was completed. A church was organized at the house of C. V. Cobb on the evening of the 27th of August. Charles V. Cobb and Thomas E. Hough were elected deacons and Sumner Hale clerk. "The New Hampshire Articles of Faith" were adopted and the form of covenant was copied from that of the First Baptist Church in Lawrence, Mass., from which some of the members had come. In the forenoon of August 29th the house was dedicated. Rev. Foster Henry of Fitchburg, Mass., from whose church Mr. and Mrs. Hale had come, preached the sermon. Pastors of nearby Baptist churches and of the Congregational and Methodist local churches took part in the interesting exercises. On the afternoon of the same day the church was duly recognized as a Baptist church by a council called for that purpose. The recognition sermon was by Rev. F. E. Cummings, D. D., of Concord.

The persons who entered into this church relation at that time were: Clement Hough and his wife, Theoda Hough, Asa Chase and his wife, Dorothy Currier Chase, Rev. Sumner Hale and his wife, Hannah T. Hale, Charles V. Cobb and his wife, Betsey A. Cobb, Thomas E. Hough and his wife, Ellen Hough, Edwin W. Hough and his wife, Martha D. Hough, John C. Worth and his wife, Mary Worth, Elias H. Cheney and his wife, Susan W. Cheney. These united heads of families, and besides, Cyrus Heath, Gilman C. Whipple, Mrs. Jennie Smith Davis, Mrs. Arabella Thompson, William D. Bryant, Mrs. Marcia J. Purmort, Mrs. Hannah Andrews, Mrs. Harriet N. Cushman, Miss Melissa Wright—26 in all.

The following Sunday, August 31, the chapel was opened for public worship, Rev. E. E. Cummings, D. D., occupying the pulpit. The congregations were large, that of the afternoon overtaxing the chapel. A Sunday school was organized at noon, with Rev. John McKinlay as superintendent. The evening was given to a social, religious, testimony service, in which a large number took part. This was followed by a general hand-shaking and heart-shaking. It was a day of intense interest to the little band.

The pulpit was supplied by neighboring preachers until October 12th, when Mr. John McKinlay of Lawrence, Mass., came as a candidate. He preached two Sabbaths, gave perfect satisfaction, received a unanimous call, accepted, and immediately entered on his duties. On Saturday, November 6, 1862, by a council duly called for the purpose, Mr. McKinlay after the usual examination, was publicly set apart to the work of the Christian ministry, and recognized as pastor of the church. The sermon on that occasion was by Rev. H. F. Lane of Boston. McKinlay was a native of Alexandria, Dunbartonshire, Scotland, a skillful pattern designer, and came to this country, with his wife, née Miss Jean Russell, in 1854. He immediately found lucrative employment in the Pacific Mills at Lawrence. Soon after he and his wife became interested in personal religion, found congenial spirits in the First Baptist Church in Lawrence, and united with it. It soon became evident that he was meant for a higher sphere. He was encouraged to abandon his lucrative employment, spend all his accumulations and more in preparation for the pulpit, and enter the ministry. He gave two years to study at the Baptist Theological School then existing at Fairfax, Vt., and one year at Andover, Mass., and was ready for duty, providentially, as he and those who called him believed, when the church in Lebanon was organized. He was a man of great strength of character, thoroughly consecrated to the work he espoused. He immediately took a high stand among the clergy of the vicinity.

The history of his ministry of six years is one of uninterrupted church prosperity. The church more than doubled in numbers, 39 members being added. He came at last to feel that perhaps the church and himself would be benefited by a change, and with this in view preached during his vacation one Sabbath at Adams, N. Y. He was simply tired, and unaware that a fatal disease lurked within him. Coming from his room the morning of the second Sabbath at Adams, manuscript in hand and the congregation assembled, his host noticed a deathly paleness on his face and dissuaded him from entering the church. He went to bed instead, lingered, suffering, during the day, and expired without a struggle just at the hour of evening service September 20, 1868. The news was a shock to the community, producing the widest sympathy. His remains tenderly prepared, were brought here in charge of Rev. F. E. Osborne, who preached the funeral sermon in the Congregational Church, courteously

FIRST BAPTIST CHURCH AND PARSONAGE.

tendered for the purpose, in view of the limited capacity of the chapel. Business was generally suspended and a large congregation assembled to do him honor and express sympathy. The remains were committed to dust in the village cemetery with solemn ceremony, in the presence of many witnesses. Mr. Osborne remained and occupied the pulpit the following Sabbath. Ministers of several denominations from the surrounding churches, and professors at Dartmouth and New London supplied the pulpit for about three months, the salary being continued to Mrs. McKinlay.

With the beginning of 1869, Rev. C. E. Cummings, D. D., came as acting pastor. Dr. Cummings was a father in the Baptist Israel, of long and distinguished service as pastor, his last two charges being in Concord. He was distinctly the founder of the Pleasant Street Church in Concord, as was Mr. Hale of that in Lebanon. From its inception he had been a trusted adviser of the latter. He had just resigned as pastor at Concord, on account of age and the severe duties required in a church of that size, but with singular fitness for such an opening. During his short ministry the present church edifice was erected at a cost of about $12,000, of which $7,000 was raised at home, $1,000 contributed abroad, and a debt of nearly $4,000 was left. The project had gone so far before Mr. McKinlay left as to secure a lot, though a change of lot was afterwards made. A building committee consisting of Charles V. Cobb, Asa Chase, Asa W. Richardson, Jasper H. Purmort, and Henry B. Hough was appointed September 15th, only five days before the pastor's decease, and in his absence. Work began in the early spring, but the first plan adopted proving unsatisfactory to many, was suspended to examine other plans, and the present house was the result. Mead, Mason & Co. had the job as before. Considerable of the cost went into the trusses which support the roof, made strong enough to admit of taking out the partition which separates the vestry, should it be necessary, without additional support. Hon. A. M. Shaw, the well-known Lebanon railroad man, said he would dare run a railway train over them.

The unexpected cost was in the thoroughness with which the work was done. The end of the year saw the structure completed. It is a singular fact that the man, Nathan F. Tilden, who was destined afterwards to be 25 years pastor of the church, began his work in Lebanon, having just moved here, by digging the trenches for its foundation, and labored upon it in one capacity or another till it was completed.

The little chapel saw its last congregation assembled for worship on the 19th day of December, 1879, and the new structure was dedicated on the 31st. Dr. Cummings preached the sermon. Appropriate service was also held in the evening, the sermon being by Rev. Foster Henry. The little chapel was sold to the Lebanon High School Association, the precursor of the present high school, and for a year or two was used for school purposes, then sold and moved to Elm Street, where it serves as a tenement house. It was in this building that Commander Harry H. Hosley, U. S. Navy, who so successfully towed the great floating dock to Manila, began his academic course.

Dr. Cummings had no sooner seen the new house completed and everything going smoothly in it, than he himself initiated the movement to release him and settle a pastor. With this end in view, in August, 1870, he invited a man to occupy the pulpit whom he thought most suitable and the people likely to appreciate, Rev. Jirah Tucker of Randolph, Vt. And they did. When Dr. Cummings resigned, two months later, taking a leave which was most affectionate, mutually, the church knew whom it wanted. The call was unanimous again, was accepted, and the church once more started out with bright hopes, save for the shadow which the debt left. The burden was made heavier for that the State Convention, which had appropriated $100 a year to this interest, withdrew its support, on the plea that a congregation which could build such a house ought to take care of itself. The blow was very severely felt and increased the difficult task of paying the debt. Mr. Tucker was a charming personality, a gifted pulpit orator and consecrated to his work. He excelled as a reader of hymns, reading so as to compel the singing, "with the spirit and understanding." But he was in delicate health, more than he or anybody dreamed, and after preaching ten Sabbaths, with great effort, he was obliged to rest. Resuming his pulpit the first Sunday in January, 1871, he found himself completely exhausted at the close of the service. He went West, among friends, hoping to regain health, but grew rapidly worse, and breathed his last at Upper Alton, Ill., April 24, 1871. Again the church was thrown into the deepest grief. But the emergency afforded another opportunity to exemplify the spirit of Christian courtesy which has marked Lebanon churches. The Congregational Church was repairing and altering its house of worship, and the church with the sick pastor invited the Congregational pastor, Rev. C. A. Downs, to occupy its pulpit, and the congregation to worship with itself. It was done, to mutual edification and advantage; and again the salary went to the distressed and bereaved widow.

The fourth pastor was Rev. Horace F. Barnes, a native of Newark, N. J., and a graduate of Amherst and of Newton. He had fulfilled a successful pastorate at Buffalo and might easily have coveted the larger city church and salary. He chose the humbler field because he found a flock which more nearly seemed to meet his ideals. His, too, was a charming personality. He was an excellent pulpit orator. He attacked the debt, put his whole soul into an effort to pay it, and he succeeded. But it was at the cost of so crippling the church's ability to raise money for ordinary expenses, coupled with the death of one liberal giver and the removal of others, with the abandonment of the enterprise by the State Convention, that it became impossible to raise his salary, and having a flattering call elsewhere, he accepted it. He resigned February 1, 1874. He carried with him ever after the warmest affection of the membership. He had a successful pastorate at Winchester, Mass., and was for a long time in mission work in and near New York. A large part of his useful life was spent as assistant pastor of the Tremont Temple Church in Boston, from which service he was summoned to the church above a few years ago.

The church was paying a debt, it is well to note, incurred when gold was still at a premium of about thirty, and prices proportionately high, and the country on the swimming tide of the prosperity which inflation engenders—paying it with gold back nearly though not quite at par and the country almost in a panic, in the effort to resume specie payment. Dollars were harder to get now. Many a church got caught that way.

The debt was paid none too soon. In a few years the church had lost by death two of its heaviest financial supporters, and three more by removal. The five were bearing nearly half the yearly expenses, and they had paid nearly half the debt.

Sunday, September 18, 1872, Rev. Mr. Barnes preached an historical discourse, covering the first ten years of the church history. This has been preserved. Mrs. Barnes has kindly forwarded it as a possible aid in the preparation of this history, and it has been found of great value. It is to be preserved.

Rev. J. H. Gannett was next called, and accepted at the salary which the church thought it could raise. He was an excellent minister, who had done good work elsewhere and who did good work to the end of his life. But conditions had greatly changed in Lebanon and in the church now. It was passing through a period of adversity, which tried its faith to the uttermost. Rev. Sumner Hale left, carrying the unbounded love of those to whom he had been so long as "the shadow of a great rock in a weary land." He retired from active labor, ending his ability to give; had given himself poor, and settled in Camden, N. J., where a few years later he died—died poor in worldly goods but rich in faith. Other liberal givers also left. It was the ebb of the tide, even if disaster had not overtaken the town, in the failure of the Sturtevant Manufacturing Co. That crippled all the churches. It seemed as if the little Baptist Church would have to close its doors. Again the pastor had to leave because it became impossible to raise the money to pay his salary. And pastors must live. Mr. Gannett read his resignation, December 12, 1875. The church parted with him unwillingly and its love followed him to the end of his life.

It had, however, among its numbers, a preacher, Nathan F. Tilden, of no mean ability, whom it had itself licensed to preach, and who had filled its own pulpit and many others in emergencies, that at Etna and the Lebanon Congregational Church among others. He was a native of Boston and educated in her schools, but without the advantages of theological training. He was now a measurer of lumber for the company that went into bankruptcy. He was thrown out of work. He owned a house and wanted to stay. He loved to preach and people loved to hear him. The church asked him to supply, and he did, taking what it could pay, and it paid as liberally in proportion to its ability as ever. He gave to Bible study now the hours he had been wont to give to business, and rapidly developed into a man fit to set apart for the ministry. The church finally settled and ordained him. There was not a dissenting voice in the council, though the examination was unusually critical. It grew not of any disposition to be severe, but from the love the pastors had to hear him talk.

He was ordained June 22, 1876, Rev. Dr. Lorimer, the noted Tremont Temple pastor of Boston, preaching the ordaining sermon. He continued in the pastorate 25 years, and under his ministry the church gradually recovered somewhat of its standing. At the end of fifteen years he had a unanimous call to the New London church, where he had often preached on exchange. The students especially were glad to hear him. But his church simply would not let him go. He afterwards held pastorates in Warner, N. H., and Fiskdale, Mass. He is now settled at Baldwinsville, Mass.

During his pastorate various church improvements were carried out. The church was made glad by the presentation to it of a very excellent pipe organ, by one of its members, Mr. A. W. Shapleigh. The audience room was frescoed and otherwise improved, and a new carpet was provided. Previous to his call to preach, Mr. Tilden had won the favor of the whole community by his remarkable efficiency as president of the Y. M. C. A.

Mr. Tilden was followed in 1900 by Rev. W. L. Stone, in a three years' pastorate, during which also the church recovered somewhat of its lost ground—lost almost wholly by the removal of members and most liberal givers. The audience room was renovated again, and a commodious kitchen and parlor were added and furnished, free of debt. He was finally recalled by the church in Sterling, Mass., whose pastorate he resigned to come to Lebanon, and is preaching there at this writing, 1907.

During Mr. Stone's pastorate, September 18, 1900, the morning hour of worship was devoted to an impressive service, commemorative of the life and work of Mr. McKinlay, 32 years after his decease. Papers were read by Gilman C. Whipple, E. H. Cheney and Mrs. Mary Emerson Pike. Tender words fell from the lips of Mrs. McKinlay, whose presence in town after long absence suggested the service. During much of the intervening time she had made herself exceedingly useful as matron of a missionary children's home at Newton Center, Mass.

The present pastor, Rev. Frank L. Knapp, came to the church in 1904, from an eight years' pastorate in Milford. Under his ministry the church pursues the even tenor of its way, meeting its liabilities perhaps more easily than ever. If it is not showing marked growth, it is to be remembered that the principal growth of the village has been Roman Catholic, for a long term of years, by the coming in of large numbers of people of that faith, with whom, since they own the same Master, it has no quarrel, but is rather content to live in peace.

The church has united at various times with other Protestant denominations in union services of various kinds, within doors in winter, and out of doors in summer, the latter in recent years. In some of these services, illustrating the better spirit now prevailing than once was wont, the Catholic pastor and congregation have been kindly commended to the common Father's loving care.

The church has had five deacons only, viz.: Charles V. Cobb, Thomas E. Hough, Gilman C. Whipple, Charles B. Ross, and David W. Aldrich. The two original deacons both removed from town, nearly simultaneously in the 70's, and Deacon Cobb died in 1884. His remains were brought here for burial. Deacon Hough has recently returned to town, but is too feeble for active service. Mr. Whipple was made deacon in 1875, after Asa W. Richardson, who soon after died, had declined an election. Mr. Ross has served since 1895 and Mr. Aldrich since 1900.

The church from its organization has taken a deep interest in and given liberally to all the missionary and benevolent work of the Baptist denomination. Its founder succeeded in imbuing it with his own lofty ideals.

It responded promptly to the Christian Endeavor movement, and was early in the field with its own local organization.

Its Sunday school has uniformly been large and efficient, in proportion to the congregation. It was never more prosperous than now, 1907, under the superintendency of Deacon C. B. Ross, with Mrs. Ross as head of the primary department, which meets separately.

The following persons have served as superintendent: Rev.

John McKinlay, Rev. Sumner Hale, Charles V. Cobb, Gilman C. Whipple, Nathan F. Tilden, Fred W. Cheney, Amos W. Gee, E. H. Cheney and Charles B. Ross.

In the early records it is frequently noted that Bro. so-and-so "preached all day." It means, of course, forenoon and afternoon. In 1875 the afternoon service was discontinued during July and August, and in 1880 altogether, in all the churches.

THE METHODIST EPISCOPAL CHURCH.

Early in the nineteenth century the "Hardy Neighborhood," so called, was visited by one or more Methodist preachers and a small "class" formed, which as preaching ceased was finally abandoned.

The writer has a letter from an aged Methodist minister, who says: "I remember when a small boy (about 1810 or 1812) seeing a Mr. Evans, who lived in Enfield, often at my father's house. He was dressed in 'ye olden style,' with long stockings and breeches or kilts, that reached below the knees and were fastened with knee buckles. I then thought him an old man, but he was probably about forty. He was pastor of a church at Enfield, and also judge of probate; he was a Methodist 'itinerant' and often preached in Lebanon, and was one of the pioneers of Methodism in the early part of the nineteenth century."

It is probable the first sermon preached in organized Methodism in Lebanon was by Rev. Robert Williams, a local preacher, who preached in the schoolhouse in the Hardy neighborhood (then called "The Village") in 1821. He formed a "class" of seven persons which was continued, and from which the present church sprung.

Mr. Williams preached in the neighborhood more or less for three years with good results, for we find that in the second summer of his preaching he baptized Isaac Fitch and Eunice Edwards in the brook running through the Colonel Alden farm (a much larger brook than at the present day), Mr. Fitch by immersion and Miss Edwards by sprinkling. These were probably the first baptisms by Methodists in Lebanon, and the service is reported to have been witnessed by a large number of people.

The schoolhouse was soon too small to hold the people, who came to hear "the preaching of the word;" the groves were often resorted to as places of worship, and one record says the first "Quarterly meeting" was held in a new corn barn on the Fitch Loomer place.

Many Methodists of the early times have blessed memories of this same Hardy neighborhood, and at least seven of its residents have since become preachers of the Gospel, to wit: Rev. Anthony C. Hardy, Rev. George Noyes, Rev. Charles H. Lovejoy (of bleeding Kansas fame) and four sons of the Rev. Robert Williams; a proud record for any neighborhood.

It is also recorded that in these days Rev. Joseph Kellum came to Lebanon and labored with success. He resided with George Storrs on the hill south of the plain, where he formed a "class" and George Storrs was appointed "leader." Mr. Storrs was born and reared in Lebanon, educated at Kimball Union Academy, and while quite young was appointed captain of a uniformed company of militia, and afterwards became major of his regiment, and was in a fair way of promotion when he became satisfied that he was commissioned from the highest of all authority to preach the Gospel. He was in easy financial circumstances and sought an interview with Rev. Robert Williams, which resulted in his uniting with the Methodist Episcopal Church and was licensed as a preacher; was ordained in 1829, and filled some of the best appointments in the New Hampshire and Vermont conference. Being a man of strong convictions, he embraced anti-slavery principles and evidently feeling the church did not take sufficiently advanced ground, withdrew. Mr. Storrs wrote several noteworthy books, and died in Brooklyn, N. Y. Mr. Storrs often preached in the Hardy schoolhouse, but after a time the Methodists began to preach in the old "Town House," when it stood on the common.

An old citizen remembers a communion service held in the old town house, where a communion rail was improvised by using planks at which to kneel. A large number of people are reported to have been present. This was about 1828.

The first mention we find of Lebanon in the general minutes is in 1825, when Lebanon is reported as a part of Canaan circuit. In 1828–'29 it is quoted as being connected with Plainfield or Meriden circuit. About this time a revival is reported and Christopher Tone, the son of a Hessian soldier, who did not fancy having his services sold to the English for the purpose of putting down the rebellion of the colonies, and who for that reason deserted their ranks at the battle of Bennington, was, with his wife, converted, and came to Lebanon to live. He was a man of great energy and perseverance, and was one of the leaders in building the present house of worship; for the record says in 1832 Marlin Downer, Christopher Tone and Isaac Fitch, seeing the need of a house of worship, took the entire responsibility on themselves, bought the land, built the church, depending on the sale of the pews for their pay, and while rumor says it was not a financial bonanza for themselves, it did prove a good investment for the cause of Christ. Their record is on high; their reward in heaven.

On January 6, 1832, Constant Storrs, Christopher Tone, Moody Noyes, Isaac Fitch and William Pardee assembled and formed themselves into a religious association, "to be known as the first Methodist Episcopal Society of Lebanon, County of Grafton and state of New Hampshire, agreeable to an act of the Legislature of said state, passed July 3, 1827, entitled 'An Act empowering religious societies to assume and exercise corporate powers.'"

They agreed to "assemble at the house of H. M. French on Monday, 23rd day of January, 1832, at one o'clock in the afternoon to organize and adopt a constitution." The meeting was held on time, but for some reason not at H. M. French's, for the record says, "The first annual meeting convened at the house of Calvin Benton in said town and adjourned to the house of Mrs. Lucinda Storrs," when the constitution was adopted. The reason for this sudden change does not appear. At the first annual meeting Nathaniel Ladd was chosen "moderator" and Marlin Downer clerk, an office which Mr. Downer held for many years.

The house was finished in the spring of 1833, and was dedicated "to Almighty God and the use of the Methodist Episcopal Church forever" by Rev. B. R. Hoyt, the exact date being lost.

At the Vermont and New Hampshire conference (then one) held at Windsor, Vt., August 6, 1833, Rev. J. W. Morey was appointed to Lebanon Methodism, which may be said to have set up "housekeeping" that year.

In 1836 five men bought a house and lot directly opposite the church, which cost them about $800, which in 1838 they deeded to a board of trustees, to be held for a Methodist Episcopal parsonage forever. This house was in 1861 moved to Elm Street and a new parsonage built.

The church edifice has been much increased in size by adding transepts, balcony and a choir chancel, and has a seating capacity of nearly seven hundred.

The church has had thirty-three pastors in its seventy-five years of existence, one, Rev. Chas. E. Hall, D. D., having served two terms, the first in 1873-74-75, and again in 1896-97-98.

The church in Lebanon has always extended a most cordial welcome to the masses, and for years has been the church home of large congregations, the present membership being about two hundred and fifty.

The church contains a fine organ, largely the gift of the late Hon. A. M. Shaw, who was for many years a liberal supporter of this church. The choir has for many years consisted of a large chorus, the policy being to utilize the musical talent of the younger members of the congregation, who contribute their services, and it speaks well for the solid character of the choir, when we say the present chorister has wielded the baton for forty-two years.

The church celebrated its seventy-five years of existence in January, 1908, with interesting services extending over two weeks, during which the history of the church was carefully reviewed.

In 1901 the society voted to make the pews free and preaching is supported by the voluntary contributions of the people, who contribute weekly as the Lord has prospered them, and all bills are cheerfully met.

The Universalist Society.

It has been well said that "the history of a church can never be written." Especially is this true when so few of the people who are active in the affairs of the most worthy objects fail to consider the necessity of recording and carefully preserving the proceedings of the organization of which they are members.

REV. JOHN MOORE.

COLBEE C. BENTON.

The task I have undertaken, to give a brief sketch of the Universalist Society of Lebanon, has been rendered extremely difficult by a failure in recording and preserving *intact* the records of its early days.

From the material at hand, however, we learn that the Universalist Society was organized *about* 1808 (the exact date cannot be given as the early records are lost), and for several years prior to their calling a minister meetings were held and occasional sermons delivered by the early pioneers of the denomination, viz. Hosea Ballou, Sebastian Streeter, Sylvanus Cobb and others.

Their meetings were held a portion of the time in the house of Thomas Packard, situated on the road to Enfield, and now owned and occupied by George E. Gile.

The construction of this house, like many others of that day, was well adapted for the purpose. In the second story was a large square room designed and used for the purpose of spinning the yarn and weaving the cloth used by the family, as was the custom in those days. At other times services were held in some schoolhouse in the town, where accommodations for the followers of this faith could be obtained. In 1811 and again in 1819 the general conventions of the denomination were held here.

The first settled minister was the Rev. Daniel Pickering. He was followed by Rev. Lemuel Willis, whose date of settlement was in 1824.

They made good proof of their ministry and were highly respected by the people of Lebanon, but no man was ever more beloved in the town than their successor, Rev. John Moore of saintly memory, whose ministry dated from March, 1828. His engagement in Lebanon was for half the time. During the other half he preached in Claremont, Newport, Hanover, Lyme, Piermont, N. H., and in his native place, Strafford, and other towns in Vermont. He had one of the most promising fields for religious culture, and well did he improve his opportunities. He was both pastor and missionary and well qualified did he prove himself for both kinds of ministerial work, and his influence for good was felt wherever he went. He was everywhere a representative and advocate of the cause he had espoused.

Dignified, yet gentle and easy in manner, plain and persuasive in his public speech, he could not fail of eliciting attention and commanding respect wherever he appeared.

In September, 1830, the Universalist General Convention was again held in Lebanon, and was an occasion of great interest to all present. Under date of January 29, 1831, I find the following recorded:

"On the 11th day of January, 1831, Enoch Freeman, James Willis and Daniel Whittemore of Lebanon in the County of Grafton, and State of New Hampshire, and others, their associates, members of the denomination of Christians called Universalists having met at the inn of Calvin Benton, Esq., in said Lebanon, assumed the corporate name of 'The First Universalist Society in Lebanon, New Hampshire.'

"Attest: Nathan B. Felton, Clerk of said Society.

"January 29, 1831."

Rev. Mr. Moore remained with the society in Lebanon until February, 1833, when he accepted a call to Danvers, Mass. Upon his withdrawal great disappointment was felt, and at a meeting of the society held just prior to his departure he entered into an agreement to return to them at the expiration of a year, should they then earnestly desire it. During the year of his absence Rev. ——— Knapp administered to the society. At the end of the year the Lebanon society claimed the fulfillment of Mr. Moore's promise to return to them, and he accordingly did so, resuming his labors in January, 1835.

It was during the year 1835 that the "Town Meeting House" was remodelled, the Universalists finishing a commodious audience room in the second story. There were 68 slips, besides a large orchestra in front of the desk. The alterations were completed in August when the house was reopened for religious worship by dedicatory services. The church organization was not perfected until the return of Rev. Mr. Moore in 1835. I find this record pertaining to the church: "We the undersigned believing our individual and mutual edification and growth in grace may be improved, the apostolic examples observed and the cause of truth and happiness promoted by the organization of a church, in connection with the First Universalist Society of Lebanon, do hereby enter into such connection, and adopt the New

REV. G. W. BAILEY.

Testament as the rule of our faith and practice. We will, therefore, invite to our communion all Christians, and receive into our fellowship any person desirous of leading a Christian life."

Rev. Mr. Moore remained with the society at Lebanon until December, 1839, when he removed to Hartford, Conn. From 1840 to 1851 the ministers were Revs. ——— Harris, John J. Putnam, Lemuel B. Mason, and John S. Lee, the latter severing his connection with the society in 1851, to assume the charge of the Green Mountain Liberal Institute at South Woodstock, Vt., where he also had a class in theology, and fitted nine young men for the ministry.

In 1852 the Rev. George W. Bailey accepted a call to the society and his pastorate extended to 1865 or 1866. At the close of Mr. Bailey's ministry, this organization was merged into the Unitarian Society. The rebuilding or remodelling of the old "Town Meeting House" into its present form resulted in the decline of interest in the maintainance of an organization of this faith, and its small fund, derived from the sale of its pews in the old "Meeting House" was divided by a vote of the society, a portion going toward the purchase of an organ for the Unitarian Society, the balance to the trustees of the Public Library, the income to be appropriated for the purchase of books.

NOTE.—From the Universalist Register I take the following: "In 1859 Dr. Lee removed to Canton, N. Z., where he was connected with St. Lawrence University as president for nine years. His health becoming impaired, he sought rest and renewed strength in a journey to Europe and the Holy Land. After his return he wrote and published two books: "Nature and Art in the Old World," and "Sacred Cities," both evincing wise and profitable observations in his travels. Resuming work in the university he was appointed professor of ecclesiastical history and biblical archaeology in the Theological School, a position which he held the remainder of his life, a period of thirty-three years. In 1874 he received the degree of D. D. from Butchel College and in 1901 the degree of LL. D. from Tufts College. Doctor Lee was a man of great industry, genial, eminently social in his nature and steadfast in his friendships. In the midst of his varied professional duties, he found time to contribute many valuable articles to the denominational papers, and from 1850 to 1891 he furnished twenty valuable papers to the *Universalist Quarterly*. All his powers were devoted to the church of his love, and he rendered long and devoted service to her institutions of learning. His death occurred in Canton, N. Z., September 18, 1902.

Sacred Heart.

The first mass was celebrated at Lebanon in 1835, by Rev. Father O'Reilley. The mission was afterward supplied by Rev. Fathers Daily and Brady until 1862. The first church was purchased by Father Brady in 1856. The Rev. Father Noiseux afterward attended Lebanon until 1870, when it was placed under the charge of the pastor at Claremont, Rev. Father Devonne. The Very Rev. John Murphy, late Vicar General of Portland, Me., also attended this mission from Laconia, where he was pastor. His successor, Rev. Father Goodwin, looked after it until the appointment of Rev. L. Trudell as first resident pastor in 1871. Father Finnegan succeeded Father Truedell in 1876. It was he who built the present neat and convenient church and also the parochial residence.

The old church was sold to a gentleman of the town and made into a factory, for which purpose it is still used. Father Finnegan was followed in 1881 by Rev. Father Sullivan, who in turn was succeeded by Rev. Father Laplante in 1882. At Hanover, a mission of Lebanon, Father Laplante purchased land and his successor, in 1886, the Rev. Father Paradis, built a very neat church upon it, which was dedicated by Bishop Bradley in 1887. Father Paradis improved the parochial residence in Lebanon and increased the seating capacity of the church. He also purchased a cemetery which was consecrated by Bishop Bradley in 1891. Hanover, Enfield, Canaan, Danbury, Potter Place and Andover are missions of Lebanon, and like it, have been attended by the several pastors of Claremont, Laconia and Lancaster.

Parochial schools under the charge of lay teachers were established by Father Paradis in 1889. Father Paradis was transferred to Littleton in 1893, and was succeeded by Rev. Martin H. Egan, who is at present the efficient pastor of Lebanon. He is assisted by Rev. Fr. Bernadin. (Rev. M. H. Egan was transferred to Keene in 1907.)

INDEX.

	PAGE.
Annual meetings	188, 214-217
Annual meeting illegal	279
Aspenwall, Zalmon, accused and tried	100
Assemblies held in private houses	59
Barbarick, John, confesses	101
Bequest of C. C. Benton	318
Bequests to the town	311, 312
Bonds issued to fund debt	302
"Boston Lot" first home spot	53
Boundaries	64, 65, 66
Boy, binding out of	164, 165
Bridge, agreement to build	31
Bridges, vote to put railings on	253
Bridge year	190
Burying ground, deeds of voted	32
laid out	20, 21
voted to clear and fence	34
also to enlarge	255
and to lay out a new one	278
Burying grounds, improvement and enlargement of, authorized	292
village burying ground fenced	287
Business mainly farming	199
Canada, final conquest of	1
Canoe trip disaster	53
Capital punishment	276
Cart bridge, voted to build	32
Cemetery purchased	190, 293
Cemetery, West Lebanon	286
Census taken, 1767	56
1775	68
1786	158
Centennial fourth of July celebrated	312

	PAGE.
Charter of Lebanon	2-4
provisions of	5, 6
Churches of the town	405-436
Congregational	405-417
organized	405-407
charter members	405
ministers	409-417
meeting house	408, 409
one for whole town	410
first Sabbath school organized	411
memorial tablet to Rev. Mr. Cutler	411
land donated for parsonage	412
total abstinence a condition of membership	412
church raise fund	412
movement to organize a new church at W. Lebanon	413
Rev. Isaiah Potter	409
Rev. Calvin Cutler	411
Rev. Phineas Cooke	412
Rev. Charles A. Downs	413
Rev. Walter H. Ayers	414
Rev. John M. Dutton	415
Rev. Edgar T. Farrill	416
West Congregational	417, 418
church organized	417
pastors	417, 418
Baptist	418-429
society organized, chapel erected, parsonage secured	420
chapel opened	421
church membership	421
Sunday school organized	421
Rev. John McKinlay	421
Rev. E. E. Cummings	423
Rev. Jirah Tucker	424

	PAGE.
Churches of the town,	
Baptist, Continued.	
Rev. Horace F. Barnes	425
Rev. J. H. Gannett	426
Rev. Nathan F. Tilden	426
Rev. W. L. Stone	427
Rev. Frank L. Knapp	428
deacons	428
Sunday school organized	421
superintendents	428, 429
edifice erected	423
debt paid	425
pipe organ presented	427
improvements made	427
Methodist	429–432
first baptisms	429
part of Canaan circuit	430
society organized	431
house dedicated	431
had thirty-three pastors	432
has a fine organ	432
Universalist	432–435
organized	433
first minister	433
assumes corporate name	434
worship in town meeting-house	434
adopt rules of faith	434, 435
becomes Unitarian	435
Sacred Heart	436
pastors	436
Cider and sewage, sale of	313
Cilley, Col., regiment of	94
Cleaveland, Tyxhall, accused and tried	100
Clocks, town	322
Coasting on highway prohibited	317, 318
Cohos country	1
Colburn Park	324
Colburn, Robert, accused of aiding in felling tree on Sunday	103
Cold Friday	232
Collector of taxes instructed	287, 288
College commencement largely attended	214

	PAGE.
Committees chosen	9, 10
Committee of Safety	100–107
members of	106
Common given to town	256
regulations for protection of	299, 300
vote to grade, fence, etc	284
meeting-house, vote to purchase reserve rights	266
Congregational Church formed	59
Connecticut river, surveying the	52
Connecticut valley, townships chartered in	2
Constitution, new, adopted	153
Continental Congress, expense for attendance voted	45
powerless	161
Continental currency worthless	157
Controversy with Enfield	66, 67
Convention for revision of constitution	185, 186
Convention held to frame a new constitution	161
also called to judge the same	162
adopted	163
Cotton factory	239
Counterfeit bill passes through several hands	104
Counterfeit money	70
County farm, establishment of	291
Culler of staves	314, 315
Currency depreciates	156
Cutler, Rev. Calvin, settled	240
Dartmouth College controversy	242
Davison, Oliver, settles and builds mill	55
Davison's sawmill	18, 21
Deer hunted and killed unlawfully	40
Division of 100 acres voted	21, 23
Doctors	240
Dog tax, balance of	322, 323
"Doubling up"	263
Downer, William, and family settle	54

INDEX. 439

Downer, William, Jr., accused
   of swearing, etc.........104–106
Dresden, incorporation of, asked
   148–150
Education facilities 70
Election, 1788 163
Encouragement for speedy set-
   tlement 1, 13–15, 17, 18
Enfield, controversy with.....66, 67
Engine Co., No. 2, voted pay... 294
Estabrook, Hobart, confesses... 101
Ferry franchise confirmed 8
Fire department, movement for
   245, 246
Firemen's pay 285
Fire precinct extended......... 305
Fire, great 384–404
   list of losses.............393–395
   insurance 395–399
   notes about 399–401
   origin a mystery............ 401
   relief work 402
   who will rebuild 402, 403
Fire precinct, etc..........370–404
   meeting called.............. 370
   voted to adopt and raise
     money 371
   precinct incorporated........ 372
   apparatus furnished.......... 372
   money borrowed on its notes. 373
   new engine house, etc., peti-
     tioned for 373
   movement for reliable supply
     of water 374
   money voted 374, 375
   officers chosen.............. 375
   hose tower voted............ 375
   pipes and hydrants author-
     ized 375
   also purchase of a chemical
     engine 375
   boundaries enlarged 376
   voted hook and ladder outfit 377
   legislature recognizes it...... 377
   motion to ratify carried..... 378
   bills ordered paid........... 378

Fire precinct, *Continued.*
   change in the boundaries..... 379
   firewards 379
   tax assessed on whole town.. 379
   contract to keep pump ready 380
   committee chosen to investi-
     gate introducing running
     water 381
   firewards elected 381, 382
   vote to introduce running
     water 382
   committee appointed to adjust
     damages 382, 383
   committee authorized to pro-
     cure necessary surveys... 383
Fires, extinguishment of...276, 277
Fish inspector appointed....... 189
Foord, Rev. John, supply Sec-
   ond Congregational church. 240
Four post routes established... 243
Freight teams and stages...... 263
Freshet, great................. 248
Glebe for Church of England... 5
Glenwood Cemetery............ 248
   purchased 293
Governor's lot, committee cho-
   sen to lay out...........30, 52
Grafton County, vote not to di-
   vide 262
Grain ground 69, 70
Grantees of Lebanon.......... 4, 5
Grievances, action to refer to
   General Assembly 151
Grist-mill privilege granted.... 18
   voted conditionally 26
   voted to build.............. 43
Groceries selling beer and cider
   nuisances 288

Hanover street bridge replaced
   by one of iron.........302, 303
Hat factory 239
Hay scales 248
   erection of, granted......... 302
Hearse for West Lebanon voted 289
Hearse voted..............294, 304

INDEX.

Health, first board of, elected.. 304
Hendee, Capt. Joshua, Co. of..92-95
Highway, intervale............ 20
Highways, prices for work on.. 190
Hill, Charles, accused of passing
    counterfeit money........ 102
    settles, West Lebanon....... 55
Hog constables first recognized. 152
Hog reeves, last time chosen 313, 314
Horse sheds, land leased for... 283
Hose, purchase of............. 299
House, Capt., Co. of........... 94
House on poor farm burned.... 294
Hubbard bridge, voted to build 31
Humphrey Wood bridge....... 285
Huskings..................... 201
Hyde, Levi, deposition of...... 159

Indians no longer feared....... 1
Inoculation for small pox..... 215
Introduction 1
Inventory, earliest........186, 187
    law of 196

Johnston's Island 53
Journeying mainly by horseback 199
Justice of the court, first appointment of 312, 313

King's highway 9, 55

Landee, Abigail, accused of
    breaches of the peace...... 106
Lakes of ancient times......46, 47
Land for propagation of the gospel 5
Lathrop, George H., receives
    vote of thanks............. 277
Law facilities 70
Lawyers 240
Lebanon, development of....144-197
    accession of inhabitants...... 144
    dam across Mascomy river
        sanctioned 144
    undivided land laid out in 50-
        acre lots 144, 145
    drawers of 50-acre division... 145

Lebanon, development of, *Continued*.
    plan of township made...... 145
    lots of 20 acres asigued by lottery 145
Legislature held as prisoners... 157
Liquors, action to secure a law
    against traffic in.......... 288
Log Cabin campaign, etc....... 258
Logging bees 201
Lots drawn.....11, 12, 16, 17, 49, 50
    laid out 49
    mode of marking............ 51
    ownership of, hard to identify 51
Lottery voted 11
Lumber sawed 69
Lyman's bridge 198, 202, 203
    movement to make it free.... 305
    controversy respecting it..306-311
    finally made free............ 311

Maintenance for Mr. and Mrs.
    Patrick, auctioned off...... 184
Male inhabitants, 1776, list of 68, 69
Mann, John, journey of, to Orford 54, 55
Manufacture of nails.......... 185
Manufacturers exempted from
    taxation 321
Manufactures, encouragement of
    295, 303, 304
Mascomy river..............46-49
Masting pines 163
Merchants 239
Meeting-house, building refused 28
    first 59
    floor plan................... 174
    gallery plan................. 176
    ground for, fixed near burying
        ground 29
    location fixed....33, 34, 37, 60, 160
    167, 170
    location changed 30, 61
    reasons for strife as to location 63, 64

INDEX.

Meeting-house, *Continued.*
  money to build, appropriated 38
                                  61, 161
  size altered 37, 38
  tax raised to build.......... 36
  proprietors assess tax to build 62
  subscriptions to build........ 173
  voted to build.......33, 34, 60, 61
                151, 155, 161, 165, 169
  voted to procure plan of floor 41
  subscribers' accounts.....174, 175
  vote to build reconsidered.... 166
                              168, 169
  voted to move............155, 255
  old, pulled down............ 168
  distances measured 171
  vote to sell pews............ 246
  pews sold 177, 178
  vote to repair............246, 265
    to repair windows......... 250
    to alter 250
  proportionate occupancy by
    different denominations.. 247
  Congregationalists build new
    one 247
  "war" 178-184
Mineral formation 46
Minister, committee chosen to
  procure 31
  provision for..........20, 24, 36
Mob dispersed 158
Money in use, paper, currency
  of England, Spanish coin... 70

Occupants, first winter......... 52
Orchards 201

Park on Hanover street........ 295
Path, first completed, 1763..... 52
Pension bureau, transcript from
                                   98, 99
Petition for ferry 154
  for peaceable dissolution of
    the Union presented in
    Senate 259, 260
  produces great excitement... 260

Phelps, Bezaleel, accused of al-
  tering bill 101
Pine Plain road laid out...... 252
Pine trees, preservation of..... 6
Plan of town accepted......... 12
Plan for a new town.......... 147
Police officers, appointment of.. 289
Political affairs...248, 249, 256, 257
       279-281, 289-291, 300, 301
Political parties 242
Poor distributed in families.... 294
Poor farm, voted to purchase.. 251
Poor house, voted to build...... 184
Postage 243
Postmasters 324
Post rider 199
Potter, Rev. Isaiah, called to
  the ministry 38, 58
  accepts 36, 58
  ordained pastor 59
  salary voted 39, 58, 231
  vote where to preach........ 187
  for settlement with 230
  committee chosen to confer
    with 231
  his son sues for arrears of
    salary 232
Pound, town voted to sell...... 300
Poverty Lane 55
Preaching, provision......15, 17, 21
                              24, 25, 57
Presidential electors chosen.... 167
                                187, 215
President Munroe visits Hano-
  ver 232, 233
Property in town, 1800.....195, 196
Proprietors, first 7
  records of 8-31, 37, 38
  taxed...9, 12, 14-17, 19-21, 23, 25
                         32, 38, 57, 58
Railroad bridges and crossing
                                288, 289
Railroad in prospect........... 254
Railroads 268-275
  resolutions adopted......268, 269
  Northern open to Lebanon... 269

442 INDEX.

Railroads, *Continued.*
   address by Daniel Webster.. 269–275
Railroad tax 286
Raisings 201
Rebellion, early volunteers..... 325
Regimental muster, law providing for 217
Revolution 71–107
   congress of the colonies 71
   military stores prohibited ... 71
   powder and arms taken from Fort William and Mary.. 71
   committee of safety appointed 72
   preparing for hostilities..... 72
   inhabitants advised to stick to farming 72, 73
   Association Test 73
   army forced to retreat from Canada 74
   decision to fortify Royalton. 74
   also Newbury 74
   Assembly petitioned for help 75
   powder and lead purchased.. 76
   small pox prevalent........76, 77
   inoculation and pest house... 77
   soldiers receive bounty...... 77
   scouting party discover cause for alarm 77
   Tories desert to the enemy.. 78
   day of fasting observed..... 78
   battle of Bennington........ 78
   scouting party recommended. 79
   Congress asked for aid...... 80
   expedition of Gen. Sullivan.. 80
   voted to raise bounty........ 80
   Royalton attacked 80
   call to the towns to rid themselves of suspected enemies 81
   tax voted to defray expense of alarm 82
   vote to guard roads 82
   voted to raise scouting party 82
   plans formed for the capture of persons 83

Revolution, *Continued.*
   army provision bill.........84–86
   Revolutionary papers 86–91
   losses sustained 80–87
   receipts for powder, etc.,...87–89
   expense and losses sustained. 90, 91
   Revolutionary soldiers 92–99
   regiment of Col. Chase.....92, 93
Rifles, vote to be responsible for 255
Road built to Plainfield....... 251
   committee chosen to clear to No. 4 ....14, 15, 17–19
Road to Enfield line voted..... 244
   also survey of, to Hanover line 233
   granted to meeting house ... 221
Roads across common discontinued 296
Roads and bridges 198–221
Roads built 70
   necessary to settlement...... 52
Robbing graves, penalty for.... 220
Rum seized 7
Rum voted for raising bridge.. 146

Sawmill owners 239
School districts, bounds of..286, 287
   occasion dissatisfaction 217
   division into ...153, 154, 214, 216
Schools, action for benefit of... 146
   selectmen to visit........... 220
   support of primary.......... 253
   vote to support.....27, 30, 40, 43
Sealers of weights and measures instructed to procure a stamp 318
Settlement of various families. 56
Settlers, early 7
Sexton for cemeteries 295
Shade trees allowed to be set out 293, 294
Shoemakers 70
Skinner, Joseph, confesses to altering bills 102, 103

INDEX. 443

	PAGE.
Slavery, extinction of, urged...	261
opinions respecting	258
Slaves mutiny, are tried and set free	258, 259
other slaves imprisoned for mutiny	259
Society for Propagation of the Gospel formed	8
Soldiers' monument	318
Spirituous liquor, vote not to license save for medicine	267
Spring, West Lebanon	321
Stage drivers	264, 265
State and town officers	229–267
State election, 1789	184, 185
first for 20 years	152
State emissions insufficient	157
Steamboat of Samuel Morey	200
Steamboats employed	241
Stores, many	199
Street lights	320, 321
Surplus revenue	254, 262
Survey of streets	304
of town	47–49
Surveyors chosen	13
Tanneries	239
Tavern-keepers	239
Taverns, country, flourished	264
plenty of	199
Taxation for worship, complaints against	244
Taxes, arrearage of, voted to pay	159
paid in barter	160
Taxlist, 1820	234–238
Taxpayers, 1800	191–195
Tax voted for laying out road	27
for making and clearing road	27
Teachers' institutes	277, 278, 281
Territory of Lebanon	45
Texas seeks admission to the Union	260
opposed by N. H. legislature	260, 261
Toleration act	243

	PAGE.
Tories	7, 8
Tomb, selectmen directed to erect	279
Town and state officers	229–267
Town clerk given right to record deeds	255
clocks	322
committee chosen to establish southern line of	42
condition of, 1775	67–71
divided into districts for school purposes	43, 44
farm deeded	294
officers, 1800	196, 197
Town hall, voted to build	60
heating and lighting	319, 320
Town house, voted to build	166
vote for, reconsidered	167
location of	167
movement for a better	296
committee appointed to consult Universalists as to their interest in	296
their report	296, 297
plan and estimate	297
plan adopted	298
gas fixtures for lighting authorized	298, 299
also finishing basement, tower and painting building	299
movement to purchase land for removal	281, 282
person employed to take charge of	282, 298
voted to repair	265
vote to remove	266
removed	282
has new bell	283
Town in 1800	190
Town line, settling the	25, 27, 28
Town meeting, manner of calling	188
Town meetings	325–329
money appropriated	325
voted to borrow	326, 328
disbursed by the selectmen	326

INDEX.

Town meetings, *Continued.*
  bounty voted 326, 329
  families aided 327
  selectmen during war 329
  soldiers serving 329–351
  state aid paid to families ... 351
  receipts 351–352
  centennial celebration 352–364
  exercises on stand 353
  toasts and speeches 353–364
  response of Rev. George Storrs 354
  Rev. C. H. Fay 354–356
  Rev. Rufus Case 356, 357
  Dr. Phineas Parkhurst...357, 358
  Dr. Nathan Lord 358–360
  Daniel Richardson 360
  Hon. A. H. Cragin 360–362
  Robert Kimball 363, 364
  memorial building 364–369
  subscriptions made 365
  building association organized 366
  money raised 366–368
  corner stone laid 368
  town makes appropriations.. 368
  various contributors 368
  lot purchased 369
Town pump 312
Town records 20, 37–41, 43–45
Townships granted 1
Town taxed 23, 34, 82
Transportation by boats on Connecticut river 198
  means of 240
Treadway, Rev. Mr., briefly town's minister 58
Trout, stocking streams with... 319
Turner, Capt. Bela, accused and exonerated 101
Turnpike from Packard's mills 210
  committee's report on 211
  courses and distances 212, 213
  officers of road 213

Turnpike from White River Falls bridge to White River voted 209
Turnpike, N. H. fourth.198, 202, 203
  shareholders 206
  town tax voted in its interest 206
  conditions of 207
  some resist payment 207
  report of survey 208
  changed 252
  vote to make free 262, 263
Tything-man 315–317

Vermont controversy 108–143
  causes of 108
  Masonian grant 109
  boundary of 109, 119
  New York's eastern boundary 110
  grants made in disputed territory 110
  grantees required to renew charters 111
  New Hampshire's grievances. 112, 113
  inequality of representation.. 113
  sympathy lacking 113
  border towns disaffected 114
  lands regranted by New York 114
  Vermont organized 114
  seeks assistance from N. H.. 115
  such assistance granted...... 115
  battle of Bennington 115
  convention of committees proposed 116
  sixteen towns decide to join Vermont 116, 120
  are received by Vermont assembly 116
  N. H. notified of this union.. 117
  reasons for this given ...118, 119
  tax of £8 voted............. 120
  not erected into a distinct county 120
  protest and retire 121
  claimed for N. H............ 121

INDEX.

	PAGE.
Vermont controversy, *Continued.*	
Congress asked to interfere	121
favors union with N. H.	122
convention adopts proposals	123
Lebanon's attitude	124, 125
Assembly claims whole of N. H. grants	125
town votes £200 for representation before Congress	125
Congress petitioned	126
Vermont determined on recognition	126
coquets with British authorities	126
movement for a new state	127
convention called and its committee favors union of all towns with N. H.	127
its report corrected substitutes Vt. for N. H.	128
reasons for change	128
terms of union	129
towns admitted	129
collisions and arrests	130
sheriff's story	130, 131
matter submitted to Congress	131
terms on which Congress will recognize Vt. as a state	131
Vermont acquiesces	132
towns east of Connecticut river without state connections	133
voted to conform to laws of Connecticut	134
Lebanon protests	134
a depreciated currency embarrasses	135
selectmen's letter to Col. Chase	135, 136
no place for records	136

	PAGE.
Vermont controversy, *Continued.*	
deed of Jane Hill	136, 137
Mrs. Truman's story	137, 138
horn of Gabriel	138
petition concerning story	138
and for redress	139
petition to be under N. H.'s jurisdiction	139, 140
settlement of controversy	140
terms of	140
statements in behalf of N. Y.	141, 142
flogging of Benj. Hough	142
town for a time independent	143
finally came under N. H.	143
Vermont emission of money voted to care of selectmen	146
Wales, Rev. Mr., town votes to have him supply pulpit	26
and to call	29, 58
his verbal acceptance not accepted	30
War of 1812	222–228
causes leading to	222
war declared	223
Lebanon in	224
soldiers of	225–227
treaty of peace signed	228
benefits following	231
Weights and measures, money for voted	41
Wheelock, Dr., requests the laying out of a new township	35
appointed agent to favor the same	35
Wheelock's school, land for support of voted	32, 33
Whitcomb, Maj., battalion of	97
White River Falls bridge	203

INDEX OF NAMES.

PAGE.	**PAGE.**
Abbott, Asahel.................214	Atkinson, George..........152, 155
Beriah.......199, 214, 226, 239	Theodore...........4, 5, 27, 65
Joseph 214	Austin, Sylvester..............368
Moses.................226, 239	Ayer, Rev. Franklin D........416
Mr......160, 161, 167, 168, 410	Ayers, James..................169
Polly 226	Rev. Walter H.........414, 415
Adams, John Q....242, 243, 259, 260	
Alden, Daniel..................170	Bailey, Rev. George W.....353, 364
Ezra 311	435
Miss Fanny.............56, 63	Jacob.............83, 123, 124
Luther............209, 292, 407	Jude 189
Mr. 363	Samuel....39, 45, 138, 181, 313
Mrs. 148	Bainbridge 224
Mrs. Luther..........18, 55, 61	Baker, Abel....................262
P. A.......................283	Alpheus..240, 252, 265, 296, 297
Zenas.................210, 214	Alpheus W....309, 365, 368, 376
Ziba..................213, 246	378, 382
Aldrich, Clark.................239	Gideon......8, 97, 144, 145, 164
David W..................428	165, 218
Allen, Abner..281, 284, 285, 411, 418	Joel 239
Asher.........171, 172, 188, 208	W. N............371, 372, 377
Comfort...............168, 169	Balduc, Mrs....................390
Diarca....97, 144, 178, 207, 244	Baldwin, Col...................94
D. H......................353	John 3
Ethan............116, 122, 127	Mr. 388
Ira.......115, 116, 124, 127, 128	O. W..............365, 366, 403
Isaac..................226, 412	Rufus..................33, 152
Joann B..................226	Ballou, Rev. Hosea............433
Phinehas..............97, 144	Barbaric, John................101
Amsbery, Ecabod...............92	Barnes, Rev. Horace F.....425, 426
Amsden, Joel..............239, 246	Josiah.................239, 252
Uriah............239, 252, 370	Mrs. 426
Andrews, Mrs. Hannah.........421	Barret, Charles................187
Army Men on Provision Bills..84, 86	Barron, Asa T.........306, 308, 309
Arnold, B......................92	Oscar.................306, 308
Ash, Robert....................329	Bartlett, Josiah..........187, 188
Aspinwall, Peter.............15, 16	Baxter, Charles M.368, 381, 389, 398
Zalmon......43, 44, 56, 100, 153	Bean, Richard................227

INDEX.

	PAGE.
Bedell, Col.	87, 92, 102
Moody	215
Bell, John	243
Samuel	242
Bellemont, Earl of	6
Bellows, Benjamin	163, 164
	184, 188
Col.	82
Bennet, John	18, 56
Mary	86
Benton, Calvin	239, 245, 247
	431, 434
Colbee C.	255, 266, 292, 318
	364, 372, 373
H. B.	302, 370
Henry	390
Howard	49, 148, 212, 213
James	364
Bernadin, Rev. Father	436
Berry, Watchman	385
Bidwell, Nathaniel	214
Billings, H. G.	399
Stephen	144, 164, 169, 171, 173
	177, 187, 213, 214, 244
Birchard, John	52
Blaisdell, Daniel	220
Elijah	266, 287
Blake, Patience	98
Samuel	98
Thomas	70, 97, 98, 144
William	98
& Johnson	98
Blanchard, Jonathan	7
Joseph	1
Bliss, Anna	71
Azariah	34-37, 39, 41, 43, 45
	59, 61, 62, 72, 100, 102, 103, 405
David	153
Ebenezer	45
Stephen	82
Vinal	71
Blodgett, Amasa	226
Anna P.	226
Blodget, Daniel, Jr.	9, 48
Blodgett, Elias H.	226
George	148, 214

	PAGE.
Blodgett, Nathan	226
Seth	226, 264
Blood, George	299
Bosworth, Alvah	148
Edward	246
Bounty, Signers of Receipts for	89
Bouton, Nathaniel, D. D.	413
Bowen, Josiah	317
Boyles, Mr.	48
Bradford, Benjamin	225, 226
Brady, Rev. Father	436
Bradley, Bishop	436
Braley, Nelson	391
Breck, John T.	379
Mr.	214
Brewster, Ebenezer	203, 204
Jacob W.	214
Brink, Alexander	40
Brooks, L. F.	360
Brown Bros.	240
Ira A.	239
John L. T.	382
Micah	206
Bryant, William D.	421
Buck, Martin	296, 297
Pelatiah	189
Bucklin, Ira	387, 395
& Miner	368
Bugbee, Mr.	44
Nathaniel	77, 78
Bullock, Watchman	385
Burdette, Charles	390
Burgoyne, Gen.	77, 94, 114, 115
Burnap, G. W.	299
O. W.	391
Burnham, John	371
Bush, Capt.	91, 97
Bushway, John	388
Buswell, Paul	239
Butman, John K.	320
Butterfield, Isaac	92
Buyers of Pews	177, 178
Byington, Joseph	169
Byles, Ebenezer	12
Camp, Miss E. M.	387

INDEX

Carter, H. W..................187
    T. J......................269
    William S................365
    & Rogers..................385
Case, Rev. Rufus....356, 364, 417
Chandler, Abijah..............210
Chapman, Rev. F. M...........416
Charles II. King..............110
Charter Settlers................7
Chase, Asa...............420, 423
    Jonathan..82, 88, 90, 93, 95, 96
        98, 135, 136
    Moses 67
    Samuel 60
Chase's Regt., Men in.........92, 93
Cheney, Elias H......374, 396, 421
    427, 428
    Fred W...................429
    Mrs. Susan W............421
Child, Jonathan................77
Chittendon, Gov......116, 121, 131
Church, Timothy..............141
Churchill, Frank C........366, 367
    390, 395
    William A................382
Clapp, Sumner...167, 169, 171, 173
    199, 205, 209, 210, 215
Clark, Oliver..................16
    W. 200
Cleaveland, Aaron....210, 211, 212
    J. Warren................329
    Tyxhall..........100, 103, 104
Clifford, B....................325
Clinton, Gov..............110, 276
Clough, John..................364
Cobb, Mrs. Betsey A......420, 421
    Charles V.....420, 421, 423-28
    Rev. Sylvanus.............433
Cogswell, Thomas.........188, 215
Colburn, Charles.........388, 395
    John...................77, 214
    John, Jr..................165
    Robert......103, 104, 159, 160
    169-73, 175, 177, 185, 187, 188
    191, 214, 256, 313, 314

Cole, Ebenezer........154, 190, 199
    239, 329
    Solomon..........372, 373, 375
    Tabitha D................226
    Timothy 226
    William...............226, 370
    William B................420
    & Son....386, 389, 390, 397, 403
Committee of Proposals........123
Committee of Safety, Members
    of 106
Conant, Jonathan..............77
Congressional Candidates......229
Coogan, Patrick...............388
Cook, Jesse.....23, 37, 39, 45, 56, 70
    97, 146, 164, 165, 170, 171, 185
    187, 214, 239
    Jesse, Jr..................214
Cooke, Phineas........406, 412, 413
Cotting, E. A.................390
Cragin, A. H...68, 279, 288, 353, 360
    R. W.....................382
Crocker Co....................321
    James...........158, 187, 221
Crosby, Dixi..................357
Cross, Capt...................386
    Col. 330
    Ichabod 98
Cummings, E. D...............325
    Joseph 420
    Mrs. Chloe H............420
    Rev. Edson E.....421, 423, 424
    Royal 400
    & Emerson................419
Curtis, G. W. P..............224
Cushman, Frances A...291, 293, 296
    297, 372
    Mrs. Harriet N...........421
    Solomon 102
Cutler, Rev. Calvin......240, 411
    Rev. Charles 411

Dacy, Daniel..................325
Dalley, Rev. Father...........436
Dana, Capt...................147
    Charles...............51, 407

INDEX.

Dana, Charles H..............418
   Jedediah....2, 9, 10, 13, 15, 24
                      49, 56
   Jonathan..21, 31, 33, 37, 40, 56
            59, 61-63, 153, 405
   Joseph..9, 14, 16, 21-23, 25, 26
            56, 58, 59, 405, 407
   William..18, 37, 39, 45, 52, 56
             88, 146, 154, 354
Davidson, Oliver..11-13, 18, 19, 21
    26, 28, 32, 38, 55, 56, 62, 69
Daniels, Mrs. Daniel...........402
Daniell, Warren................148
Darcent & Simons..............283
Davey, John...................181
Davis, James A................304
   Ferdinand........365, 366, 368
   Mrs. Jennie S..............421
   Pliny E...298, 299, 304, 372-375
   Mrs. P. E........387, 390, 399
   & Kendrick......385, 398, 402
Dearborn, Gen.................225
Decatur 224
Delano, Luther................239
Densmore, Jason...........368, 400
Dewey, Elijah.............23, 55, 56
   Elijah, Jr..................151
   Jesse E........365-69, 313, 399
Devonne, Rev. Father..........436
Dinsmore, Samuel..............242
Dole, Charles A............382, 383
Doty, Isaac...................250
Douglas, Stephen A............363
Dow, Charles..................390
   Moses............152, 163, 188
Downer, Marlin 431
   William.......35, 37, 39, 54, 56
             139, 171, 354
   William, Jr.......104, 105, 106
   Zacheus......33, 45, 59, 70, 405
Downs, Charles A...364, 366-68, 384
            413, 414, 425
   C. A. & Sons..293, 304, 313, 320
Drake, Charles M..............319
Drew, J. L....................283
Driscoll, Daniel...........391, 398

Dudley, D. B..................363
   John 150
Duke of York..............110, 141
Duncan, James.................199
   William..........304, 374, 375
   William H..................241
Duplisse, P...................390
   Watchman 385
Durant, Edward J.....298, 300, 371
                375, 381
Durkee, J. A..................363
   Moses P...............372, 379
   Nathan.................97, 144
   Ziba 295
Dustin, Sally.................226
Dutton, Rev. John M.......415, 416
Dyer, Carlos..................368

Eager, Dr. George........102, 103
Eaton, A. S...................373
Edwards, Eunice...............429
   Rev. John H................418
Egan, Rev. Martin H...........436
Ela, Jacob....................214
   John 221
   Theodore 199
   William S...241, 277, 283, 288
            305, 308, 329, 364
Elderkin & Wales..........76, 370
Eldridge, Watson K.......265, 276
Eldredge, Zuar............97, 144
Elliott, Capt..................96
   G. A............387, 396, 402
Ellis, Col.....................82
Emerson, D. B.................379
   F. F.......................382
   Samuel 188
   & Cummings................419
Estabrook, Hobart..44, 101, 153, 214
   Leonard A..................418
   Molly 408
   Nehemiah..9, 10, 13-17, 19, 21
     30, 41-44, 56-59, 66, 71-75, 81
     89, 100, 104, 106, 110, 111, 116
       117, 120, 125, 137, 146
   Nehemiah, Jr................44

Estabrook, Nehemiah, 2d 97
    Rodolphus 200
    Samuel......31, 41, 52, 56, 171
                          172, 175
Evans, Henry..................141
    Mr. 429

Faney, Thomas...........391, 397
Farman, Henry...146, 151, 168, 409
Farrar, Timothy...............188
Farrill, E. T.........402, 416, 417
Fay, Barnabas.................214
    C. H.................353, 354
Fellows, B. F..................252
Felton, Nathan B..............434
Fenton, John...........72, 73, 136
Finnegan, Rev. Father.........436
Fire Losers................393–95
Fisher, John....................7
Fitch, Isaac..............429, 431
Flanders, Rev. C. R..........416
Folsom, Maj.-Gen..........77, 132
    & Peabody..................80
Foord, James..................240
    Rev. John.............410, 411
Foss, M. B....................390
Foster, Abiel....164, 185, 187, 189
    Joel 103
    Mr. 55
Fox, John.....................153
Freeman, Capt..................147
    Col. 225
    Daniel 239
    Edmund..30, 86, 105, 152, 158
        161, 167, 184, 225, 227, 314
    Enoch............214, 231, 434
    John S....................319
    Jonathan....42, 43, 66, 77, 163
              164, 184, 185, 188
    Otis 408
    Roger 214
    Russell..........190, 202, 205
    Zilpah P..................227
    & Richardson.........388, 396
Freeto, P. H. & Sons..............

Fremont, John C..............258
French, Horace...............418
    H. M. 431
Fuller, Benjamin.......31, 70, 218
    James................41, 184
Fulton, Robert................200

Gage, Samuel..................199
Gallup, Benjamin.........240, 294
    Thomas 65
Gannett, Rev. J. H............426
Gates, Gen.....................76
    Ira...................251, 410
    Mr....................213, 240
    Thomas 65
Gedney, Lieut.................258
Gee, Amos W..................429
Gerrish, Charles..............153
    C. W.....................383
    Helen M..................366
    Joseph W.....296–298, 300, 303
                          373, 375
    Joseph W., 2d.............366
    Mrs. Joseph W............366
    Samuel B.................221
Gilbert, Benjamin J...........205
Gilden, Joel..................163
Gile, George E................453
Giles, Squire.................130
Gilman, John G...............190
    John S..........188, 190, 217
    John T...............216, 219
    Nicholas.............164, 188
Goodrich, Harlan P.......368, 379
                          381–83
    Joseph 232
    Mr. 410
Goodwin, Rev. Father.........436
Granger, H. P.................388
Grantees......................4, 5
Graves, Rufus............203, 204
Green, Capt...................102
Greenough, Moses.............239
Grimes, Alexander............240
Griswold, Ahirah.............240

Griswold, Elizabeth P...........226
    John...28, 30, 32, 33, 35, 37, 41–
        45, 56, 61, 66, 72, 76, 102–104
        146, 151, 152, 161, 226, 313, 314
    Rev. John.................409
    Joseph 226
    Maj. 90
    Oliver...........28, 35, 37, 41
Gustin, John..............283, 316

Haddock, Rev. Charles B.......413
Hains, Walter 144
Hale, Col.....................130
    Hannah T. 419–421
    Rev. Sumner .419–421, 426, 429
    William 220
Hall, Andrew 104, 105
    Aruna 417
    Andrew 104, 105
    Rev. Charles E............432
    Dr. 146, 357
    George 60
    Mr. 374, 375
    Nathaniel ...9, 14, 20, 21, 32, 33
        39, 40, 48, 52, 56
        104, 105, 151, 169
        173, 201, 313, 314
    Nathaniel, Jr. 158
    Obed 220
    William 325
Hamilton, Jonathan 218, 226
    Lathrop 226
    Polly P. 226
    Ziba 226
Hanks, John 9, 48, 52
Hardy, Rev. Anthony C. 430
Hardy, Daniel 250
Harper, John A................220
Harris, Joseph 325
    Rev. Mr. 435
    Walter, D. D. 409
Hartshorn, James 56
Haseltine, Mr. 400
Hatch, Horace 283, 286, 292, 298
Havens, Rev. C. E.............418
Hayward, John 181

Haze, Samuel 42, 66
Hazen, Asa 209
Hazzan, Joshua 74
    Richard 109, 110
Heath, Cyrus 421
    Jesse 138, 393
Hubbard, James 104
    John 51, 54
    Mr. 32
Hendee, Joshua, men in com-
    pany of............92, 93, 95, 96
Hendy, Capt. 90
Henry, Rev. Foster 421, 424
Herrick, Timothy 246
Hibbard, Jedediah..21–23, 30, 31, 38
    40–44, 56, 62, 66, 72, 153
Hill, Charles 9, 11, 13, 16, 18–39
    41, 45, 48, 52, 55, 56,
    58–63, 65, 92, 98,
    102, 103, 136, 138
    313, 354
    Charles, Jr. 31, 103
    Jane 136
Hilliard, L. F. 368
Hinkley, Daniel 239, 305
Hinckley, David 145, 199
Hobart, Col. 95, 96
Hoffman, C. M. 377
    William 214, 232
Hoisington, Mr. 387
Hosley, Harry H...............424
Hosley, Jewett D.......309, 366, 379
Hough, Benjamin 142
    Clement 421
    Daire 161
    Daniel 89, 155, 171, 172
    David...146, 151, 160, 161, 163
        164, 166–170, 173, 186
        189, 191, 208, 210, 211
        213–215, 219, 251, 252
        313, 314
    Edwin W..................421
    Mrs. Ellen 421
    Enoch F. 295
    Frank G. 295
    Guy 214

INDEX.

Hough, Henry B..............423
   Lemuel......39, 41, 78, 159-161
           169, 171, 184, 185, 313
   Mrs. Martha D. 421
   Theoda 421
   Thomas 175, 214, 219
   Thomas F. 420, 421, 428
   Wetherill 153, 154
Houghton, S. S...........388, 397
House, Capt.................94, 98
   John 81
Hovey, Josiah.................153
Howe, Corporal................340
   Edward 248
   Edward A.....227, 255, 266, 353
   James................218, 221
   Richard S.................287
Hoyt, Rev. B. R...............431
Hubbard, Orren................239
Hull, General.............224, 228
Huntington, James........105, 106
   Lieut..................91, 97
   Samuel 153
   Theoph...81, 82, 136, 160, 161
                   166, 221
   Uriel 199
   William...............160, 161
   Ziba 407, 408
Hurlburt, Amasa..............240
Hurlbutt, C. O................388
Huse, E. B....................401
Hutchins, Mrs..................289
Hutchinson, Aaron....151, 160, 161
   165, 166, 169, 170, 174, 184-86
   203, 204, 207, 214-16, 240, 314
   A. B......................352
   James......42, 66, 219, 220, 240
Hyde, Elihu..81, 82, 105, 106, 127
   129, 137, 151, 155, 165, 169, 185
              188, 313, 409
   John 37
   Levi..13, 18, 24, 25, 28-30, 32
   33, 37, 39, 45, 52, 56, 159, 354
   Robert 145

Ingalls, Mr...................363

Jackson, Andrew..242, 243, 248, 249
   Charles 7
   President 361
Jefferson, Thomas.............216
Jewell, Stephen...............240
Jewett, Haynes................240
Johnson, Charles...............67
Johnson, Hezekiah 34, 60
   Joseph 66
   N. S......................406
   Thomas 83
Johnston, Charles 53
   Michael 53
Jones, Mr.....................224
   James...23, 28, 37, 39, 45, 55, 56
     86, 90, 138, 171, 172, 201, 313
   S. D......................390
Jordan, Patrick 388, 396
Joslyn, G. S..................381
Judson, Judge 259

Kellogg, Enos 200
Kellum, Rev. Joseph 430
Kendall, W. M................383
Kendrick, E. A................300
   F. B......................322
   George S.........266, 370, 371
   Henry L..................363
   J. H......................372
   Stephen..190, 214, 215, 218, 239
            245, 277, 411, 412
Kendrick & Davis......385, 398, 402
Kenne, Mr. 31, 58
Kenrick, Timothy..239, 266, 276, 279
Kenyon, P. M..................389
Kilbourn, Asa......20, 23, 28, 30, 56
Kimball, Benjamin.........190, 214
   Ebenezer 417
   John 190, 214
   Miss Mary 402
   Nathaniel 169
   Richard 62, 213, 252, 417
   Robert 255, 363
King, Elijah 103
Kinsman, Aaron 208
Knapp, Rev. Frank L.......428, 434

INDEX.

	PAGE.
Knight, F. A.	304
William	8
Ladd, Nathaniel	431
Lafayette, Gen.	400
Lamont, Oneil	8
Landee, Abigail	106
Lane, Rev. H. F.	422
Langdon, John	163, 216, 217, 219, 220
Woodbury	7
Laplante, Rev. Father	436
Lary, Dan	331
Latham, Arthur	209
Lathrop, Elisha	81, 155
Lathrop, George H.	251, 252, 277, 353
Gordon	169
Human	167
John	243
Joseph	169
Lois H.	226
Samuel	146, 226
Sluman	163
Urban	169
William	39, 226
Lawrence, Mr.	224
Leach, Silas	239
Ledyard, John	241
Lee, Rev. Dr.	435
Rev. John S.	435
Lemay, Peter S.	388, 396, 402
Lincoln, Abraham	361
J. F.	388, 396
Liscomb, Elisha P.	276, 364, 365
Livermore, Samuel	163, 165
Loomer, Fitch	286
Loomis, Israel	181
Lord, Rev. Dr.	353, 358
Lorimer, Rev. Dr.	427
Losers in great fire, list of	393, 395
Lot Drawers	11, 12
of one acre division	16, 17
of 50 acres	145
of 100 acres	18, 19
second division, 100 acres	49, 50
Lovejoy, Rev. Charles H.	430

	PAGE.
Loveland, Joseph	209
Lowe, Abel, Jr.	284, 370
John	252
Lull, Frederick	240
Lutwyche, Edward G.	7
Sarah	8
Lyman, Abel	74, 93, 104, 105
Elias	155, 204
John	45
Justin	204
Richard	175
Lynch, Mrs.	390, 397
Madison, James	219, 229
Magoon, F. L.	363
Mahan, C. P.	379
Mahurin, E. H.	225
Male inhabitants, 1776	68, 69
Manchester, C. W.	304
Mann, John	54–56
Marsh, Joel	210
Joseph	76
Marston, C. E.	388, 396
D. W.	366
N. B.	372, 387, 396
T. B.	390, 395, 400, 403
Mason, Jeremiah	184
Joseph	240
Rev. Lemuel B.	435
Reuben	409
Martin, John	153
Joseph	33, 35, 37, 39–41, 45
Mathews, Samuel	165
Maynard, Heman	325
McFee, W. P.	388, 396
McKinlay, Rev. John	421, 422, 427, 429
McKinlay, Mrs.	423, 427
McNeil, Col.	224
Mead, Mason & Co.	239, 379, 380, 385–89, 398, 420, 423
Mecham, Samuel	22, 40, 56, 104
Meeting House Subscribers	173
Merrill, Rev. Charles H.	416
Messenger, C. M.	292
Miller, Col.	224

454   INDEX.

	PAGE.		PAGE.
Miller, G. A.	409	Orcutt, J. H.	368
Millington, David	97	O'Reilley, Rev. Father	436
Miner & Bucklin	368	Osborne, Rev. F. F.	422, 423
Moore, John	255	Owen, F. L.	305, 318
Rev. John	433–35		
Monroe, James	232	Packard, Abner	252
Montgomery, Gen.	92	David	207
Morey, Col.	90	Ichabod	207, 211
Rev. J. W.	431	Thomas	433
Samuel	200	William	207
Morgan, Frank	388	Paddleford, Jonathan	104
Morrill, David	242, 430	Page, Jeremiah	67
Morris, Gov.	271	Paine, John	101
W. H.	368, 402	Lemuel	102
Morse, Nathan W.	368	Samuel	45, 75, 90, 91, 97, 100
Prof.	274	Paradis, Rev. Father	436
Wareham	239	Pardee, William	431
Moses, W. S.	372	Parker, Ephraim	11
Muchmore, Orimel J.	365, 376	Mr.	153
& Whipple	368, 389, 395	Nahum	215
Murch, James	283	Parkhurst, Phineas	207, 209–11, 213
Murdock, Jonathan	9, 13		240, 357, 358
Murphy, Rev. John	436	Partridge, Isaac	209
		M. & Co.	283
Names of Protestants	134	Patrick, John	164, 184
Napoleon	222	John, Jr.,	164, 165
Nash, Harlow S.	279	Molly	164
Nelson, Capt.	91, 97	Pattee, Lewis C.	298, 299, 305, 308
Nevins, James	8		309, 373, 374, 381
Newell, Rev. Mr.	412	Patterson, James W.	353
Newhall, Dan.	391	Payne, Elisha	76, 77, 80, 82, 88, 90
Nichols, Col.	96		123, 128–30, 141, 146–48, 151–
Niles, Rev. Mr.	405		53, 155, 158, 160, 161, 163, 164
Niles, Samuel	214		166, 184–86, 188–90, 202, 204
Noiseux, Rev. Father	436		205, 208, 210, 226, 313, 314
Northrop, M. A.	368	Elisha, Jr.	226
Norton, Henry C.	325	Elisha, 3d	226
Noyes, Rev. George	430	Gov.	146
Moody	431	John, Jr.	145
Mr.	353	Noah	92
Nutt, Capt.	241	Peter P.	226
		William	230
Olcott, Bulkley	59, 405	Peabody, Frank	221
Col.	126	& Folsom	80
Olcutt, Peter	137	Pease, Rev. Theodore C.	418
Orcutt, Hiram	308, 309	Peck, Azel	240

INDEX. 455

	PAGE.
Peck, Eliel	169, 214, 237, 254, 410
Jahleel	214
John	283
John W.	205, 317, 370
Simeon	81, 82, 136, 151, 167, 168, 190, 208, 214
Solon A.	167, 208, 300, 319, 320, 329, 364, 383
Walter	93, 144, 214
Penhallow, Samuel	8
Percias, Ezra	93
Perkins, Barnabas	70
George C.	381, 382
James	153
J. M.	353
Perley, Edwin	70, 214
I. N.	389
Moses	213
W. G.	286
Persons, Moses	169
Peterson, Turner	199
Petitioners for Plan of Town, 147, 148
Petitioners for Redress	139
Petitioners Respecting State Jurisdiction	140
Pettie, John	53
Pew Buyers	177, 178
Phelps, Bezaleel	101, 103
Daniel	170, 188
Pickering, Rev. Daniel	433
John	164, 184, 197
Pierce, Benjamin	243
Pike, Luther	214
Mrs. Mary E.	427
Pinkney, C. C.	216, 219
Plastridge, Charles B.	366, 374
Caleb	240
Plumer, Gov.	225
Porter, Dea.	311
Eleazer M.	92
Rev. Experience	409
John	153, 154, 214
Lieutenant	28
Nathaniel	17, 25, 27, 31–35, 37–39, 42, 56, 61, 62, 65, 66, 155, 170, 171, 188, 201, 207, 354, 412

	PAGE.
Porter, Nathaniel, Jr.	45, 412
Post, Andrew	239, 254
Capt.	96
George	284
Postmasters, List of	324
Potter, Barrett	354
Rev. Isaiah	35, 36, 39, 58, 59, 171, 187, 214, 215, 220, 227–32, 240, 354, 406–409, 411
John	363
Powder, etc., Signers of Receipts for	87–89
Power, Chandler	383
Powers, Mr.	56
Prescott, Jacob S.	311
Presidential Electors	164, 187, 215, 216
Protestants, Names of	134
Pulsifer, C. E.	389, 395, 403
J. T.	27, 208
Purmort, Jasper H.	420, 423
Mrs.	420
Mrs. Marcia J.	421
O. T.	388
Putnam, Rev. John J.	435
Quimby, Jonathan	169, 214
Ralston, James	213
& Winneck	199
Randlett, Capt.	340, 353
N. H.	365
Redington, Enoch	97, 226
Huldah	226
William	226
Reeves, Deer	39
Representatives to Congress,	187, 215
Revolutionary Soldiers	98, 99
Rich, A. B., D. D.	418
Richards, Rev. John	413
Richardson, A. C.	389
Asa W.	423, 428
C. A.	322
Daniel	287, 292, 329, 360, 417
David	417, 418

456 INDEX.

Richardson, Rev. Elias H......417	Simons, Hiram A...............371
Jacob C....................219	& Darcent..................283
William H.................298	Simmons, T. D................402
& Freeman...........388, 396	Mrs. T. D..................402
Rix, A. W................387, 397	Skinner, Joseph..........102, 103
Robertson, Moses...............132	Slack, Mr......................56
Robinson, Daniel...............185	Slacks 49
Rock, A.......................388	Slapp, John....21, 26, 32-34, 36-40
Rogers, C. C..................402	43-45, 56, 59, 61, 62, 70, 72-74
Mrs. C. C..................402	78, 97, 102, 104, 120, 153
& Carter...................385	154, 405
Roper, Rev. C. Fremont.......418	Edward................77, 97
Rose, Mr......................388	Simon 70
Ross, Charles B...........428, 429	Simon P...............71, 240
Russell, Charles T.............269	Smalley, Adoniram.............292
Miss Jean..................422	Smith, Abner..................214
	Benjamin 329
Saction, Charles................45	Carlos D..............382, 383
Salter, John.......9, 10, 15, 16, 19	Francis.............94, 96, 137
Richard 145	Jeremiah....185, 216, 219, 220
Sargent, Jonathan E...........288	Jonathan 215
Justus 390	Judge.................306, 307
Miss Mary.................402	Lorin............282, 371, 372
Sartwell, Roswell.........252, 281	L. W.................388, 397
Sawyer, P. R..................374	Soldiers, Capt. House's Co.......94
Saxton, Charles................171	Col. Cilley's Regt............94
Sayre, Frank..................382	in Civil War...........330-51
Scilly, Col.....................90	Revolution..............98, 99
Scott, C. I.................395-97	1812 225
Dan 386	Southworth, Constant.....14-16, 20
Searle, Cuff...................230	Spaulding, Mr.................400
Seavey, Charles C..............325	Sprague, Elisha.............38, 40
Moses 226	Elkanah...............105, 214
Selden, Samuel............240, 245	Philo 240
Selectmen During the Rebellion, 329	Samuel 152
Sennett, Joseph................325	Spring, J. L..............381, 382
Shapleigh, A. W...........365, 427	Stanley, Matthew..........207, 210
Shareholders of Turnpike......206	State Officers..229-34, 248, 249, 256
Shattuck, William..............141	257, 279-81, 290, 291, 300, 301
Shaw, A. M...366, 368, 381, 382, 398	Stark, Gen.................94, 115
403, 423, 432	Stearns, Nathan.............54, 56
Mr. 353	Nathan B......49, 292, 417, 418
William F..............374, 387	Nathaniel 62
& Wright..............387, 397	Oliver L......28, 329, 364, 417
Sherburne, John S.........185, 187	Stephens, Isaac................40
Simons, Arad..................144	Stevens, Elias............206, 210

INDEX. 457

Stevens, Hasley R.....252, 266, 364
    John 65
Stickney, Col...................96
Stone, Rev. W. L..............427
Storrs, Aaron..17, 20–22, 24, 25, 29
       33, 34, 38, 42, 49, 56, 57, 60
       62, 66, 70, 77, 101, 102
    Abel..................51, 155
    Amarian........8–10, 12, 13, 15
    Constant..155, 161, 166–69, 173
       201, 202, 204, 205, 214, 215
    Dan 295
    Experience 16
    George 354
    Rev. George...............430
    Horace 221
    Huckens..23, 26, 28, 31, 33, 35
       36, 38, 41, 43, 48, 49, 56, 61, 62
       69, 70, 82, 313
    Huckens, Jr...........9, 21, 56
    John 9
    Judah 11
    Mrs. Lucinda..............431
    Nathaniel..45, 56, 81, 82, 86, 97
       136, 146, 155, 170, 171, 175
    Samuel....9, 10, 14, 17, 19, 21
       56, 57
    Thomas....10, 11, 13, 16, 18, 19
Streeter, Rev. Sebastian..,......433
Stubbs, Capt....................168
Sturtevant, J. C.....292, 293, 296–98
       303, 372, 379
    J. C. & Co.....375, 376, 379, 426
    Jesse E...................298
Subscribers Towards Building Meeting House...................173
Sullivan, George...............220
    John 158
    Gen. John...95, 98, 157, 162–64
    Rev. Father...............436
Swetland, Josiah................89

Tax-payers..........191–95, 234–38
Thompson, Mrs. Arabella.......421
    Captain 15
    Judge 259

Thompson, W. W...............368
Tickney, Elisha.................93
Ticknor, Elisha....66, 146, 147, 151
       152, 161, 185, 216
    James G..................312
    Judge 402
    Lieut. 79
    William D................364
Tiffane, Gideon.................150
Tilden, B. T..............387, 395
    Charles 159
    Daniel...............181, 183
    Joel 199
    Joseph..23, 25, 28, 29, 32, 56, 101
    Rev. Nathan......416, 423, 426
       427, 429
Tone, Christopher........430, 431
Toothaker, Charles.............214
Town Officers....196, 197, 219, 220
       229–33, 290, 291, 300, 301
Townsend, Mr..................388
Tredway, Rev. Mr....22, 24, 58, 405
True, Bradley..................30
    Osgood 239
Trudell, Rev. L...............436
Truman, Mrs.........137, 226, 227
Tucker, Franklin..............390
    Rev. Jirah................424
Turner, Bela..35, 37, 39, 41, 43–45
       59, 62, 101, 125, 137
Turnpike Shareholders.........206
Tyler, Pres....................411

Vose, Roger...................220

Wales, Rev. Mr................405
    Mr................26, 27–31, 58
    & Elderkin................76
Walker, Capt....................96
    C. N.....................388
    Daniel 142
    Richard 210
Walton, F. & Co................389
    John 214
Warner, Seth..................114
Washington, Gen..........131, 361

458   INDEX.

PAGE.
Waterman, Polly...............408
   Silas.......17, 20, 21–23, 25, 28
      31–33, 35–37, 39, 41, 44, 45, 56
           61, 72, 105, 152, 351
   Thomas..214, 216, 217, 219, 244
   Thomas P..................305
Waters, Hezekiah..39, 41, 43, 86, 151
           155, 166–69, 213
Waters, Luther................200
   Mr. 408
Weare, Mesheek...117, 121, 138, 152
Weathers, Samuel..............164
Webber, Capt. 96
Webster, Daniel...288, 259, 269, 275
   Levi 175
   Noble A...................401
   O. W......................370
   Watchman 385
Weed, Joseph..................214
Weeks, William B.........308, 309
Wellman, James...............406
Wells, Thomas............159, 207
Wentworth, Benning....1, 2, 4, 30
                  72, 110
   Hugh H.....................7
   John....................7, 67
   Mark H.....................7
West, Benjamin................163
Wheatley, Andrew....102, 103, 214
   John........20–31, 33–37, 39–41
      43–45, 49, 56, 58, 59, 61, 65, 70
      72–74, 89, 95, 100–06, 116, 120
      137, 143, 146, 159, 160, 405, 406
   Luther.................77, 95
   Math 161
   Nathaniel.....71, 158, 161, 167
Wheeler, Corliss C............325
Wheelock, Eleazer..33, 35, 137, 184
             233, 242, 406
   James 207
Whipple, Gilman C...384, 403, 420
             421, 427–29
   Lyman..........380, 381, 383
   Mrs. Lyman...............402
   & Muchmore......368, 389, 395
Whitcomb, Maj.................97

PAGE.
White, Mrs. Fanny.............370
Whitelaw, James...............206
Whitley, Rev. John E..........405
Whitmore, Giddings............231
Whittemore, Daniel............434
Willard, O....................137
William, King...................6
Williams, Dr...................77
   Jesse 210
   Rev. Robert..........429, 430
   William 182
Willis, James.............251, 434
   Rev. Lemuel...............433
Wills, Abiel...............45, 152
Wilson, James.................220
   Lucretia 71
Wingate, Payne......187, 188, 189
Winneck, John.................240
   & Ralston.................199
Winton, Mrs...................103
Wood, Ben.....................239
   Rev. Benjamin.............409
   Ephraim..188, 200, 202, 218, 239
             251, 281, 283
   Henry G...................417
   Humphrey............285, 317
   Jeremiah...............54, 253
   John..................285, 417
   Joseph..28, 30, 31, 45, 56, 58, 78
      86, 145, 171, 199, 206, 213, 231
        239, 250, 313, 413, 416
   Joseph, Jr.................172
   Rev. Luther...............409
   Mr. 26
   Samuel...............417, 418
   Samuel, D. D.........409, 411
   Samuel, 2d...........364, 370
   Thomas 417
Woodbury, Levi................242
   Mr. 214
Woodward, Bezaleel..77, 100–02, 110
        123, 137, 152, 163, 188
   Charles 387
   David....34, 42, 60, 66, 74, 101
                102, 104
   Henry..................45, 146

	PAGE.
Worth, John C.	421
Mrs. Mary	421
Worthen, Enoch	169
G. W.	251, 294
Wright, Abel	45, 104, 105, 146, 313
Jonathan	77
Miss Melissa	421
Wright, Phinehas	77
Thomas	153
& Shaw	387, 397
Young, Ammi B.	240
Samuel	240, 246
Walter	214

Milton Keynes UK
Ingram Content Group UK Ltd.
UKHW040058180324
439604UK00007B/1103